Ironopolis Media Ltd
Acorn Lodge Studios
Chop Gate
Bilsdale
North Yorkshire
TS9 7JR
England
www.ironopolismedia.com
www.ironopolismedia.co.uk

First published in Great Britain in 2008 by Ironopolis Media Ltd.
Copyright Ironopolis Media ©

Typeset and designed by Ironopolis Media Ltd.
Printed in Great Britain by Studio Print. Redcar. Cleveland.

A cip catalogue record for this book for this book is Available from the British Library

ISBN -13-978-0-9560694-0-5

IRONOPOLIS
MEDIA

FOREWORD

I hope you all enjoy reading the story of my friend Johnny Hammond. He truly was unique. He could snatch defeat from the jaws of victory like no other comic I know! We met in the 1976 finals of the TV talent show New Faces. I was so cock sure of myself.... Until I saw Johnny. He was sensational and had us all in hysterics. Johnny really was the comedian's comedian, ahead of his time and completely unaware of his talent. I miss him......

Jim Davidson OBE.

...So I said to myself: Why not write a bestseller? Everybody buys them, everybody reads them, they make more money and it doesn't take any longer to write a best seller than it does to write a book that nobody buys!'

I locked the doors, closed the curtains, took the phone off the cradle and slipped into my Ernest Hemmingway best-selling writers jacket, the one with the brown leather patches on the elbows identical to the one the iconically acclaimed, happy go lucky, never say die Hemingway was wearing when he shot himself.

I filled my Sherlock Holmes pipe with an exotic aromatic tobacco, punched up the chair cushions, switched on my personal computer and sat staring at the blank monitor screen for three weeks, aching for that earth-shattering flash of inspiration that refused to materialise. I'd gotten writers block on my very first assignment.

Most authors would have thrown the towel in, but not me.... especially the way I was dressed. But what to write about?

Then, like a bolt out of the blue it struck me.

<u>ME!</u>

I've known me for seventy-eight years and in that time I've spent more time with me than I have with anyone else I know. I've certainly seen life... from cowering on the ice-rink deck of a crazy pitching Destroyer named HMS Oribi on the 'Suicide Run' between Scapa Flow off the northern tip of Scotland and Murmansk on the Northern most tip of Russia, in the treacherous North Atlantic winter, starved of sleep, shivering with bone numbing cold. Pounded by mountainous seas in howling Arctic gales... Dodging shells, bombs and torpedoes from Nazi bombers, surface craft and U boats and somehow miraculously surviving against all the odds... only to drift, aimlessly like a piece of flotsam into an equally stressful post war gut wrenching career, still cowering, this time in broom-cupboard sized dressing rooms dreading the sound of the M C's voice as he was about to throw me to a blood thirsty drink crazed Saturday night mob in some dingy North Eastern back-street Workingmen's Social Club.

So that's what my book is going to be all about... and as you read it I hope you can experience with me the horrors of situations not of my making, from the mind-numbing wartime scenario, through the harshest 'Showbusiness' schooling to the excitement of finally being accepted into the bosoms of huge and appreciative audiences in the heady Golden days of Clubland, Cabaret, Theatre, Radio and Television… and even a couple of forgettable movies…devouring and savouring the poise at the top, albeit waiting with bated breath for the steady slow downward slide, back from whence I'd come as chief support to the booze, barracking and Bingo.

Believe me, when it was good it was Heaven…And when it became Hell, the hardest part was finding a dignified way out.

I relished the warm heady seasons as stoically as I accepted the inevitable winters. And more importantly I learned that as much as there was an art of living out the role of the successful headliner, it was as equally important to perfect…

The art of dying.

The <u>second</u> loneliest job in the world is that of the stand up comedian

Johnny Hammond's

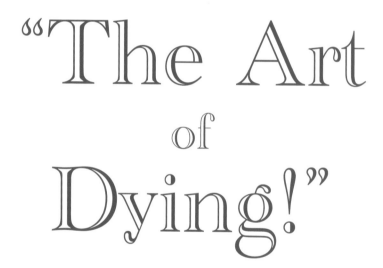

The 'loneliest' job in the world' is that of a 'Workingmen's club' stand up comedian

To
My Wife,

Jeannie

In appreciation of her love,
guidance and undying devotion,
who never for one second lost faith in me,
Even through the hungry years when I lost
faith in myself.

'The Wind Beneath My Wings'

Acknowledgements

Jim Davidson

*Who put me on the rocky road of comedy
writing and to whom I owe*

more than I could ever re-pay.

Bob Monkhouse

For his invaluable help and encouragement whilst failing

to warn me as to what I was letting myself in for.

Eric Morecambe

*For relentlessly hounding me to
'Write that bloody book!'*

Mike McCarthy

*A good friend, we should have been a writing double act!
We are working on a great TV script and
getting this sodding book published.*

My mentor

Terry Laffin

*For his invaluable insight
into the rapidly diminishing
Art of real comedy*

&

*Those of my peers who contributed
to this book willingly, selflessly, or under duress,
…as did those indomitable readers
who stayed awake past page 4.*

Break a leg!

Oh yes…..

And

Thanks

&

God Bless you

C̲l̲u̲b̲l̲a̲n̲d̲

You showed me that the light at the end of the tunnel wasn't always a train coming the other way.

IN THE BEGINNING

'The first critic I ever saw shot himself in the middle of my first joke.'

Murton Democratic Miners Social Club stood in the middle of the coal-mining village a stones-throw from Sunderland, Tyne & Wear in the industrial North East of England. It was no different to hundreds of other Northern Workingmen's Clubs that were mushrooming all over the industrial North immediately after the 1939-45 war.

The club was a foreboding, sombre, two-story brownstone building consisting of large vestibule, games room, bar, ladies lounge (women weren't allowed in the 'Men Only' bar... and in this chauvinistic male dominated society members were discouraged from fraternising with the opposite sex within the parameters of the men only bar).

There was a large 'Committee Room', the domain of the seven officials elected by the voting members for the length of their tenure. These officials were, in line of seniority: President; Chairman of Committee; Concert Secretary (the Entertainment Booker and glorified Compere): Treasurer: Sports Committee and Bar steward... and Geordie (The Bard) Miller, the omnipresent octogenarian doorkeeper.

It is written that every village has an idiot... and Geordie Miller possessed all the essential qualifications in spades. He was nicknamed 'the Bard', because, though totally illiterate, he would quote, pidgin fashion, passages from the great historic tomes. At the drop of a hat and the bribe of a pint of the local brew, he would dredge up gems like, "Them bloody Greek's has got a word for it y'knaa... but I can't for the life of Jesus remember what the hell it is now."

A master of the faux pas, Geordie Miller once told an incoming act who was lost and had phoned in for directions: *"Come straight down the road from Sunderland unless you're coming up the other way from Hartlepool or left over from Durham what will fetch you face to face with the pit-head directly behind you on your right. If you come to another road on your left...or your right if you're coming the proper way over from Sunderland, follow that as far as you can and when you come to a fork in the road, take it. If you come past Chicky Gasgoines paper shop you've gone too far so you'll have to go back to the 'Iron Coffin' (an ancient cast iron horse trough), turn left at the Iron Coffin and come straight on. You'll pass Jonty Jackson's farm on the right and at the second left farm gate take a sharp 'U' turn at the signpost what says 'Esh Winning'. Don't turn left at the first sign what says "Pick your own strawberries" as this is now obsolete since old Jonty died on his motorbike in the back of a bus in 'Pity Me' high street. Come on for another couple of miles and we're on the left. Now then, be bloody careful here cos if we're on the right you've come the wrong way down the turnpike so you'll have to go up to the traffic island and make sure to look over your shoulder where the old school used to be before it was bombed by the Germans on the first day of hospitalities and 1939... then come back on yourself and when you see a club on your left now with our name over the CIU sign, that'll probably be us. If you still can't find us, ask for me when you get here and I'll see if I can tell you an even better way next time."*

Interviewed by a reporter from the Sunderland Echo on reaching his centenary, Geordie Miller was asked the secret of his longevity. He replied: *"I think it's cos I stopped smoking a couple of weeks ago."* Undeterred the hack soldiered on.

"If you had your life to live over again, what radical changes would you make?"

Without a pause Geordie said; *"I'd part me hair down the middle... and if*

I knew I wouldn't get caught I'd like to be the Club Treasurer."

When 'The Bard' finally succumbed at the age of 101 the 'Sunderland Echo' reported: *'All the village turned up for the funeral celebrations in the Co-operative Hall where there was a buffet with 'Wingy' McCallister, the three fingered accordion player from the Labour club, and a concert party, 'The 'Morpeth 'Always Look on the Bright Side of Life' Glee Club'... On the top V.I.P table the local gravedigger and stonemason Gilbert Woolinson carved an amazing lifelike effigy of the deceased in potato salad.'*

The following week one of the Memorial acknowledgements read:

"TO GEORDIE WHAT WE USED TO DOTE ON,
WE'LL NOT FORGET TO PUT YOUR TOTE ON."

"From *the staff and all the lads at Joycey's bookie's shop."*

On the first floor of 'The Club' stood the concert room, a large soulless barn of a place with twelve large windows through which, on this particular summers evening, the sun cast blinding shafts of sunshine like a dozen spotlights... which was twelve more than the club could boast. Chairs and tables were either bolted or nailed to the floor as a precaution against repeats of the Armistice Day Celebration riots. Left of the entrance stood a bar, maybe thirty feet long (or short, depending on the calibre of the entertainers billed for the night).

At the far end of the hall was a wall-to-wall stage on which stood an upright piano, An ancient drum kit, several brushes, mops and buckets and bottles of cleaning fluid (unused)... and the Bingo caller's lectern. Behind the stage was the dressing room against whose far wall laid several stacks of decrepit two legged stools, three legged chairs and topless tables... souvenirs from the aforementioned Armistice Day Celebrations debacle. A heavy wooden thirty-foot ladder was wedged in the corner of the tiny six by four foot room, half of it disappearing through a trapdoor in the ceiling and probably poking through the roof. Visiting mathematicians must have long ago given up trying to figure out how it was possible to get a heavy wooden thirty foot ladder through the six foot six inch door of a six by four foot box-room and guide it through a twelve inch square hole in the eight feet high ceiling...unless perhaps the club had been built around the ladder. The most feasible solution.

In one corner of the dressing room was a washbasin minus taps or 'U' bend; its plughole stuffed with cigarette ends... a nuisance for anyone relieving him or herself in the receptacle. A row of nails doubling as coat-hangers protruded from the wall and there was a Yellow 3x3ft patch where once, probably decades ago had hung a mirror.

Above the dressing room door, in fading yellow chalk some long dead disillusioned clown had scribbled the warning to fellow thespians:

'COMEDIANS GO HOME COS THEMS ALL BRAINDEAD IN HEAR', which members obviously took as a compliment because it remained there till the mid eighties when the whole club and outbuildings mysteriously but conveniently burned to the ground the very day before the brand new club opened opposite 'Crabby' Gildersleeves wet fish shop, shoe repairs and haberdashery.

The three remaining dressing room walls were covered, floor to ceiling with graffiti defaced 10x8" glossy photos of female singers swallowing microphones artistically re-drawn as vibrator sex aids. There were action shot's of male vocalists swallowing artistically airbrushed penises and comedians With words like 'unfunny bastard' and defamatory remark's about their mothers and sister's nocturnal occupations scribbled across their faces.

The solitary dressing room window was secured by a bent and rusted six-inch nail, a precaution against cat burglars. This however was a point of conjecture because outside the window was a sheer seventy-five foot drop to the beer crate littered yard below, hindered only by the corrugated iron roof of the club official's bike shed.

A chipped Tannoy microphone hung centre stage from the flies and a single flex 40 watt light bulb barely illuminated the sombre scene.

Let me point out that, even at this early point of my career I would not normally accept this kind of gig but it just happened that I was 'resting' at the time and out of the blue I'd received a 'May Day- S-O-S- May Day' telephone call from my best friend and arguably the North East's greatest comedian of the post war era, Bobby "The Little Waster" Thompson.

Bobby Thompson was an icon in North East club-land just after the 39/45 war.

He'd acquired the synonym through his habit of transferring, at the very last minute, his allegiance to the highest bidder for the sake of an extra couple of shillings.

It was said that if Thompson was booked at the London Palladium for a fee of £3.10 shillings and at the last minute was offered an extra two shillings to appear at the local reference library, within minutes of reaching the venue, he'd have his audience rolling off the bookshelves.

Bobby and I had started our careers round about the same time, in 1945-6 and remained close friends till his death several decades later.

I'd recently been demobilized from the Royal Navy at the age of eighteen and a couple of months and Bobby boasted that he had also 'done his bit during the war'. He was too modest to elaborate but in an occasional state of inebriation he would pull out of his trouser pocket a fistful of assorted medals from every theatre of war, awarded to him by "my mate King Geordie" for his selfless devotion to duty in the face of imminent danger as a front line foot soldier in the relief of Maffaking, a Ghurkha scout in the Burma campaign, Field Marshall Montgomery's batman and a Field Commander in the Desert rats. I wouldn't directly, to his face, accuse Bobby of lying but I do think he was a stranger to the truth. For such a heroic gargantuan, he stood no taller than 4ft 6" in height and never weighed more than six stones. He and was also so cross-eyed he could watch a tennis match without moving his head.

I once asked him how he got through the strict armed forces medical examination. He gave a sly wink and nudging me with his elbow, said in his thick Geordie dialect "I lied about me health". Bobby used to say that, at his passing out parade the recruiting sergeant looked him up and down and barked "That man is too small for a rifle... give him a catapult."

Nevertheless, he swore he was up there, not only with, but actually leading the lads into that 'valley of that shadow of death thing.' Bobby Thompson's comic routines about his days in the army went something like this: "I was standing outside Buckingham Palace with Field Marshall Montgomery when the Queen peered over the balcony and turning to her husband 'King George'; 'who's that down there with little Bobby Thompson?'" Lines like that made him the most sought after comedian in the glory years of 'Clubland'. And I never heard him use a four-letter word… on or off the stage

Today's comedians couldn't live with him. Like hundreds of other great comedians of that era, he relied on good clean family humour. But, maybe those wonderful old funny comics would have starved in today's 'anything goes' society. Nowadays 'fuck' is funny. In those days only funny was funny and someday God willing, funny will once again be the only kind of acceptable humour. Bobby Thompson was funny. Bob Monkhouse, Eric Morecambe and Ernie Wise and Jimmy James and Eli were funny… and Frank Randal, and Lucan and McShane, and Laurel and Hardy…

After Bobby's demobilisation from the forces and his hero's return to civvy street, he was expected to follow his forebears into the coalmines…and he told me he almost certainly would have followed them into the coalmines had he not failed the miner's intelligence test.

I enquired, "How come"? He replied, blank faced, "When I was asked question number '6' 'Do you know your gas safety regulations?' I replied, "Well, I know it shouldn't be any higher than mark '7' for Yorkshire puddings."

But the coal industry's loss was the North East club-land's gain.

Overnight he reached the pinnacle of his profession and stayed there till he was finally called to his greatest gig in his seventies.

So it came to pass that Bobby rang me from his 'office' (a public telephone-box a few feet from his front door) and asked me if I could do the show that night at Murton Democratic Miners Social club because the original 'turn' (artiste) booked for that evening had contracted tonsillitis and he (Thompson) had been asked to recommend a top class replacement.

"Naturally bonny lad, straight away I recommended thou."

I thanked him and promised to return the compliment someday.

Arriving at the club I went up to the concert room, which was a beehive of nervous activity. They were hanging from the rafters and I got a warm glow to think that, even in this early period of my chosen profession I could draw such a crowd.

It wasn't till I was approached in the dressing room by the concert chairman that I learned that the 'Star Turn' booked for this particular evening was in fact the aforementioned 'Little Waster, Bobby Thompson'. Apparently, on realizing he would be 'guesting' on an Amateur Talent Night he'd decided to acquire a life-threatening ailment. Knowing Bobby's track record I should have read the signs more clearly but I needed the money and didn't wonder why Bobby had pulled out of this kind of gig. Thompson was a 'Star' in club-land and nothing fazed him. He'd been weaned on the hardest venues, and anyhow, being the 'Pro' on an amateur show was the easiest type of job on the circuit. Talent show wannabee's were usually so bad that the audiences would be praying for the 'Star Turn' to come on at the beginning of act one. I suspected however that, true to form, 'The Little Waster' had been swayed by and accepted his thirty pieces of silver and to hell with the club, his fans.... and me! (I said he was funny... I never said he was a nice guy.)

Tonight's show was unique in that it was a two-act amateur talent contest plus the pro star turn. I was the 'replacement' professional 'Star Turn' because I was being paid a set fee of three pounds ten shillings. I was soon to realise the real reason why Thompson had pulled the plug, and at the same time discovered that my chances of success on this night were on a par with skiing backwards up Mount Everest.

The reason there were only two amateur contestants on a show which would usually attract a score of wannabe 'Stars' was because the two contestants were Little Billy Wanless and Miss Mary Bagley.

Little Billy Wanless was billed throughout North East Club-land as the 'Little Singing Angel'. The eighth son (there were also three daughters) of a miner fatally injured trying to save several of his doomed comrades in a mine-shaft roof-fall, 'The Little Singing Angel' helped eke out the family's meagre income by winning every talent contest from Lands End to John 'O'Groats and from The Wash to the Isle of Man. Billy was only seven years old with a mass of bubbly blonde curls and two saucer sized blue eyes. He looked like Shirley Temple in drag. Greatly boosting his chances of a landslide victory was the fact that he also wore a cumbersome surgical boot secured to his little withered right leg by two shiny steel callipers. This handicap (?) aside he really did have a beautiful voice that could charm birds out of the trees. He especially laid them in the aisles as he hobbled painfully around the stage, arms held high above his head carrying a large picture of his heroic father, tears rolling down his pale, quivering cheeks as he sobbed his gut wrenching show-stopper,

"Daddy please don't walk so fast".

After every show he laboured agonisingly back to the dressing room as his bedraggled mother and her remaining ten ragged urchins scurried around the stage shovelling up the ankle deep nobbin's that showered like hailstones from the auditorium. Seasoned professionals, Sir Laurence Olivier and Frank Sinatra included, would rather walk across the burning Sahara with a live scorpion in each sandal than appear within a fifty-mile radius of 'Little Billy Wanless'.

And The Singing Angel was only half of my troubles.

The other half was 'Miss' Mary Bagley.

Miss Mary Bagley was the recently widowed wife of a former war hero from 'The battle of the Somme' and founder member of the Miners Union movement and one of the organisers of the unforgettable Jarrow March. He also doubled as the local fire and brimstone lay preacher. To say James.J.Bagley was a popular man was like saying Jesus of Nazareth had a few followers. The great James.J.Bagley's newly widowed spouse was also the village midwife struggling to feed her fourteen offspring on a paltry widow's pension and the few hand-outs she was paid for delivering 99.9% of Murton's overworked and underpaid population.

A tireless charity worker, she was the organist in the chapel (non-gratis) and was adored by the local kids, especially when she encouraged them to stroke and cuddle her faithful guide dog, 'Old Shep'. I omitted to relay to you that Miss Mary Bagley (her stage name) was totally blind. To increase her chances of getting the first prize of five pounds and a large hamper of badly needed victuals, she had chosen as her party piece the guaranteed heart rending tearjerker, 'When I leave the world behind'… and when she reached the line,

"I leave the songbirds to the blind" the rest of the lyrics were drowned out by an uncontrollable wailing swelling up from audience.

On to-nights show the local bookmaker couldn't get a bet on the winner, but the loser in this three horse race was a foregone conclusion.

I had begun to doubt my chances of receiving the club-land equivalent of a Hollywood Oscar when on entering the amphitheatre 'the two combatants took almost an hour to fight their way to the dressing room through the hero-worshipping, backslapping, grovelling, boot licking fans.

Numb with fear and feeling like a rat in a mouse trap I made my way to the bar, ordered a pint of the local brew, looked casually around at each and every hostile face which seemed to return my nervous friendly smile with raw unadulterated hatred and with my scrotum shrinking to the size of a pinhead and my buttocks clamped together in a vice-like grip I shuffled into the gent's toilet.

I immediately reversed out, took a deep breath and headed back to a cubicle, dropped my penny entry fee into the slot and entered for a second time where, for the next few minutes, with lungs bursting, I read with hooded amusement odd odes like; "It's no use standing on the seat, the crabs in here can jump three feet' and "When you enter these marble halls use the paper and not the walls."

Half way up the wall to my right someone had scribbled, "Masturbation stunts your growth" and following a scrawled pencil line down to the skirting board some other wag had grudgingly written, 'Now he tells me!".

It was only momentary relief. My ablutions completed, my heart suddenly missed a beat when my gaze fell on the unintelligibly worded notice pinned to the back of the toilet door.

"Because of the theft and pinching of lavitery materals from this club, anyone what's wanting a bit of toylet payper should ask Alma behind the bar."

I had a vision of a dozen putrefying men, trousers and long johns trailing around their ankles forming a queue which snaked from the toilet, along the corridor and through the crowded concert room to the bar.

Panic stricken I rifled, unsuccessfully through my pockets for a leaf of paper, an envelope, a bus ticket... or even a ten-shilling note. Finding none I scanned my surroundings and my blood pressure suddenly slid back to normal. Someone, obviously a regular client or an Irritable Bowel Sufferer had come suitably armed and had stuffed a couple of pages of the 'Sunderland Echo' behind the rusting cistern pipe. Or maybe he was a critic from 'The

Hartlepool Northern Daily Mail'. Regardless, he saved my life. I flushed, washed my hands and, on leaving paused to smile at the graffiti on the newly installed "Durex Condom" dispenser, which read:

The contents of this machine have been passed by British Standards...' under which some wag had scribbled, *'So was the Titanic!'*

I stepped back into the concert room and scanned the faces of the male members. I was trying to pick out the ablutions artist. He's the guy I'd work on.

The proceedings started with three houses of Bingo. The fact that I, an interloping and much-hated foreigner won the first house prize of ten shillings distanced me even further from the hostile crowd. I retreated to the comparative sanctity of the dressing room, which was full of fawning attendants turning the chubby, rosy-cheeked 'Little Angel' into a grey skinned emaciated bedraggled Tiny Tim. In the opposite corner, supporters of the opposition transformed the moderately attired Miss Mary Bagley into a carbon copy of something from the nightmarish imagination of Charles Dickens. I stood ignored and forlorn in a neutral corner, feeling as deserted and alone on this ocean of kitsch as the doomed 'Mary Celeste'.

Bingo over, the entertainment started with "The Singing Angel" and while his renditions alternated between nauseating syrupy ecstasy one minute to soul searing anguish the next, I spent an unbearable hour barricaded in the stifling dressing room trying to claw out the six inch securing nail embedded in the window frame with the intention of flinging myself to oblivion on the cobble-stoned yard seventy feet below.

Little Billy Wanless had the audience eating out his hand. On his performance I realised that I couldn't have had them eating out of my hand if I'd worked in the pet's corner of the zoo. The concert room was awash with tears and reverberated with heart-rending sobs as 'the Angel' reached a climax which brought forth from the darkened auditorium a 2000 megaton atomic blast of adoration as the tiny mite dragged himself agonisingly back to the dressing room, where he miraculously recovered sufficiently to afford me an unconcealed 'Follow That', stare.

But 'The Little Singing Angel' had serious competition.

Miss Mary Bagley's offering was greeted with the equivalent of the recently combined 1939-45 Victory celebrations in Trafalgar Square, The Arc de Triumph and the ticker-taped New York Times Square, aided and abetted as she was by her shaggy friend, 'Old Shep' who joined in the chorus with a howling rendition of his own,

causing the piano player to fall prostrate onto the keyboard, tears extinguishing the cigarette dangling limply from his trembling lips, while the other half of the orchestra sat bolt upright on his percussionist's stool, eyes welded to an invisible spot on the ceiling, arms outstretched as he held his number 3 sticks before him in the shape of a cross. As the screaming, sobbing throng threw themselves at the stage in an historic interpretation of Santa Anna's ragamuffin troops storming the Alamo, I crouched like a trembling cowardly wretch on the steps of Madame Guillotine.

Back in the dressing room, sweating profusely, Miss Mary Bagley groped her way to the only chair, fumbled into her handbag and, awarding herself a cigarette from a five pack of Woodbines, stuck the weed between her lips, lit up, looked with unseeing eyes to the heavens and blew a perfect smoke ring which drifted slowly down and hovered like a ghostly halo above her head.

'Old Shep' dragged his adoring gaze from his mistress, looked me straight in the eye, bared his fangs in a satanic smile and relayed his telepathic version of "Okay asshole, follow that" with even more venom than 'The Singing Angel.'

The award of a draw seemed fair to me but the supporters of both camps thought 'their man' was robbed and showed their disapproval by ripping the furniture from it's mountings and bludgeoning each other into pulp.

The concert chairman heroically took to the stage and requested that hostilities be transferred to the legally designated battleground, the sporting field, behind the club.

This cut my audience down drastically to a table of seven drunks, hunched in the semi darkness at the back of the room.

The concert chairman announced me on stage. As I reached the microphone and before I had a chance to open my mouth a voice from the gloom called, *"NEXT."*

Under increasing handicaps I soldiered on, and maybe ten or less minutes into my act one of the inquisition hollered, "You're doing the same fucking jokes as you did the last time you were here".

Squinting into the expanse of gloom I hollered back; "I'm getting the same fucking money as I got the last time I was here!"

The lush topped my retort with a loud belch and, "You're kidding, we thought you were doing it for free." That was the cue for the remainder of my audience to stagger to their feet and head for the third world war raging on the pitch of 'no-mans-land between the club and the hastily boarded up premises of Crabby Gildersleeeves

foot and mouth emporium. Being the consummate pro, I performed the last fifteen minutes of my set to one loyal old man sitting feet from the stage, who steadfastly stayed the course with me, albeit glued to the sports page the Sunderland Echo. I turned to the Pianist to ask him to play me off only to discover that he and the rest of the orchestra, (the drummer), had deserted the sinking ship at the firing of the first distress flare and were probably now lying comatose, their shirt's torn asunder on the now silent battlefield. So gingerly did the musicians depart that the drummer had time to throw a heavy tarpaulin sheet over his kit miraculously without rattling the cymbal. After I'd left the stage to the sound of my own footsteps I thanked the old man for his undying loyalty in staying till the end. He stood up, drained the dregs from his pint glass, stretched, yawned and said, "Aye well, I had to bonny lad, it's my turn to lock up."

As I made my way to the bus stop, I passed maybe a dozen or more bloodied and broken, male, female and infant bodies sprawled, moaning and twitching on the grass verge outside the now darkened club.

I peered into the gloom hoping to see, among the fallen combatants, the shapes of 'The Little Singing Angel', his mother and at least some of her brood...but there was nothing... not even Miss Mary Bagley choking on her halo... Nothing except an eerie, ghostly distant howl of, what I fancied was, *'Old Shep'!*

This is my life

I was born Hugh Cecil Hammond into a semi Show Business family in that my mum had trodden the boards with such theatrical giants as Frank Randle, George Robey.. Gracie Fields. G.H.Elliot and George Formby Snr.
'GEORGE WHO?'
George Formby Snr!
My mother swore on her mothers eyes that it was on her lap that George Formby Snr finally rested his head when he dropped dead in the wings of the Empire Theatre, Middlesbrough…
But when she'd had a few Gin and tonics she also recalled cradling the same old comic's head when he expired in the wings of the Sunderland Empire, Manchester Garrick, Leeds City Varieties, London Palladium, Crazy Horse Saloon in Paris and the Hippodrome Theatre, Cleckheaton.
(In researching for this book I discovered that there never was a Hippodrome Theatre in Cleckheaton.... and it was rumoured that it was Toulouse Lautrec who succumbed at the 'Crazy Horse' in Paris…Although this too is open to conjecture… but if it was true you can guarantee that he took his last curtain-call with his head in my mother's lap.
When the glory days of working the 'B' variety circuit came to an end mum and dad teamed up as a gipsy song and dance act called 'The Romany Rovers', (which is what Gypsy's do.) I don't think my parents spent many sleepless nights racking their brains thinking up a title like that.
My dad would stroll around the auditorium wearing a red polka dot rag on his head and large brass curtain rings tied to his ears playing the gipsy violin, while my mother danced round the audience picking pockets and selling clothes pegs. They were real pros and even when she was heavily pregnant with me she never missed a show. On November 16th 1927 my mother gave birth to me on the stage of the old Hippodrome Theatre in the West Hartlepool docklands. My delivery went down so well with the audience, my folks decided to keep me in the act. However I was missing out by not going to school so my dad taught me all he knew, which was pretty limited as he could neither read nor write… or think.
Soon the 'Romany Rovers' retired from living in penury and dad, tired of reaching for the stars took a non-clerical job as a coal-wagon shunter on the London and North Eastern railway on the Hartlepool coal dock staithes.
I was the fifth of seven kids... two of whom died in infancy before they had a chance to audition for whatever role life could offer them.
Actually my paternal grandfather, who was a rascal of Irish gipsy stock, had changed his name from Jack Lee for some reason. He was the first recorded Hammond in the variety halls in the late 1800 to early1900's.
Till I came along he was the only entertainer in the dynasty to make any money.
'Granddad' Hammond had the milk bottle concession on the Blackpool's Golden Mile during the great depression. He ran a 'Knock the bottles down to win' pitch at the end of the Central pier. There were twelve milk bottles set in four uneven rows, similar to the pins in a modern ten pin bowling alley and the punters had to try to knock them down with a 50lb cast iron cannon ball, a souvenir from the Boer War. The prize was usually a coconut, a 'Kiss me Quick' hat or a penny Clay Pipe. In the several years he was in the business not one person in all the hundred's of millions of Blackpool holidaymaking contestants ever won a prize.
Just hitting the bottles with the cannon ball was not good enough. Almost every contestant did that. To win your mind-blowing prize you had to knock the bottles over. And no one ever got near to doing that.
But it all came to a sudden and dramatic end in the 1932 typhoon, the worst in living memory when Blackpool was almost decimated by hurricane gales, monsoons and the first

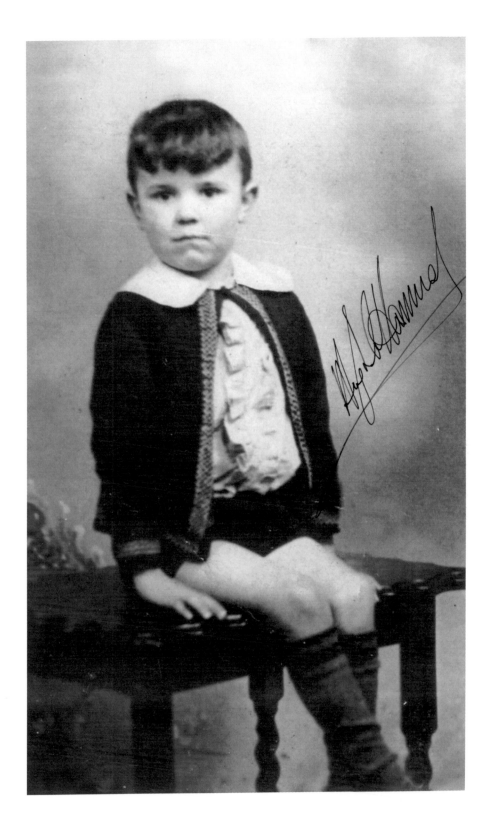

ever-recorded tsunami in North West England. When the storms finally abated and the sun sheepishly reappeared through the clouds the only things left standing were the Blackpool Tower, the Central pier and granddad Hammond's twelve milk bottles.

The old man then sold damaged fruit, which he repaired with bees-wax and shoe polish, but his business venture crashed when the resorts first ever would be suicide, deranged because he'd gambled his train fare home trying to knock down twelve milk bottles and still carrying the cannon-ball he hurled himself from the top of Blackpool Opera House and landed on granddad Hammond's pushcart. Fearing this could start a vogue in air to ground holidaymakers the old rogue decided to move indoors to the Opera House, which at that time was running variety shows. He worked for a short while as a Comedian (which he wasn't). Soon he honed his old skills and became a comedy-pickpocket, an act that he performed with uncanny skill and great alacrity. Unfortunately, during one performance he was apprehended in the middle of attempting to bankrupt the unsuspecting local police chief who just happened to be in the audience, and was dragged forthwith before the Magistrate.

He performed the next three summer seasons in Liverpool's Walton Prison.

His time served he once again put his knowledge of skulduggery to good use and became a Theatrical Agent, which kept the wolf, but not the Gendarmerie from his door till he succumbed to an early demise when he unwittingly booked a Russian strong man - act solely because he had an eye for Petrushka, the giant Cossack's comely spouse.

One fateful day Igor Borominovitch came home early from the beer tent and staggered in on granddad Hammond playing dogs and bitches in his horse drawn boudoir with the aforementioned Petrushka.

When the posse finally recovered granddad Hammond's grizzly remains they discovered that he had been drawn and quartered. Borominovitch hadn't even bothered to hang grandpapa first. In fact the old man was so professionally diced that he was only identified by his denture prints on Petrushka's buttocks.

As the killing of Lotharios was in those days deemed a crime of passion, Igor was let off with an early form of community service and six days later he returned to the Blackpool Tower circus. He divorced the unfaithful Petrushka and married the bearded lady who was already several months pregnant with their first child. Asked by a reporter from the Blackpool Gazette if they preferred a girl or a boy, Igor, a dyed in the wool trouper replied, "Ve don't care, just so long as it fits in the cannon".

It was not till my mother, many years later teamed up with my father and became the better half of the 'Romany Rovers' that the Hammond name finally reappeared on the 'Employment Wanted' pages of the Showbusiness tabloid, 'The Stage', where they remained till their deaths respectively fifty seven and sixty two years later.

Incorrigible ham's, in all those years they never gave up hope of appearing on the International Pubs and Flea- pit Music Hall circuit and to this day they still hold the record as the longest serving fully paid up 'resting' Equity members in the history of show-business. In all that time the Hammond name remained only slightly above the printers name and address at the foot of theatrical bills. In fact they were so far down the bill, audiences assumed they *were* the printers. There were many embarrassing 'don't call us, we'll call you' retorts before number four son finally made it to the dizzy heights of the North Eastern Workingmen's Club Circuit…but not till I put my career on hold to play my part in the downfall of Hitler and the decimation of the Imperial German Navy.

Hail the conquering hero

In 1941, two years into the Second World War, and at the age of fourteen years and a couple of weeks, I joined the Navy, Army & Air-force Institute, **(N.A.A.F.I.)**
(Those initials would come to have a bearing on my attitude and aptitude to a chosen post-war theatrical career, 'No Ambition And Fuck-all Interest.)
I was installed in His Majesty's service as a non-combatant Junior Canteen Assistant on the fish quay on the Hartlepool docks. The job entailed being a glorified shop assistant. There was a staff of five. The manager was Thomas Hanson., a midget of a man who, in his chief petty officers uniform resembled a latter-day Colonel Tom Thumb. Leading canteen assistant Bruce Wildflower was the outrageously gay second in command who's greeting to the matelot's at opening time each morning was a whooping camp 'Come and get me boys'.
Third in pecking order seniority was Robby (The Executioner) Branston, the psychotic son of a trawler skipper who one day in a fit of pique attacked me with a bacon boning knife and inflicted my first wartime wound by almost hacking off my left thumb.
Our book-keeper was Wren secretary 'Daisey' Crocket whose main contribution to the war effort was to spend as much time as she could with her **W**omen's **R**oyal **N**avy **S**ervice regulation brassiere and knickers stowed in her gas mask case as she hammock hopped around the crews quarters of the myriad of naval torpedo boats, minesweepers and the deep-sea trawlers of the Hartlepool fishing fleet.
Daisey Crocket had been one of the early Wrens contingent in the Home Fleet Naval Base at Scapa Flow off the northernmost point of Scotland where it was said she ran a successful cathouse in a delightfully picturesque white painted thatched croft she rented from an ancient one eyed, hook handed, peg-legged Blue bearded Orkney pimp. In record time Daisey Crocket acquired an anti social disease, which spread like the bubonic plague around the Orkney Islands and almost wiped out the entire native population and two thirds of the Home Fleet…. A feat that the combined forces of the Axis war machine could not achieve.
The knock on effect of this was the decimation of 90% of the sheep stock on the islands.
However, Daisey's wartime efforts were rewarded when the fighting men of the Home Fleet dedicated a song in her honour on the lines of the theme tune dedicated to the famous American frontiersman of the same surname, Davey Crockett.
The maritime version went thus; **'Daisey, Daisey caught it, and gave it to the whole frontier.'**
In staff pecking order I took bottom billing as junior canteen assistant 'Jackie' Hammond. My main task in the Hartlepool NAAFI store was taken up with the slicing of cheese, opening wooden packing cases, scrubbing floors, tipping garbage into the picturesque harbour and, in my rest periods, sitting at the high window in the darkened back store- room massaging my hairless nether region while I peered up the WREN staff courier's skirts as they dismounted from their bicycles laden down with sacks of large brown O.H.M.S. envelopes.
At the time this was my only contribution to the war effort but I did help my mum and dad start up a lucrative sideline. For almost two years they 'fenced' crates of eggs, sides of bacon, huge tins of ham, cheese, boxes of chocolates, barrels of soap, cartons of cigarettes and shag tobacco high jacked from my place of employment.
Once we had the dry goods concession wrapped up we started to re-export alcohol which had just hours earlier been life-threateningly imported in convoy from the Americas as a token of their appreciation for our taking on the brunt of the entire German and Italian forces while they lived in luxurious fat cat neutrality.
Our scam was never in any danger of being discovered because my 'fence' was non other than the diminutive 'Fagin', Canteen Manager/Chief Petty Officer Thomas Hanson. Twice a week he would arrange transport for us in a naval staff car where he would escort me safely home.

There behind chained, barred and padlocked bombproof doors he would graciously accept my parents hospitality of large measures of illicit Jamaica rum, purloined ham and cheese sandwiches, exotic fruits and Havana cigars.

Before continuing his journey home, mum and dad and he would retire into the front room with the 'Blackout' curtain tightly secured and there they shared their ill-gotten rewards while I crammed the contraband into our specially reinforced air raid shelter in the backyard.

No-one in those hostile times had a good war, but ours was made a little more bearable thanks to this manna from heaven and points North-West.

As an organisation we were suddenly beginning to show an unnatural affection for the Nazi's with each stock take. After a short while mum and dad and 'little Caesar' made it to the hierarchy in the illicit 'black market'. 'Tommy' Hanson was the supplier, dad was the carrier and mum was director in charge of sales. I was only added to the board of directors because I knew too much. We acquired a very upper class clientele of 'fences' including councillors, senior members of the judiciary and other sworn up-holders of the law. Dad even had business cards printed, and this was his undoing because jealous starving law abiding citizens revolted. The upshot was that my parents were dragged before the magistrates and with a wink and veiled reprimand were convicted and fined 5 shillings each.

However a small core of untouchable law-men persevered with their clean up campaign and a few weeks later at an ungodly hour several large men in trilby hats skidded to a halt on their bikes outside of No 10 Greenland Cottages, renamed 'Fingles Cave.' The scam was broken and designated to the historical 'heinous' crime files in Scotland Yard's 'Black Museum'. They not only confiscated the stock of food, cigarettes and chocolates and small change but they also impounded the side-board, couch, chairs and the piano which they took to the local market and auctioned off to the needy. Nonetheless, Mum and Dad had siphoned off a small fortune and disappeared from public life. Tommy however was a smarter cookie. He kept receipts and records and the names, addresses and coded phone numbers of all his influential law-abiding clients, (and his former partners in crime, i.e., Mum, Dad and even my good self), and after hostilities went, I believe legit and lived in sumptuous comfort into his nineties.

Three days after my 16th birthday I was kitted out with the single breasted, white shirted, black tie'd, peaked capped uniform of His Majesty's Royal Navy, (N.A.A.F.I Non Combatant Division) and posted off to Chatham Barracks in Kent where I, and hundreds of other bemused and bewildered urchins were given four weeks brutally intensive tuition in whoring, clumsily fitting on condoms, boozing, brawling, mugging, adeptly fitting on condoms, and fighting off packs of paedophiles in preparation for our journey through the valley of the shadow of death and into the unknown.

But in doing so, I had to suffer the greatest embarrassment of my entire life.

It had started the day of my birth when my parents decided to bestow up on me the Christian names 'Hugh Cecil'. Hugh after my maternal grandfather, the drunken psychopath Hugh Marks, and Cecil after the great South African leader, Cecil Rhodes. The connection however has always evaded me.

Minutes after arriving at the Royal Naval Barracks at Chatham in Kent I signed on as a member of 'the Andrew', which for some unknown reason the Royal Navy was nicknamed. I was ordered to strip and join an endless queue to be medically examined in the base's hanger sized drill hall. We were all stark naked except for our newly acquired caps, boots and socks. The rest of our clothes were piled up against a wall, guarded by an armed matelot bearing an unloaded 303 rifle.

Weighing in at 10 stones seven pounds, I was as white as one of granddad Hammond's (bolted down) milk bottles. But what I lacked in physical stature I made up for in film star looks. I was beautiful with long dark curly hair, huge chocolate brown eyes, and soft silky skin and

Betty Grable legs. I could get turned on just by looking at my official photo in my paybook. Up till that point I had never thought of myself as anything special in the looks department till I realised I was being ogled by hundreds of large hairy arsed anthropoids, would be stokers, seamen, sub-mariners and royal marines, doubling as perverts.

I stood out like a rose in a garden of weeds.

My predicament became more untenable when I noticed that as each man stepped up before the medical board, he was psychologically, physically and sexually assaulted by three naval medics and name-tagged by two beautiful blonde, rampant and panting WREN secretaries. The first medical officer would raise the victim's penis with a bamboo baton and roll back the man's foreskin looking for contraband, and finding none would vent his spleen by roughly gripping the man's testicles and screaming into the victims tortured face: *"Cough!"*

The recruit would adhere to the request, then, at the command from the second medic: "That man, One Pace Forward March. Halt. About Turn, Touch Toes" The man would swing round with his back to the table and offer his anus up for inspection. The inspecting officers (and the two Betty Grable look-alikes) would be confronted with a large hairy rectum and a pair of bruised throbbing testicles.

The third officer would then unceremoniously ram a Vaseline covered rubber gloved finger into the man's tightly gripped orifice causing him to throw his head back and bellow like a pole-axed buffalo. The victim was then ordered to "Stand to Attention...Look to the front and call out, *"loud and clear, That Man's Full Name"*. This occasionally brought forth derisory peals of laughter from the several thousand 'already done' and 'about to be done' volunteer's. The sound of a loudly squealed camp Egbert, Wilberforce or Horace elicited the loudest guffaws. However, these were few and far between.

There were mostly Georges, Charlie's, Stan's, Bert's, Dave's, Alf's and even a 'Rocky' who cringed at the stinging retort, *'THAT MAN WHAT CALLED OUT ROCKY...THAT IS NOT THAT MAN'S CORRECT NAME. SHOUT OUT YOUR CORRECT NAME WHAT IS 'ROCCO', THAT MAN!'*

Seconds before I was to step before the inquisition I fell madly in love with both of the alabaster breasted secretaries and looking down I was horror stricken when I realised I had an erection, which caused me to receive a stinging a rap on the cock from the first officers baton and the giggled command to

"Control Yourself, That Lovely Man."

The whole hall went suddenly quiet. All eyes were focussed on me. I looked for a bolt hole to crawl into but there was no escape, and my torment was magnified tenfold when I looked beseechingly at the nearest of the two sex Goddesses and noted that she had purposely loosened the top two buttons of her straining white shirt exposing a heaving sweating cleavage and hitched up skirt to reveal an expanse of milky white thigh and a smidging of her regulation navy blue elastic legged cotton knickers... And this at the very second when the medical officer steered his hand around my organ and gripped my newly fallen testicles, causing me to ejaculate a stream of sperm over the gold braided rings on his sleeve.

This brought a deafening roar from the ecstatic onlookers and a sliver of spittle from the pouting crimson lips of the climaxing pair of cock teasers.

Bye-passing the command to 'cough, about turn, touch your toes', the lieutenant in charge yelled; *"NAME?"*

"Hugh Cecil Hammond, sir" I whispered.

"What? Speak up... *NAME?"*

Tears running down my flame red cheeks, I stood on my tippy toes and tried to whisper into my tormentor's ear, "Huge Cecil Hammond sir."

Wiping his stained sleeve on his white smock, my torturer snarled: "I'm warning you, you little bastard... one more time... *now lets hear it..."*

"HUGH...CECIL...HAMMOND, SIR"

I screamed in a falsetto I thought I'd broken two years previously.

My name bounced off the walls, floor and ceiling, along corridors, through open windows and across the huge parade ground and beyond the outer perimeters of the base.

As I cowered and shivered with embarrassment the whole room vibrated into convulsive laughter as large, multi-shaped men (and the two apparitions), coo-ed, wooed, whistled and guffawed.

In that instant I became a man... and after the pain of my initiation into His Majesty's Royal Navy, (N.A.A.F.I division) nothing the Germans, Italians or Japanese threw at me could even come close to that first 'near death' experience.

Four weeks from the day of waving myself off from the West Hartlepool railway station to 'join up,' I greeted myself back into the fold.

I was given five days leave, but as I stepped through the front door of my former home my father met me almost on the doorstep with an ear to ear grin on his face, pushed a one way rail pass into my top pocket and handed me an admiralty telegram ordering me to about turn and make my way up the coast to North Shields, Tyne and Wear and report to the Master at Arms aboard the county class cruiser,

H.M.S. Devonshire. And the sadistic bastard capped off his delight by saying, "good job really, we rented your room off."

Disembarking from the overcrowded train at North Shields tiny railway station I handed my papers to a small weasel faced Petty officer and was herded unceremoniously into the back of an already crowded royal naval lorry and 15 minutes later was delivered to a long wooden gangway, leaning precariously against the hull of the aforementioned County Class Cruiser, H.M.S. Devonshire.

I stood transfixed on the quayside and was mesmerised. She was the biggest, most beautiful sight I'd ever seen. For a second my mind flew back to my father's gloating face and I silently said a 'thank you' to God for cutting the umbilical cord and freeing me to find my own way in the world. As I thought of my brother Dick, still tied to that uncaring bastard I felt a heavy sadness and wished he could have been sharing with me this, the greatest moment of my life.

Struggling to carry my kit bag up the crowded gangway my foot went through a hole in the rotting, blue painted number 7 gangway and I stumbled.

Helped by' a shipmate' I made my way, after a fashion to the ships N.A.A.F.I canteen where I introduced myself to my immediate superior, Leading canteen assistant Cliff Keeble, who in turn introduced me to the Canteen Manager, Chief

Petty officer Alex Hammil. I snapped to attention and saluted.

'The Chief' screwed his face into a wince and said, "Cut that out you prick...inside these bulkheads I'm 'the chief' and, nodding to his second in command, "and he's Cliff... we're all mates y'see son." Then showing me the first sign of affection I'd seen in years he put his arm round my shoulder and said, "and if you're a good learner you'll make more money with us than you'll ever see for the rest of your life". We may have to bend the rules a little but stick with the team and we're going to get along just fine. Welcome aboard the skylark, son!"

I smiled inwardly to myself that they were going to have to up the ante to compete with the racket I'd had to put trustingly into the hands of Canteen manager, Chief Petty Officer Thomas Hanson., railway shunter Joseph Hammond and my mother, Jane Florence, *'till the end of hostilities'.*

The next few weeks was to be the shaping of my manhood, and my entry into 'the league of gentlemen pirates.'

The N.A.A.F.I. canteen had a staff of five. Apart from Alex, Cliff and me there was an old school mate named Trevor Swinbourne and a tall gangly youth from Bolton in Lancashire called Lofty…(to this day I don't remember if he had a surname.)

The ship itself, buzzing with frenzied activity, was, in my eyes, a floating city. She was also spotlessly clean.

Within hours of joining the crew of the Devonshire Cliff Keeble took me down below-decks to the 'mess' that was to be my new home for the unforeseeable future and ordered the duty mess steward to look after me.

Trevor Swinbourne greeted me. "Jesus Christ, Jackie, where did you come from? I didn't know you were shipping with us… oh boy, we're gonna love this war."

Cliff gave us a few hours off to 'find our sea legs, and Trevor, who'd already been aboard a week showed me around. Every nook and cranny was a voyage of discovery to me. We wandered around the focs'l, sniffed our way along midships and aft as far as we dare venture to that holier than holy, 'The Quarterdeck'. I was shown the galley where, as the once weekly 'duty mess steward', I'd collect the meals for my mess, and on to the ships armament from the huge 8inch gun turrets to the broadside Pom-Poms and Orlekon anti-aircraft guns.

We went to the N.A.A.F.I. goffa (lemonade) bar, which was today run by 'lofty'. The 'goffa bar' was the rest area…a kind of small social club where we would share alternate duties making ice-creams and soft drinks for the off duty crew. After my first ever mess-deck dinner I collected and signed for my hammock, heavy-duty sea gear (sea boots, thick sweaters, balaclava, gloves and duffel coat… an inkling that we weren't heading for the South seas). I stencilled my name and number to my hammock and every item of my kit right down to my toothpaste. I was appointed a 'hammock sling' (my very own sleeping space) and after a soft drink and smoke on deck I realised it was time to turn in.

I'd slept in a hammock for the past four weeks in the Chatham training base so I had no problems 'slinging' my hammock and swinging, monkey fashion into the swaying canvas and rolling over three times to cocoon myself in my solitary blanket.

I lay awake, wallowing in the wonderful way my life had suddenly become my very own. Then in the midst of my reverie all the lights went out and soon I was being serenaded by a couple of dozen snoring 'shipmates. Later the bars, which supported the rows of hammocks, began to gently vibrate as sexually aroused youths fantasised with dreams of recent or future conquests. Then, with a silent 'goodnight' to my brother Dick, I drifted off to the best sleep of my life.

Six thirty the following morning the unmistakeable screech of a 'bosun's pipe' and a gruff voice over the Tannoy brought us back into the real world. Suddenly all was bedlam. The night watchman heavily nudged us awake and anyone who thought they could take liberties suddenly found themselves dangling head first as the watchman came back and tugged free the head end hammock lashings, with a rousing but jocular, "Come on you horny bastards… wakey-wakey… hands off cocks, on socks." I spent the first night of my life aboard ship.

Today I was going to be a sailor.

Immediately after breakfast the scenario, from quayside to inboard was a hive of activity. A fleet of trucks were unloading tons of food. Countless sides of frozen beef, sheep and pig carcases and huge sacks of fruit and vegetables were slung aboard by   dockside cranes. The gangway was cluttered with men, scuttling like a plague of ants, struggling up board with stores and dashing ashore to collect more.

All around the ship, men were dashing about the deck under the watchful eye of the gunnery officer, unloading a massive range of ammunition for the huge guns and smaller armoury …there was even a catapult-mounted seaplane. The furore gave us an insight of what life aboard fighting ship was really like…manic, hectic and mind-boggling. All that was missing was the slave-master with the bullwhip. Then over the tannoy came the screech of the bosun's pipe and the call from the quartermaster 'stand easy'… then "Up Spirits", an order that had mess stewards dashing to queue for the mess's rum ration which was collected in shining steel 'mess fannies' (pans)

And now it was Dinnertime… then more manic thrashing about then, in no time it was the bosun's pipe again, this time calling us to tea. Then in late afternoon the call *"Liberty Men, fall in!"* This meant that off duty hands were allowed ashore.   Two days later, armed, stored, shipshape and Bristol fashion, there came the now familiar sound of the bosun's pipes and the stern message summoning the cable parties to muster fore and aft where they toiled at the capstans to slip our moorings and hand our fate over to the crews of the tiny tug-boats straining at the bow and stern hawsers, hauling us away from the quayside. Slowly at first we headed midstream up the river Tyne. A short time later we approached the river mouth and casting the tug tow lines adrift we watched the pilot shin down the port ladder onto his cutter. Long minutes later we rendezvoused with an armada of mine sweepers, escort destroyers and frigates and went 'full ahead' into a brilliant sunny but choppy North Sea, heading for the farthest tip of Scotland. It seemed that we'd all been too busy to notice the rising and falling of the ship as we headed into the wider expanse of the North Sea… then there an added movement as the ship climbed a huge wave, the rolled sideways down the trough, huge waves of spray saturating everything and everyone above board. Then the ships rails were suddenly cluttered with groaning vomiting seamen as we ploughed through the most treacherous waters in the world next to those of Cape Horn, the Pentland Firth… and on to the cold wet and clustered Orkney Islands and our new Home Fleet base mooring at Scapa Flow.

Sadly my old schoolmate Trevor Swinbourne was so ill with seasickness that he was put ashore in the Orkney Islands and I never ever saw him again.

In all my years afloat in some of the fiercest storms we could encounter, I was never once seasick. Today I can't watch a sea going movie without a bucket between my feet.

Once at anchor the whole ships crew were mustered on the quarter-deck and informed by the Captain that we were now an integral part of the Home Fleet, performing the dual role of protecting the north Atlantic convoys and seeking out.

Enemy surface craft, U-boats and Heinkel and Stuka dive-bombers of the Luftwaffe.   And although I was only a few weeks into my sixteenth year, I was on the threshold of becoming a fighting man long before I'd started shaving.

Because of the war, Cliff Keeble had had a promising career as a professional middleweight boxer put on hold, so he fashioned his own gym in the goffa bar and kept in trim by training every chance he got. He boxed in all the Northern Command championships and never lost a fight. He became a mother hen to me and taught me (among other things) how to protect myself from bullies and 'arse bandits'.

(the omnipresent paedophiles).

From the day I stepped through the gates of the Chatham training barracks I was aware of older men making passes at kids of my age. So we'd work and play in groups…like a pride of young lions. In short we'd watch each other's back's…. especially the lower regions.

I remembered that very first night at Chatham some perverted duty officer of the watch groped us in our hammocks. Nothing heavy, just a feely touchy situation which would be halted with a loud 'fuck off, dirty bastard' and the shadow would head for the hills. However, one guy, a middle aged officer was more persistent.   Reporting offenders to your duty officer was a waste of time as most of them were members of the same sex offenders association. So around ten of us had a war council and decided to handle it our way. We made 'monkeys fists' out of hammock lashings and when the groper (he turned out to be a lieutenant) came to play in the early hours we loured him into a false sense of security allowing him to grope his way through the hammock's till he was in the centre of the hall. Then at a signal from one of the kids we retaliated lashing out and making more noise than the London blitz. When several guards broke in and turned the lights on they found this badly cut and battered semi conscious officer writhing in agony.

A court martial followed and the man was dishonourably discharged…. drummed out of the service before the entire mustered 'ships company'.

It meant the offender was paraded before everyone on the base, found guilty and stripped of his Rank. This was done by a master at arms tearing off the offenders cap badge, epaulettes gold braiding and buttons. Then he had to march, under armed guard the full length of, and out of the parade ground in step to the beat of a drum.

So, after a few uneventful weeks aboard the *Devonshire* came that unforgettable nightmare, while I was taking a lone late night shower, the ships Master at Arms accosted me. He stood and ogled me for a few minutes then offered me a drink from a half empty bottle of rum. I refused and made a move for the door when he grabbed me forcing my hand down to his genitals while forcing his other hand over my mouth. Immediately Cliff Keebles training came to fruition. The man was drunk, disorganised and with both hands occupied he was now completely defenceless. I suddenly grabbed his balls and sunk my nails in…he moved his hand from my mouth and his head fell back in a silent scream. I measured him up and butted him on the point of his chin, then as he staggered back I swung my fist at him with all the power I could muster catching him flush on the bridge of his nose. He fell backwards and collapsed in a heap under the shower. As I left I picked up the half bottle of Rum and poured it over him, turned the cold shower directly over him and watched him squirm for a few seconds then, throwing a towel around my nudity I strolled back to the mess and swung proudly and merrily into my hammock.

The following morning, at Captains rounds I stood to attention as the entourage made their inspection. The master at arms was nowhere to be seen. Word was that he'd accidentally fallen down a companionway and was at present in the sick bay.

So he was still aboard.

He was a very good photographer and the following week while making a purchase at the canteen he asked Alex Hammil if he could take some pictures of the canteen crew. He took one of me standing in front of the 8 inch guns of 'A' turret… and he not only presented it to me in person, but he smiled as he graciously signed it.

I have it to this day, framed and hanging with pride on the wall of my office. I never mentioned the altercation to anyone, and the only evidence of it was an inch long scar on the bridge of the 'Masters' nose.

I'd stand in my off periods and stare in fascination at the fleet, from little escorts to massive battleships tied at anchor in between the scattering of tiny unlit islands.

Since the end of the 1914 World war, the waters of Scapa Flow were littered with the upturned wrecks of the defeated German Fleet. Rather than surrender to the 'enemy' they decided to ignominiously scuttle their own ships.

It became a silent message to us all as to the futility of war… and this while we were fighting the same enemy over again. *When will we ever learn?*

Coming from a seaport I was used to the smell of cold salty air, but here, standing alone in the pitch black of night, the smell was different. There was still the salty air and an even icier bone chilling wind, but now there was an added ingredient to it all. A scent of excitement…constantly accompanied by the choking sickly aroma of diesel oil. There was also a more sinister phenomenon…of the unknown, and though, in all my days at sea I was foolishly never afraid, there was always a prickly feeling in the pit of the stomach, an ominous feeling of something drifting on the breeze and floating just below the waterline. We'd sway in our hammocks while our hooded unsleeping eyes flashed images across the blackness of the deck head just inches above as if waiting for something, we didn't know what….but in all my voyages during hostilities. And the only time it left us was when, during a lull in the tension we'd be allowed to go ashore for the shortest of breaks.

The first two days in 'Scapa' the Chief, Cliff and I went ashore to the nearby island of Hoy... and though my memory plays tricks in my dotage I seem to remember landing at a place named Lyness where we went to an old seafarer's pub in a side street, and in a scene straight from Robert Louis Stephenson's 'Treasure Island', I was kept out of earshot, and Alex, Cliff and three huge heavily bearded shifty looking seafarers spent several minutes in hooded conversation. Not only did I learn why later...but soon I was as bloodied as the rest of this loyal band of smugglers.

The following week we were ordered to sea to join our first convoy. This was 'it', the real beginning of the greatest adventures of my life. Next morning I came on deck and was amazed at the amount of ships, large and small, multi national all heading north to the first rendezvous in the Faroe Islands. I borrowed Alex's binoculars and scanned the horizon from South to North and back again.

I was doubly fascinated at the little destroyers that zigzagged between the forest of swaying masts... like sheepdogs darting to and fro through a massive flock of nervous sheep, herding the slower ones who strayed out of line, the occasional 'whoop-whoop' of their sirens echoing across the rolling expanse, snapping at the heels of their charges. And suddenly we could see nothing... as if a mighty hand had switched off all of the lights in the world. Then, on an invisible cue came the breath-taking phenomenon of the Northern lights as dozens of brilliantly coloured beams swept in huge alternating arcs to the four corners of this magical world accompanied

by billions of twinkling flakes of snow which lit up the inky black backdrop of the Arctic heavens, softly and faintly serenaded by the soft dulcet tones of the two forces favourites Vera Lynn and Anne Shelton fighting a losing battle to break the hypnotic panorama the Good Lord had laid out for all, friend and foe alike to drink in like an intoxicating heady wine.

Most of the ships 'new hands' stayed on deck most of this mysterious night.

In the early hours, with the fading of natures firework display all was silently black and cold like the breath of the grim reaper. Then the silence was broken by the sound of an aircraft... somewhere on the outer perimeter of the convoy.

Was it midships? Ahead? Astern? The sound got louder and unbelievably a tiny beam of light at the far side of the convoy flashed across the gloom... just for a few seconds... then the plane zoomed directly above us. Several of my new shipmates had joined me shivering on the forecastle as we pressed against the huge cold steel housing of the 8 inch 'A' gun turret for sparse comfort. As we looked skywards a rapid blinking of an Aldis lamp sent an indiscernible message from the cloudless sky, once again, just for a few seconds, then the plane moved in another direction and was soon swallowed in the freezing blackness. A disembodied voice in the blackness grunted; 'One of ours!'

"Thank fuck!" came another voice.

A young seaman standing next to me puffing on a cigarette was suddenly lifted off his feet by a dark duffel coat hooded figure and a voice snarled, "Put it out.... Put it out or I'll throw you over the fucking side.... *Name...gimme your name and number... now you cunt."*

The recipient of the assault seemed to have swallowed the still smouldering weed and was coughing and spluttering his name and number...then the spectre turned and disappeared into the murky night. We held our breath for minutes but there wasn't a sound...apart from the whooshing of the sea speeding along the hull of the ship. We turned and groped our way to our allotted mess-decks where we quickly slung our hammocks and fully clothed swung up into our gently swaying nests and half slept, occasionally staring through drooping eyelids at the deck-head just inches above.

I tried to figure how a ships signaller could exchange coded messages with a plane over the foreboding blackness to be seen for miles, and an unthinking matelot dragging on a shielded

cigarette butt was threatened with keelhauling for such a
Misdemeanour.... but *'Our's is not to question why... our's is but to do or... die'.*
Dawn brought a weird kind of mayhem aboard. We all toiled, performing our duties, breaking open crates and filling the canteen shelves with stores, but in all the hub-hub, despite the roar of the engines, we all worked without speaking. It seemed like e were waiting for that inevitable 'something' outside in the freezing mist that must surely make an appearance... but only in it's own time. There was not an element of real fear aboard... just an uncomfortable expectancy of a something we all dreaded would suddenly call us to account.
Several hours later as we sailed further into the frozen North Atlantic ploughing through mountainous seas, blinding snow and lashing hailstorms, we felt, rather than heard a low muffled thud, followed immediately by the alarm bells summoning us to our action stations. As I made my way clumsily along the starboard side of the ship my eye was drawn to a cloud of smoke in the middle of the convoy...there was no substance to it...just a cloud of black smoke out of which slowly emerged a blazing black hulk from which several people jumped into the icy water. Everything seemed to move in slow motion, then suddenly the cloud turn into an inferno. I was still running to my station when a huge explosion from the stricken ship hurled a large piece of debris, possibly part of the deck through the blizzard, which landed on top of the survivors... then nothing. A destroyer swooped out of nowhere maybe a hundred yards from me and the depth charge crew were rolling 'ash-can' depth charges over the stern of the ship, while feet away more depth charges were sent flying through the air and dropping into the boiling seas. Several huge plumes of water rose in the destroyers wake then I was dashing headlong into my action station.
Less than an hour later we were ordered to stand down. I emerged back into the daylight and watched silently as the convoy carried on pitching and tossing almost peacefully onto whatever lay ahead.
As darkness once more settled on the scene I made my way back to my place of work, the canteen. I pushed the bottom 'stable' door open and crawled in, where I lay on the deck in the canteen alongside Cliff, Alex and a couple of matelot's and pitched headfirst into confused oblivion. I was still rigged out in my lifebuoy with its 12 inch inflation tube and the little light and a whistle attached to the shoulder strap.
I suddenly snapped awake seeing those poor souls being pitched into that icy black void, and I started to sweat profusely as I came to realise that at any moment, night or day I might be down there, bobbing about in that frozen waste.... screaming to God, any God and my mother for help knowing that neither would heed me.
I lay all night exhausted and semi conscious wondering what the hell I, ordinary sixteen years old Jackie Hammond from the nondescript little fishing port of Hartlepool was doing freezing the middle of a real man's war. In the space of a few days I had become a man...and I wasn't sure if, in my haste to escape the tyrannical regime of home, I hadn't leaped from the frying pan into the fire.
Last nights loss was the only one I saw that week. We escorted the convoy only part of the way to its destination. Then we altered course South-South West and met up with the rest of the Home Fleet strike force of Battleships, Aircraft carriers, heavy and light cruisers, Destroyers and Frigates. There wasn't a Merchant ship in sight.
Some weeks later the whole length of the ship was alive with a buzz that we were into something even more important than shepherding cargoes to Russia. Word was that we were now heading for Alton Fjord in Norway where we were going to 'get' the scourge of the 'Murmansk run', the German Pocket Battleship 'TIRPITZ'.
That victorious battle came on a beautiful balmy sunny evening in 1943. But now, with such a valuable prize at hand we were more than a strike force. We were an Armada and the main strike force were the pilots and crews of the combined Royal Air Force and Fleet Air

Arm and those insanely courageous two man human torpedoes. This day we were to witness acts of bravery and sacrifice that would be engraved in the pages of heroism for all time. And although mine was a microscopic part in the battle, I knew I could now and forevermore boast that '*I was there*'.

Wave after wave of heavy bombers of the RAF were joined by those little torpedo carrying 'Fairy Swordfish' biplanes from the Aircraft Carriers Victorious and Furious which flew before our unbelieving eyes, into the jaws of hell and the pages of history. Then it was over, and a message went around the free world and gave a glimmer of hope to the occupied countries and ignited a burning pride in us all, an emotion we were about to experience more and more from this day on.

The tide of War was slowly but inexplicably turning.

12 November. **TIRPITZ SUNK**

Beautiful Booty

Sadly our little money making scheme, born that night in the dimly lit bar in the Orkney capital of Kirkwall all came to an abrupt end when back at the Scapa base we were taking stores aboard from the N.A.A.F.I supply barge.

Cliff was operating the crane and I was as usual guiding the incoming cargo of cigarettes, spirits and lesser important stores like food into the hold.

As I'd done several times before, I would guide three loads of stores into the 'N.A.A.F.I store room hatch and one load of 'contraband' onto the docker's barge tied up on the lee-side of the ship. Afterwards we planned as usual to meet the 'head man' in the same pub in Kirkwall and share the spoils.

Unfortunately this trip we had taken aboard a new eagle eyed (and incorruptible) young midshipman. He immediately spotted the sting, fired a distress flare and yelled; *'PIRATES'*. Court martial followed. Alex Hammil was reduced to the rank of Petty officer,

Cliff Keeble was given detention in the brig at Kirkwall and because I was so young I was put ashore for two months at the X1X Royal Marine Auxiliary base on a small floating carbuncle of earth called 'Flotta'.

Believe me, my punishment was by far the most extreme.

The X1X Auxiliary Marine Battalion base was a reception camp for the recuperation of battle fatigued marines and naval personal. Most of these people believed they'd been hidden away from the world. When all their hopes and dreams of ever becoming normal human beings again were blown away on the constant icy north winds, the only relief for the occasional battle weary, confused men, deemed lucky to have survived the nightmare of battle was to take a 3.03 rifle, shove a live round in the breach, tie a boot-lace to the trigger, loop it round the butt of the gun, press the muzzle hard to the forehead, jerk the lace upwards and blow their brains out.

I remember one day when I was on counter duty a marine sergeant major came to the counter and purchased a "good strong pair of boot laces!" Less than five minutes later we heard the 'bang' that ended his misery. The whole X1X Marine battalion attended the man's funeral as he was buried, as one war weary hero snarled.

"With full useless military fucking honours!" That nightmare still haunts me to this day.

Boredom mixed with some of the most atrocious weather in the world helped tip the balance between insanity and an eternal queue for a seat on the right hand of God. Having recently fitted myself out with a criminal record, they naturally didn't supply me with a rifle or a bullet. So instead of noisily removing my own brains, I handed that task to my fellow man and joined the base boxing team.

I should have shot myself. You don't have to go into strict training, it's quicker, and apart from a stinging split second, it's less painful.

First I was ordered to stop smoking, which, for a 16 years old kid who'd been fighting the habit since he was five years old gang member, was an almost impossible task, but after reading a couple of books on world boxing champions, I got the bug and gave up on the dreaded weed.

My first fight was as a featherweight. My opponent was a forces flyweight champion but as I was the only opponent on the island within pounds of the champ's weight he agreed to concede a couple of pounds and accept the overweight contest.

Overweight I may have been. A contest it wasn't.

As the timekeeper raised his little hammer above a borrowed ships bell to herald in the first round, the pocket Marciano tore across the ring and knocked me into oblivion while I was still in a semi sitting position. All I remember is the first bell and a very angry looking midget walking towards me. The rest was all lights and flashes and then darkness. I woke up in the sick bay sometime later. It could have been a week later I'm not sure.

I was concussed and spent two days in the sick-bay, where I was visited by the team's trainer. He'd brought my losers award, a silver (plated) ash tray, engraved thus: *CNX/703625. C/A HC Hammond, "BOXING. SCAPA FLOW.1943"*.   As I fondled my prize with mixed emotions through half closed eyes and mumbled my gratitude through cut and swollen lips, my trainer imparted some great advice. He didn't, in so many words, advise me to try another form of suicide but he did say that should I wish to take up smoking again it was okay with him and the rest of the team... *'and you already have a new ashtray'*. But I persevered. My record still reads. C/A HC Hammond. Contests. (4)   (1) Lost. KO. 1st rnd.   (2) Lost. KO.1st rnd.   (3) Lost. KO.1st rnd.   (4) Failed to appear, Disqualified. Retired.

It was my third fight that put the seeds of doubt into my trainers mind. I staggered to my corner and asked my trainer what round it was and he said, "when the bell rings it'll be the first"... and his pre-fight instructions put the lid on my aspirations;

"Just go out and hit anything in front of you, except the guy in the white shirt and black bow-tie"

Am I crazy? They catch me committing a minor misdemeanour so they take me out of the fighting and cast me adrift on a barren island. So what do I do?

I become a fighter.

I got occasional letters from home but mainly from my brother Dick. Now and then I'd get one from my mum but things hadn't gone so well since I'd left.

Thomas Hanson didn't call anymore and Mum and the old man were now struggling like the rest of the world. I was happy with that... Tommy and I had built up a great little scam between us, and Tommy needed me as much as I needed him. And my folks definitely needed me more than I needed them. Now Tommy was a one-man band... and with the way things had been going him and I figured that my folks had been lucky to be in the orchestra in the first place.

Dick was trying his damndest to get into the forces but his job in the railways was classed as a too important to allow him to follow his dream. But at least he was a reaching manhood and the old man had eased up knocking him around because Dick was bringing in more cash and was now the main breadwinner.

I heard that my sister Irene was thinking about getting engaged to Tom Stainthorpe, who incidentally was a sparks (radio operator aboard the destroyer Whelp) and also based in Scapa Flow... He once came aboard the Devonshire to see me and I loaded him up with a year's supply of loot. Tom Stainthorpe was a nice guy and he finally did marry my sister.

My brother Les was in the merchant navy still, and was still mum and dad's hero. Her letters to me were full of their admiration for him. But as he and I hated the sight of each other, always did, and to this day still do, I began to check the writing on the envelopes at mail time. If they were in Dick's handwriting I'd open them... if they weren't, I'd give them to the fishes. I wasn't being disrespectful. I'd had precious little respect in my growing up years... now I was choosey who I gave mine to.

And to add to my folk's problems, Hartlepool docks, shipyards and steelworks had become a favourite dropping off base for the bombers of the Luftwaffe... I used to smile to myself sometimes listening to the BBC news during action breaks when reports came in about bombings in the North East. I visualised my folks crammed into their air raid shelter with all that contraband... and no one to sell it to. Still, I figured if they were going to die in the blitz, they'd be the healthiest and wealthiest corpses in the cemetery.

Maybe the reader will think I'm a hard man, but this was war, and seeing as how, in all the time I was in the navy I never got one solitary letter or good luck card from my father, I should worry more for the people who shared my war with me.

For the record, during my stay the total headcount on the island of Flotta was a variable 800 men. One (passable) WREN and 10.000 sheep (the place was famous for its sheep which, it was rumoured were often the only sexual diversion for miles, and which, it was said got prettier and more desirable the longer one stayed in their company)... There were also twenty five boxers. The two main pre-occupations on the island were fucking and fighting.... and as I knew I was better at the former than I was at the latter I decided to hang up my gloves. I was unique in that I was the only patient in the sick bay suffering from obvious wounds. 95% of the other patients were suffering from the effects of booze, nicotine and the dire effects of rabid bestiality. Most of the islands great romantics would begin their nocturnal meanderings by heading first for the N.A.A.F.I beer bar where they would get blind drunk on cheap hooch. Then feeling horny would head for the hills for a night of debauchery with a quadruped of their choice, ignoring the warnings on a myriad of giant posters pinned up around the base suggesting that, in the interests of hygiene and longevity, after the final goodnight kiss they should immediately dive headlong into the nearest carbolic sheep-dip.

Often, in my reverie I make a nostalgic return trip to Scapa Flow, my mind clogged with curious memories and mixed emotions. Strolling onto higher ground I wander knee deep through heather, gorse and sheep and am amazed how many of the older quadrupeds resembled former comrades, and I found myself calling out to them,

'Hi Ginger'... 'Wotcheor Geordie'... 'Hello Neville'. I am relieved to note that not one of them had a broken nose or cauliflower ears.

Now I'm sitting on a small heather covered hillock, my thoughts drifting back over the years as I observe the ghosts of my comrades shaving and combing their hair to line up for early shore leave, dashing off into the hills to be to get the best looking ewes."Comon Dusty... hurry up".

"What's the hurry, there's ten thousand sheep on this island!"

"I know, but you don't want to get an ugly one, do you?"

I smiled as I thought of my old partner in crime Cliff Keeble making a fortune on Flotta selling cheap hoof sized engagement rings to all those lovesick seamen.

And then I drift to that fateful day when the order came from the duty officer to report to the base draft office and now I'm almost marching through a tiny village of camouflaged Nissen huts anchored to the frozen earth by steel hawsers, and my heart misses a beat as I espy a paint peeling notice which reads; 'X1X Marine Auxiliary Battalion.' I stop at a deserted windowless hut, the door hanging on one rusted hinge, but still bearing the red painted initials; 'RSM' and my memory swirls back through the mists of time as a marine sergeant major calls me into the office and says:

"I think you've served your penance son...fancy a cruise?"

And with that he handed me a small envelope on which was typed "ORIBI G66"

"What is it?" I asked then.

"I haven't any idea, son." He frowned "but I don't think you've won the lottery."

He reached out, ruffled my hair and said, "Good luck son..." and as he turned his back on me he repeated, almost in a whisper, 'yeah, Good Luck son.... Christ knows, you're gonna need it"

Now, today I look out over the now calm waters at the peaceful scene as I re-lived that day 40 odd years ago. I see myself dash back to my room in the main canteen and joyfully throw my belongings into a kit bag. And my mind swimming I shout a hurried final farewell to the other hands and, I'm making my way down to the little jetty. Within an hour of leaving the RSM's draft office it's bitterly cold and in the swirling fog I look around the crowded fleet barge. Occasionally we'd pull alongside a completely blacked out warship and watch shadowy forms struggling aboard their designated berth as we disappeared into the frozen mist. The coxswain on the bow of the barge wielding a boat hook turned to me and called:

"What's you berth, Winger?"

"Oribi" I said, checking my slip and shivering against the icy spray.

He pored over his saturated clipboard. *"G.66."* and his voice echoed through the eerie blackness. After an eternity of silently steering between steel hulks he suddenly called back.... *"There she is."* I squinted through the gloom at the ghostly camouflaged hull of a destroyer, framed against the backdrop of a scuttled World War 1 German Warship. The barge pulled under the bow of the ship and cutting the pinnacle's engine we drifted along the starboard side of my new berth displaying in 3ft tall white lettering **"G.66."** She didn't stir up the same excitement as my first ship. The 'Devonshire' was a 'Big ship'. A three funnelled floating town.

In comparison H.M.S. Oribi, an 'O' class destroyer attached to Russian Convoy escort work, was a village. A destroyer is classed as a boat. A little boat with little guns and littler promise of any feature comforts. I remembered when, aboard the Devonshire shepherding the convoys up into the Arctic, I'd watch these fragile little whippets streaking in and out of the lines of merchantmen, their sirens 'whoop whooping'…. geeing the stragglers to keep up… 'Or else'. In inclement weather they bobbed happily around like a cygnet on a warm summer's park pond. In big seas, and the north Atlantic is notorious for it's big seas, they'd either plough through the waves, or, caught broadside on, would perch momentarily on a mountainous crest, then heel over like a rolling Spitfire breaking formation, into the boiling trough. And I was soon to learn that when a destroyer at top speed ploughs into a thirty-foot wave, it is tantamount to driving a speeding car into a ten-foot solid block of concrete.

There were postings in every war as bad as Russian convoy work. There were none in all the wars in history, worse.

As I huddled in my duffel coat and wiped freezing spray from my stinging eyes a large grizzly bearded member of the barge crew flung my kit-bag onto the quarterdeck and with bated breath and heart gripped between my teeth I waited for the coxswains call to 'go' I grabbed a Jacob's ladder dangling from a boom jutting out from right angles to the ships deck, and I clung to the frozen rung of the swaying rope ladder as the coxswain threw the barge into gear and disappeared around the stern of Oribi, leaving me terror stricken, swinging for long terrifying minutes, my rubber booted feet flaying above the icy black waters of Scapa Flow. With my freezing, aching fingers occasionally missing a rung, and just when I was about to give up and crash into the inky void, I was suddenly and roughly grabbed by the collar and hauled aboard landing like a hooked fish in a heap on the deck.

Getting to my feet I turned to the quarterdeck to salute only to be stopped in mid arm swing by a scruffy duffel-coated P/O who hollered against the wind, *"Cut that shit out...hurry up… I'm fucking freezing"* and sticking an upturned gloved hand in my face, hollered, *"Chit?"* I handed him the soggy slip. *"Fucking NAAFI"* he sneered.... then nodding his directions toward the sharp end of the ship he yelled, *"through the foc'sle…third door starboard...that's the canteen...the manager should be in...But he's probably pissed somewhere... drunken Scots bastard."*

Then bending against the lashing spray the man turned on his heel and staggered amidships ducking behind the torpedo tubes where he vanished behind a heavy tarpaulin curtain.

Grabbing the lashing of my kitbag I dragged it for'ard and made my way through the heavy blackout sheet into the forepeak, which was dimly illuminated but warm.

The space before me was sectioned off into several tiny steel alcoves each divided by a mess table. Each alcove was packed full of seamen seated in gloomy surroundings in semi darkness, laughing, smoking, drinking from mugs and laughing out loud at the mess deck banter. A couple were writing letters to mothers, or girlfriends… none looked old enough to be husbands. A couple of them looked up at me, called out a greeting and then went back to the game at hand, while barely above their heads hammocks hung limply in the gloom.

I flicked on my cigarette lighter and tried to read the names of the brass plates above the small steel doors. The third one read 'CANTEEN'. I kicked on the door and it swung open to reveal a small bundle of fiery red bearded duffel coated something barely illuminated by the lights of the mess deck. He just stood and stared through bloodshot eyes, trying to focus on whatever had intruded on his reverie as he drank himself to oblivion in the dark miniscule but cluttered space of the ships canteen.

The whiskey bottle froze half way between his belly and his beard.

"Aye, who the fuck are ye?" Snarled the canteen manager *"Why did ye no knock, ye ignorant bastard?"*

"I did knock, chief," I said.

"See yae... dinnae gimme non o your lip ye snotty English bastard or I'll head ye. Noo, who the fuck are ye?"

"Hammond, Chief" I said. *"Your new hand."*

The man pulled the hood back from the duffel-coat, put his uniform cap on, pulled the hood back into place and finally getting my face into focus said; *"Yae? Jesus Christ, you're only a bairn...aye, well, fuck me they get younger... ye know what to dae I suppose...good luck to ye son.....noo, oot 'o' my fuck'n way...I'll see ye."* and he was gone.

I never knew his name. He seldom reported for duty...he never checked on me... I only clapped eyes on him when he'd storm angrily into the canteen to rifle the stock, then without a word he'd storm out again and vanish.

There came a time when I didn't see him at all. I never reported him missing... and nobody ever asked.

Checking that the port dead lights were closed I found the light-switch, flicked it on and looked at the notice pasted behind the steel stable-type door;

'Open 07.30. Close 09.00. Open 12.00. Close 13.00. Open 1600. Close 18.00. Except during Action Stations.' A pointless remark

On the small steel counter was an open envelope on which was written:

'C/Asst. H. C. Hammond. 2 Mess. Action Stn. 'B Turret gun hoist. Rpt. L/H R.Gallagher.'

As I was reading the message a tall stocky matelot stepped into the tiny space and tapped me on the shoulder. I turned and he smiled...somebody in this day still smiled?

"You NAAFI?"

"Yep".

"Gallagher. Welcome aboard. Call me Ray. You?"

"Jackie"... I said.

"Make it Jack from now on... or they'll think you're a hatter." (a homosexual!) *"There's some broth and a fanny (large metal bowl) of kye (regulation cocoa) in the mess if you want...oh, and listen carefully, you open after time for no-one but me, okay?....and I don't pay for nothing, but I mean, NOTHING, okay? You look after me and I look after you... we're wingers...get it?*

I nodded.

"...So, where you from, Jack?" he asked leaning past me and taking two cartons of cigarettes and a handful of chocolate bars from a shelf and pushing them down the front of his duffel coat.

"Hartlepool".

"O, a fucking monkey hanger.... Liverpool me! First ship?"

"No, I was on the Devonshire but me and the Manager and the killick (leading hand) got caught swinging stores onto the docker's barge.... Alex got dropped one.. Cliff got jankers in Kirkwall and I got put ashore over on Flotta."

Ray smiled. *"Cliff Keeble... the killick...? he's my mate...him and Alex Hamil... bent bastards.. I think Hammil's on the 'Welp' now... I only think though...but that's his problem...you're*

To my two
best friends
Maureen & Bob.
All my love
John

gonna be okay.... we're wingers now and I'm..."
The conversation was cut short by the boson's pipe, then a voice over the Tannoy."
'Attention... Attention...Cable party muster fore and aft..... Cable party muster
fore and aft. All hands make safe. Stow all hammocks.'
Ray cursed: *"What?....Bastards...what the fuck...we're not supposed to move till Sunday...*
well, the lousy bastards. See ya Jack..." and he was gone.
I looked around at my workspace with its cluttered untidy shelves of cakes, cigarettes,
chocolates, and small first aid kit. ('That should come in handy if we're hit by a torpedo' I
mused') I picked up a cardboard packet bearing a Red Cross label which read. 'Crab Paste...
not to be taken orally'. Several sides of smoked bacon hung on steel hooks by a small hand
operated slicer... and a hammer lay on the deck beside a dead blood-soaked large brown rat.
"Aw shit" I said... "Dirty scruffy Scot's bastard...aw,' I retched. "Shit. SHIT!"
I was suddenly jarred back to my senses by the rumble and grind of the fore and aft capstans
and men yelling orders. I switched off the light, reached up and, securing the deadlight, I
opened one of the two portholes. 'Two port holes, this is luxury on a grand scale..' Between
finger and thumb I picked up the still twitching rat by the tail and dropped it out into the
black freezing water of Scapa Flow starting an aerial war with a squadron of huge seagulls
squawking and fighting for the prize...then I slammed the porthole shut and securely clamped
the heavy port deadlight, locking out the outside world.
I looked at my watch '6.15 pm.' I'd stepped off the jetty and aboard the barge at
5.25... Fifty minutes. A cold watery sun was shining when the RSM had handed me my
pass to hell. I just didn't know it yet...but I had that 'too late to turn back' tight knot in my
stomach. Like maybe I'd stepped over the line once too often, and now it was 'pay back time!'
Switching on the light I glanced around the untidy canteen. There was a dirty apron slung
half across the bacon slicer. I took the stopper from a large bottle of lemonade and poured
the liquid over the thin trail of blood running up from deck to the porthole. Wiping the blood
from the counter and the bulkhead I finally dropped the
apron over the sticky mess and scrubbed it with the sole of my sea boot...
'I'll give it a wash after I've had my broth' I told myself, stepping out of my prison.... but
when I reached into the mess-deck oven, somebody had beaten me to my dinner. "Pirates....
Everybody's a fucking pirate!"
I looked around at my newfound shipmates. One stared back and said in a thick Birmingham
accent; "Don't look at me mate. I never touched ...er...that is...
whatever's been pinched." The duffel coated seaman to his right grinned and said "You're
lucky pal...it was fuckin' poison."
I smilingly shrugged and turning struggled with the double heavy tarpaulin sheets and
strolling out of the forepeak onto the deck I sheltered under the foc'sle ladder and the
bulkhead of the lower bridge superstructure. It was only then I noted the sensation of
movement as the almost indiscernible shadows of different sized ships drifted slowly by.
Apart from the now subdued activity and the odd shout from the foc'sle above me, Oribi slid
almost silently through the icy waters surrounded by the blacked out shapes of the Orkney
Islands. Occasionally a flashing light from a distant aldis lamp would send a coded message,
and across the inky blackness came spasmodic eerie far distant sounds of bosun's pipes
summoning a dozen cable parties to their stations.
Pulling my cap down over my eyes and fastening the neck toggle of my duffel coat I braved
the marrow chilling cold. Occasionally I'd start suddenly as a ghostly figure would appear
out of the fog for a brief second and with a grunted greeting would disappear through the
tarpaulin and into the for'ard crew's quarters.
I cocked my ears in the direction of voices calling from the small craft of the boom defences
guarding the entrance/exit in the anti U-Boat nets. They would create just enough space for

us to slip through before they closed the gap. Squinting into the
night I could make out the shape of ships steering the same course as ours, and occasionally
we'd sail close by an escort heading in the opposite direction bearing the battle scars of a
recent trip North/North East.
I looked at my watch.19.00 hours. I was glad in one way that I didn't have to open the canteen
tonight. In the space of a couple of hours I'd been uprooted, pushed bodily onto the deck of
a nanny barge, soaked in icy spray, had all my worldly belongings snatched from me and
flung who knows where, left dangling alone from a bosuns ladder over an inky black sea,
manhandled by a saviour, verbally abused by a man I'd
known no longer than a few seconds and never see again, forced to perform a humane
sea burial, and had my dinner stolen. I was alone in a freezing black void where I was the
only person I knew…apart from…what was his name again? I wasn't yet seventeen years old
and I didn't know from one minute to the next if I'd ever reach the tape. I was on a scruffy
little ship I speeding through strange waters taking me either to I didn't know where… or
why… I'd had a bit of a stressful day…I was going to go back into my little haven I'd share
for the length of my stay with rats as big as cats…. And right now I didn't care. I'm going to
sleep.
I headed for'ard and pulled the tarpaulin aside and hurriedly stepped into the warm below
decks. I gingerly opened the bottom half of the split doors and crouching entered my domain,
kicking out and making as much noise as I could to let any king sized rodent know that I was
back. I treated myself to a bar of nutty and a cake. Then I climbed onto the counter and as the
Oribi made her way through the cluster of German wrecks and tiny islands out into the open
hostile North Atlantic, I curled up, pulled my duffel hood over my head and slept like a babe.
A frantic banging on the canteen shutters and the sound of several angry voices awakened me.
I looked bleary eyed at my watch. 7.35.
I unbolted and lifted the steel plate flap to be confronted by, what appeared to be the whole
ships company. And they were angry. I was almost deafened by the cacophony of calls for
'three pounds of bacon… a dozen eggs… three pounds of
Bangers (sausages) two loaves of bread… powdered milk…tomato-sauce..soap.. Rizla fag
papers… razor blades… hurry up you cunt… c'mon for fucksake… the demands and abuse
came thick and fast. The one-hour opening seemed to go on all day… then suddenly there
was silence… apart from the throbbing of the engines.
I looked at my watch again… 9. 01. Jesus Christ… what happened?
I was brought back to my senses by the homely smell of frying bacon collected from the
galley which wafted through the still opening canteen serving hatch as it was carried to the
forward mess by the duty stewards. A lad around my age strode up to the window with a
plate of food and said, "hey naffi… are you on a diet or summat… get down to the mess now
while there's still something left".. and still carrying his breakfast he turned and disappeared
back down the hatch. I slammed and bolted the shutter on the canteen hatch and dived after
my new saviour.
My mess, number two was a hive of activity with men noisily gorging themselves, play
fighting, shouting insults at the occupants of mess one and mess three… and
Tormenting the three or four matelot's crouched vomiting into buckets and moaning.
The kid who'd gave me the warning call to breakfast asked me where I came from. I told him
Hartlepool, which as always brought the retort 'who hung the monkey'
A sailor in mess1 stood up and said to me, "hey winger, I'm from Hartlepool… Dyke House"
and I realised I too now had a 'Winger' (friend) aboard. It was only later that I realised that
he and I had gone to the same school at the same time. His name was Tommy Peckett and, at
18 he was a year older than me.
From leaving the U Boat boom nets at Scapa Flow to returning a couple of weeks later and

several years older, we never changed our clothing nor bathed. In harbour we slept in our hammocks. Outward bound, once past 'the Boom nets', hammocks were a hindrance in such a small area during action stations and were banned, so we slept where we fell. If we were lucky we'd confiscate a 'biscuit' to lie on. Biscuits were small cushions from the steel seat lockers welded to the bulkheads in each mess.   The early birds always got the biscuits…the less fortunate of us would just roll up in our duffel-coats against a bulkhead on the mess-deck and try to wipe out of our minds the thoughts that there was someone out there silently watching us through a periscope.

I believe the booze soaked Manager crawled into the hammock locker with two years supply of cheap Russian Vodka and to my knowledge he is still there.

Now and then we'd note the change in the sound of the diesel engines and a slowing down of the boat as we approached yet another obstacle on our trip north, then with a surge we'd head for the next hurdle where the whole procedure would occur again…

Groaning, straining as we climbed up mountainous waves and down into bottomless troughs… to pause, shudder and repeat the whole act over and over again.

Unhindered yet by a convoy we ploughed at full speed through the pitch-blackness on an endless carousel.

That second night aboard Oribi, although I had made myself known to my shipmates in my allocated mess but few, if any ever made a lasting relationship. We ate slept, laughed at the same endless jokes, make up stories about our sexual prowess or swap information about air-raids on our home towns and cities and worry as much about our families as they worried about us.

We'd go ashore when possible in small groups but apart from one or two special mates we didn't really bond. There was always the fear that at any time your best friend could become your ex best friend. From 'cable party' to 'tying up' if we were lucky enough to get to the other end of the cruise, time was taken up by working, eating, and sleeping. And as the ship rose and fell and writhed in agonising contortions, those who weren't permanently crouched over buckets were too tired to make chummy conversation. I was never in either band of the aforementioned victims. I don't know why I was never seasick. I do know that I was one of a very rare breed. But I felt sick for those of my mates who were. It must have been purgatory. In such a confined space of the boat every smell permeated and staled the thin breathable air. The close proximity of the 'heads' (toilets.) The ever present stench of vomit mingled with the aroma of freshly cooking food and the stink of stale leftovers which we weren't allowed to throw overboard during daylight hours because it was like a written invitation to U-boats, surface craft and aircraft alike. Tempers were constantly frayed and fights would break out over the most innocent of situations. To be a member of the Russian convoy run was bad enough. To be expected to cope with the constant sickness and its cause was unbearable. And through it all was the expectancy of sudden or lingering death, the constant 24-hour throb of the engines and the thick choking lung searing presence of the diesel fumes
which hung like a reeking blanket from port to starboard and stem to stern.

Yet somehow everyone would find some humour in all his or her misery. Someone would fart and the rest of the mess-deck would cheer, take deep breaths and say, "Ah, that was like a breath of fresh air."

My second night aboard 'ORIBI' I learned a very important lesson on seamanship, an unnecessary lesson on the big ships.

Before turning in for the night I decided to go to the heads. The crew's heads were below decks and in a large (for a destroyer) forward compartment. There were six door-less toilets port and starboard. Privacy was non-existent. I took my place on a seat less metal pot on the starboard side and fell into conversation to the man in the next cubicle. There were several other crew doing their thing, most of them facing the 'bog' to regurgitate their last meal, then immediately about face and carry on with their ablutions.

I was perched on the starboard side of the ship. Finishing the conversation I rose at the same time as my new friend. I cleaned myself up, adjusted my dress against the cold and turning to the bulkhead I leaned over and pressed the toilet flush release button with the palm of my hand. In that instant my colleague shouted 'NO… NOT YET!' But the warning came too late. The ship was already heeling over to starboard. And all my efforts came back to haunt me. With a loud 'hissing whoosh' I was covered from head to toe in a mixture of freezing seawater and shit.

Minutes later I was standing fully clothed in a miniscule shower as my shipmate sprayed me down with a fire hose. I made my way back to the mess-deck and shivering violently I stripped off and changed into my 'other' gear amid much 'ohhing' and 'pooing'. What few friends I had I lost that night.

Leaving my gear in the shower I returned to the little canteen, wrapped myself into a thick course hammock blanket and climbing up onto the counter I rolled into a ball and lay, wide eyed until dawn.

The next morning after I closed the canteen at 0800 Ray told me to take the main lashing from my hammock and tie all of my reeking gear in a bundle.

That done we went up amidships and, tying the loose end of the rope to a cleat on Ray's order I tossed the bundle over the side.

The ship was ploughing through the waves at top speed. A couple of hours later we both went back on deck and retrieved my clothes. Ray told me to follow him and we inched gingerly amidships, hanging on for grim life to the hand loops tied to the fore to stern wire safety hawser above our heads. At the torpedo tubes we unhitched from the lifeline and pulling aside a heavy tarpaulin curtain I followed Ray into a wide alcove. This was the same bolthole the duty bosun who had dragged me from sure death on the swinging boom the night I boarded, had made for. There was an open hatch and the heat coming up from the engine room was intense. With Rays help I hung out my 'dhobying' on several lines and we sat on the hatch cover smoking and chatting about anything and everything that came into our minds.

From that day on I spent most of my spare time in that warm and cosy haven with Ray and my new shipmate, Tommy Peckett, my new 'winger' from Hartlepool.

Around noon we had a dummy run at action stations. Ray's station was at port quarter depth charges. My action station was 'B' gun turret supply.

I made my way up to the lower bridge compartment directly under the wheelhouse and was ordered to open an ammunition supply hatch. This done I pressed a large red Button on the hatch rail signalling the magazine to send up the shells.

A small hoist containing four shells arrived and I unclipped the first shell, took it from the hoist and laid it on a metal cradle. This was angled to a hole in the bulkhead to 'B' gun deck outside. Tommy Peckett then positioned the shell, which rested on a 'fist'. The fist was in turn manipulated by a cable on the end of which was attached a cross bar like a 12 in piece of broom shank. Tommy would grab the bar and pulling down briskly would send the shell through the hole to a gun layer out on deck who would collect the missile and shove it into the gun breach. It sounds archaic, but it worked perfectly. The drill lasted about half an hour and we were then deemed 'B' gun turret supply. That was it. One didn't have to be an Einstein to realise that hardly anything could go wrong… and if it did it wouldn't happen a second time.

After lunch I'd open the canteen for an hour serving the bare essentials needed on a convoy escort destroyer. These were in order of importance; Toilet paper, Cigarettes, Cigarette papers, Rolling tobacco, Matches, Chocolate, and if we were lucky enough to come out unscathed at the other end and acquired a girl friend, soap, razor blades and Brylcreem.

Then eggs, bacon, sausage, bread and cakes, writing paper and envelopes. That's it.

I also learned, after my first altercation with the customers because I was five minutes late opening, that as canteen assistant/manager (as I now was) I was greatly favoured by every member of the crew, from the lowest hand, through the ranks to 'the Skipper'. I was especially fawned upon at each end of a cruise… especially as

Having learned from my Mafiosi mates on my previous berth that a stock of cheap perfume and a couple of dozen pairs of silk stockings would raise my stock one point higher than even the Captain. Even a Quasimodo look-alike could pull a mannequin with a pair of genuine American silk stockings and a watered down re-bottled shot of aftershave.

Day three, we dropped anchor in the Faroe Islands as we waited to pick up the convoy we were to shepherd through the foulest of weather with the added danger of attack from U boats, surface craft, (usually German Cruisers and Pocket Battleships), and the guaranteed attention of the Luftwaffe from the Nazi bases on the Norwegian coast and the northernmost German garrison on Bear Island.

Today, here in the Faroe's it was bitterly cold but sunny. Ray, Tommy and I hopped on a liberty boat and went ashore.

We took a few cartons of cigarettes, beads and other trinkets to trade with the natives. I swapped a carton of cigarettes for a beautiful Fair-isle polo necked sweater. I only wore it once. It was like being enveloped in a roll of barbed wire, but the Faroe islanders wore them non-stop… even for socialising. Those folk were made of teak. And after all the trouble I had cleaning my soiled outfit I only wore that once. It shone with a luminous glow, but the salt water had turned the lining into sandpaper. I had to wait till I got to Murmansk where, for a few cartons of cigarettes and a block of carbolic soap I rigged myself from head to toe in new gear. Of course it was not navy issue but on the convoys you'd wear your duffle coat twenty-four hours a day. No one saw or cared what you wore underneath it. My headgear at sea was a beautiful Russian blue fox fur hat replete with the red star badge pinned to the front flap.

You could wear a Ballerina's tutu and no one would have noticed.

We caught the liberty-boat back to Oribi and a short while later we upped anchor, set a course and took our positions on the outer perimeter of the armada of merchantmen, old and new. Tankers, cargo ships large and small, fast and slow. Dotted around this

gaggle were the escorts, Minesweepers, Frigates, Destroyers, Cruisers (large and small,) Aircraft carriers, Battleships and air-cover from Coastal command. It gave some cold comfort to our looming predicament.

I didn't realise that that was the last time I'd see sunshine for a couple of weeks, but the nocturnal display was breathtaking. The 'Northern Lights' painted in all of Gods brilliance across the night skies made up for the shortfall in daylight.

Beautiful as it was, I had more important duties to perform, mainly trying to keep the rats from eating all the stores…and staying alive.

Ray took me under his wing like a mother hen…and I made sure he lived like a baron. The first part of his contractual duties was point out the thieves, which (including myself) accounted for 99% of the crew. He also pointed out the perverts who would make a beeline for a fresh 17 years old kid. As an extra precaution he made me a 'monkey's fist', The 6inch length of rope with a wrist strap at one end and a brine hardened knot at the other I'd first used on the 'perv' in Chatham barracks. However, all the time I was aboard Oribi I had no need of it. From leaving the Faroe's we were all too taut and tired to think of anything but making it to Murmansk or Polyanoe in one piece. Several guys paired off as lovers but I was never bothered,

and in icy weather it's almost impossible to get an erection …your own warm hand and a good imagination sufficed…and I had a good imagination… I once read a whole volume of Lady Chatterley's Lover with one hand. In the other hand I held a bottle of baby oil and a box of tissues.

The trip from Scapa Flow to Russia was an endless nightmare, not only because of constant attacks from the enemy but also because of the weather. I was unfortunate enough to berth aboard Oribi at the onset of the winter. Although the summers weren't exactly exotic cruises, in comparison to the 'winter trips' they were a punt on the park lake'.

As we headed further up into the Arctic Circle the ships became laden down with ice, which had to be, chipped away, non-stop every day, which cut stand easy periods down to the absolute minimum. The seas were huge, the cold froze the bone marrow and the storms were terrifying.

I was still never sea sick... no matter how big the seas.... but as I said earlier I was the exception. I've seen men so ill they've begged the Germans to sink us.

"Oh God, where's the nearest land?"

"Two Miles!"

"Which direction?"

"Straight down!"

"Bastard!"

Merchant and warships were constantly being sunk by the U-Boats till later in the war when it was the U-Boats turn to face the nightmares of their own making.

Depending on the time of year, it was believed that the longest a human being could last in the water was three to seven minutes.

I was a witness to the horrors of almost scooping my fellow humans from the freezing sea when, at that very moment of rescue, a U-Boat warning would ring out and we'd have to become the hunters and steer through the screaming, begging, dying souls as we went again into action.

Again and again, I saw this happen. I never got used to it. I never to this day forgot the sight and sound of it.

You quickly learned the danger points for the convoys, like strikes from the Norwegian coastal batteries but if there was possibly a more dangerous patch to sail through it was that thin line between the farthest point on the Norwegian coast and
the German Luftwaffe garrison at Bear Island.

We, every single one of us were sitting ducks, at the mercy of the might of the German Army, Navy and Air Force. It was a miracle that anyone ever survived those horrific few miles, but unbelievably, most of us did.

Yet the closest I ever came to death was during a quiet period in the action. It came about thus. Although we'd been on constant red alert, we were at stand easy at our battle station. I was ordered to go down to the mess, get a large white metal jug and go to the galley and top up with 'purser's kye'. This was liquid chocolate, which tasted like mud in which the whole crew had washed their socks. Armed with my prize I made my way back up onto the starboard forepeak then climbed up onto the 'B' gun deck. The seas were wild with waves a tall as houses. Gripping the large jug of boiling cocoa with one hand I was inching along the narrow deck to the bridge station when the ship swung suddenly and sharply to port.

Caught off balance I fell backwards onto the guardrail. By some miracle I caught my right heel in the 2 inch steel rail that sealed the deck. As Oribi turned in a full circle the deck was awash. I felt the hood fall from my duffel coat and made an automatic grab for it, tilting my head back at the same time. All I saw was water speeding inches from my face, and to my horror I realised that I was hanging upside down over the rail...still gripping the jug of 'kye'. In seconds the ship came onto an even keel, righted herself and I released my foot and finally made it back to my station where I relayed my story to the crew who chided me... and they howled with laughter when the chief said, 'you didn't spill the fucking kye did you...if you had you bastard you'd have gone back for seconds.' As I write this 60 years on I still get a queasy feeling in the pit of my stomach... and the thought that, in the war of all war's I may have given my all for that jug of putrid hot chocolate.

On reaching our destination of Polyannoe, in the Northernmost regions of the Soviet Union, we would head for the Red Star club where, for a couple of packs of cigarettes and a bar of chocolate, the locals would melt a little and make the agony of our stay a little more bearable.

From the age of 16 I learned more sexual deviations from the

Fraternising sheep on Flotta to those Russian girls, thanks to a carton of cigarettes, a block of carbolic soap and a couple of bars of chocolate, than I have ever learned before or since. Of course the sheep didn't smoke or imbibe... they were happy with a bouquet of freshly gathered heather.

I also learned that as the only guy in charge of the ships canteen, therefore Lord of all the necessary requirements to make life a little more bearable I was a very much-respected member of the crew. You look after me and I'll give the okay to an extra carton of cigarettes... rolling tobacco, and little presents to send home if and when we ever got back to Scapa. In fact I became the second most desirable part of the crew.

Thanks to Alex Hammil and Cliff Keeble in my short stay aboard the Devonshire I'd learned to stock up with nylon stockings, make-up and perfume for when we hit a feminine friendly cove. As we were heading for our home port even the officers... including the skipper would warm towards me, and chat like old mates for several minutes before they 'wondered if I could... er... perhaps let me have a few...er... little bits and pieces for my wife and kiddies back in austere blighty?"

Even in inhospitable places like Murmansk, Polyanoe and Archangel I, and my N.A.A.F.I counterparts became known as Bluebloods who, if shown respect could make ones plight a heap more bearable.

After a while even the sheep felt left out.

I remember going ashore one time in the approaching yuletide season and cabling £75.00 home to my parents at a time when they existed on £12.50 a week.

£75.00 was a lottery win.

In Polyanoe we'd go first to the Red Star club, get pissed, try to lay as many local girls the time would allow and go to the makeshift football ground and play a game of soccer with the up and coming local Georgie Best's.

On my third trip we turned up for a game to be informed by the local coach that the fixture had been cancelled because there had been an execution that very morning. Drunk with cheap Vodka and curiosity the other guys checked it out and found both goals adorned with the frozen swinging bodies of several men and women who had been despatched for fraternising with the enemy. As we were many miles from the Russo/German battlefront we wondered, quietly, who the enemy were.

At sea I think that boredom was as soul destroying as the constant watches.

Aboard the Devonshire there was entertainment... Housey-Housey (Bingo) Boxing, Movies (blue), a handful of homosexuals and a sort of a gym... and she was big enough for joggers to trot around the deck.

Aboard the Oribi there was the occasional game of 'Housey between the torpedo tubes', arm wrestling, looking at dirty photographs and masturbating, reading and writing home. Some of the crew passed their time knitting or fishing while others became proficient model makers... using nothing but a razor blade and match-sticks which they'd collect or save and turn into unbelievably beautiful models and pictures. But most of time we were too tired for anything but sleeping.

I remember one cruise when a huge crazy stoker a Welshman had a bet that he would fight a large brown rat he'd caught. The rat was tied on a leash, one end of which was nailed to a mess table. To make the contest fair the 'Taffy' had his hands tied behind his back. The fight, with teeth, lasted maybe a quarter of an hour and was won when the badly bitten

stoker finally grabbed the squealing rat by the neck and shook it to
death. He tried to make it a regular attraction but no one could stand a repeat of the sickening
spectacle.

I'd spend time with Tommy Peckett during his duty watch and we'd chat about our early days
in Hartlepool.

But one watch at dawn we were so carried away with stories of home and admiring the
glowing, twinkling phosphorous from the bow wave when I brought Tommy's attention to
an arrow straight white line that seemed to be drawn on the water and pointing towards our
starboard bow.

Suddenly Tommy hit the alarm bell and screamed into my face,

"It's one of them. Ya daft bastard… Torpedo...Oh GOD, Torpedo...on the......... HELP. It's
…starboard bow."

All pandemonium broke out with alarm bells ringing and sirens screeching as we turned
sharply to face the missile, rapidly shrinking the target between life and death. Seconds later,
we peered, petrified over the side as the 'tinfish' whooshed past us with feet to spare.

The following night Stukas and Heinkels from Bear Island attacked us. I was at my action
station in 'B' turret supply. Bobby, our friend from North Shields was running to his station
towards the stern when the Heinkel came in low on the starboard beam. Bobby must have
seen the flashes from the planes cannon and heard the thud and
whizz of shells ricocheting off the Oribi's hull and superstructure.

The sky was a patchwork quilt of tracer shells as the plane came in almost touching the water
and as the pilot soared off in a hail of our gunfire we heard several cries of "Man Down".
Bobby had been hit in the lower jaw and almost decapitated by a cannon shell.

They said he was dead before he hit the deck. He was 18 years old. At that time I was already
learning there's an art in dying.

I don't remember a sea burial for Bobby, but I do remember my horror when, on getting back
to Scapa witnessing an auction of all his clothes and naval belongings.

This was normal practice in the navy, but Bobby was the first person I saw killed in close-up.
Yet it wasn't so much his death as the 'auction' that was sickeningly foreign to me.

However, his personal belongings were checked, parcelled up and sent to his family

in North Shields. I'd made up my mind someday to call on his folks and tell them he didn't
suffer, but in the words of Robert Burns,

"The best laid plans of mice and men will often gan awry."

The opportunity never came, and nor did my pilgrimage.

Bombs from one our covering aircraft hit the offending UBoat, and as she surfaced Oribi
rammed her. I was in shock for days after the attack. Oribi suffered structural damage. But
the enemy suffered a worse fate. There was only one survivor… the U-Boat's commander…
everyone else aboard U-365 were lost.

No one on either side had anything to cheer about. A lot of sons, sweethearts, husbands and
fathers were lost in those few minutes.

On a lighter note, after depth charges exploded, the sea would be covered with dead
fish, and I've seen crewmen from following boats lean over the side with small nets and scoop
up much appreciated fresh cod.

'To the victor go the spoils of war.'

On my penultimate trip I went with Ray to the Red Star club and we met up with Cliff and
Alex. Alex had a beard and Cliff had a broken nose, presented to him by some bullying
thug in the 'Glasshouse', and a couple of days after his release he joined the Alex aboard
the Destroyer HMS Welp, and the first guy he bumped into (literally) was his glasshouse
tormentor. Cliff immediately dispatched the man to the hospital in Kirkwall.

We were in Polyanoe for two days and we were pissed every second.

On my fifth convoy, we were, as usual attacked by Stuka dive-bombers from the Nazi base at Bear Island. I was at my action station,'B' turret supply and as the ammunition arrived on the hoist from the magazine in the bowels of the ship I took a live shell off the hoist and was about to lay it in position when a Stuka dropped out of the sky releasing a bomb which exploded just feet off the port beam.

The whole ship shuddered and keeled over to starboard and I lost my footing and fell backwards down the companionway. I bounced off every steel stair and landed flat on my back on the deck below, breaking my nose left arm and right collarbone in the process, and still hugging the live shell.

"Wounded in action" never appeared on my discharge papers so I assumed that my falling down two decks was my own clumsy fault. Even the fact that I didn't drop the shell was put down to 'self-preservation'. I was patched up in the sick bay and later hospitalised in the naval hospital in Greenock, Scotland. I was given sick leave. My brother Dick met me at West Hartlepool railway station and we caught a bus to Greenland Cottages. It was a Saturday and as I walked, still heavily bandaged into the kitchen of my parents house my dad was sitting at the small table listening to the wireless and crossing off the football results on his coupon. Although I hadn't seen him for months he didn't even look up as I entered the room.

I said "Hi dad... I'm back!".

He looked up with a face like thunder, threw his pencil onto the table and said, "Aw, you noisy bastard, you made me miss the football score!"

To Dick's horror I leaned over and shoved my plaster covered nose into his face and said: "Fuck you... and fuck your football coupon."

The atmosphere was electric. Then with a bewildered look on his face the master of the house stood up, took his railwayman's cap from the hook on the back of the door, shoved it on his head and stormed out.

I turned and Dick stood stark still with a look of horror tinged with admiration on his face. It was two days before the old man faced me again and asked how I was. I looked him straight in the eye and said; "Guess!"

I spent most of my leave boozing with Dick and my best friend, Bobby Laycock.

One morning, after sleeping late I came downstairs and discovered Dick, dressed in my uniform standing to attention and saluting in front of the mirror.

He didn't see me and I had the good manners to back out and leave him alone with his fantasies.

If you don't have dreams...

Discovering my artistic bent!

Had I had any show business aspirations I could have reached the top of the tree.
I could sing, a gift passed down to me by my mother who possessed a beautiful soprano
voice... and I acquired a sharp, ad-lib sense of humour, without the vitriol from my father.
My brother Dick taught me to play the piano (badly, and only on the black notes).
My school teacher, 'Pip' Pearson, despairing that I was unteachable in two of the three
'R's' noted that I had at least the ability to write compositions and perform on stage before
an audience without the slightest trace of nerves. However, they were my whole worldly
academic acquisitions. As an entertainer I had it made... as a scholar at least two thirds of me
was thicker than two short planks.
Like most homes in those days we had a piano and at the first opportunity mum, the greatest
ham in the bacon business, would organise impromptu concerts for friends, relatives and
neighbour's...strangers even.
The highlight of these would be a turn from my sister Irene (Dads favourite). Actually my
sister Irene hated to sing and the rest of the family hated to hear her but my dad thought she
had the makings of a diva. This was brought on by almost total deafness through his close
proximity to non-stop howitzer fire during his four-year sojourn fighting in India on the
Khyber Pass in the First World War.
It must have been sheer torture for my little sister to stand up and sing to all those people, but
when dad said, "sing", she sang.
Irene would be embarrassed to stand in the middle of the living room and perform, so mum
would allow her to stand in the hall with the door open.
I remember one night just as she was building up to a top 'C' my Uncle Sam got up and
closed the door.
I think that's the last time Uncle Sam was invited to one of Mum's musical extravaganzas.
Irene had been in the chorus at her school's production of 'The Gondoliers' and knew most of
the score and dad bribed an agent to pass her on an audition for a touring
Variety show. She joined the show and the first date she got was a week at Sunderland Empire
theatre. Unfortunately the theatre manager heard her sing at rehearsals and cancelled her.
She never made it into the big time but she still holds the record, seventy-five years after the
audition for the shortest career in the history of show business. Later she got a job as a bus
conductress, but the bus company put a proviso in her contract that the first time she broke
into song she would be asked to hand in her cash bag and ticket punch.
My favourite Uncle Sam had once been a stoker in the merchant navy and he taught me all
the crazy songs he knew. His favourite was 'Granny hold the candle while I shave the chien's
lip'. Or 'Don't sit on the gas ring granny, you're too old to ride the range.' I learned some
great song from my Uncle Sam. This led to my downfall at the Dyke House junior school's
Christmas nativity concert when, aged seven I was chosen to sing in the crowded main hall
before the entire school to a mixed audiences whose ages ranged from 5 to 14 plus the entire
teaching staff and the Reverend Roland A Long. Uncle Sam, a lifelong wannabe operatic
basso rotundo was delighted that his sole discovery was about to place his size 3 foot on the
stairway to stardom and encouraged my to sing one of his latest hits, which went something
like this.

"Ohhhh, have you ever seen a woman make water?
She doesn't half make a stream!
She can piss for a mile and a quarter
And you can't see her arse for ...."
Before I reached the word 'steam' I was dragged from the stage by the headmaster Pip

Pearson aided and abetted by a Posse which included Irene Boydon, playing the Virgin, Cackie Malabar, playing Joseph, and Bam Hamilton as the ass doubling as Pilate, and taken before the schools Christmas organizing committee where they took turns in giving me a severe beating with birch branches and banned me from nativity plays sine die ....FOREVER! This was during that part of the war when the blanket bombing of the shipyards, steel plants and docks was at its height and most parents were evacuating their kids to the country-side for safety.

When my mum and dad were called before the school P.T.A committee to answer the complaint about my oratorio offering they decided that I too should be evacuated.

It was a unanimous decision signed on a petition by every pupil in the school, the entire PTA, the Church and all of my family, their families and their family's families.

A few days later I stood on the platform of the West Hartlepool railway station slightly disorientated with both my arms in plaster casts and my head turbaned in bandages. Wailing, sobbing kids clung to their parents begging not to be sent away. I stood alone designated to the far end of the platform. My dad couldn't be there to see me off because it was a Saturday afternoon and he always listened to the football results on the wireless around about train take off time. My mum also couldn't be there because she was at the Odeon Cinema matinee sobbing her heart out at the plight of the similarly crippled 'Tiny Tim' in Charles Dickens "Scrooge".

A crowd of frightened kids stood in a tight group with their little gas mask boxes slung over their shoulders, labels pinned to their balaclava's bearing the address of their new homes. The Laycock boy's labels read 'Scarborough'. George, Jimmy and Mary Gooding's labels read 'Whitby" and the Murray kids were tagged for 'The Isle of Skye.' My dad wrote down the family's choice of destination for me to which my mum eagerly gave her consent and pinned the label to my jacket lapel…it read; **'DUSSELDORF.'**

I decided against ever again performing my Uncle Sam's compositions again and later in my career I became a much-respected Singer, Musician and Comedian.

In later years Irene Boyden, the proud product of a strict Catholic upbringing became the madam of several cathouses in the North East and later caused ructions in the church when she ran off and married a much-respected homosexual Presbyterian minister.

'Cacky' Malabar got his synonym because he never wiped himself properly after his ablutions. At school he was never allowed to join the rest of the students in line-up.

Our sports master, Harry Burnham, acquired and old airfield Windsock, which he erected at the far end of the schoolyard.

It depended in which direction the windsock was pointing as to where Cacky Malabar stood in line. If it was facing North/ North West, Cacky would be strategically placed in a position South/ South East…. Etcetera, Etcetera and so on.

A year after giving my all for my country I was embraced into the land fit for hero's and took a job as vocalist with the Jimmy Preston orchestra in the Borough Hall, in the old town of Hartlepool. Jimmy Preston auditioned me and said I had a great singing voice and Frank Sinatra goods looks. All I needed now was the ability to sing… whatever was thrown at me. I had spent so much effort trying to sound like my hero Perry Como… and his was in my favour. In 1945/46 nobody this side of the Atlantic had heard of Perry Como… and every male singer in the country was a poor replica of Sinatra. Most if not all could struggle through the whole Sinatra repertoire. My own Perry Como repertoire consisted of "Till the End of Time." Period. If anyone of my fans called out "encore" they got "Till the End of Time" till they hated it.

And until Perry did finally make it to these shores his handful of British fans thought he sang in a broad Hartlepool dialect. Jimmy Preston's first move was to make me sound like Jack… JACK? … nah… lets make it Johnny…Hammond! The first song he and his pianist Arthur

Smith taught me was the Como version of "If!"

It took them three weeks to change my "Ef, they made me a King" To IF they made me a King...but I did it... They also spent time on me singing songs in a dance tempo because on my first ever-professional gig the dancers had to hop to my timing. I was catastrophic. The band finished the songs 5 bars before I did and the crowded dance floor resembled a highway snarl-up. But Preston, Smith and the rest of the cast persevered and in six months I was accepted into music business. But I had a long haul ahead of me.

But, back to Cacky Malabar.

One night just after I left the Jimmy Preston rostrum a handsome pair of dancers approached me and the young man in white tie and tails asked me if I recognised him.

I said I was sorry but I didn't.

He beamed and said 'Malabar.'... Do you remember me now?

Taken aback I said, "of course, you're Cac... Cac... can I buy you both a drink?"

But the damage was done and he shoved his bottom lip out petulantly, stuck his nose in the air and, his black patent leather shoes flashing like a Hummingbird's wings, he

whisked his beautiful partner into the centre of the crowded dance floor.

I was amazed. 'How did the old Cacky Malabar change so much... and more so, how did he attract such a doll as the one now clinging to his like a limpet?'

As I was watching them glide away from me the girl suddenly threw her head back and sneezed loudly.

'Ah, that's it' I smiled... 'She has a cold in the nose.'

Bam Hamilton acquired his title by being the most ferocious bully in the whole infant school. He got the nickname because he'd stride around the schoolyard punching all the kids in the head. He would accompany each punch with a loud vocal, "Bam.... Bam...Bam".

While I was still living with my first wife in Hartlepool I began to suffer chest pains, which I attributed to living with my first wife. I decided to go to a private physician but the cost of £150.was prohibitive... then I met my old adversary Bam Hamilton. We were now adults, and friends and he told me he suffered similar symptoms to mine. So feigning concern I told him more people were dying of heart attacks than had died in the recent war...and that he should have an examination immediately.

His mother borrowed the £150 and Bam went private. He had a myriad of tests and finally the physician told him all he was suffering from was indigestion. I was happy for Bam and even happier for myself because I had saved myself One Hundred and Fifty big ones. A few days later I heard that Bam was dead...

"I don't know what happened" my informant droned, "but I hear that one minute he was here and a second later he was dead."

I flew into a panic and called a former Harley Street specialist who told me to get on a train immediately and check into his place. He also said I should bring his fee of £15.000. I phoned my bank manager and signed over my house and within hours I was wired up to ten machines in a very exclusive Harley Street clinic.

After an exhaustive examination my beaming physician brought me the diagnosis.

'INDIGESTION!'.

I was suicidal.

When I got back to Hartlepool I decided to go see Bam's mother. She said her son's death was indeed very quick.

I asked her if it was a heart attack, and she said, "No, he just stepped off the pavement and the bus ran over him!"

As long as I can remember I loved to sing. It was something inside me that just had to come out. If you had something like that inside you, you'd want it out, too.

Even now I never stop singing non-stop at home or in the car, but because I'm now a professional I always keep the windows closed. If people want to hear me sing they have to pay for it.

At parties in the early days I was a great asset. If things got a little dull I'd jump right into a two or three hour set. But this was long before Jimmy Preston and Arthur Smith transformed me from an unknown into an "Er. What's his name again?"   Sometimes I jump in even before he party got dull.

I'd plump for one of Uncle Sam's more acceptable numbers… like the aforementioned "Granny hold the candle while I shave the Chicken's lip." It was a great favourite in the First World War and on Old Comrades functions they loved me , but the new Madonna fans avoided me like the plague.

I went to one of Bob and Jackie Monkhouse's famous parties. Bob opened the door, put his hand on my chest, pushed me aside and let my wife Jeannie pass and closed the door in my face. Knowing Bob as a wag, after a couple of minutes I rang the bell. This time his lovely wife opened the door. I said, "Hi Jac, it's me Johnny… Bob locked me out."

She said, "I know" and closed the door in my face again.

So I became a dancer and that made my peers, which are few and far between even more jealous. I had all my shoes fitted with American jingle taps. This was a bad move however as now they could hear me coming two hundred yards away which gave them plenty of time to turn off the music, put out the lights and hide behind the furniture. After twenty or thirty of these snubs, I took the hint and Rang Jimmy Preston and Arthur Smith. But they were now suffering from amnesia and I was getting desperate. I was out of work and still owed the bank thousands for my non-Indigestion operation.

That's when I became a comedian. Nobody ever gets jealous of a comedian... unless he's an exception to the rule. Once you learn the number one rule, you're in. The number one rule is don't be funny. I've stuck to that rule for close on sixty years in Show business and it's never let me down. Some comics have to work hard at not being funny. To me it came as natural as dying.

The great Bob Monkhouse paid me a huge compliment when he likened me to the late song and dance comedy superstar, Dickie Henderson Jnr.

Dickie Henderson Jnr had class in spades.

Just how Dickie Henderson Jnr. would have fared in the workingmen's clubs however, with his laid back style is open to conjecture, but when you have so much class like Dickie Henderson Jnr had you don't have to worry. Anyway, Dickie Henderson Jnr would have been too expensive for the workingmen's clubs. He'd have out-priced himself.

The top fee for a club comic in those early days was £3.10 shillings per week.

Dickie would have wanted double that.... plus travel allowance, accommodation and personal injury insurance. Dickie Henderson Jnr was the most laid back comedian on the variety theatres and he was a huge success.

At £7 a week he could afford to be laid back.

Most of the clubland comedians I know spend a lot of their careers also laid back, usually comatose in club car parks. That's why a lot of class comedians won't touch workingmen's clubs.

But nothing fazed me in those days. I was fearless. I'd try anything.

Some years ago my ex-manager, the great north eastern impresario, Hector 'Bullets' Brancepeth got me a booking as a warm up comedian for 'Brancepeth's Beasties, a five piece Geordie group who had just returned from a tour of The Great Wall of China and had become the greatest ever band and a small threat to the era's top groups, not only in the whole world but any other country you'd care to mention. The Brancepeth Beasties had, just that week signed up with the brilliant Whitley-bay agent and bookmaker Rodney Einstein who had just been voted the North East of England's Greatest

Manager in the World
It was an open secret in the business that my manager Hector'Bullets'Brancepeth was jealous
of Einstein because he feared that when Einstein heard me he'd try to steal me from Hector.
I've always been inspired by that great Irish poet Jock McKinnon who once said to
the world famous Dublin Chiropodist, ''Bunions' O'Bannion, 'me fate are in your hands'…
and it never rang truer than this night. And fate can be very cruel two-pronged tuning fork.
Fate was cruel to Hector 'Bullets' Brancepeth, yet it smiled favourably on Rodney Einstein.
Today Hector 'Bullets' Brancepeth is scraping a meagre existence as a lowly public
convenience (Toilet) operative somewhere in the North West while the great multi-billionaire
and fabulously successful agent Bertie Einstein is dead.
You win some… you lose some!
The 'Beasties' show was on the football ground at Wembley Arena and there were maybe two
or three hundred thousand Beasties fans there.
The crowds came from every favourite corner of the world and Hartlepool.
The audience was littered with the greatest names and the most famous faces in the world of
entertainment. But there were thousands of famous faces in the crowd. I was the only guy
there I didn't recognise.
The late, great Tommy Cooper once said to me, "Johnny, never take a Gig in the open air.
You can't be funny in a field". But I didn't listen to him.
(*Actually it was Bob Monkhouse who said 'Johnny, never take a gig in the open air. You can't
be funny in a field', but I didn't want to give Monkhouse too many plugs in my book…he told
me he loved me but he didn't give me a mention in his.*)
But if the Beasties wanted me to help out, how could I let them down. The Brancepeth
Beasties were nice kids and I'm sure if ever I needed a group to help me out on one of the
Sunderland working-men's club Sunday lunchtime stag shows, the Beasties would have found
a way to get out of it. But if they wanted me to help them on this, their greatest night, I was
happy to return the compliment.
I had to walk out and do a ten minute set to all these kids who'd saved their last pennies and
walked hundreds of miles to London because all the trains were full and the motorways hadn't
been built yet. The event was billed as 'The Greatest Show on Earth' and the fans had eyes for
nobody but their idols, The Beasties.
The whole show was costing two million two hundred and fifty pounds. The Beasties cut was
two million two hundred and twenty five pounds.
My manager, Hector'Bullets'Brancepeth had demanded twenty-five pounds for me because
he'd rented me a suit for the gig. He wasn't, as yet a great manager like Einstein, but he was
doing his best. And he needed money for a new suit because the suit he'd rented me was an
old one, which had belonged to him in the first place.
On the big night the air was electric. If I said I didn't have butterflies I'd be lying but this was
my big chance.
I walked out without so much as an introduction or even a musical play on, which in a
field can be daunting, and I have to admit that I didn't knock them cold with my opening
gag. Matter of fact only about three people in the crowd even noticed I was there...and they
thought I was the sound technician checking the microphones.
I'd been talking to myself for seven or eight minutes till someone saw me and
Called to the rest of the Beasties fans, "Give the kid a chance".
I did my ten minutes in complete silence and threw in my last gag.
I couldn't believe it when it got a big laugh. It was the greatest feeling.
I thought, 'I can't walk off now that they love me, so I stayed on for another forty minutes.
Suddenly I realised I was dying again and the audience were all getting edgy and leaning
over sideways to get a glimpse of the five guys with the guitars and drum-sticks in the wings.

I turned and threw a joke at the boys and, trying to help me out they pretended they didn't get the gag and they booed and waved their fists and their guitars at me and their lead singer arched his back and pretended to masturbate while their drummer threw his sticks at me…and it worked because this brought great cheers from the audience.

But this also put me in a bigger quandary because I thought it would be bad manners to walk off now that I had the Beasties helping me out so I stayed on maybe another hour, hour and a half, during which time I looked to my left to see what the commotion was and noticed the four boys and their great manager, Bertie Einstein getting into a stretch limo and as it pulled away Spud, Geoff, Stan, Phil and

Bong Bong leaned out of the windows and gave me the finger.

Einstein just arched his eyebrows and put his tongue out at me and buried his head sobbing into a pink silk handkerchief.

The crowds watched in silence as the taillights from the limo vanished into the night then hundreds of fights broke out among the disappointed crowd. The police called in army reinforcements with tanks and helicopters, which the crowds set on fire.

After the audience had left, the stage manager turned the lights off.

I looked at my watch and was surprised to see that I'd been on stage over three and a half hours, so I decided to end my set.

Back in my dressing room I found an empty wage packet on the floor with my name on it and a four worded message which read 'Call Us Next Tuesday.'

Bemused I changed and went to my car. I didn't notice at first but a lot of the audience, maybe eighty or ninety thousand Beasties fans were hiding behind cars and coaches armed with golf clubs, iron railings, paving stones, boulders and knuckle-dusters, and as I got to my car they all leaped out and, screaming like banshees, they attacked me. They beat me mercilessly for maybe two hours. I don't remember exactly how long they beat me because as soon as I saw them running towards me I fainted. But before I succumbed I recognised one of my assailants who was inciting the rest of the mob to disembowel me, and later I identified him from a huge folder of police mug shots. A few weeks later he was arrested in Casablanca and sent to jail for six months.... and that's why I'm now looking for a new agent.

A verbal contract isn't worth the paper

it's written on.

In the late 1940's, at the time of my crucifixion at the Murton Democratic Miners Social club, I was already deemed a seasoned 'pro' I'd 'served my apprenticeship' on the workingmen's club circuit of the north east of England and I was still in my early twenties... but entertainers mature faster in clubland than they do in any other branch of the entertainment industry.... and no one matures faster than a club comic.

Comics take one of two routes... fight or die, in what is the hardest training ground for entertainers in the whole spectrum of the business.

An actor, singer, dancer or musician needs years of tuition, dedication and practice to master his or her art. A club comic has one hour to achieve the impossible, but if he can remain vertical for that tortuous 60 minutes and still have his ambition intact, he can call himself a club comic on his first throw of the dice and is automatically placed on every agent's social calendar.

Of course, to make it onto the *Agent's* Christmas card list you have to suffer, unflinching through an initiation ritual similar to that of a Zulu Warrior or a Chippewa Indian brave.

You don't have to be another Bob Monkhouse, a Jim Davidson, Tommy Cooper or an Eric Morecambe or another anybody. Talent is irrelevant. As dying is a predominant part of the club comic's lot, you have to emulate those brave musicians on the Titanic... Or worse, the backing band in the Sunderland Survivors club. I know. In 54 years I've been deflated more times than a communal condom.....You need a technique.

During my days touring the cheap variety theatre's before stepping backwards and downwards several rungs into club-land, I was fortunate to work several times with the man who was the uncrowned king of heckler put-downs Tommy Trinder.

Trinder said; "Johnny, you can't be funny in a field."

I said, "Bob Monkhouse already told me that a couple of chapters back."

Tommy Trinder blanched and said; "Fucking Monkhouse...okay, try this... If you have a heckler on your right you move stage left and converse with anyone in the audience interested or sober enough to listen to you. The heckler will suddenly realise he is talking to himself. Once he is subdued you make your way stage right and attack the unsuspecting asshole with a barrage of vitriolic put-downs which, if delivered correctly can have the moron looking at the floorboards for some woodworm burrow to crawl into."

Tommy Trinder, however never drew the short straw condemning him to earning a living on the northern workingmen's club circuit. To work Trinder's routine in a docker's or miners club you need, first of all, the courage of a Roman centurion to eyeball the offending party who is usually ten storey's taller than you. Then you need the ability to dredge up an insult which will immediately send the rest of the morons into paroxysm's of laughter and in so doing will not only disarm your tormentor but will lift your stock at least three points higher than you would have believed possible.

Little ball breakers like: "We're glad you could come.... it's a pity your father did", or "You won't get me off, I'm a pro like your mother was" are a couple which spring to mind.

While he scratches his shaven head with a large chunk of flint he'd gouged from the wall of his cave and gropes for a suitable answer, you deliver the coup de gras with a gem like. "Save your breath pal, you're going to need it to blow up your inflatable girlfriend."

He may be smart enough to impress his friends with, "Er...Oy er, what do you do for a living?" That's when you sink him with, "I get clients for your sisters."

Of course there are the standard put downs that have been around since the first Neanderthal funny-man was heckled at his attempt to tell the one about the 'giraffe necked, three horned duck-billed pterodactyl' and flattened his tormentor with the old chestnut; "Last time I saw a mouth like that it had a hook in it" or "go put your head against the wall, that's plastered too." However, in the several million light years since that historic night, comedic put down's having come along in leaps and bounds into an art form.

A good club comic will have the ability to ad-lib... to invent new insults at the first sign of trouble.

I used to practice mine on the way to the Gig. With the type of agents I worked for you knew the second you put the phone down you'd not be appearing in the concert room of the Vatican in Rome for an audience with the Pontiff.

One or two heckler stoppers that I favour in these technological times seldom fail.   I'd turn to the rest of the audiences and break the place up with; "This guy makes two short planks look like a fucking computer." or "I bet if I asked this asshole his name he'd have to ask the audience, go fifty- fifty or ring a friend." Are 'expletives' essential? I think so.

For instance; Say you're trying to entertain a mob of Rugby fans in the Sunderland Stevedores Whist Drive and Social Club on a Sunday morning stag show with several strippers who didn't come in the first 300 places at Crufts Annual Dog Show and you're the only guy in the place with two ears, trying to put down some anthropoid, complete with the hairy knuckles and eyebrow ridges who just that day has learned to walk upright, with; "This boring fellow makes two short planks look like a damn computer," the fusillade of empty Newcastle Brown Ale bottles, tables and chairs heading in your direction will tell you that your putdown 'had fallen well short of the mark!'

Some years ago, before cowardice forced me into writing gags and sketches for radio and television comedians, I got commissions from Workingmen's Club comics to write mainly heckler put downs.

But even with Herculean courage and a brain full of smart-ass insults, the main ingredient still has to be a Rhinoceros-thick hide and the ability to withstand the pain and humiliation of verbal (and often physical) abuse. This will put you in that tiny corps of unique performers, hailed, with genuine reverence as *'Workingman's Club Comics'*.

I've stood in the broom cupboard dressing rooms of some of the most frightening amphitheatres in the British Isles and listened to the opening act being dissected by a mob who at best resemble extras from 'The Texas Chainsaw Massacre', knowing that as soon as he or she succumbs, which 99.9% of them do, it will be my turn to be dragged before the inquisition and be mentally hung, drawn and quartered for the mandatory sixty minutes.

Walk off at your peril! It'll have cost you the expense of the journey to the venue, the torture of suffering the slings and arrows of outrageous fortune.... plus your paltry fee.(*It was common practice in many (but not all) clubs in the North East of England to have comics overcome all the hurdles, reach the finishing post and still not get paid for their considerable pains.*)

The first time it happened to me when I asked the concert chairman why I wasn't being paid he said, "You did two forty five minute spots and were crap both times!"

I said "Then why didn't you tell me after my first spot."

Slipping *my* hard earned wages into *his* pocket, he replied, "Well, I thought you might get better as the night went on."

It was also a thinly veiled clubland secret that your withheld-wages may even be later shared by certain or all members of the committee. However this is only well informed hearsay.

There is a jealous streak among committeemen, which makes them loath to pay a comic, just for standing on a stage for an hour telling jokes, the equivalent of their combined week's wages sweating at the coalface. Club committees were also cocooned in the knowledge that never, *NEVER EVER* would a sole club act be foolhardy enough to stand in the middle of a committee room full of huge miners, docker's, steel workers, ship-builders or weather beaten leather skinned, muscle-bound trawler-fishermen and *demand* his wages.

Of course you could always complain to your agent, but the agent to whom you were paying 15% of your fee to find the work for you was also the agent for the clubs, and you didn't need to be an Albert Einstein to work out where the agent's allegiance lies when it comes to the toss up between a one night comic or a 365 night lottery win.

"You were crap" from a chorus of irate, money-strapped committeemen was your cue to bite the bullet, grab your street clothes and head for the comparative safety of your 'digs'... with it's waiting flask of lukewarm tea and stale spam sandwiches with the customary curled up crust.

And it's not only comedians who acquire this jungle art of survival.

Sometimes it rubs off on the occasional girl singer, Git Voc (Guitar Vocalist), speciality act or pop group.

The first time I met the late Marti Caine was when we were both working a back-street comedian's abattoir in Chester-le-Street, Co. Durham which had that very evening waived the 10 pence cover charge in celebration of the switching on of the club's newly acquired neon sign. As is with all such awe inspiring clubland occasions, the bar had opened around 10am and stayed open till the beer ran out in the early hours of the following morning.

The opening act was a tall handsome black vocalist from Hull named Leon Ryles, who on the publicity poster in the club foyer Leon was billed as 'Taties (Tahiti's) Nat King Coal' Even though the singer was, and at the time of writing, still is, an icon in club-land, the concert room was only half full, mostly with panting females and the solitary local 'fruit', because Nat King 'Coal' was a sweet voiced ebony Adonis.

However, the other 50% of the anticipated audience were missing because this night there was championship boxing on the television in the 'Men Only' bar.

Nevertheless, 'Nat' had the knicker throwing audience grovelling at his patent leather clad feet. Then just as the last of the climaxing throng were aiming their panties, thongs and frilly underpants at the object of their desire, the door to the right of the stage opened and a small pockmarked individual dressed in jeans with twelve inch turn-ups, hob-nailed boots, a black shirt with yellow ruffed front and a greasy flat cap poised at a rakish angle, clumped across the wooden floor, leaped onto the stage and without glancing at the artiste, snatched the microphone from the singers hand, head butted it three times, yelled 'hello hello, testing testing...one two, one two, can you hear me in the car-park' into the mesh mouthpiece, and as the organ music droned to a halt, the mini gladiator held his fist high above his head, called for order and turned the warm friendly atmosphere to ice with; "Ladies, lads n' lasses, I'm sorry to stop the show like, but if we have any boxing fans here in the audience tonight, the news has just come from the bar that Jack London flattened the nigger in the seventh round." There was a deathly silence interspersed with embarrassed clearing of throats as the oaf turned to hand the microphone back to 'Nat'. His mouth dropped open as he looked for the first time into the handsome shining black face, gulped and said, "Oh shit... sorry pal."

Marti Caine was second 'turn' on the bill. I was the rest of the show, and as I was the comedian, Marti, an excellent comedienne in her own right agreed to cut her comedy and just do a singing set. Later in her career she became one of our greatest and best loved radio recording and television entertainers. But tonight she was just, in northeast clubland jargon, 'the tart singer.'

Marti floated onto the stage, an apparition in a slinky flame red diamante spangled creation, which plunged down from her neck to her navel and split up to the waist

revealing shimmering white panties and a pair of legs that reached up to her armpits.
The men lusted and the women loathed, and the fat little lady organist with the Groucho Marx moustache made sure that that was all Marti was going to show off
tonight and proceeded to murder her opening song by hitting some of the worst chords I've ever heard since Les Dawson's cod piano act. Here was a future Las Vegas star being destroyed before our very eyes. Finally Marti called for (and got) some semblance of order... and in a sultry voice she laid Leon and I in the aisles with the following announcement; "Well ladies and gentlemen it seems like I'm wasting my efforts, your time and the clubs money by trying to entertain you tonight, so, with your permission I'll leave the stage now and slip into something more practical...*like a Fucking taxi.*"
Leon flicked a coin, I called 'heads,' it came down 'tails, but what the hell.
Marti Caine, Leon (Nat King Cole) Ryles and I left the now kicking, spitting, scratching rioters to their own devices and headed for the hills.
A tortuous decade later Marti Caine appeared on National Television in a Trade Show called "New Faces" and was immediately rocketed to Icon status. From the MGM Grand Hotel in Las Vegas to Australia's Gold Coast, the South African Casino World in Sun City to the London Palladium, Marti Caine was one of the entertainment world's brightest lights. Tragically, at the height of her career she contracted cancer and died. But she had received the highest accolade any entertainer can achieve....

A perpetual place in the hearts of the International Entertainment World.

All for one......ME!

In most industries, downtrodden workers with the battle cry of 'All for one and one for all'
will strike for fair play, but if you try that ploy in a workingmen's club, there's a good chance
that you'll find yourself draped, comatose across the bonnet of your vandalised car long after
your tormentors have reeled off to their beds for the night.

A club comic's billing is usually fifth in line behind the opening act, bingo, the raffle, and the
hot pies, in that order. A club-wise comic will insist on number three spot, because a dozen
well-aimed hot pies can cause irreparable damage to a grossly expensive stage suit.

Some years ago I sat in the dressing room of the Alexander Theatre in Birmingham with one
the country's greatest and best loved comedians, Eric Morecambe. We were appearing in a
midnight charity show, one of the many arranged by my friend and continual benefactor, Jim
Davidson.

Eric and I immediately bonded into a friendship which lasted right up to his untimely death.
We chatted about show business and my sides ached with laughter at the great clowns stories.
But when I told Eric I was a 'club comic' his 'funny stories' were immediately put on the
back burner, while he grilled me as to how anyone could walk onto a stage without any
scripted material and work for an hour plus to an audience whose main aim of the evening
was winning the bingo, getting pissed and demeaning the comic... seven nights and a Sunday
noon, every week, for fifty two weeks a year.

Eric said; "Give me and Ernie an Eddie Braben script and a good warm-up-man and we can
be the funniest guys in the world...but throw us in at the deep end of a workingmen's club as
they do to you fella's and we'd die a million deaths."   As we relaxed over a drink I told Eric
my favourite story of the Stockton Fiesta Club*

Now it was his turn to go into convulsions.

After the Charity Show which included Jim Davidson, international singing star Frank Ifield
and comedy actress Sheila Staefel, the whole cast congregated in the bar and Eric got me to
repeat *the story,* then another and another. I made a lot of new friends that night.

A couple of weeks later I was doing the warm up front-cloth spot in a Cardiff Theatre with the
fabulous Dallas Boys and singing star Lita Rosa. We were all in the same digs run by 'Mrs
Jones, a former midwife whose claim to fame was that she was the person who delivered the
future diva, Shirley Bassey into the world!' and our stay it was a seven-day party. During the
week the Dallas Boys had to go up to the BBC London studios in Shepherds Bush to record a
show with Morecambe and Wise, and for some reason they happened to mention that I was in
the same digs.

Eric Morecambe said to the groups lead singer, Stan Dallas; "When you get back to the digs
tonight ask Johnny to tell you the story about his week at the 'Fiesta Club' in Stockton-on-
Tees". So I adhered to their request and told them Eric's (now) favourite story, and from then
on wherever I went some act would sidle up to me and say, "We were with the Dallas Boys"
or "We were in the studios with Eric Morecambe." or "We were with Jim Davidson".... and
they'd go on about *'The story.'*

Several years later Eric was heading home from a Gig and he had a massive heart attack, from
which, thank GOD he recovered. When he left hospital and went home to recuperate I rang
and was delighted to hear from his son that Eric was on mend. Although Eric was not taking
calls, when he was informed that I was on the line he massaged my ego by taking the phone
and asked me if I was still doing *'The Story'*.   I said I was and he said "you won't believe this
Johnny but driving home from the gig that night and I was re-capping on *'the* story'. I was
howling with laughter and the next thing I remembered was *'boom'*. So please, shelve your
stories or take out insurance on them.... especially that one. It's bloody lethal."

Later, zany Dancer Billy Dainty rang me and said, "Eric said from now on I have to check out all your stories, water them down and if they're safe, pass them on to him.... okay, gimme number one."

I related Morecambe's favourite tale to the great frenetic hoofer. As I delivered the tag, over the phone there was a strangled "oohaaagh," followed by a loud crash then silence, which lasted a full half-minute. In a panic I yelled Billy's name down the phone. After what seemed an eternity Dainty's cackling laughter erupted in my ear, followed by... "'Ere, Eric was right, that's bleedin' lethal."

I got a call from Eric just a few weeks before his death. He said, "I just dug out your number, how are you? I'm just thinking about that...oohahh oh aah..." After several seconds there was a click and then nothing. I knew Eric was kidding, but that was the last time I shared a laugh with him. Some weeks later I was watching television when news of Eric's death was flashed on the television screen. But instead of weeping for him I went up to my office, dug out a "Morecambe and Wise Special" and did what he would have wanted me to do... I laughed at him and for him.

As I remembered those magical moments together and locked in my brain is the night I told him I could get him a season on one of the more horrendous Sunderland Social Clubs and with outstretched arms he crossed his forefingers, exorcising me and said "I'll do it for ten million quid....plus funeral expenses".

I like to think that when he finally went to the great 'Palladium in the sky' he went out on my story.

Just let me add a 'naughty but well aired Morecambe gag', which creased me and the few close friends he'd trust it to. He said he was walking along the sea front in Bournemouth with Ernie and his great friend, the evergreen Max Bygraves. The great old 'ham' Max was holding court when suddenly Eric excused himself and strode into a music shop leaving his two pal's outside. After a few minutes he came out flustered and, doing his famous double take to make sure the coast was clear he did his famous wince and said; "God that was awful".

Ernie asked him what was wrong.

Eric said, "I went up to the counter and asked the buxom blonde behind the counter if they sold condoms. "The girl blushed and dashed into the back shop… so I did ditto and bolted out of the shop."

"It's a music shop, for Gawd's sake" said Bygraves.

"I know that" said Eric... "Actually I wanted a Des O'Connor record but I was too embarrassed to ask".

You've probably heard that story a thousand times and each time the locale is different but the name's the same.... Morecambe.

Actually I got that story as a gift from Bob Monkhouse but I gave it him back. Bob never gives away anything that works for anyone else… but before I returned it I called my bank and cancelled the cheque…Naturally that was after I'd put it in my gag file.

* The Fiesta Club story is chapter 38: "If I can make it there I'll make it anywhere"

WHY DO WE DO IT?

While a club comic can work any audience in the world, his legit peers would rather dive into a cauldron of boiling tar than venture into at least seventy five per cent of the country's workingmen's clubs. I have spent a lifetime... well, at the time of writing, fifty-four years on and off in this environment so I feel qualified to speak with some authority on the subject. *So why do we do it?*

Well, the bread (wages) is above the national average. The hours are good, and there's always the chance that one could be performing on stage one night when by a gigantic fluke, some influential television or movie producer's car breaks down outside your venue and, for warmth and sustenance the impresario finds himself seated in the concert room on one of your illusive good nights.

This however is a long shot, comparable to trying to shove butter up a wildcats arse with a white-hot poker. And I'm only one of a thousand club comics in the country.

I stayed most of my working life in Clubland and I must confess that 75% of that life was fabulous... but you don't go to the bullring to see the bull win.

For over 50 years ago I've been a close friend of the wonderful writer and radio producer named Frank Wappatt. He'd heard about me while driving home through early hours and he was fascinated by the stories. He contacted me and said he wanted me to perform in a Geordie radio show he was putting on for BBC Radio Newcastle. It was to be made before a live audience at a small but friendly Miners village club in Pelton Fell, County Durham. This was a novelty in itself. *LIVE* audiences in Workingmen's clubs are as rare as rocking horse manure. Frank was, and still is a lay preacher, but one with a ribald sense of humour. And I was not noted in Club-land for jocular niceties. So, just to be on the safe side Frank recorded the show before a live audience. Every act on the bill was superb and I, much to the chagrin of Frank and his script editor excelled with my hilarious double entendre. I finished my eight-minute set with my comedy piano act (which incidentally Frank still plays on his successful daily radio show to this day 50 years on.)

Several years later a young BBC radio producer named Michael Hurll who was destined to become one of the country's most successful and respected television and film producers was searching for new talent for a new TV series he was recording in Blackpool called Seaside Special. He was looking for something different from the normal spotlessly clean radio comics and having a tough time putting his finger on what he was really looking for. Late one afternoon he found himself sitting in his car in a typical London traffic jam and to ease the boredom he flicked on the car radio at the penultimate gag on the 'Frank Wappatt Show'... my comedy piano routine. He said later 'I'd never heard anything so original in all my years in the business'.

(This was many years before Les Dawson was in showbusiness). When Michael got to his home he started phoning around the studios to find out who was this guy, and more to the point the name of the show.

Finally getting Frank Wappatt on the phone in the early hours he asked how to get in touch. Frank put Michael in touch with my then manager Mike Batty in Newcastle and asked Mike where I could be viewed WORKING? Batty said he wouldn't know till he opened his office in Gateshead later in the morning.

At 9.15 the following morning Mike called Michael Hurll and informed him that I was appearing for a week in the Yorkshire Workingmen's clubs. Hurll asked for a date and venue and Batty gave him one at random. Of the seven gigs I was appearing in, Mike Hurll had to pick the worst of the tour. Although its one of the biggest clubs in Sheffield it was the nemesis for comedians.

So it came to pass that while I was being drawn and quartered by the inquisition a liveried chauffeur entered this aircraft hanger full of disinterested imbibers, and directed by the doorman strode down the length of the concert room and introduced himself to my wife Jeannie. She looked horror-stricken and mouthed the message to me that Mr Hurll was about to enter. I felt sick, but was too occupied with my battle with the drunken hecklers to notice the great mans entrance. In fact I was only drawn to him because not only was he the only person in the room laughing… he was also solely applauding my stand against the ever-increasing abuse being flung at me from all directions. However, as is my wont, I decimated the opposition and left the stage to a modicum of applause. Jeannie entered the dressing room followed by a glowing, beaming Michael Hurll.I started to apologise for his wasted journey but the great man held up a restraining hand.

"You were wonderful…no, you were fabulous… God, I can't believe it… how the hell… I mean… Oh my God, you were brilliant." And turning to my wife he said, "I've heard about these places… I've even visited a few and watched in horror at entertainers being destroyed… but this was an experience I shall take with me to my grave…the experience of a lifetime… and pumping my hand continuously he beamed… I'll see you at Pontin's, Blackpool on…" (he mentioned the forthcoming date to Jeannie.) and led by his chauffeur he strode head high from the room and out of the club.

The following week I had a call from my manager Mike Batty that not only was I booked for the "Seaside Special Show" but also Michael Hurll will spread 'our' name around the business like wildfire. Batty also related to me, off-handedly that he'd had an accident and had a badly broken leg.

The following week I was commanded to appear at Pontin's Holiday camp in Blackpool. On a scorching hot summers day Jeannie and I turned up bright eyed and bushy tailed at the 'big top'. I was introduced to the compere, Roy Hudd who beamed as he told me about Michael Hurll's description of my 'baptism of fire' at the hands of the Sheffield mob.

A couple of hours later during a break in rehearsals several of the crew and artistes were laid on the grass outside the 'big top' basking in glorious sunshine being chatted to by Michael Hurll when he suddenly looked up and exclaimed, "Fucking hell… it's Captain Ahab!". We all turned and stared at the figure of my manager hobbling towards us on crutches, his right leg encased from toes to groin in glowing white plaster and formally attired, complete with tie and pocket handkerchief.

As he reached the tape the whole crew and cast roundly applauded him.

The show was the best of the series and Michael Hurll kept his promise and spread my name far and wide in the television world.

For now at least, I'd arrived.

The Rollercoaster ride.

There must be thousands of stories, unwritten, which could tell the good (?), the bad, and the ugly side of my chosen profession. I'll attempt to give you some idea of the trials and tribulations in life as first a club entertainer and finally a club comic.

But first I have to go back to my earliest childhood which lacked most of the essentials to a good Christian upbringing. But no matter what fate threw my way, I have always abided by a quote from the greatest laughter-maker of them all, Charlie Chaplin who said; "A day without laughter is a day wasted!"

I was born in the fishing port of Hartlepool in the industrial North East of England. We were Mum, Dad, Cyril, Irene, Leslie (named after Joseph Leslie who died aged two) me, Audrey (who died aged eight months) and Bryan. I and my siblings were born at Number 10 Cleveland Road, Central Estate in a microscopic three roomed downstairs tenement slum surrounded in close proximity to the docks, the ship-building yard, the railway marshalling yards, the cement works, the timber yards, the fish quay and the kipper curing sheds. For the first five years of my life we lived in a constant stinking, noisy, smog choked atmosphere. From 7 o'clock every morning till 5 pm, six days a week we were bombarded by the staccato rattle of dozens of rivet guns, sirens, the crashing collision of the buffers of coal carrying railway trucks, the thunderous non stop rumble of cement trucks   passing within feet of the front door and the ever pervading choking clouds of cement dust and smoke hanging like a dirty grey blanket over and inside the houses and lungs of the populace

The central estate where I was born was a mini metropolis of three sets of tenements set in a diamond shape…with a diamond shaped garbage tip as a play area in the centre.

Looking back over the years it amazes me how my parents brought up such a large family under the conditions we lived in but whatever they did, it worked.

Dad's weekly wage as a railways wagon shunter was twenty-seven shillings a week, which in today's currency was £1.60 p. That was it. FULL STOP.   No family allowance. No Health insurance.   No community handouts.

On his income tax returns dad used to put 'food and clothing' down as 'Entertainment.'

Like most families we barely had money to buy food, but coming from a seaside town nature, more than often laid food at our feet.

Our playground was the Hartlepool fish dock. My elder brother Dick would play the Jews harp and I'd do my song and dance act while kind-hearted trawler-men would hurl fish at us. From those early beginnings I suffered early for my art.

In truth the locals would walk the half-mile to the beach surrounding the harbour

And dash back and forth dodging the crashing surf and snatch up stranded cod, crabs, lobster and shrimps from the slippery seaweed covered rocks. And hoards of kids would flock around the kipper curing houses after school and, for a penny we could purchase an armful of 'broken' kippers. These were fish, which had come apart in the curing sheds and didn't present an appetising picture in the fishmongers display slab.

Every man and boy within a wide radius of the estate became a first class angler, standing for hours on the pier casting home made lines and hauling in enough fish to feed the multitude. We never needed to pay for coal. Instead the men and bigger boys would go down to the sands and scrape up the coal dust that washed up from the slag tips of the mining villages of Blackhall, Horden, Easington and on to Sunderland. And firewood was always handy from the tiers of pit props stacked yard's from the front door. The younger kids would keep a lookout for the dock police and the older ones did the stealing. Nature is a great provider. Looking back over 78 years I find it difficult to see more than a hazy picture of my early childhood.

Life got a lot better for me personally when aged two I decided to leave home in search of my destiny. I took a fifty-yard stroll around the corner of my street and stopped to rest on Barton's front doorstep.

Old man Barton was a small market gardener. He and his wife had three sons, Harold, a giant of a man who opened a butcher business. Stanley worked as a plater in the shipyards and Eddie who was disabled when as a youth he was involved in a crash on his motorbike. After many months in hospital he returned to the world as a hunchback. There were also two daughters, Mary, a ravishing beauty who stayed in my life for some years and Hilda, a plain matronly girl. In comparison with the rest of the Central Estate populace the Barton's were fabulously rich. The story goes that I became the family mascot, and my mother used to tell me how the staid old man Barton would take me to his allotments on his handcart, the girls would mother me and the boys would unashamedly spoil me. When they discovered my parents had named me Hugh Cecil the Barton boys said that of all the kids in the area I was certainly not a Cecil, and laying me on the living room table, they baptised me with tomato ketchup and rechristened me 'Jack', a name that stayed with me through my infant and junior school days, through the navy and up to the doorstep of showbusiness, when I joined the Jimmy Preston Band as their new vocalist as Johnny Hammond.

My father was at that time a poker straight, handsome ex soldier…. and an unashamed womaniser.

I was aged around two when my mother gave birth to the ill fated Audrey who died the same week as Alice Hewson, an attractive teenage girl living in the upstairs garret with the Readmans, gave birth to my father's first illegitimate child. When Audrey died I remember my distraught mother picking me up and showing me 'the little doll in the white box' atop of the chest of drawers. Minutes later a horse drawn handsome cab arrived at our front door and as my Aunty Peggy held me, a large top hatted man came into the room, put a lid on the box and carried my sister off. As my father unashamedly aided my mother out of the house she went with the sound of Alice Hewsons healthy newborn baby screaming her lungs out in unison with me. I can see now, in my minds eye, the big man handing the tiny coffin to my dad seated beside my mother in the horse-drawn handsome-cab, then, after closing the coach door the cortège, led by a small high hatted boy in a black silk suit moved slowly off past the window and vanished from sight.

Three years later we, thanks to another of dad's infidelities the whole family packed up what sticks we had and caught the dawn 'milk train' out of 'Old Hartlepool' railway station. Like an old 'B' western movie, we just made it ahead of the posse.

Later that day, after several station changes we arrived at my father's hastily arranged new place of employment. He was now stationmaster at the beautifully picturesque village of Ampleforth (two trains a day) railway station. This was Shangri la.

It's strange that my father's indiscretion had forced us out of the choking smoke and noise filled Hell and into one of the most heavenly villages in the Yorkshire Dales. Each time I see that wonderful fairylike film "The Railway Children" on television my mind spins back to that glorious period. I'd swear that the author of that book had paused here on his dreamlike travels and watching our blissfully happy and healthy throng, picked our story for his wonderful novel.

We were housed in the centre abode of three tiny railway cottages. Our neighbours to the left were an old couple, Mr George and Mrs Alice Stainburn. To the right were Fred and Annie Woods. Fred, like old George was a railway plater doubling as telegraph lineman working the line from Ampleforth station south to Coxwold. George had spent all his working life looking after the track down from Ampleforth to neighbouring Gilling. The Stainburns were York folk who'd moved into the cottages immediately after their wedding as eighteen year olds. In rapid succession they had three sons and two daughters who had grown into honest healthy God-fearing citizens and in their own time had courted local swains, wed in the old church and flown the nest and settled in the four corners of the county. Old George was the part time church warden, and it was he and his little dumpling of a wife who took us under their wings and inaugurated us into the tiny beehive communal church, under the auspices of the youthful reverend Lawrence A Long. He had a congregation of thirty-eight 'country folk'...and six townies. We, the Hammond's were a young family. Cyril, the eldest of us was twelve. Irene was nine, Leslie was seven and I brought up the rear as a chubby five years old. Mum used to say, when we first arrived we looked like starving Russian Jews in comparison with the rest of the 'robust well fed and apple cheeked flock'. We were so pale skinned and undernourished that we looked like ghosts. But as children will, we were soon 'as country folk as the rest'. Life seemed to be taken up with eating, hiking, eating, church, eating, cricket, eating, hay making, slaving joyously on the neighbouring farms and becoming decent God fearing citizens. Mum, with her beautiful soprano voice immediately became a leading chorister in the church. She even formed a small concert party and travelled the county giving shows in the surrounding church halls, the receipts going to local charities.

The White's farm was half way between the station and Ampleforth Village, which was a mile away 'as the crow flies'. They were Mr and Mrs White (no-one ever called them by their Christian names). My memory fails me after all these years but the whites had two great strapping sons, one who was called Stanley... but the name of the younger one escapes me. They had several hired hands and Mrs White was assisted but a pretty girl of eighteen who had been castigated from the village because she had fallen 'with bairn' through an affair with a student from the Ampleforth Military college. The Whites took pity of the girl and more or less adopted her and the baby. At harvest time Mum, Cyril, Les, Irene and I would work from dawn till dusk, first on the Whites farm then onto the Colemans.

The Coleman farm was on the crest of a high hill and looked down onto our cottages and the lush rolling countryside.

Our new neighbours went of their way to befriend this ragamuffin tribe who'd been literally dumped into their midst.

The Colemans and the Whites owned hundreds of acres of lush farmland. As far as the eye could see natures canvas was awash with green fields, white farms, multi coloured trees, ancient stone churches and halls on a backcloth of cloudless blue skies.

We attended school in the equally picturesque village of Coxwold, a few miles 'up the rail track'.

From spring to late autumn mum and my sister and brothers and I worked for the farms and were paid in food and kindness. We even joined the flock of the reverend Lawrence A Long, and we'd go to church in a pony and trap that Charlie Coleman would bring to collect us. To this day I can still visualise the scene... I can even remember the name of the pony... Biddy. Mum joined the tiny church choir and we kids would perform with the other players in the seasonal plays in the church hall. Christmas seemed that it was made only for Ampleforth's idylicall happy residents. It really seemed that the good Lord and looked down on us and rewarded us with a permanent plot in the Garden of Eden.

Then, in the middle of this Heaven all hell suddenly broke loose, thanks to my father's uncontrollable libido or more to the truth his obscene disregard for the code of decency. Almost overnight we had to once again, up-stakes and flee... we knew not where... till after several hours of journeying the train stopped at the now un-familiar West Hartlepool Railway station...We were back to the industrial North... the stench, the noise, the filth and the long forgotten greyness.

The old man acquired a 'railway house' at 18 Greenland Cottages in West Hartlepool, in close proximity to the railway goods-yards, the timber yards, the shipyards and the docks and the fleas and the rats and the legions of pale faced half starved families, and to add to our mothers pain, we were housed almost within sight and sound of his 'other' offspring.

The minuses were that with our father's track record we never knew for how long we'd be staying. The dubious plusses were that the country was plunging headlong into a second world war...A war that would split the family asunder and free me, a 16 years old ill-educated kid, to make my own way through life's minefields, fortunes and misfortunes. But the adventures my brother Dick and I longed for were still a lifetime away.

In our new cluttered home our parents had one bedroom, Irene had the second and we four boys (Bryan had taken over the mantel of Audrey) shared one large bed in the third.

We sweltered in the summer and in the winter Dad would throw a couple of rugs on top of the bedclothes.

Then, at long last came for the war.

When the old man joined the Home Guard we'd wear his army greatcoat in bed. He'd spread it out and the two sleeping on the outside would slide a leg into each sleeve and we had no problems with that. When the bombings started Brian, Les and I started wetting the bed... Bryan could swim before he could walk.

It was thanks to those bombing raids that many years later Brian became the only member of the family to get a silver medal for the hundred metres breaststroke in the 1965 Olympics. He could have won Gold but you can't practice the breaststroke with your feet trapped in the pockets of an Army greatcoat.

Living in a fishing port our main fare was the famous Hartlepool Kippers, which we had seven days a week. Mum would serve them fried, dried, baked, flaked, roasted, toasted, grilled, chilled, poached, boiled, soiled, fricasseed, mashed, trashed, bashed...and on sandwiches. She even baked them as desert with custard.

You never tasted anything like her kippered hot cross buns. Visitors would give an eye tooth for one of her kippered scones with mum's famous clotted cream.... made from sour milk and kipper juice.

She even made starters of Kipper soup. She'd boil them in a large pan. Throw in a bottle of ketchup, some black pepper, a couple of diced carrots and unpeeled potatoes. It was gorgeous.... and her jellied kippers with castor sugar and a flagon of crushed cowslip and nettle wine were a gastronomic adventure.

In the early days of the War we used to run along the pier dragging a baited fishing line and on a good day we'd reel in maybe a dozen seagulls, which, when sautéed with Cameron's best bitter ale tasted like seagull.

Mum was rewarded for her War effort. Towards the end of hostilities the RAF dropped some of her recipes over the Rhineland. Hitler's official Russian food-taster Yuk Das Shiesen sampled the concoction and immediately expired followed by Joseph Gobbles, his wife and kids and within hours the hostilities ceased.

Because of the lack of fresh food we'd suffer occasional mild maladies, for each of which Grandma Marks had a remedy. In the winter a thick slice of raw potato wrapped tightly round the throat with an old wet lisle stocking saw off the inevitable swollen glands. However, the tourniquet had to kept constantly moist.

Our next-door neighbour Mrs Ethel Laycock (nee Scott) applied Grandma Marks' patent potato tourniquet to the neck of her octogenarian father, 'Old' Barnaby (Badger) Scott. The next morning he was found dead in his bed, his eyeballs resting on his chest. His purple lips wider than an open mineshaft in a silent gasp and his tongue protruding almost to the gas light bracket above the bed from which dangled his upper and lower dentures. The heat from the coal-fire in the bedroom had dried out the cotton tourniquet and the old man was strangled in his sleep.

However Grandma Marks' cure for constipation has never, even to this day been improved upon. It was a guaranteed success. It worked like this. While the patient sat in the privy at the end of the back yard, straining and groaning while staring in horror at a Tarantula spider's illuminated eyes glaring menacingly back from a dank corner above his head, Grandma Marks tippy toed down the moonlit yard and, ear pressed to the door of the operating room she would time her operation to the one most extra excruciatingly long and laboured strain and would rend the night air asunder by suddenly splintering the door with a heavy cast iron coal shovel, at the same time hollering and screeching like a demented banshee.

As GOD is my witness, it never failed.

Our father, (who I doubt art now in heaven) was promoted to goods guard on the trains that used to shuttle from the docks to the goods depot. As we lived in uncomfortably close proximity to railway line, the trains used to pass within yards of the back of our street. A five-foot wall separated the goods-yard. The old man would tell us what times he'd be passing and all the kids in the street would stand on the wall with our short pants round our ankles and yell childish obscenities and rehearsed insults as the train chugged by. Dad would yell back at us and wave his fists in false fury and throw huge lumps of coal from the engines tender in our direction. Then when the train disappeared from sight we'd pull up our trousers (and knickers because the girls were also in on the ploy) jump down into the siding, collect all the coal and pass it over the wall where the adult neighbours would be waiting with buckets, tin cans and one wheeled barrows to share it out.

When you work out that Dads train would make maybe twenty journeys a day seven days a week, the residents of Greenland Cottages ended up with more coal than the London and North Eastern Railway Company. After three months of this the Murray's at number 20 stopped burgling houses and became one of County Durham's biggest coal merchants.

I got my fine singing voice from my mother. I know this is not much of a boast when only her family and a few close friends knew that she'd been in Show Business. In fact she was so much loved and was such a great success that she'd been retired thirty-seven years before anybody missed her. Nobody ever heard of George Formby Snr, Frank Randle, W.H.Elliot or all of the other 'stars' of the Variety Theatres that she'd boast about treading the boards with, but she had her dreams and if you don't have dreams you don't you have anything.

I got my humour from my dad, although he was never a comedian, never stood on a stage and never said anything funny in his life. Matter of fact, he holds the record for being the un-funniest guy I have even known. He wasn't intelligent enough to be funny... but he was a walking disaster...if the old silent moviemaker Mack Sennett had stayed with us for a week my old man would have pushed Laurel and Hardy, Charlie Chaplin, Chester Conklin and Harold Lloyd off the screen.

In between his extraordinary marital liaisons Dad did things to try to improve our lot but they seldom reached fruition. But considering he was always running around with his trousers at half-mast, any, if not all of his planned home improvements suffered.

We were the first family in the street to have a 'cat's whisker' wireless.'

Don't ask me to describe a 'cat's whisker wireless.' It was indescribable, and the grating screeching noise that emitted from its .1 amp speaker was horrendous, but the greatest brains of today would never be able to re-invent one. Thank God!

My early memory in this field was of all the family sitting around this tiny contraption as it crackled, whistled and whined. We each had a pair of earphones which the old man had wired together to make a kind of cartwheel, with the 'wireless' as the hub, the connecting cables as the spokes, and the family as the rim. I always remember my brother Brian at a mere three hours old wearing his tiny earphones, sucking my mum's breast and howling at that unforgettable (no matter how much we tried) comedian, Stainless Stephen, who in his long showbusiness career was even unfunnier than my father. My dad would be wired up to mums other breast. Breast sucking in those days wasn't deemed a sexual nicety, but mum had two breasts, one baby and seven mouths to feed... and one of us were always hungry.

Dad, being head of the family had first choice of the menu. Later we exchanged the 'cat's whisker' for a small 'box-wireless.' It was perched on an old sideboard (if it had been perched on a new sideboard it would have been in someone else's house) and as we didn't have any fine aerial wire dad linked up three bike chains together to act as an aerial. He soldered one end to the back of the wireless and the other end he wedged half in and half out of the kitchen window. As it was a heavy chain and for years it hung in a deep loop across the kitchen. Anyone passing through the kitchen to reach the back yard had to duck low under this obstacle. In those days a wireless also needed an accumulator, which was a thick glass battery filled with acid, which had to be topped up once a week. The local grocer, Mr Lionel (Buck) Buttry held the accumulator filling concession, till one day he had an accidental spillage over a large part of his loose potato stock. He tried to conceal the accident and carried on business as usual, but within three weeks he'd wiped out 37% of his clients and closed down every chip shop within a five-mile radius. He had inadvertently acquired the dubious distinction of being Hartlepool's first serial killer. He went to prison for five years, but he was an attentive student and when he was finally released with time off for good behaviour he went into politics having possessed all the necessary qualifications to be a Member of Parliament.

Later in his career he was ostracised for 'pulling rank' by arranging for his brother, the local Presbyterian Church minister to jump the queue and get the recently vacated position as assistant Hangman to Albert Pierrepoint Jnr, the public Executioner.

But I digress. The wireless accumulator had a carrying handle and it was given to me the task of taking it to be charged and collecting it each weekend. I was on my way home with my friend Bobby Laycock (he was also carrying his family's accumulator) and as boys do we'd be swinging the things over our heads. One time, in mid swing I felt a punch on the back of my head, which brought me to my knees.

I looked up and dad was hovering menacingly over me.

"You bloody idiot," he screamed, "no wonder all the stations are mixed up."

After a few years we moved on to a more modern radio. The bike chain aerial was taken down and for the first time through innumerable horrendous arctic winters we could finally close the kitchen window.

However, old habits die-hard and I remember that for years afterwards, we'd still automatically duck under the imaginary aerial on the journey from the fireplace to the pantry… and visitors to our house never seemed to make a return call.

However, the new 'radio' still needed an aerial so one moonless night the old man had us stand sentry while he shinned up the telegraph pole outside the Tram depot and snipped off twenty yards of overhead trolley cable. It would still need to come through the window but as it was super strong we could just link it through the aperture and slam the window shut before securing it with a six inch nail. Now winters were a gas, but the tropical summers were a nightmare.

Some years later Dad got word that the "Greenland Quoits and Social Working-men's Club" was about to dispose of it's old twenty five foot wooden Boer War flag pole and purchase a new metal one, so he offered to erect the new metal one in exchange for a free transfer of the old wooden one.

The pole delivered, my dad and a couple of hefty neighbours helped him bolt it to the back yard wall. He then stripped to the waist, slipped a hammer and a few nails into his waistband, then gripping one end of the new aerial wire in his dentures he slowly, laboriously shinned up the rotting ex Greenland Quoit and Social Working-men's Club flag pole.

Hanging on for grim death he took hammer and nails and secured the wire to the top of the wildly swaying, groaning and creaking pole.

The task completed he started to slide slowly and *painfully* the twenty five feet return journey down to the safety of the back-yard and my mothers open arms.

As he turned revealing his blood soaked face, chest, arms, and stomach, we all recoiled in horror. Blood even ran in rivulets down his trouser legs. He was carried, stiff as a board into the house by neighbours, Bert 'The Lush' Laycock, Harry 'The Horse' Sedgewick and Jack 'The Bengal Tiger' Murray. Mum spent the next couple of weeks armed with eyebrow tweezers pulling hundreds of thousands of wood splinters from his face, neck, torso, genitalia, inner thighs, knees, ankles and toenails. I was six years old at the time and I remember taking my turn on the death watch as he lay mummified on the front room couch. I was sitting at his side stroking his laminated head when I whispered in his earhole:

"Dad?"

"Aherrooarrrwhat?"

"I was just wondering."

"Oh God...Ow...Oh Lord Jesus.... what?"

"Well, I was just wondering...why didn't you nail the wire to the top of the pole before you bolted it to the wall?"

His resurrection was immediate. His eyes shot open and with every last ounce of strength he could muster, he knocked me flying across the room.

That winter we had the worst thunderstorms in the town's history and one well placed bolt of lightning struck the newly erected metal flagpole of the Greenland Quoits and Working-men's Social Club setting fire to the outbuildings and burning the Club to the ground.

A couple of day's later dad received a letter from the committee housed at the temporary headquarters (an old horse drawn Romany caravan parked in Benny Cox's Coal yard) of the once proud Greenland Quoits and Workingmen's Social Club asking the old man to return his club membership lapel badge and refrain from making contact with them ever again.

Jack of all trades... master of none.

As we were a growing family dad decided to get rid of the tin bath hanging on the backyard wall and build us a fitted bathroom. Some years before he'd already built a lean-to shed against the back of the house enabling mum to cook out there instead of having to stoke up the coal fire to heat up the kitchen range every mealtime.... and the heat from those old kitchen ranges was stifling in the summer. Great cook, as my mother was she was not infallible. At Christmas the turkey looked like it had been killed by a hand grenade... in fact it could only be identified by its dental records.

Of course we could never afford a turkey but this one had followed dad home from a stroll in the countryside after it gobbled up a hooked piece of bread being dragged innocently behind him on a fishing line.

As we were always short of cash the old man secured an old cast-iron bath from a junkyard. He dragged it into the shed and built a partition wall and door and, PRESTO... we had a bathroom.

There was no plumbing... and no running water, but in the backyard but we had a huge wooden rain barrel and in the lean-to shed dad had fitted a tin gas boiler.

One of the boys would scoop out buckets of water from the tub and transfer it to the boiler. This was done twice a week...on a Monday for washday and on a Sunday morning at bath-time.

When the water was hot enough dad would fill the buckets and transfer them to the bath. However, because the rain-tub was static it always contained a fair amount of pond life, tadpoles and newts mainly, but we always had the occasional frog and as the area was adjacent to the docks we had more than our share of rat infestation...and these weren't the flyweight variety... these guys were the Muhammad Ali's and Arnold Schwarzenegger's' of the rodent world.

We had a nest of them in the coalhouse and we kids kept them as pets. Honestly, I kid yee not! In the yard we had a tiny air raid shelter with bunk beds and during an air raid we'd be dodging bombs and shrapnel and bludgeoning rats at the same time.

Dad would put down cage traps and two or three times a week he'd pick up the cage containing a live rat and drop it in the rain tub to drown it.

How we never caught bubonic plague I'll never know but apart from the food shortage, we seldom ailed anything all through the war.

On bath day, Sunday morning, Mum would be first in the bath, then Dad then Irene followed by Dick, then Les. I'd follow Les, then baby Brian would bring up the rear.

Baby Brian was dirtier when he got out of the bath than he was when he got in.

Sunday mornings, after we were bathed and dressed we were allowed to sit in the 'front room' and listen to the wireless. While we were preparing for the dubious weekly treat dad would be out in the back yard chopping sticks, Dick would be given the task of crumpling up old newspaper and Les would fill the coal scuttle. Then the old man would light the 'front room fire'.

To make a roaring fire he would use a 'blazer'. This was a thin sheet of metal on which he'd riveted a handle. He would sit the 'blazer' over the fire and cover this with a sheet of newspaper 'to draw the flames'. Invariably one of us would be given the task of holding the newspaper in place. And just as invariably the newspaper would catch alight and drawn by the screams of the youngest of us, dad would dash into the room, grab the blazing paper and hurtle through the kitchen (in the earlier days, before a radio aerial was replaced by conjoined bicycle chains he'd almost decapitate himself) and dropping the blazing mass into the yard would stamp it out with an enviable impression of the Arapaho Indian rain dance.

Another problem with the Sunday morning ritual was that, when both of the room doors were opened at the same time, the back draft would cause clouds of choking smoke to engulf the whole downstairs of the house.

So our father decided to borrow some chimney sweeping brushes he found tied to an unattended chimney sweeps handcart.

Suitably equipped he draped a heavy canvas cover over the fireplace, holding it in place on the mantelpiece with a flat iron, a 14lb hammer and the full coalscuttle. He screwed the round flue brush to the first section of pole… then, shouting 'bastard' he unscrewed the round flue brush from the first section of the pole, removed the holding articles from the mantelpiece, placed the brush into the chimney space, pushed the first pole through the tiny hole in the sheet, replaced the round flue brush to the first section of pole and replaced the 'dust-sheet'. He screwed on a couple more of the twenty sections of the pole to the first then told us to go into the back

street, stare at the roof and let him know when the brush appeared through the chimney pot.

We'd been in the backstreet for maybe half an hour answering a mouth to mouth Telegraphed 'NO' to his "can you see it yet?" call.

His next message was "Hang on, there's somebody at the front door."

The somebody was Police Constable 'Cliffy' Greenleaves. He asked my father if he was responsible for the gigantic traffic hold up on the main road outside the front door.

The traffic jam started at the flue brush resting on the road and stretched at least three miles to the old Hartlepool fish sands. And this during the lunch break when all the workers were dashing home for their dinners.

Stepping into the road at the request of the constable the old man realised his gaff.   While his offspring were dutifully staring skywards at the rear chimney pot, the brush, and thirty jointed lengths of bamboo pole hung like a weeping willow from the front chimney pot.

The fine of five shillings plus the loss of a morning's wages for the court appearance, plus the cost of a professional chimney sweep put an end to his flue cleaning aspirations.

Sea-coal is a commodity unique to the North East coast of England.

As the area is dotted with coalmines, when the black gold is finally mined and washed, large buckets slung on an overhead cable system take the waste and deposit it into the North Sea. This in turn is washed back up onto the beach at each high tide into a fine black combustible powder and the local 'sea-coal warriors' rake it into manageable heaps, pack it into huge sacks and, like beasts of burden they can be heard from a thousand yards, pushing, shoving, dragging, gasping and farting as they transport it on tyre-less, pedal-less bicycles, where it's touted from door to door and sold for a pittance. It is back breaking, soul-destroying toil but the 'sea-coal warriors' argue that it's better than working for a living.

Of course only the poor people would buy sea coal. The main reason was, apart from the fact that it was dirt (which it mainly was) cheap, it was also a hazard, in that, when the men were raking the coal dust up on the beach, they would also scoop up a fair quantity of smooth sea-shells and hard round pebbles, which, when heated exploded like mortar bombs, and the shrapnel would ricochet all around the living quarters. The mortality rate among North Eastern sea-coal users was the highest on the planet.

The trick was to first get a roaring wood-fire going, then, while a member of the household stood with a sturdy steel mesh fireguard at the ready, the stoker would throw a shovel-full of sea-coal onto the pyre and the guard was immediately locked into the safety mode position.

I remember my dad telling us that when he was a kid they had hanging on the opposite wall to the fireplace, a picture of Napoleon Bonaparte in his usual pose with one hand thrust into the front of his tunic. Dad said as soon as anyone approached with a shovelful of sea-coal Napoleon immediately took his hand out from his tunic and held it in front of his face.

As the War progressed the railways started sending Army stores through the marshalling yards where dad was now the equivalent of a Mafia 'Capo di Capi .

Daddy had reached the highest pinnacle. He was now 'The Godfather'

On a moonless night we and the neighbour's would don dark clothing, smear our faces with soot and attack the sealed wagons running from the docks to the marshalling yard, topping up the larder - and local shopkeepers - with victuals to sustain us through the winter and most of the war. Life was so good that we'd add a little prayer as we knelt by our beds asking God to give the Germans strength to hold out for a couple of more years. In fact, life had taken such a favourable turn that when the train robbers came to a van loaded with rifles they'd remove the firing pins and hide the ammunition with the intention of prolonging hostilities forever.

After our army lost several major battles through their inability to repel the local constabulary's baton charges, the War Department stopped sending good's wagons through dad's yards. So for a short while we went hungry, but every member of the family had a rifle…including baby Brian and Grandma Marks.

Because of the wartime rationing, rabbits became part of the staple diet and soon kippers were relegated to the foot of the menu.

For a long time we wondered why while constantly feeding the whole nation the rabbit population was never decimated. Then animal lovers noted a dearth in the pussycat population. After all, cat tasted like rabbit, rabbit tasted like cat...and without their fur coats, they both looked the same.

As the war moved away from mainland Hartlepool to Europe Mum boredom drove my mother into cinema addiction.

She'd visit the several local movie houses every night of the week. She'd even do the shopping then take the victuals with her to the cinema.

In our street we had a gang of around twenty five kids;   The Laycock's, Murray's Sedgewick's, Gooding's, Lacey's, Watson's and us, the Hammond's.

We were as normal as kids can be when brought up in a lower than low working class environment. I guess because of the stress of poor living conditions, overcrowding, starvation wages (nobody was ever out of work in those days), and to a lesser degree, the air-raids, all the parents seemed to be at each others throats every time they set eyes on each other. Greenland Cottages became a mini war-zone of kicking, punching screaming matches from dawn till dusk, seven days a week, three hundred and odd days a year. We kids followed suit and we'd be at it, battling it out non-stop. But immediately after each fight we'd all be friends again. We, parents and kids alike lived hard and played hard. One game we played was called 'Which Way'. All the kids in the gang would stand in a circle and we'd blindfold a kid we'd kidnapped from another gang and stand him in the centre of the circle. Then our leader, my bother Dick, would step forward and hit the victim over the head with a shovel, and we had the guess, which way he'd fall. We even had a mini bookmaker who held the bets made up of Woodbine cigarettes and glass marbles.

We seldom ever got toys. I remember one Christmas when Santa brought me a hardly used colouring book. He also brought my brother Dick a small tin of paints and a brush. Santa, attired like a railway's shunter looked on lovingly as we tore the newspaper wrappings from our presents. Then, tilting his railway cap to the back of his head, Father (Joe) Christmas explained that if I let Dick use my colouring book he'd in turn let me use his paints.

Christmas was just as exciting in those austere days as they are in these technological times. And that cheap little gift stirred in me the need to study art.

As soon as I was old enough to set up an easel I enrolled in the Hartlepool College of Art, fulfilling a fortnight's ambition to be another great painter.

My hero's were Johann, Sebastian and Bach who were the three most famous painters in the world.

I set up my easel and a large folder of canvases and artiste's paraphernalia. I even bought an old already paint spattered smock, a large black velvet beret, grew a Van Dyke beard and took a pitch on the Hartlepool promenade and tried my hand at painting. That didn't work out either. But I learned why all the great masters are posthumous achievers... they all starved to death. The only time I made any money was when I sold my brushes.

Saturday morning was the time of the week to get rid of ones frustrations. Immediately after breakfast every set of parents in the street would start a cacophony

of jungle noises, screaming, throwing anything at hand, jumping up and down and sometimes hitting each other. I swear if there'd have been a tree at hand they'd have been swinging from branch to branch.

This was a signal for all the kids to tear a few chunks of bread from a loaf, fill a couple of bottles with water and take off. There'd be twenty five or thirty of us and we'd swarm together like bees and head in which ever direction we were facing at the time. Sometimes to the sands, the docks, the fish quay or the promenade where we'd shin down the old iron runged steps set into the breakwater wall and shin down to the rocks some thirty feet below (an adventure which would nowadays give the average parent a coronary) and we'd dig among the rock pools for crabs, limpets or stranded fish. When the pangs of hunger struck we'd all sit in a circle and pass around chunks of bread and bottles of water. The last kid to get the bottle would shake it hard and cause a snowstorm of swirling breadcrumbs.

Sometimes we'd walk the five miles to 'the Monkey Forest' at Crimdon Dene, which was a local beauty spot. It got the name from the scores of squirrels that scurried up and down the trees. As squirrels were a new addition to North East wildlife, the locals, unsure of the species decided they were 'little monkeys'... hence the name Monkey Forest.

Monkeys, or to be precise, 'a monkey' is an integral part of Hartlepool folklore...one which the town was never proud of. In fact, for several hundred years the story of the hanging of the Hartlepool Monkey has been a source of great embarrassment to the local populace and great glee to the rest of mankind.

It came about thus.

During the Napoleonic wars a French warship ventured into the heavily fortified Hartlepool bay. When the ever-alert militia realised after several hours that the huge four masted Man-o-War was not a local fishing boat, Ralph (Kipper) Herring was sent for. Ralph held the post of Lord Honourable Keeper of the telescope.

He focussed first of the intruding vessel, then atop it's mainmast and ascertained that the flag fluttering there as 'not one of ours'. The militia, who were several local fishermen immediately sprung into action.

They charged up to the highest point overlooking the harbour and after much huffing and puffing and cursing, finally rolled the 20lb cannon ball into the breach of the gun.

Tommy 'The Crab' Boagey, who was in turn the village idiot, Mayor and keeper of the flint box struck a spark and ignited the three-foot fuse, which immediately fizzled out. However, the wife of a nearby crofter came to the rescue with a strip of burning dried seaweed and the shot was finally fired. The first ball demolished the old wooden lighthouse but this was of no consequence because, in heeling over to starboard, the Frenchman struck the Lighthouse Rock and ended up wedged under the pier. Immediately the French sailors jumped into a little boat and rowed as fast as they could for the horizon. This brought great gusts of laughter from the local fishermen who knew that when the Frenchies reached the horizon they'd fall off.

The following morning a piece of driftwood was espied yards from the shore adjacent to the Fish sands...and clinging to it was a tiny uniformed 'French sailor'.

He was immediately captured and apprehended in the local jail where he was interrogated by the local magistrates. He did not refuse to give his name and rank, nor would he utter a word about the intentions of his now doomed and deserted vessel. It is written in the

Hartlepool archives that all the prisoner would do was show his fangs, chatter and bristle the hairs on his forehead and swish his tail… and once he broke free of his bonds and shinned up the sheer wall of the chamber and sat on a ledge screeching at his tormentors.

Recaptured he was shaved, given a last meal of eggs, bacon and fried bread which he flung into the face of Rupert 'Panner' Cranston the jailer and great great grand-dad of the thug who knifed me in the hand decades later and dragged back from whence he came (the Fish sands) where he was booed, hissed at and ridiculed by the now drunken horde. A gallows had been hastily erected by Chuck 'Chippy' Sutheran, the local shipwright, and amid much jubilation, singing and dancing and drinking of mead, the poor wretch was slowly and painfully dispatched.

It wasn't till a couple decades later when, during the visit of a zoologist to the town, that the learned man was regaled with the tale of the French spy where-upon he informed the posse that they had 'hung a monkey'.

The stigma has hovered like a stagnant black cloud over the town of Hartlepool to this day. But they are slow learners in Hartlepool, and proof that history does repeat itself.

Several years after the 'hanging of the monkey' two crofters were sitting on the wall of the pier smoking 'penny clay pipes' and talking in whispers about the lynching, when a brightly coloured bird landed on the wall a few feet from them.

Bedazzled by the strange but striking plumage, they decided to capture it and take it to the now resident zoologist.

While 'Dutt' Wallace offered the fowl a morsel of fish he had taken from his line, James Markham, who had acted as executioner on that fateful day many years prior, a deed that harnessed him with the nickname, "Jimmy the Murderer" sneaked up from behind and grabbed the bird.

"Arr, me pretty creature" uttered 'the murderer', "and 'oo do we 'eve 'ere then?"

The bird fluttered its plumage and squawked "Pieces of eight", "Come aboard Squire Trelawney" and "Show us your tits, Miss Purity".

Recoiling in horror, his one un-patched eye popping from his head, Jimmy gently placed the Parrot (for that's what it was) back on the sea wall, doffed his sou'ester and said; "We'll be beggin' your pardon for our ignorance, ma'am, we thought you wuz a bird."

The Birds, the bees and the real stuff.

I never noticed girls till I was around the age of seven. We didn't have pin up pictures in our bedroom. We'd fold our hands into different shapes in front of a flickering candle and make shadows on the ceiling of the girls of our dreams. My favourite was Rita Doughty although she didn't reciprocate. The first time I saw her I fell head over heels in love.

It took me weeks to pluck up the courage to beg her to be my girl, but when at last I handed her a note at school asking her if she'd like to come to the pictures with me but she just turned the slip over and wrote in block capitals, *'KISS ME ARSE!'*

I didn't know if that was a sexual come on or a ribald rejection so I left well alone. But I don't know where she learned words like that. Her daddy worked as a first mate aboard one of the three masted barques that shipped coal from Hartlepool to the continent and returned laden down with cheap French wine, contraband cigarettes and small fine rubber envelopes which the locals called 'French letters'.

A few weeks before, the only shadow images I could do were an Alsatian, a Butterfly or a Bunny Rabbit. My brother Les could do all of these and, as he was older and bigger than me he'd stand in front of the candle with his shirt tucked up under his chin and do a brilliant Python and a baby's arm with an apple in it's hand.

I went off Rita when I heard she used to get cigarettes for her kid brother by running a peep show behind the school bike-sheds letting the boys have a quick look down her knickers for a Woodbine. For a Capstan full strength you could have a long gaze and a sigh.

She must have been good at it because when he was fourteen her brother changed his mind about being a Spitfire Pilot and opened a chain of tobacconist shops in the high street.

I remember taking Ruth Farrar to the Palladium cinema at Hartlepool to see Gordon Harker in 'The Phantom Light.' It was about a haunted lighthouse and it was scary.

By now I was ten. Ruth, who was year older than me hid her eyes and buried her head in my shoulder. I tried to feel her breasts but she didn't have any…not even nipples. The girl opposite me had breasts and nipples but she was at the time seeing the aforementioned 'Bam Hamilton' now aged eleven and taking a gap year from the Durham junior remand home so I settled for Ruth Farrar resting her head in my shoulder.

If I'd found anything resembling a nipple I doubt if I could have concentrated on it because when I left the house my mum was down with a bad fever and I worried about her.

Suddenly, as often happened in those days a message was flashed up on the screen; ***"WILL JACKIE HAMMOND PLEASE COME TO THE FOYER IMMEDIATELY?"***

"Mum" I thought and without another word I jumped up, first gallantly pulling Ruth's vest down and tucking it into her Gym skirt, and dashed to the foyer, to be stopped by my friend Cuthbert 'Cushy' Cowley.

He said, "Hiya Jackie."

"I can't stop now Cushy," I gasped, "I have to get home. They just flashed my name on the screen."

Cushy smiled and said; "That was me!"

You? "You flashed my name on the screen… waddya want?" I panted.

Cushy beamed and said, "Can I borrow your bike pump?"

Without thinking I punched him in the mouth.

He must have taken it badly because on the Monday he swapped desks with a kid nobody wanted to sit next to who we nick-named (the also aforementioned)

"Cacky Malabar."

One Saturday afternoon after Mum had gone shopping and cinema-hopping Dad whizzed into the back street on his bike and called a POW WOW.

"We're moving," he said, and marching us into the house he commanded, "you take that

67

chair, you grab the frying pan, and you catch Donald" (by then we'd gone into the poultry business). I swept the squawking Christmas dinner up in my arms and awaited the old mans next command.

The reason for the mass exodus was that word had got around that the Middleton's at number 10 had done a moonlight and dad remembered that Rupert and Florrie Middleton had recently had Guy de Maupassant Slack, a local street sweeper doubling as painter and decorator, in to transform their hovel into the most desirable residence in the street. Dad had immediately cut a swathe to the railway offices and secured the key to number 10 and informed us that he wanted the change to be made as a surprise for Mum when she got back from her weekly shopping cum cinema spree. It took maybe twenty minutes, including a tea break, to complete the transfer from the dilapidated slum at number 18. By 5pm we were the new residents of the gleaming number 10 Greenland Cottages.

At 7 o'clock we'd devoured the last of the weeks kipper and pussy cat cum rabbit pie and by 9pm we kids were wrapped in Dads Home Guard greatcoat and the rug from the head of the stairs and were deep in slumber, while he settled in front of a roaring coal-fire to listen to Valentine Dyall, "The Man in Black" on the brand new second hand radio-gram. At 11 o'clock Mum struggled off the last bus, and, loaded down with shopping bags struggled through the wartime blackout across the road.

Propping the groceries against the wall she stuck her fingers through the letterbox and pulled the length of string, which held the front door key and let herself into Number Eighteen Greenland cottages. She stepped into the darkened front room and flicked the light-switch. Apart from the echo of the click-click-click of the switch, Nothing!

Frantically clicking the switch she called out into the eerie blackness.

"Hello?" Her voice echoed nervously off the bare walls. "Hello...Hello...Hello...Josie...Josie... Josie?"   Nothing.   She upped the decibels

"...Cyril...Cyril...Cyril... anybody...body...body...body" Feeling the skin on her face tighten to an ice cold mask she backed out of the darkened hall into the front street, fumbled in her handbag for her torch, flicked it on and leaned back into the house. Stricken with horror she played the weak beam over the empty room... swung the light onto the carpet-less stairs the let out an almighty scream. Mr and Mrs Gooding from number sixteen dashed out into the street, followed by the Farrow's from number fourteen and seconds later the Laycock's from number twelve.

It was Mrs Ethel Laycock who informed our now prostrate mother of the quick change in our living quarters.

Minutes later, Dad, who had fallen asleep was rudely awakened by a way off boinging noise which got louder and more painful till he realised he was being beaten to pulp by Mum's latest acquisition, a new cast-iron sauce-pan. This was followed by much shouting, screaming and swearing, then, after a while, peals of laughter. An hour later we were awakened by the rhythmic tempo of boinggging bedsprings from our parent's new bridal suite. And it continued right through the whistle and thud of bombs, the whine of ricocheting shrapnel and the boom boom-boom of the anti aircraft gun emplacements dotted around the town.

All seemed to be well. The war, for the present was forgotten and dad was well and truly forgiven.

Dreams and nightmares

During my sick leave from the navy I courted my future wife. I'd known Sally Lumley since she was four years of age and she blossomed into a beautiful shapely blue-eyed blonde. I made the mistake of marrying the most beautiful (and sought after) girl in town. However, we were not your regular Romeo and Juliet.

It came to a point where I was competition for the competition…. and frequently at the tail end of the queue.

A marriage made in hell… It unbelievably lasted 26 years and she gave birth to seven kids. I hung around till all the kids were grown up and with a clear conscience, having done my parental duty, flew the nest, leaving behind all my worldly goods and an impressive and much desired four bedroom semi-detached abode.

I worked in many menial jobs… labourer… steelworks crane driver… grave digger… steel erector… this for a guy whose nose bleeds when I walk on a thick carpet… I even worked as a slaughterhouse porter… then I re-kick started my showbusiness career by taking a job as a dance band vocalist. I never looked back… and it lead me to meeting my present wife and, to date, 45 years of absolute ecstasy.

Some years after my divorce I heard that my ex-wife met and married a local guy.

He sold his house and she sold *'ours'*. They then pooled their joint and ample resources, took the vows Till Death Us Do Part and before the paint had dried on the new 'Déjà vu' plaque, her new beau dropped dead in that comedian's graveyard of graveyards, the Owton Manor Social Club.

And he wasn't even in showbusiness! (Those Owton Manor Social club audiences they don't differentiate.)

Several years ago I learned I had another son from a brief encounter with another local girl…a discretion I'm not at all proud of, more so for the mother who gave birth to my 'other son' and, suffering in silence never mentioned it to a soul. Over the years I've prayed for the courage to contact her but it took till recently and a push from 'our son' Scott to finally make contact.

With my wife, Jeannie's blessing Sylvia and I spoke for a while on the phone, then she settled back into her own life with a wonderful guy she never married, but who gave her more happiness than she once thought it impossible to achieve.

Once we met up, Scott and I bonded into an idyllic relationship… and he turned out to be a most wonderful son any parent could wish for.

The strange part of the whole affair is that he is a mirror image of me… a Doppelganger… so I don't lie awake nights wondering about this one. Unlike some of my 'other offspring' he looks, walks, talks, thinks and acts like me. He has even written several books. He never misses a celebration or an anniversary. He's a hugely successful business executive with a Swiss/American company in China.

A few years ago he married a gorgeous Chinese girl named Penny, and in turn Penny gave birth to my first Chinese granddaughter, Leona and she's as beautiful as her mother. Scott had previously presented me with another two granddaughters who in turn have made great headway in their lives. He never remonstrated about my affair with his mother and we are an extended happy family.

All of the boys from my first marriage did okay for themselves, One, Terry is, and I'm told, a successful hotelier. Tony became a Major in the Army. Mark, like me is the Jack of all Trades, Master of none.... the type of guy who, if he fell into the sea he'd come out with a pocket-full of fish. Actually Mark is the only one who didn't get divorced… and he heads the happiest family of them all. Martin, the youngest is the only one who followed me into the entertainment business. He was, last time I heard, a guitarist in an average band somewhere doing the same round of lousy clubs I did in my younger day.

The girls, Carol, Jackie and Julie all married and divorced. Carol was in the throes of a divorce when her husband Mike, one of the greatest guys I ever knew, contracted cancer at an early age and left her a widow and their only daughter a semi orphan.

I believe Carol married again and is living in the North of England.

Julie divorced and never married again. I heard that her ex husband settled down happily with another lady to an idyllic life… then a short while ago he was tragically killed in a car crash. He too was a great guy… and his kids were distraught when he died.

After a catastrophic marriage, which gave her two wonderful kids, Jackie broke loose. Later she found a gem of a guy, Richard, who is her rock. In fact Jackie is the only one of the family who kept in constant touch. Like Scott she is 'MY' kid from the top of her head to the tip of her toes. She and Richard brought the kids, grandkids and great grandkids to celebrate my 75th birthday. Then in time the calls got shorter till silence finally reigned.

At the last count I have 7 kids including Scott and Jeannie's and my daughter, Helen. They in turn gave us16 grandkids and 19 great-grandkids. I may not be rich but I'll never be an island…

. I haven't heard from the others in many years, but they're all parent's, and grandparents themselves now. Like me they all made their mistakes and they all sorted themselves out.

I sometimes try, with great difficulty to remember what they all looked like.

Time, like love is a great healer.

The American Dream

Back in 1944, freshly recovered from my nightmare altercation with the U-Boat and the Stuka dive-bomber, I received a telegram from the Admiralty to report to the Naval dockyard in Greenock, Scotland.

I was ready to fling myself back into the fray but was instead given the ignominious post of canteen assistant with the NAAFI on Greenock docks.

On 'VE (Victory in Europe) night' I went out on the town to celebrate the end of the hostilities in a dockside pub with my new friend, Jock McKinnon…and got into a private war with a very large, very drunk and very aggressive docker. I accepted his invitation to follow him into the street and while I was taking off my jacket he kicked me in the balls, butted me on my recently re-constructed nose and proceeded to undo in ten minutes what it took the whole medical staff at the Greenock naval hospital six weeks to repair. I was back 'in dock' for another five days.

A couple of weeks later, thanks to Jock McKinnon's sister who worked in the naval draft office we were posted to the Far East to see if we could educate the Japanese in the errors of their ways. I was always a slow learner and I was rapidly running out of blood and guts to give to my King and country.

We boarded the troop ship Ile de France in Gourock on the river Clyde and got as far as New York where Jock McKinnon and I and a couple of hundred more British service-men were temporally billeted in Pier 92 on the Manhattan waterfront.

I was seventeen years and a few months old… and still not shaving.

I stayed in the Big Apple for a few hazardous weeks, in which time I was mugged more times than any other human being since the landing of the Founding Fathers. I joined the U.S.O. boxing team but spent most of my time between fights in traction before I realised that I wasn't going to dethrone anyone who could fight back.

My record read, 38 fights, drew 1, lost 1 and chickened out of the other thirty-six.

There is an old gag about a guy being thrown out of a bar three times in a night by the same bouncer. The third time he looked up from the pavement and said to his tormentor, "How many bars do you own in this town?"

I swear, hand on heart that I was that man. I was a 17 years old war veteran and on the periphery of alcoholism. I was an obnoxious asshole and as such I was also a living punch bag.

To this day I have the scars to prove it.

I did however achieve some world recognition as the world's greatest pain in the arse. The penultimate lesson came in the famous' Jack Dempsey's' bar in New York City. It was situated at and angle on three corners of a street on Times Square and because of my youth, but more so because I was an obnoxious asshole, I was heaved out. I rose shakily from the sidewalk, staggered round the corner...spotted another boozerie and entered where I came face to face with the same gorilla that'd seconds before deposited me in a heap in the gutter. Seconds later I got up, staggered round the next corner and unknowingly re-entered and was immediately re-exited from the 'Manassa Mauler's' domain for the third and last time.... calling out to my tormentor: "how many fuckin' pubs do you own in this town?"

I was even ousted from the old boxing stadium, Madison Square Garden for causing a fracas. Later that same night a young American sailor in another bar offered the hand of friendship. I rejected it and invited him outside to show him what a real fighting man was. He refused my offer and broke his ass trying to make up.

Finally, and after a barrage of abuse and taunts, he picked up the gauntlet I'd contemptuously thrown at his feet. Making Mr Dempsey's henchman look like a rank amateur, he bounced me off every wall in Times Square and so far up Broadway I could see the Catskill Mountain's.

He kept pleading with me to call it a day and I kept throwing punches from a horizontal position. He finally shoved me into a taxicab and took me back to my base at Pier 92 where I lay comatose for the next four days.

When I finally regained my senses the first face I saw as I lay in a cot in the sick-bay was the last face I'd seen as I lay in the gutter in The Big Apple…. my conqueror.

He introduced himself as Steve Taylor and apologised for having to half kill me, but said that he'd sat by my bed every day since the massacre.

We became friends and remained so, albeit pen pals for many years after hostilities ceased. Last I heard from him he was the President of a Bank in Wilmington, Delaware, U.S.A.

One day, mended and back on the town, Jock McKinnon and I went to a Penny Arcade off Times Square where they had pinball machines, sideshows and a 'What the butler saw' machine. I put a dime in the slot machine and as I put my eye to the peephole I got a terrific electric shock that threw me to the floor. The owner came running over and asked 'what the fuck yez doing'?

Jock, always a epitome of diplomacy grabbed the guy by the throat and told him his machine was dangerous and he was going to get a cop.

The man calmed down, peeled two five dollar bills from his pocket and, helping Jock get me vertical, stuffed them into my hand, "say nuthin', okay?"

I gave Jock a five and kept the other one.

Above the din, a barker was trying to have him-self heard. I caught something about "one of the greatest fighters ever and former 'Champeen' Jack Johnson."   McKinnon and I had spent most of our nights at the fights in the old 'Madison Square Garden' before I was barred sein die, so we joined the small crowd at a curtained off stage on which stood the barker. He was dressed in a red white and blue striped shirt with armbands and bow tie, a Derby hat and baggy pants. In his hand he held a cardboard megaphone. He also had the first instant camera I'd ever seen, dangling round his neck.

"So, hey, c'mon" he yelled. "C'mon and say 'hi' to the former heavyweight champeen of da woild... Jack Johnson."

After much tugging and tearing, the curtain opened and a huge bald headed Negro in old style boxing strip stepped onto the platform. Jack Johnson shuffled around the tiny stage throwing punches at the air. I was mesmerised, and at first a little dubious. What the hell would one of the greatest boxers of all time be doing in a dump like this, but it was the old fighter. I'd seen and read enough to know this was the real thing. In the flesh!

The barker roared above the crowd: "All ya need is a buck tez ast the champ any questions ya like about his time as the greatest... don' ast him nuthin' else or yez'll get a bust in the kisser!" And he and the ebony giant roared with laughter.

The crowd were as stunned as my partner and I, and a little shy.

After a while a black guy piped up with a question about white chicks.

"We don't answer no poisonal questions ya bum... and we don't answer no questions for nuthin either."

The black heckler turned and shuffled off.

I found myself with my hand in the air.

"Hey" bawled the heckler "we gotta hero here... watcher wanna know kid?....... er, cash foist."

"I've only got a five" I said, holding my newly acquired fortune above my head.

"The barker looked at his charges long johns and said, "The champ ain't got no pockets, son" and snatching the five out of my hand he said "We don't give change....waddya wanna know, sailor?"

"Ask Mr Johnson what he thinks of..." but I was stopped mid question by the showman.

"Waddya mean waddya astin' me for? You ast him... it's your buck... talk to the champ."

I looked up into the sweating face of arguably, up till then, the greatest fighter in the history of prize fighting.

"What do you think of...?"

The big man looked down at me and held his gloved palm up and silenced me in mid sentence.

"Hey, see here...How old are you son?"   The voice was gentle but had the sound of a bass Drum.

"Seventeen...so what do you..."

"You seventeen? How long you bin a sailor?"

"Er, since I was fourteen and a half."

The champs face creased into a watermelon grin... his whiter than white teeth looked like a piano keyboard.

"Damn!" He said, shaking his head slowly.

"Er, anyway," I said "er, what do you think about Jack London?"

The big man looked up at the ceiling, pondered a while then said; "Jack London is the best book-writer what ever lived.... man...did y'all read his book, 'The Call of the Wild'?

The crowd roared as I corrected him. "No, I mean Jack London the British Heavyweight Champion."

Johnson looked bemused and said sarcastically, "Dey got fighters over there?"

Embarrassed I shot back defensively, "Yes, we have thousands of them... we've been fighting for you guys the best part of the war".

The area around me turned into a fridge. Jock McKinnon almost had a coronary, but the amiable giant roared with laughter and called me up onto the dais, where I had a photograph taken shaking the hand that shook the world. I never found out what he thought about Jack London, the fighter... nor did I care. Jock and I wandered around the arcade and after a while the barker called me from a pinball machine and handed me my photo. I walked slowly to the street and turned to look back at the champ. "Hey, what about my change?" I called.

Johnson stood with his gloved hands by his side, looking at me. He gave an incredulous smile, shook his head and gave me a little wave.

A couple of days later Jock McKinnon and I were strolling through Times Square when a car pulled into the kerb ahead of us. As Jock and I drew alongside a familiar voice boomed out and a huge black guy leaned out of the rear window and offered his hand, "Hey its mah main man, Jack London. Howya doing li'l sailor?"

Before I had a chance to take his hand he withdrew it and fumbled in his shirt pocket, then again held out his hand. I took his huge mitt and as we shook hands he squeezed a dollar piece into my palm. "Here's your change" with a massive grin he gave a casual wave, a wink and as the limo moved off he shouted back:

"Ya'll take care now, and watch them damn japs".

And he vanished into history.

As I turned an old guy with a busted up face asked me, "Hey sailor, d'yez know who dat guy is?"

I said, "Yeah, he's the champ. That's Jack Johnson. He's a friend of mine. He just returned a dollar I loaned him" and I held the coin in my palm for the small crowd to see. The old pug stared at the silver dollar glinting in my hand. "Hold on tight to that buck son." he said... " Some day it'll be woith a fortune."

A few minutes later Jock and I sat on a couple of high stools at a window table of a deli' in 'the Square' drinking a cold banana milk shake.

Jock took the coin and examined it closely, then with mock indignity he said; "Yon's no the one yae gave him.... yours was five dollar bill... and it was worth a hellofa site more than

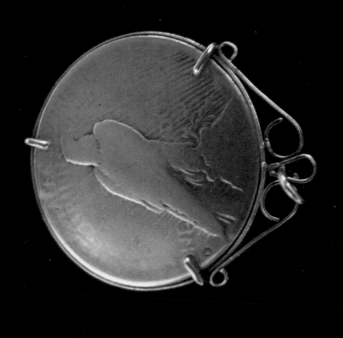
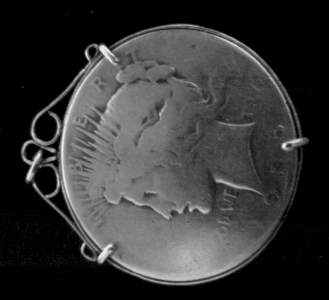

yon.... ye paid him five new dollars for one ould one, this ones a bloody 1935... the skinny black bugger" And he burst into fits of laughter.

Back home I gave the treasured photograph of "Jack Johnson and me shaking hands" to my brother Dick and after he died I tried to retrieve it, but search as I may, it, like the only brother I ever loved, was gone.

I gave the Dollar to my Mum and she had it mounted and hung on a chain. She used to boast that the great World boxing champion Jack Johnson gave it to her son, but nobody ever believed her.

The night before she died we went to see her in the Hartlepool General Hospital and as we were leaving she called me back to her bedside. "Here bonny lad, this is yours" and she had me bend down while she hung my 'Jack Johnson Dollar' around my neck. Years later the chain snapped and I never had it repaired.... but I still have

'That Buck'. 'Jack Johnson' couldn't know but I did take care, never got to grips with them 'damn japs' and I lived to tell the tale.

And The Silver Dollar? Sorry! It's not for sale.... not even for a Kings ransom.

Nobody would believe my story anyway... but it's not important...and

If you don't have dreams,.............................!

PERRY

One afternoon a crowd of us sailors were invited through the auspices of the USO to a Bond rally in New York's Central Park. They put on regular Shows and featured the most famous 'Stars' in the world, every one an icon. That day I fell under the spell of one, Perry Como who was sharing honours at the time with the up and coming Francis Albert Sinatra from the parish of Hoboken, New Jersey, just over the Hudson River.

Great as Sinatra was, from the moment I heard Como sing I was sold on him. At the rally I bought a record of Perry's current hit "Till the End of Time".

I spotted him later signing autographs and never the shy type I took my record across and asked if he'd sign it.

He asked me how old I was and I said "you're the second one to ask me that... Jack Johnson asked me the same question a couple of weeks ago."

Perry gave me a quizzical look.

"I'm seventeen." I said,

He raised his eyebrows. "You should be in school".

I told him we were ready to head off to do battle with the Japs in the Far East. He winced then wrote across the H.M.V. label. "To Jack, Best Wishes, see you in Tokyo kid. Salute, Perry Como." Along with my 'Jack Johnson Dollar' that label was one of my most treasured possessions.

Perry Como became the greatest influence in my change of direction for the rest of my life. I stopped boozing, whoring and street fighting. I started using my free honorary U.S.O. pass to the Broadway Shows, discovered my singing voice and got myself a few little (unpaid) Gigs in U.S.O. Shows. I copied the style of Mr 'C', and my efforts paid off one night in the Crystal Club on 52nd street when some of my pals pushed me onto the stage to 'do a number' with the house-band.

That night I put my foot shakily on the bottom rung of the Show Business ladder.

I even secured a regular Gig at the Club for $8 (then £2) a night.

I was now a Pro.... although I didn't mention the fact to the Royal Navy that I was moonlighting on their time.

I gigged three nights a week with the band, which were actually a quintet...and all black. I was the only coloured guy in the outfit.

Nights off I'd go with Jock McKinnon and with six buck's to burn we'd hit the town... not the old way... (I'd hit too many walls with the back of my head or too many sidewalks with the front.)

We'd use our U.S.O. guest passes and see shows, and go backstage and meet the Stars, or we'd spend nights in the world famous Stage-door canteen.

'The Stage-door Canteen' was a small downtown Manhattan Club where Hollywood Stars would drop on a duty rota to say hi to the fighting boys. People like Alan Ladd and Veronica Lake, William Bendix, John Garfield, George Raft, Betty Grable.

We'd go to Radio City Music Hall and see Stars like Peggy Lee, Ella Fitzgerald, Louis 'Satchmo' Armstrong and Harry James and his Orchestra.

Tough guy James Cagney and his best friend Pat O'Brian would drop in to the Pier 92 base and Cagney would spar with all comers. Everyone who was anyone appeared at Radio City and when Perry Como was booked I'd be first guy in.... front row... and I always made a point of getting backstage to say 'hi'. He'd give me a hug like I was his best pal, and I milked the part like the brand new, wet behind the ears 'pro' I now was.

Many years later when I was a full-blown 'real entertainer' touring Australia I was offered a weeks work in the old MGM Grand Hotel, Las Vegas.

It was lounge work, and although I did okay with the Brits in the room, I hated it.

Mid way through the week the 'booker' asked could I do five nights the following week in Galveston, Texas as a support to *PERRY COMO*

"Is the Pope a Catholic?" I screamed at to the Agent… "Do Bears shit in the forest…?"

I and three other acts flew down to the Gig on the Monday. We walked into the Club in time to catch Mr 'C'.

My name was so far down the Bill people were wiping their feet on me and as a bonus I was also working with the fantastic George Carl…

I was under the same roof as these icons.

I did my comedy piano act to great acclaim.

It was a great show and the greatest honour of my life. In fact in the 54 years I spent on the periphery of stardom, I can say, hand on heart that Perry Como was the greatest, nicest most loveable person among all of the great acts I had the honour and pleasure to appear with.

A couple of years later I was on my second tour of Australia for the Brian Fehon Agency in Sydney, Australia. Perry Como was there at the same time and he'd chosen a great English friend of mine to act as comedy MC.

Don Crocket was, like me a product of the 'workingmen's clubs' and he'd bled and sweated to become one of the finest comedy impressionists I ever knew!

To be chosen above all the top American and British comedians to support Perry Como is no mean feat. But Don Crocket was the best in his field.

I asked Brian Fehon could he arrange for me to get backstage to see Don and perhaps rekindle my friendship with Mr 'C' at the same time.

I caught the show on the last night and was invited back to the wrap party afterwards at the Hotel. All the cast were there along with some of the top Aussie Radio, Television and Movie people. However, as Perry was flying out on an early flight the next day he had to take a rain-check on the festivities, which incidentally was being held in Don's room across the hall from Perry's suite.

The rule was to enjoy yourself but keep the noise down. But entertainers being what they are and Aussies being what they are, around about 1.am the quite party turned into a full blown Mardi Gras.

Suddenly everyone froze at a frantic banging on the door. Shushing everybody,

Don Crocket walked gingerly across the room and taking a deep breath slowly opened the door. There, dressed in flowered shorts and carpet slippers and carrying a bottle of Champagne under his arm stood Perry Como. He gave a 'toot-toot on a toy trumpet to which he'd tied to a balloon and shyly said "Hi guys… can I come to your party?"

He was carried shoulder high round the hotel to the amazed stares of the guests. There were never greater singers in the world and there was never a greater guy than Perry Como.

Don Crocket had his fifteen minutes of glory and ended up back on the Workingmen's Club Circuit. A couple of months after his hugely successful Australian tour, Don was heckled off the stage in a Workingmen's Club in Gateshead.

Totally stressed out he didn't even stay to pick up his wages…and he never worked again. He suffered terrible depressions and a short while later he died of a massive heart attack. My dad used to say, "Hard work never killed anyone".

But my old man never stood on the stage on a Saturday night before a tribe of hostile natives fired up with "Newcastle Brown Ale", 'the strongest hooch in the world'.

The Cinderella Man

Back to 1946.

Just as I was warming to Show Business and edging towards the bright lights of Broadway, His Majesties navy posted me off to Boston, Massachusetts to join the crew of the newly refitted light cruiser, H.M.S. Leander which had suffered a horrifying battering from the Japanese.

A couple of weeks later I was pushed by my shipmates onto the stage of the
Old Howard Theatre in Solly Square, Boston, Massachusetts. I sang the Perry Como hit "Till the End of Time" to great acclaim.

The Star of the Burlesque Show was a lady who later made it to Hollywood as a runner up to Gipsy Rose Lee. Her name was 'Lilli St. Cyr' and I fell hopelessly in love with her. She took me under her wing for the full weeks stay and told me I was destined for stardom...though I think she was being more patriotic than realistic.

Forever the Cinderella man, the midnight chimes struck and my career was cut short when someone dropped a couple of 1000 megaton atom bombs on the Japanese cities of Hiroshima and Nagasaki.

Some years later I met a Japanese magician who was working in a munitions factory during the War. Taking a few days holiday he told me he'd decided to go see some relatives in the city of Hiroshima.

He said, "I stepped off the train at the precise second the "H" bomb exploded.

Unhurt but badly shocked I decided to get back home pronto, which I did, and seconds after I stepped off the train in Nagasaki........."

Well, it was funny when I heard it.

I was on my way to becoming a redundant sailor at the age of seventeen and a few months.

We first headed for Montreal, Canada where, heavily guarded we loaded the ship with treasures including the Crown Jewels that had been dispatched from Britain to Canada for safe keeping during hostilities. After a few days in Canada we set sail for home. The first part of the cruise has stayed in my memory all these years.

We cast off from the quayside in Montreal and cruised on an autumn tide slowly down the St Lawrence River. That short cruise bordered on both sides by endless acres of Pine forests, painted by the sun in several of shades of gold. We sailed past Tepee strewn Indian reservations under a multihued sky unhindered by the roar of warplanes or pock-marked by a million exploding death dealing shells and bombs that had become an integral part of mans inhumanity to all that is good in God's creation.

It was like the creator was laying before us a canvas of such beauty which we all, in our haste to destroy each other had, for too long forgotten.

Even now when the enemy had been vanquished we still sailed with an expectancy that this was all a dream that any second another nightmare would loom up out of the inevitable mist. Days later I leaned on the starboard rail on the foc'sle of HMS Leander as we sailed slowly and without ceremony down the ugly fogbound River Tyne to a vacant berth and watched idly as dockworkers took the thick hawsers and secured us to the 'Geordie' quayside. Long minutes later amid a cacophony of sound from a host of ghostly voices and ships sirens a crane manoeuvred a heavy wooden gangway into position amidships. An emotion almost overtook me as I stared at the fading blue number '7' on the worn and splintered handrail, and seconds later my eyes fell on the different coloured plank board which covered the gaping hole I'd fallen through while heading into the unknown aboard my first ship, that other cruiser, bigger and more beautiful, HMS Devonshire.

How long ago was it? 23 months?

No... I can't have crammed that lifetime of pain and horror into 23 months.

23 months ago I was a nervous young kid… three weeks into my sixteenth year… and now I was just one month from my eighteenth birthday… in 23 months I'd been, with hundreds of thousand of other kids to hell a thousand times over. And I could still hear, smell and feel the ingredients of it all… The silent fear… the cold and hunger… the brutality and the ear shattering noise, and in that icy cold I imagined I could still clearly hear those voices coming up from the black depths crying and begging for help when there was none to be given….

And in my clogged up brain I was already beginning to miss the horror of it all. Those fading personal nightmares. 23 months ago the alternatives were just coming to fruition…

Life with an uncaring father or this second choice, which I had unknowingly taken. Now I was back to square one…and at this minute I was more at home with the devil I knew than the one he'd replaced. But this time there was no choice.

And now the drill was a quick meal, grab your belongings, a mumbled cheerio over you shoulder and God knows what.

The next 24 hours was a mind-blowing hurricane of disorganisation. 'Gangway… mind that fucking hole…you hit it the last time. The navy transport lorry jammed to the gunwales with former comrades… The rush and punching for a berth on the train… the train that seemed to stop a thousand times before you spilled out onto the platform at Chatham. And a queue for the non existent navy dockyard truck… now the march…full pack, muscles aching from the battering from there to here… then the barracks… no easy way out… and in a few hours in bedlam you find yourself on the platform at London's Kings Cross station… with extra baggage… a large cardboard box… your demob suit… they didn't even let me try it on…I told the man the shoes were too tight and he said "just take them son and fuck off!"…No salute… no quarter asked of given. In all the time I was in the 'Andrew' the first officer I see after I did my bit tells me to "just take them son and fuck off!"… Then the milk train back North… but the boring trip home was made bearable when I cracked it with a middle aged WREN… and she lets me screw her in the trains lavatory… her and me against the washbasin and a marine with another bird going 'doggy' on the bog seat. Now I'm on the platform in Darlington… watching a load of matelot's kicking shit out of some Yankee airmen… Someone calls for help. 'Fuck you pal!' I think… where were you when I needed you in Times Square?…or when I was laid out in that back street in Greenock and that big ugly Scots bastard was dismantling me?… And do you remember when I was tangled in the boxing ring ropes in Scapa and that little bastard was beating me to pulp… where the hell were you then?' I'll have a little sleep in the corner of the carriage…

What? What the..?.

"HARTLEPOOL"… did the porter shout Hartlepool?

I look out of the window… Jesus, I'm home. There's Dick…He's on his own… but I knew if anybody was going to welcome me back into the fold it would be Dick.

It's March…1946. I was aged eighteen and a few months and still officially 703625 C/a H C Hammond…By today's standards I'm still a kid, but like hundreds of thousands of other kids, I'm a veteran … I can't take in what I'm a veteran of yet, but I'm a veteran… and I grudgingly owe it all to my father.

Meeting 'The Queen'

Home was the conquering hero... to a job as a piano player in the Lord Clyde pub on Hartlepool's dockland. I couldn't play the piano properly but as the place was more a glorified whorehouse and black market warehouse than an emporium of entertainment, no one noticed my lack of musical excellence. I've already mentioned that my brother Dick had taught himself to play a few chords on the black notes. He in turn taught me all he knew... which was 'Chopstick's on the black notes.'

However, I was unique in that I could play the Piano (after a fashion) sing self accompanied and as I was tough enough to have kept bouncing back into Jack Dempsey's New York hostelry, I got the job...and as no one had heard of Perry Como in the Britain of 1946, I was a first.

I was paid five shillings (50p) a night.... a fortune in those days, with free beer and free favours of the hookers.

After mine-host Hughie Muldoon realised that I could drink with the best of them he upped my wages to seven and sixpence a night....'buy your own beer'. I was becoming something of a celebrity in the town, and although every pub worth its salt had a Piano Player, none of them had a self accompanied Singer.... who could sing like the unknown Perry Como and was a friend of Jack Johnson.

We were packing them in seven nights a week, the whole nine yards. We were stealing custom from the surrounding pubs and as trade boomed, we started to attract a better class of moron, who in turn attracted a better class of hooker, who attracted a better class of mug who attracted a better class of mugger.

Though most of the pubs suffered in silence, one, which up till a few weeks previously was the 'in place', frowned upon this piracy and so, one Saturday afternoon I answered a knock on my parents front door, to be confronted by two very large gentlemen, and Walter "Ducky" Merriweather.

Walter Merriweather was a local oddity. He was a homosexual... a poof. This was in the days when such people existed only in closets venturing out only after dark to buy provisions from the local corner shop. In the Navy most ships had at least one gay... the little ships that is... Battleships and Aircraft carriers had as many as three. If a ship found itself short of a gay they'd rely on volunteers. If there were no takers the crew slipped back into the old 'Press gang' mode.

There was of course a price to pay for this service. The fee was usually two pounds ten shillings. Ten shillings was for the victim and a pound each for the two sailors who held him down......because usually he didn't like it.

'Ducky' Merriweather was one of the first to 'Come out'...... almost fifty years prematurely. He wore shoulder length blonde hair, heavy make-up, silk blouse, pink slacks and wedge heeled shoes. However, he went about his business unaccosted.... mainly because he was also the most fearsome street-fighter in town. It is rumoured that he once spent a night in a dustbin full of alley-cats and came out without a scratch. He was also the Star Attraction in the Mainsforth Hotel which was in close proximity to my place of employment, the Lord Clyde. Lately however, he had gone, in a few short weeks, from hostessing full houses, to singing to a mere hand-full of patrons.

Called to account by his boss, 'Ducky' had made exhaustive enquiries and discovered that the root of their troubles lay in the now booming Lord Clyde, just yards from his front door. Further enquiries brought forth my home address and in turn a personal appearance at my door that fateful Saturday.

'Ducky' however was the epitome of diplomacy. He conceded that I was a formidable talent, wasted in such a low dive as the Lord Clyde and his boss had sent him to request my free transfer to his more salubrious establishment.... where I would be more appreciated and respected, afforded Top Billing and would not be needed to play the piano as they had a first class accompanist - he'd obviously heard of my musical shortfall... but that I would be expected to perform my self-accompanied act from 9 – 10pm. I would receive the same remuneration as I was being paid by Muldoon and I was expected to bring back not only previous deserters but also the galaxy of new whores who had recently moved to Muldoon's Shangri la.

I said "what about Muldoon" but they had already called on the amiable Scot and convinced him that my transfer was is the interest of my career and Muldoon's continuing good health. I made my debut as 'Star Cabaret' at the Mainsforth Hotel and I couldn't complain, the drinks flowed like water, (which was 60% of what they were), the girls adhered to 'Ducky's request that they tended to my every fantasy, the piano player didn't fear for his job, the management were delighted with the meteoric rise in their fortunes and I was getting three hours wages for one hours work.

In a space of three weeks, The Mainsforth Hotel had taken on the mantle of a fully-fledged 'Cabaret' bar.... before anyone knew what a fully-fledged cabaret bar was.

I was sent off to the local tailor who fitted me with my first stage suit...gratis… to replace my austere 'demob' suit.

'Ducky' attended the fitting and drooled as the tailor measured my inside leg. At the end of the fitting the tailor asked me if I required anything else. I replied, "Well, I did want a cap but I think I'll have another pair of trousers." This sent 'Ducky' into paroxysms of laughter and cemented our friendship, platonic as it was, for the rest of our time together. He also protected me from the thugs and hecklers. I was a happy individual. Oh, that 'Ducky' Merriweather were alive today.

One night, after about six hugely successful weeks , 'Ducky' informed me, after I'd just left the rostrum to thunderous applause, that the 'boss' would like to meet me. It hadn't struck me that there was a boss, so well did 'Ducky' run the joint.

"Where is he?" I asked my perfumed protector.

"Up the stairs.... along the landing, last door.... the big oak one......'good luck'" he cooed.

I went up the darkened staircase, along the landing and came to a large oak door, with a brightly polished brass sign which read 'PRIVATE'.

I tapped on the door.

"Come in Jackie," (my name then) called the voice from within.

I entered a darkened room, lit only by a huge coal-fire in an ornate hearth. As my eyes grew accustomed to the dark I noticed that the room was decorated entirely in red. Red velvet curtains, red plush pile carpet, a large round table covered by a red velvet cover, with red velvet tassels. In the centre of the room with its back to me was a red velvet chaise lounge. A voice cooed from its depths, "Come in Jackie... close the door, love."

I pushed the door till it clicked on its catch and turned to see the figure of a very large man rise to greet me. He was wearing a shoulder length red wig.... a red satin basque, and as he walked round the couch to greet me, I noticed he was wearing a red negligee, fishnet stockings and red knee length patent leather boots.

As I backed to the door he came to me, offered me a wine glass, dropped it, grabbed me, forcing me back to the closed door and pressed his salivating crimson lips over my mouth, almost smothering me...at the same time grabbing my hand and pushing it down to his crotch. Déjà vu!

My mind flew back to the time aboard H.M.S. Devonshire when I found myself in the ships sluice (bathroom) accosted by the Master at arms....

He had pushed my hand down to his crotch too... and I grabbed his balls as I grabbed the balls now in my hand, crushed them, tugged down hard, twisted them and as I'd done when the

Master at arms had thrown his head back in an agonised scream, I butted this fruit under the chin.

He reeled backwards and fell over the chaise lounge, crashing heavily into the fireplace.

I didn't stay to assess the damage but turned, wrenched the door open and headed for the hills. For the next few weeks I forbade my parents to answer the door but I was never bothered again. Some time later I heard that the Mainsforth Hotel had changed management... and a few years later Walter Merriweather went to the great cottage in the sky

The Fall of the Empire

It took several years before I appeared on the stage of the 'West Hartlepool Empire Theatre', but my luck was bound to run out sooner or later. My mother suggested that I try my hand at the 'Variety Theatres'. I had visited the local Empire Theatre and fallen in love with that branch of the business.

I arranged a meeting with the manager Gerry Robson, who informed me that the great wartime comedian Frank Randall, an icon in the variety halls, was looking for a junior lead that very week. I met the producer and was ordered to rehearsals that afternoon.

I had no idea what a junior lead was, but it transpired that this junior lead had to ride onto the stage on a bicycle, dressed as a post office telegram boy and knock on a door. When Mr Randall answered my knock I'd hand him the telegram and a pencil. I'd ask him to sign for the telegram and he would reply in his thick Lancashire dialect, "I can't reet... I'll draw thee a duck."

My other duty as a 'junior lead' was to go out for the fish and chips between houses. On the last night of the show I was ordered to escort a heavily inebriated Frank Randle to the stage door. Outside, I helped him to this new sporty 'E' type Jaguar car.

Mr Randle had difficulty getting into his seat and more trouble starting the thing. I leaned through the open driver's side window and turned the key at the same time as the great man released the clutch taking a panic stab at the footbrake missed and slammed the accelerator to the board. The super high powered car shot backwards, hurtles over a junction and crashed through the plate glass window of a fish and chip shop. Horror-stricken I dived back into the theatre.

Later, I heard that after the crash Randle leaned out of the open window slurred, "could I have a large cod and chips, salt an' vinegar and a large portion of your celebrated mushy peas." True or false, these are the stories that make great comedians immortal.

I toured for four weeks with "Randle's Scandals" and when some years later the great old comedian died, he took my last week's wage of three pounds ten shillings wages with him to the grave.

My favourite "Frank Randle" story was about the time Bob and Alf Pearson, two Geordie brothers who became icons on Radio during and after the war found themselves 'resting' and were offered a week 'second top billing' on the Frank Randle Variety Show at the Middlesbrough Empire Theatre.

After the contracts were signed the boys discovered that they were to close the show every night.

This meant that Frank Randle, as headliner would be the main spot immediately before them - and I know from experience that no one could follow a superstar of Randle's magnitude. Bob and Alf died every one of the six nights.

After the last show they were making their way back to their homes in Sunderland when, passing through a mining village of Ryhope, they swerved to miss a dog which had dashed across the road and into their path. The car struck the kerb, spun out of control, overturned several times and crashed into a telegraph pole. The boys were seriously hurt and hospitalised for a couple of weeks. I decided to drop in and see them as I was passing through the village on my way to a gig in Newcastle Both heavily bandaged they looked terrible. I asked how serious it was.

"Bad.... really bad" said Bob through swollen lips.

And in true pro style, Alf moaned, "But it wasn't nearly as bad as following that fucking Randle."

Many years later I was doing a show with Arthur Askey and Vince Hill for Tyne Tees Television. During a break in rehearsals, I took a stroll into Newcastle and was pleasantly surprised to bump into Bob and Alf who were now two very old men...and an almost forgotten entity.

They hadn't worked for ages and worse, they'd got themselves an agent who put them onto the Workingmen's Clubs. The audiences murdered them, so now they were reluctantly 'resting'. We went into a cafe and chatted over mugs of tea and scones. After a hilarious time chatting about the old times I decided it was time to get back to the studio. On the street we shook hands, hugged each other and as we parted for the very last time. I called after them, "I'm sorry things aren't so good right now boys."

A couple of paces further on the boys stopped, turned and in unison called back to me, "Aye, but it's a lot better than following that fucking Randle".

It was while I was at the West Hartlepool Empire that I met a young man who, like Perry Como was to have a profound effect on my career. He introduced me to the art of comedy. His name was Terry Laffin.

He was sixteen years old at the time and employed at the West Hartlepool Empire Theatre as assistant stage manager. Terry Laffin was the epitome of the funny man and a natural comedian with impeccable timing. It is said that Comedians are born.... this kid was made in heaven.

He had the sharpest wit I ever experienced in all my years in show business.

He was one of those phenomena who never tried to be funny. As a matter of fact he was the most doleful character you could wish to meet. I believe he was the closest one could get to Tony Hancock. He was never a professional entertainer. Always the semi pro but he was invaluable to any aspiring comedian.

Once, while we were both 'resting' and avoiding any work that was not associated with the stage while being subsidised by the social security, the Social Security officer was questioning Terry.

"Name?"

"Whaddya mean, 'name'... you ask me the same question every week."

"Name?"

"Laffin...Big L, little a, two little fs, one i and a nnnnn. Terence."

"Married?"

"Yes... me and Olwyn."

"Children?"

"No... she's eighteen and I'm nineteen."

"Any children?"

"Paul and Mandy. Paul's the lad.... otherwise I'd have drowned him....."

"Why's that?"

"Would you keep a son called Mandy?"

"Have you been looking for work?"

"Yes, but my union says I can't take a job outside my trade."

"What's your trade?"

"I'm a Zeppelin fitter."

The officer sighed and slowly shook his head. "Any money in the bank?"

"Seventy five thousand pounds."

The official exploded, "Stop talking so bloody stupid."

Terry yelled back, "Well, you bloody started it."

One particularly bad winter, when asked by the chief clerk why he refused a job as a snow shoveler, he replied, deadpan, " I can't stand the cold... offer it to me in July or August."

I was by now a seasoned theatrical doing a run of Moss Theatres with a hotch potch of variety shows. I even did a tour with a Mini Circus...as a self contained piano player singing (the now famous) Perry Como's "You must have been a beautiful baby" to a Chimp dressed in crinoline dress and bonnet. I also threw in a few gags.

I was delighted when the show was booked for a week at the West Hartlepool Empire Theatre. It really was a lousy show but I was in my hometown and I'd see my wife and two kids again, and working with Terry Laffin, I'd top up with new material.

The show consisted of twelve way past their sell by date chorus girls, a Dog Act called Rachinde's Performing Poodles, a front cloth comedian, and two speciality acts, one a slack wire act and the other a girl who wrestled with a fifteen foot python.... I was there to give a little culture to the shambles.

Sunday afternoon was always 'Band Call' for the new week's show.

The conversation between the West Hartlepool Empire house manager and Nelson, the Stage Manager (who was also a wit) went thus:

Manager: "Rachinde's Performing Poodles?"

Nelson: "Correct."

Manager. "Twelve chorus girls?"

Nelson; "Right."

Manager: (Worrying about bitches on heat) "Are there any Dogs?"

Nelson: "Three or four... but they can dance at the back."

As Terry Laffin was the assistant stage manager his job was to attend to supervise the rigging and the setting up of props.

Monday to Friday the show did dreadful business but regardless of quality, Saturday nights were always full houses on the Variety Circuit in those days.

The Saturday night of the Magical Mini Circus was no exception. The place was sold out, and even the acts were pleasantly surprised with the reception each received from the family audience. During the interval Terry and his crew toiled at setting up the slack wire rig.

At this point I should explain what a slack wire act does. It's similar to a tight rope act, but the wire is slack and the walker, dressed in white tie, silk top hat and tails usually portraying a drunk staggers up and down the swaying rope performing breathtaking 'prat falls'. The performance builds up to a crescendo with the artiste balancing a card table, stacked with rattling bottles and wine glasses, on his chin to his cue music 'The loveliest night of the year' which was usually murdered by the bored and equally inebriated house orchestra which consisted of a Piano, Bass, Tympani (drums), Trumpet player doubling on bells, Trombonist doubling on vibes, Violinist doubling on Sax and a Cellist doubling on Accordion. Mister Bert Hewitt was the Conductor.

The girl wrestling the python would follow the slack wire act and I would close the show. Cue music...curtains, lights, enter stage right, (staggering,) the slack wire act.

Once Terry Laffin was happy that the act was up and running he'd make his way to the under-stage space to collect the props for the penultimate act. The young assistant stage manager groped his way through the semi darkness to the basket containing the giant reptile. Approaching rather gingerly he gripped the stout cane handles and braced himself for the lift. Like a weightlifter he exhaled, stooped bent legged gave a might heave and went flying backwards. Looking at the basket he noticed that the lid was missing.....and so was the fifteen foot python.

Slowly standing erect, his tongue sticking to the roof of his mouth and his rectum shrunk to the size of a pin head Terry, eyes watering with fear, made his way to the exit where he edged himself out and slammed the door behind him. Then dashing backstage, he informed Nelson that the snake was loose.

Nelson said it was nothing to do with him and inform Sabrina, the snake girl. Unfortunately, Sabrina was not on the premises. As speciality acts are not exactly overpaid, Sabrina would supplement her meagre wages by doubling as a hooker, plying her trade behind the obligatory pub attached to all Theatres. Terry dashed out into the night and found Sabrina eating chips from a newspaper while being humped by a large man wearing a turban. When Terry tried to attract her attention he was rebuked by a queue of multi national soldiers, sailors and airmen, also devouring chips while they waited patiently in line.

However, Terry did finally attract the girl's attention and blurted out his story.

Minutes later she and Terry were under the Stage trying to coach 'Alexander' back into his basket.... at least, Sabrina was coaxing.... Terry was clinging to the girl like a second skin.

As the artiste swung her flashlight around the dimly lit space, Terry suddenly cried out;

"There he is."

"Where" whispered the girl.

"There... well, he was there... he's just gone through the trap...... into the orchestra pit."

"Oh, shit," spat the girl...."look, you tell the conductor... I'll go up and see if I can catch him out front..."

The seriousness of the situation hadn't yet struck the young assistant stage manager. He slowly opened the door which led into the orchestra pit.... made sure the python was not within striking distance and opened the aperture wider. He raised his eyes and realised he was looking up the nose of the conductor, Mister Bert Hewitt.

Bert had a fixed smile on his face as he cut a swathe with his baton at the musicians, as occasionally he would turn to patronise the regular front stalls customers and pass on pleasantries.........

"Hello, Mrs Baxter how's little Tommy?" Over the fever.... oh good..."

To an attractive young girl. "Good evening Stella...."

"Bert" Terry hissed. The music droned on... a ripple of applause for the man on the slack wire.

"Bert" called Terry upping the decibels over the din.

Bert turned, looked first over his left, then his right shoulder...

"Bert... for Christsake!" Terry croaked loudly.

"Hello Mrs Wilson," cooed the conductor, "missed you last week.... how's..."

"Oi, Berrrrt... down here man" Terry tugged the conductor's trouser leg and almost screamed, over another ripple of applause, followed by a gasp as the man on the slack wire performed a well rehearsed near catastrophic pratfall.

Bert looked down in the direction of the voice....

"Huh?"

"Bert...I...."

"Yes, yes... what is it?"

"The python...Alexander.... Sabrina's...it's....

"What? I can't hear you... what are you..."

"The Python... the snake... it's loose..."

"It's loose... what's loose...?"

"The Python...Alexander.... Sabrina's...the snake!"

Mister Bert Hewitt stooped till his nose almost touched Terry's. "Well, don't tell me... tell Nelson... go up and see Nelson..."

"I've seen Nelson..."

"Well, where's Sabrina... she'll be in the back-street...behind the pub. Go see..."

"She knows.... she's up there... out front... O- U- T   F- R- O- N- T... she's going to try and catch it if it comes out there..."

"Out where? Damn it boy, what are you saying?"   Slowly Mr Bert Hewitt was grasping the situation.

"Where is it...the Py...er," looking first at his feet, then at his charges.

"It's in there.... in the pit...WITH YOU......."

Mister Bert Hewitt looked over his shoulder at the house. It was Saturday night and every seat was taken. Men, women and children... and an old lady in a wheelchair blocking the emergency door...

The Pianist was the first to get the feeling that all was not well.

"Wassup Maestro?" he slurred.

Bert was now conducting the orchestra and occasionally lashing out with his baton at the floor around his feet. He edged backwards and eased his buttocks up onto the polished brass rail that cordoned the orchestra from the front row of the stalls... stretching his legs so that the toes of his elastic sided patent leather shoes rested on the lid of the Grand Piano.

"Nothing" the conductor hissed. "Just remember there are women and children ....we don't want to cause a panic....stay calm.....just stay calm... it's nothing to worry about... THE SNAKE'S LOOSE!"

"what's what?" rasped the Trombonist out of the side of his mouth as he tried to follow the flailing baton. He spoke first to the Pianist, then the Violinist, then swivelling back to address the maestro.

"Did he say the... did you say the s-n-a-k-e's loose?" shouted the percussionist as he climbed up onto his tympani...

Bert looked over his shoulder. The first five rows were already standing up and stamping their feet and lashing at their shins with rolled up programmes. The Musicians were taking the tempo from the conductor's baton...and as it sliced crazily through the air the beat increased tenfold and the slack wire was spinning like a skipping rope while the man on the wire tried to keep his balance, the card table arcing in unbelievable curves... bottles and glasses rattling noisily. Now patrons in the balcony and the 'Gods' were on their feet stamping and screaming. A huge obese man, standing on his seat in the first row of the stalls turned and, with arms akimbo addressing the biting scratching kicking throng, screamed, "The lion's loose.... don't panic...there's a loose lion...think of the women and children" and with that he dived like an Olympic swimmer head first into the heaving mass swimming over arm for the exit.

Pandemonium broke out as people clawed their way to the emergency exits...The old lady in the wheelchair was used as a battering ram as the emergency door was taken off it's hinges, the panicking crowd surging forward, taking the old lady and the chair forward like a surfboard..

The man on the slack wire swaying crazily yelled above the din, "Oh, No, noooo...help... HELP ME...heyeeeee...aghhhh..." as he plummeted down into the now deserted orchestra pit. An eerie silence followed broken only by the tinkling of glass as the wire walker tried to disentangle himself from the mangled Xylophone.

Terry Laffin was the main instrument in my adding comedy to my piano vocal routine. Because of his presence, I acquired the act that carried me through many years and countless venues in every facet of Show Business....

Thanks old friend!

As I write, I have just been informed by phone that Terry Laffin died yesterday, 5, July, 2002. I am saddened. But I will always remember the old trouper through the words of an Irving Berlin song we both used to sing, and whose lyrics are synonymous to our warm, hilarious lifelong friendship.

The perfume of roses in May
Returns to my room in December
From out of the past where forgotten things belong
You keep coming back like a song

(Irving Berlin)

I learned so much from the old pros while 'treading the boards.' I met, worked with and became friends to some of the greatest artistes in the world of show-business.. Frank Randle, Jimmy James and his stammering nephew/stooge Eli Woods, Sandy Powell, The loveable drunk, Freddy Frinton, Jimmy Wheeler, Hylda Baker, Gracie Fields, Eric Morecambe, Bob Monkhouse, Bobby Thompson and a thousand more who were the crème de crème of 'real' Show Business.... and I remember each and every one of them... who, in passing took with them the true art of entertainment. Their likes will never be seen again.

The Days of Wine and Roses

In the late forties my Concert Party, 'The Johnny Hammond Show' consisted of Cyril Wycherely, a pianist who had spent most of the war in a Japanese prison camp. Jackie Barton, an outstanding singer and musician... who was as popular right up to the time of his death in his seventies as he was in his twenties.

Mabel Bew, a gorgeous, full of fun young 18 years old who sang remarkably like the (at that time) internationally famous Jo Stafford.

George Kellett, one of the worst comedians who ever 'trod the boards', but he was a formidable street fighter and an asset to any travelling troupe of entertainers touring some of the hardest clubs in the country.

Jean Mack, (my mum) a great singer.

Gerry Glancey, one of the handsomest of men, and a tenor could have worked the great opera houses in the world.... had he been in right place at the right time. He married his childhood sweetheart and the day after the birth of his first baby, while working as a steel erector, he fell 180 feet from scaffolding on the North-Tees Power station and died instantly. It was heartbreaking to read in the Birth's column of the local paper the notice of his daughter's arrival followed in the Obituaries, the notice of Gerry's death.

I made up the number.

My dad who acted as our manager was as good at management as George Kellet was at comedy. But (George aside) we were good... we were the best, but in post war Britain we all worked at day jobs.

George, Jackie, Gerry and even I, worked as steel erectors. The day after Gerry Glancey fell to his death, I was working a couple of hundred feet up on a girder with Jackie Barton and George Kellet when I missed my footing. Jackie Barton grabbed me and certainly saved my life. Minutes later I was an ex-steel erector.

Jackie didn't want me to pack in and told me I should go back up onto the girder I'd almost fallen off. "Your spirit is up there" he said.

That was 50 years ago and as far as I know my spirit is still up there.

A couple of years later George Kellett had his lower body crushed when a crane cable carrying a five ton furnace door snapped directly above him.. He survived the accident, but immediately contracted cancer and died within eight weeks.

Jackie Barton, Mabel Bew and I carried on for a few more years, then Mabel married, Jackie took work with a dance band, and I carried on for a while as a freelance entertainer.

I even went back onto the theatres as half of a 'Martin and Lewis' type double act.

I was Dean Martin to ex miner Jackie Robertson's Jerry Lewis. We were good enough to share top Billing with the top song and comedy act of the day, Malcolm Vaughan and Kenny Earle.

I wrote an act for us (my first stab at Comedy writing... an art which would help feed my family in later, leaner times) but the Variety Theatres were closing in favour of Bingo and television.

In the fifties North East, clubland was taking hold with an iron grip.

After a long solo run I was approached by Mr Jakey Brumwell, who ran his own rag bag concert party, "Jakey Brumwell's Happy Six."

Jakey Brumwell's happy six had started with four singers, a comic and a piano player, but by the time I agreed to join them there were alternately between fifteen and thirty-two performers on the show at one time. I suggested we pick another name for the show but Jakey refused to re-name us because he'd had letterheads printed and it would cost 'at least five quid' to replace them.

Jakey Brumwell was a very large, tough coal miner. He came from the pit village of Horden, which was seven miles North of Hartlepool. Miners in any part of the world are hard working, hard living people. The miners of the North East of England are no exception. They work hard, drink hard and play hard.

Jakey Brumwell had yearned to be an entertainer but on his first ever gig, a novice's talent contest, the whole audience had attacked him. So he sold his box of motley and went into management.

He was fiercely loyal to his friends and a champion of his beliefs.... right or wrong.

When I had headed my own show, we split the money equally, mainly because no one was deemed better or worse than the other.

Jakey shared the same beliefs, but he was wrong on one important factor, every act in the Happy Six Road Show was worse than the next guy.

Apart from Mabel Bew, who'd made another comeback, Sirus Bunny, the shows alcoholic accompanist (he once belched at a funeral and turned it into mardi gras) and myself, a pro for several years standing, the rest of the acts would have been flattered had you called them novices.

But they were great drinkers, greater fighters, great friends and great fun and loyal to each other and as there were usually around thirty of us that made us an implacable, immovable and formidable force.

No club in the country would turn away a coach load of marathon drinkers and in our case, no one would dare to refuse us entry anyway. We commanded the top fees of any concert party in the North East. The average wages for a show in those early days was fifteen pounds. The Happy Six got twice that but shared between thirty 'turns' it was not a viable proposition to a guy with a wife and, by then, four kids.

So a solution was reached whereas Mabel, Sirus and I would get a wage, and the rest of the fee went into a kitty for the shows expenses, travel, booze, insurance, court costs, and probable funeral expenses.

We travelled in a 32-seater coach with the name of the show emblazoned left, right, front and back. As clubland has an excellent grapevine, we were soon as well known as a shipload of Barbary Coast Pirates.

The 'close' came suddenly one Saturday night in Leamington Miners Comrades Working-men's Club on the outskirts of Newcastle upon Tyne. The coach had collected some of the acts before stopping off at Blackhall Colliery to entice Sirus Bunny aboard.

I say 'entice' because Sirus had been a budding concert pianist of some repute before going into partnership with O'l John Barleycorn and ending up almost in the gutter.

When in a seldom state of sobriety he would stare aghast at the human flotsam he had taken aboard as soul mates and avoid us like the plague. However, being in a constant state of penury he found it impossible to imbibe without the help of this uncouth warrior troupe.

The ploy each week was to stop the coach outside his lodgings, place a crate of Newcastle Brown Ale on the coach step, and when his addled brain took the scent he would float out like a spectre, resplendent in threadbare dinner suit, crumpled shirt and black bow-tie, and fondle the crate... which the driver would reel in like an angler till Sirus was safely aboard and berthed in steerage.

We would then proceed to the next mining village Horden where the rest of the troupe would stagger aboard.

The venue this particular night was the aforementioned Leamington Comrades Club.

Should anyone today visit the Leamington Comrades Club, they would not recognise it from the establishment I describe here. It is, and has been for many years a showplace for entertainment in the North East and it boasts one of the best audiences one could wish to play to.

However, at the time of this story it resembled a dilapidated church hall.

It had a large bar, and an even larger concert room with an un-carpeted highly polished wooden floor. At the far end of the room was erected a miniscule uncurtained stage on which stood legs and keyboard of a full sized concert grand piano, while the rest of the instrument jutted out into the auditorium, the third leg supported by a white painted wooden extension not dissimilar to the artificial leg worn by Captain Ahab of Moby Dick fame.

A yellowing badly written note requested anyone in the vicinity not to knock the piano leg. The trouble started before we even entered the club.....even though the show was well advertised. It appeared that word had got around that this was the best show on the road and the place was accordingly packed. So packed in fact that there was no room for the artistes... so an Extraordinary Committee Meeting was held and the result was that thirty two loyal members were asked to move themselves to the bar area.

And as there were so many artistes to get on in the legal three hours left, our leader insisted that the club committee should forego tonight's Housey-Housey (Bingo) upsetting the lady members somewhat.

So with the scent of blood in the air, the curtain went up.

John L Dunn who shared mixed ambitions to be both a prize fighter and a comedian had modelled himself on the old bare knuckle fighter John L Sullivan and the old variety star G.H.Elliot opened the proceedings with a song in the middle of which he threatened to render unconscious some youths in the audience unless they refrained from joining in. A move that immediately cut his fan club to shreds.

Chuck Gracie was the next act on. A sparring partner to John L Dunn, he didn't just reiterate John L's feelings, but actually leapt from the stage and attempted to dismantle a whole table of hecklers.

After the fracas calmed down, Mabel Bew wearing a chiffon evening gown took to the stage and electrified the audience with her rendition of Jo Stafford hits.

Unfortunately, in the middle of her rendition of the great American songbirds "Cross of Calvary" some drunken protestant objector staggered to his feet and screamed, "Gerrorf you screaming Catholic cow."   This prompted our Comedian/Minder, Pop Porter to step forward and punch the heckler on the back of the neck, dropping the man to his knees and sending him skidding across the polished wooden floor and crashing into the wooden leg supporting seventy five per cent of the piano.

As the leg collapsed the piano crashed to the floor causing the keyboard to whip upwards catching Sirus Bunny under the chin, propelling him backwards through a small open window and crashing onto what is now the car park but what was then the committeemen's bicycle shed. In seconds the scene resembled the battle scene of 'Custer's Last Stand'.

Outside one of the locals fired a flare summoning the local Gendarme, who arrived in minutes on his bike, saw the futility of his task and returned to the station house where he locked himself in, took the phone off the hook and retired early to his bed. Unfortunately, someone knocked the treasurer unconscious and we left the battle scene empty handed, which didn't bode well with my wife, who said that I should decide between Mr Jakey Brumwell Happy Six and my starving unhappy FIVE!

I reasoned that not only was blood thicker than water but that, if I stayed much longer with the Jakey Brumwell Happy Six my blood would sooner or later be running like water. I knew that I'd miss the camaraderie and the excitement but I had to go with the family. Anyway, I'd learned the dangers of tangling with hecklers from the great Dean Martin and Jerry Lewis.

I recalled, many years previously when I was honoured to sit in the company of an ageing Dean Martin as he related a terrifying ordeal his then partner, Jerry Lewis faced one night while doing Cabaret in New York's Copa Cabana club.

Between shows Dean was drinking at the Casino bar with the owner.

Jerry was drifting through the crowd giving them a taste of the mongoloid mayhem to come. He was getting laughs when a gorilla of a man at a gaming table shouted, "Why don't you knock off that shit and shut the fuck up."

Jerry stopped in his tracks. He thought the guy was either kidding or too drunk to appreciate the humour.

Still in character Lewis laughed idiotically, looked at the man, and threw off the old chestnut; "See what happens when cousins marry."

Dean winced and his drinking partner raised two fingers to his temple.

The gorilla rose and stuck a finger in Jerry's face. "That's not funny, you stupid sonafabitch. You open your mouth again, and you won't have no teeth."

As Jerry froze Dean stepped between them and said to the man; "My partners a little young.... he didn't mean any harm." The man glared at them then turned away. Dean told Jerry to apologise, which he did and the man looked at Dean and said "Okay, only keep the little bastard away from me. You tell him he's lucky I got a sense of humour."

The man 'with the sense of humour' turned out to be a man Jerry had often heard of but had never encountered before, the guy the newspapers liked to call the Lord High Executioner of Murder, Inc.

Dean took his shaken partner by the arm and whispered into his ashen face; "For your information, schmuck, that was Albert Anastasia."

(This story is related in the brilliant book "DINO" by Nick Tosches.)

From then on I learned to make sure I could handle a heckler before I put him down.

In my many years in the Business and handling thousands of hecklers I only came unstuck once...in a dreadful hall of horrors one glorious summers evening in Newcastle when I misread my quarry. As I finished my act he strolled smiling up to the dais I was standing on, smiled, wished me a Merry Christmas and knocked me out.

The Champ.

I left Jakey Brumwell's Happy Six Road Show without giving formal notice and hid in
the Cleveland Hills till Jakey got me out of his system and found a suitable replacement.
However, Jakey had already decided to relinquish his title of Concert Party Manager and
move over into the less hazardous occupation of Professional Boxing Management.
This was brought on by his admiration for the haymaker Pop Porter delivered to the neck of
the heckler in the Leamington Comrades massacre.
He decided that Pop could make more money in a few fights than he could in a lifetime as a
coal miner/minder/entertainer. He convinced the hapless Pop that no man, no matter how well
conditioned, could take a round hander like the one Pop landed on the neck of his victim at
Leamington Comrades debacle.
They would go into strict training that very day.
Jakey acquired an old bicycle for himself and training kit for his future champ. This consisted
of a gum shield and a pair of sandshoes.
Jakey would be Pop's Manager doubling as trainer, thereby cutting out the middleman and
pocketing the extra cash.   He arranged to be at Pop's door at the beginning of each shift
where he would mount his bike and ride at a steady pace alongside his trotting, sparring
protégé.
At the end of the shift, Jakey would meet Pop at the pit head and make sure his man jogged
the full quarter of a mile back to his home, throwing roundhanders, straight hooks and
underarm nine-pin bowling spins.
After a meal of the famous Hartlepool kippers they would head for the picturesque Crimdon
Dene where Pop would don a pair of miners boots onto which Jakey had screwed inch
thick lead soles, and Pop would stagger a mile each way up and down the beach while his
trainer sat on a sandy hillock drinking beer as he bellowed instructions through a home made
cardboard megaphone.
After a half hour's beach work, Pop would stagger back to his home and batter the stuffing
out of an old rucksack filled with rags which dangled from his mother's clothes line.   Then for
recreation they would go to the Horden Workingmen's Club
and consume as much ale as members of Pop's new found fan club could afford.
After a week of intensive training, Jakey contacted the Hartlepool Boxing Promoter Mr
Walter Hazeltine and requested a place at the earliest instant on one of
Mr Hazeltine's Bills.
By an amazing co-incidence, Mr Walter Hazeltine had just that very morning had one of his
fighters pull out of an eight round contest against a young fighter named Jimmy Gill, 'The
Nottingham Jockey', 'and maybe Jakey's man could step in as substitute.' The contest would
take place at the Hartlepool Engineers open air arena on the Monday four days hence.
Being an astute business manager, Jakey accepted Hazeltine's terms. Pop would be paid on
his performance 'Per Full 3 minute Round'.
Jakey hot-footed it round to his fighter's training quarters, the bar of The Horden
Workingmen's Club just as his fighter jogged in from his shift at the coalface.
Pop, not the brightest of men was aggrieved because that day he'd crawled for an hour in an
eighteen inch seam a couple of thousand yards to the coalface, just to have to reverse all the
way out after discovering that he had his shovel the wrong way round.
Jakey informed Pop of his debut fight and ordered his man to go into a harsh four-day regime
of training...as soon as the bar closed. He informed the future champ that his mining days
were almost at an end and the light at the end of the tunnel read 'Middleweight Champion of
the World'.
Come Monday, Pop clocked off at the pithead at 6 a.m. from the night shift. He showered at

the pithead baths, donned his sand shoes and ran the full quarter mile to his mother's house, where he ate a hearty breakfast of kippers.

Jakey ordered an hour's relaxation from the rigid training routine and Pop hung a dartboard on the pantry door and he and his mentor played three games of nearest the bull before packing Pops kit.

A kiss from his mother as she pressed a charm in the form of a lucky rabbit's foot (which incidentally had brought little good fortune to its previous owner) Pop then trotted off beside Jakey who was riding his bike as pacemaker, the seven miles to the weigh in. All along the route they were cheered on by crowds of local well-wishers. Unfortunately after only seven minutes into the journey, the chain on the bike snapped, so Jakey cast the biped into a nearby hedge and they both caught the next bus to Hartlepool.

At the 'weigh in' Pop met his opponent, a flyweight who was at least six inches shorter and five stones lighter than he was. Not wishing to lose his promoters licence Mr Hazeltine decided he would bill the fight at catch weight.   However, what 'the Jockey' lacked in stature he amply made up for in experience. A National Schoolboy's Champion (undefeated), a National Junior Amateur Champion and undefeated as a Pro in nineteen fights, he had also decimated the opposition at International level. This weighed against Pop's one success in the Leamington Comrades Club fracas plus several no contests in the Horden Labour Club Car Park influenced the betting heavily against a victory for the miners.

After the 'weigh in' Pop and Jakey headed for the bright lights of the town, which on a hot summer's afternoon were decidedly dimmed. They headed for Kirby's cafe in the dock area and partook of a couple of plates of Pop's favourite fare...Hartlepool kippers, washed down by his favourite tipple, several pints of the local brew, Cameron's Sparkling Ales. This was followed by a relaxing nap on the beach at nearby Seaton Carew.

A light snack of kippers and a jog brought them to the capacity full venue.

However, not even Pop assumed that the throng were there to usher in his debut to the realms of pugilistic fame. In fact the local favourite Brian London who was soon to hold the two titles, British and Empire Heavyweight Champion, recently vacated by his fighting father, Jack London snr, was upstaging him.

Pop Porter and his opponent were the first contest on the Bill.

Pop didn't have time to contemplate his future. Within minutes he was attired in his strip and heading for the pit of punishment. If his pugilistic expertise left a lot to be desired, his outfit put this shortfall into the shade.

He stepped into the ring wearing brown sandshoes, knee length yellow socks, knee length green canvas shorts and a dyed navy blue army blouse with the name and title of his great hero, "Jack Dempsey, the Manassa Mauler" hastily daubed across the back in still wet white paint.

The miniscule Jimmy Gill entered around the same time in red and white calf-length boxing shoes, red white and blue silk boxing shorts and a blue and gold velvet dressing gown with the crossed flags of Great Britain and the United States of America embroidered in gold from shoulder to shoulder.

As Pop and Jakey caught a glimpse of the young mans athletic sun-tanned body, they exchanged bemused expressions, which, deciphered read, "What the Hell are we doing here?"

A low rumbling deep in his bowels told Pop that he should have had an enema before leaving the dressing room. He suddenly lost the ability to speak. He felt the skin on his face stretch into a hideous grinning mask. His tongue stuck to the roof of his mouth and his eyes began to water. His body went icy cold, his asshole shrunk to the size of a pinhead and to add to his misery he felt an erection coming on.

The voice of the referee calling the combatants to the centre of the ring brought him back to his senses. He heard Jakey telling him that the ref wanted him and felt his mentor pushing him towards the official and his executioner.

Jakey decided to stay where he was safe in Pop's corner and while the combatants were getting their instructions, he slid under the ropes and knelt on the rough ground, eyes peering over the ring apron, watching the ritual unfold before him.

Jimmy Gill had his manager, trainer, cuts man (a mere formality) and two corner men in attendance. Pop stood forlorn, like a condemned man facing his nemesis. He looked pleadingly into the eyes of his opponent, silently begging the young man to forgive any trespass Pop may have made against him.

"Touch gloves" the ref intoned.

Pop grabbed at his opponents shiny red leather instruments of torture and clung to them like a limpet and had to be separated by his opponent's corner men. As Gill stared menacingly into Pop's eyes, the miner smiled and said the only words he could muster, "You wouldn't believe it but I've never done this before you know."

As he made his way back to his corner he looked down into the horror stricken face of his manager. Jakey shrugged and looked down at his own feet.

'Doinnng'. The bell tolled.

Pop walked out to meet his executioner, but even at this late hour he smilingly, pleadingly offered both gloved hands in a token of friendship. Gill stepped between Pop's outstretched arms, pulled his right arm back no more than three inches and buried the leather bound ramrod deep enough into Pop's entrails to dislodge his spine. Pop let out a loud whistling whine. His gum shield shot out of his mouth and stuck on the corner post behind his opponent and as 'the Jockey' extricated his arm, Pop disgorged at least a gallon of Cameron's Sparkling ale and several portions of partly

masticated famous Hartlepool kippers which covered the first five rows at ringside and hung like Christmas decorations from the surrounding trees.

Pop retired with just one defeat on his Professional Record.

Jakey also retired from boxing management, reasoning that the hire of the bike, two and sixpence for a gum-shield, the return bus fare to Horden Colliery and the fact that Pop had not lasted the obligatory three minutes, had not made the journey into the world of pugilism a viable proposition.

Going Solo… But No Lower!

I tried starting my own Concert Party again. Once more Mabel Bew came out of retirement and I discovered a seventeen-year-old vocalist named Larry Mason. He stayed with us for a few months till the newly established Tyne Tees Television snapped him up. Mabel retired again (she held the showbusiness record for comebacks for several years when it only was bettered by Frank Sinatra) and I looked around for someone to look after me.

In the early mid fifties I signed an agency contract with the Doris Boagey office in Sunderland. This was at the time when clubland was just about coming into its' own. I was very proud that one of my discoveries, Larry Mason had made it from clubland to television in one giant leap - and most deservedly.

Larry made over five hundred appearances on Tyne Tees Television. He was a big name in the North East of the country. Sadly the BIG 'big time' forever eluded him. More a case of lousy luck than lousy management. On his way to that illusive penultimate rung of the ladder this kid must have broken more mirrors than the 'Wicked Witch in Snow White'.

His luck seemed to change when he was booked to appear in Tel Aviv for a two week high class Cabaret stint. During the second day of rehearsals the six day war broke out. For a week he did nothing but look at the scenery and dodge bullets and shells sent over spasmodically by the Arabs. Larry was the first passenger on the first plane within seconds of the Arab capitulation.

He did several World Class shows with the biggest star names which always brought him better reviews than the Top of the Bill, and this was his undoing.

He suddenly stopped getting chief support roles on the big television musical shows, mainly because he was too good at least for the stars. It's an unwritten law in show business that one should never work with children or animals... they should add a rider which says you should never work on a show where you are better than the headliner. And Larry Mason was light years better than most of his peers.

Stars refused to work with this young up and coming singer and as the powers that be had sunk fortunes into their headline attractions, they didn't want their charges to appear second best... and around this time Angels, (rich backers who sink money into up and coming stars,) were pretty thin on the ground.

Larry's climb to the top of the show business ladder stopped that one step below the penultimate rung of his career and this was at a time when other TV stations were springing up all over the country. Larry Mason missed the gravy train and it was our loss. He was that good…but that's Show Business.

At this time, two young Geordie businessmen hit on the idea of building a Cabaret-Club Circuit, which put first their own North East of England, quickly followed by the whole of Britain on the Entertainment map.

John Smith and Stan Henry became the 'The Bailey Organisation'. Starting on Wearside, they rapidly took over Tyneside, Teesside, Yorkshire, the Midlands, Scotland and Wales. Suddenly Clubland was reeling. Acts became Artistes and dressed the part. They threw away their half crown copies of music and began to have special arrangements made.

The Bailey Empire added a Las Vegas lustre sadly lacking in the austere workingmen's clubs of that time. The Top Club Acts became Stars overnight. Tony Christie, Marti Caine, Dukes and Lee, Little and Large, Cannon and Ball, the Krankies, Bobby Thompson, Larry Mason, Showaddywaddy all started in the Bailey Clubs. The Bailey Organisation turned the best 'club acts' into some of the finest Entertainers in Britain television, theatre and Cabaret..

Most of them went on to super-stardom, and one, Mike Preston actually made it to Hollywood and the super big time.

Soon the clubland stars were joined by International stars…Johnny Mathis, Louis Armstrong,

Shirley Bassey, Tom Jones, Matt Munroe, Engelbert Humperdink, Dorothy Squires, Tony Bennett...the list was endless.

Larry Mason was up there with the best of them.

One night Larry Mason rang me and asked would I like to be his guest ringside at the British opening of the American Superstar Singer Billy Eckstein's Tour at the sumptuous Bailey's Dolce Vita club in Newcastle.

I leaped at the chance.

There, as Larry's guest I was wined and dined with the Stars of the day, one of whom was an icon in the business at the time, the afore-mentioned Dorothy Squires.

A handsome young man whom she introduced as 'Roger' escorted her.

Roger Moore later went on to become one of our greatest film stars. They married and then 'Roger' traded in Dorothy for a younger model. Thanks to Dot Squires he became super famous and super rich. She stayed in the Superstar league for a few more years, but inevitably hit the slide and ended her days a broken lonely old woman in a tiny rented terrace house in South Wales.

'There's no people like Show people.'

American icon Billy Eckstein was the biggest singing star of the day and his act was a mixture of rapturous singing, side-splitting comedy and Las Vegas glitz. At the conclusion of his act he introduced his backing band. Finally turning to his accompanist, Eckstein quipped..." and this is my great friend, Benny Payne... not only a great Pianist, but also a great Arranger, Composer, Trombonist and Sex Maniac." The audience fell about. When the laughter died, Eckstein concluded "I'm only kidding ladies and gentlemen...He doesn't play the trombone." This was pure Americana, and both Larry and I memorised the line and used it for many years and to great effect in our own acts.

Like all Cinderella stories, the good times had to end.

The Bailey Empire wasn't spared and was hit by the massively rapid growth of Television. The Big Night-clubs slowly went off the boil. Then the government of the day put a ban on gambling Casino's..., which were essential to the Cabaret Clubs. Without the gaming Casino's, they couldn't afford the great American, European and British Acts.

In desperation, all those hopefuls who nearly made it headed back to the Workingmen's Club Circuit. Larry Mason was no exception. Now married with a young family to feed, he followed the sad and disillusioned herd back from whence they came.

One night Larry was booked to do a show in a Miners Club in Barnsley, South Yorkshire. It was a run of the mill Miners Workingmen's Club. 'Two turns.... girl singer, top on't bill, hot pies an' 'Bingo.'

Arriving at the club Larry made his way into the dressing room where the girl singer was going through her 'band call'.   He introduced himself to the drummer, a short fat bald man, with a cheery red face and a personality to go with it.   Then he offered a hand of friendship to the organist, who ignored the gesture, took Larry's portfolio of music, scanned through it, shoved it under his arm and walked onto the stage, where he took his place at the organ.

Larry noticed that as the musician stepped into the platform, the audience suddenly went quiet. Larry asked the drummer what the problem was but the drummer just shrugged his shoulders and said there was a 'bit 'o' trouble like.... but not to worry'.

Mason was determined to make friends with the organist, so at the end of his opening number he bowed low to the accompanist and turning to the audience, he beamed; "Ladies and gentlemen. I usually wait till the finale before I throw brickbats or bouquets at the backing, but I must ask you to join with me in congratulating this brilliant musician behind me".

NOTHING!   No reaction, from the audience at all. Larry pressed on.

"Aw, c'mon ladies and gentlemen... you are listening to an outstanding musical talent here -

and not only a great organist. This man is also a great pianist, arranger, composer, trombonist and *Sex Maniac."*

With that the organist bristled, leaped from the instrument, dashed into the dressing room, grabbed his street clothes, disappeared out of the stage door and vanished into the night.

At the same time, the club steward leaped over the bar, hurtled down the room and sailing through the air punched Larry on the chin knocking him and the drummer sprawling into the curtains.

All hell broke loose as committeemen and members of the audience ran to the singers rescue. Minutes later, bathing his wounds in the dressing room, Larry asked what the hell he'd done wrong".

"Well," said the drummer, "It wasn't a wise thing to say under the circumstances... about Syd being a sex maniac."

"But it was a gag" said Mason through broken lips."

"Well, we didn't think it were funny" interjected the concert chairman.

"But it was a gag" repeated Larry. "We... Johnny Hammond and I, we pinched it off Billy Eckstein."

The official looked puzzled.

"But how did Billy.... whatever his name is.... how did he know about it?"

"Know about what?" Larry almost screamed, spitting blood.

"The drummer looked puzzled for a few seconds, and then he turned to the several committee men surrounding the fallen entertainer.

"Gentlemen" he intoned "I think this 'ere young man is a victim of circumstances."

Then turning to Larry he said, "You see, the problem was you said the wrong thing at the wrong time... of course, you weren't to know that last night the steward went out searching for his seventeen years old daughter after the show, and caught the organist shagging her on the fire escape.

Theatres were being transformed into Bingo Halls, and great variety acts were finding life hell as club entertainers, such had been the discipline on the variety circuit.

I remember bumping into a once great clubland favourite Mark Raffles who did a comedy pick pocket act. He said work was almost non-existent and he, like hundreds of his peers, was having a rough time. I said "Well Mark, if a pickpocket can't make a living what chance have we got?" I don't think he appreciated the gag... he turned and shuffled away muttering, "PRAT!"

A few weeks ago I was walking in Hyde park in London when a car... Not any old car... a liveried chauffeur driven limo...pulled alongside me. The rear window slid silently down a slightly familiar face hailed me. "Johnny? Is that Johnny? Johnny Hammond?"

I stared trying to put a name to the face.

"It's me...Rock...Rock Vanderbilt..." he smiled

I recoiled. "Rock? GOOD GOD. Rock Vanderbilt.... How are you Ralph? "

(Rock was his stage name) I eyed the car. "Silly question but what the hell are you doing down here in a car like that... last time I saw you were ...er. Well you were out of work... not that that puts you in a league of your own... but what happened.. You hit the lottery?"

Rock opened the door and slid off the plush calf leather upholstery.

He was attired like a tailors dummy... a Saville row tailors dummy.

"Last time I saw you were down on your uppers... and Belle, are you still with Peggy?"

(Belle was her stage name.)

Rock stepped onto the sidewalk and gave me a hug. "Yes, we're still together. You look well Johnny...and you. You're still in the business?"

I said I was now a struggling writer... scripts, gags, and a few television commercials.

I could see Ralph was not really interested in my plight, so I changed tack.

"So come on you lucky bastard. How much was it. Two? Three. Ten million?"

"Three point four... who's counting?" The old ham laughed.

"You hit the Lottery for Three..."

"No, you Schmuck... let me explain" he gushed. "When the clubs closed down, and the business went pear shape I was like a lot of the other guys, down and almost out...we lost the house. You heard about that?"

I gave a 'yeah, I was sorry to hear'.

"So, we came down here to London and tried to get work in the business but it's as bad down here as up North... The best gig they could offer me was singing the National Anthem at Cockfights... so we scraped and saved and in a few months we rented a run down property in Peckham... we intended to take in a few lodgers. Then asylum seekers... anybody...even club acts.... Pro digs like. But it didn't work for us, so we opened a brothel... went to see the housing officer, Aristotle O'Brian, got the nod and, nudge nudge know what I mean? We sold up and bought a three story slum.. did it up and opened a new age sex emporium. On the ground floor we have Prostitution. On the first floor we have Homosexuality and on the top floor we have Bestiality. We struck Gold...less than a year we have it made. A penthouse flat in Knightsbridge. An estate in Cobham, Surrey, a Castle in Ireland, a yacht, and wait for it...our own plane."

I was flabbergasted. "Wait, let's get this straight... from a three story brothel... in a few months you've got all this plus three million in the bank?"

Bert shrugged. "Give or take a million."

"You must have a huge staff," I reasoned.

"Not at all" beamed my old friend... "There's just me, the wife and the dog!".

High Noon

Doris Boagey, my current manager in the early fifty's rang to inform me that I was to appear at the Downhill Workingmen's Club on the following Sunday noon. A Sunday noon Show invariably meant that I'd be on with at least two Strippers.

I argued that it was too soon for me to make a return appearance.

"But you haven't been back to the Club for nearly three years," said Mrs 15%.

"I know" I replied, "but I believe no one should have to go back there without at least a twenty years break."

"Do it" snapped Doris, and dropped the phone back onto its cradle.

I did all in my power to get out of the contract, but to no avail. So it was that at the ominous time of '*HIGH NOON*' on a glorious summer's day I pulled into the car park of the dreaded club..

The sight that greeted me was immediately uplifting to the spirit. The place was ringed with police cars, their blue lights flashing in unison. A couple of ambulances stood in readiness by the stage door. A large uniformed policeman guarded the 'Springbocktoir' entrance.

As I applied my brakes there came a loud tapping on my offside window.

Outside, stood several urchins of indiscernible ages. I rolled down my window.

"Half a crown". said the shaven headed elder of the group who was maybe 10 or 11 years old..

"Huh?" I replied.

"Half a crown!" We'll mind yer car... gizza half a crown and well make sure nowt 'appens territ."

A quick translation of the request came out as 'if you don't gizza half crown, we'll make sure summat *DOES* 'appen territ.'

I noticed that several of these trainee thugs were carrying baseball bats.

I forked out the half crown and handed it to the leader who turned and handed it to a youngster aged around seven or eight, who dropped the coin into his trouser pocket. He was obviously the mob's accountant.

Without so much as a thank you the leader spat on my windscreen and at the sight of another vehicle they all turned and bore down on the new arrival.

I got out of my car and walked towards the guarded dressing room door, passing a newish Mercedes car surrounded by the Capone mob. The driver, a gorilla of a man and his passengers had already alighted and the driver was addressing the micro Capo di Capi Tuti of the Black Hand.

"Fuck off you scruffy little bastards" he snarled and raised a ham like fist in the air in a threatening manner.

The mini mob backed off.

On my way across the car park I noticed that several of the unattended Police cars also had a goblet of spit on their windscreens and I allowed myself a wry smile.

'These kids don't discriminate'.

At the Stage door a uniformed Policeman who asked my business stopped me. When I told him I was today's Comedian, his stare glazed to a mixture of admiration and pity. He was obviously a local man and probably a member of this very Club.

I entered the Club and made my way up some stone stairs and into the Dressing Room, which was full to overflowing with uniformed and plain clothed Policemen, several Committeemen, the two Musicians, three Strippers, (unclothed), and their minders. Everyone was talking heatedly and gesticulating at one tall grey haired uniformed man with three silver symbols on his shoulder epaulette.

"Ah'm not gannen oot there for naebody" yelled the ginger Stripper.

"Nor us" said the ebony black lady, who's pubic region was shaved and vaselined to a shiny mound.

"Aye" said the third girl with the Rose tattoo. "We's got men and bairns at home, and we're not ga'an oot there in front of that mad bastard, not for nowt nor summat...... money isn't worth it, man."

A small fat man standing by the door spotted me.

"Ah Johnny, ah knew ye'd come. Good lad... (to the throng)... now we've got nowt ter worry on.... Johnny'll gan on.... he disn't give a frig for naebody, he disn't... he's done the Boilermakers on a Saturday neet... Nowt'll faze him..."

The Chief turned to me. "Hello Tommy.... well, are you willing to go on?"

My expression told him that I was unsure as to the situation.

"You" to a young constable "take Tommy out and brief him on the delicate situation we have here."

"Johnny, say nowt!" yelled the black Stripper, as the light from the single flex bulb in the room caught her erogenous area and illuminated it like a neon sign. Tapping me on the shoulder, the young officer intoned, "Follow me, mate," and slid sideways out of the room and sidled, back pressed against the wall, towards the drawn curtains, the other side from which came the sound reminiscent of gala-night in Sodom and Gomorrah. At the curtains the cop stopped, causing me to bump him.

"Hold it" he whispered, which seemed ridiculous considering the mayhem that came from the auditorium. He moved the edge of the curtain, peeked out, then whispered,

"There... can you see?"

"See what?" I whispered back.

"There" he said... "what can you see?"

"Morons" I said.

"Aye, but apart from that... can you see him?"

"Who?"

"Him!" he nodded in the semi darkness... "The kid with the gun

"The fucking what?" I yelled.

"There.... at the front table."

I leaned past the officer and pulled the curtain back. The Concert Room was a beehive of activity. Men and women swayed back and forth like flotsam ebbing and flowing on a sandy shoreline. The noise was deafening. There was a five deep queue at the long bar... The lucky ones carried trays full of pint bottles of Newcastle Brown ale.... and one glass.... the afternoon quota.

I brought my gaze from the mob down to the front table. A lone young man occupied it in his early teens. In his left hand he held a bottle of beer... in his right hand was silver .38 snub-nosed revolvers. The lad looked nervously around him, finger on the trigger, his thumb trembling on the hammer of the weapon.

"See him?" asked the cop.

"Yeah... I...."

"Move out." said my companion, and squeezing passed me, he moved slowly, body pressed tightly against the wall, back to the Dressing Room. The action was as ludicrous as his whispering. The curtains were drawn and there was no way we could be seen from the auditorium, even had the curtains been missing altogether.

'Procedure' I thought.

As I re-entered the Dressing Room it fell into silence, all eyes on me.

"Well?" asked the Chief.

"Well what?" I replied.

"Do you want to go on?" asked the Chairman of Committee.

"Not even if the place was filled with admirers" I replied.

"Ye dae reet!" echoed the girls in unison.

"What's going on?" I said.

"Well, let me put you in the picture Sir." volunteered the Chief.

"It appears that this young man out there comes home from a party in the early hours of the morning and walks in on his step father kicking the shit out of his mother." The terminology seemed out of place for one in such high authority.

"So he pulls out this .38...where the hell he got it.... although round here, nothing surprises me...." he shrugged "anyway, he pumped five bullets into the old man."

"Is he dead?" enquired one of the Committeemen.

"No, but he was mortally wounded." replied the Chief.

"But that's the same thing more or less." I said.

"Aye well" countered the embarrassed senior officer, "but that's not the point.... the point is that we have to get in there and get that gun off the boy before he snaps and starts indiscriminately killing everybody in the room."

"Which wouldn't be a bad thing!" I joked. "Look gentlemen..."

"...And us Johnny, speak tiv us as well man." The ginger Stripper was offended at my omission.

"Sorry Andrea" said the Committee Chairman... "Johnny didn't mean nowt."

I continued... "I've worked this Club when nobody was armed out there, and I was almost killed by the stress... I don't think that my standing up there like a frigging Aunt Sally is conducive to my intended longevity."

The girls applauded my observations, although I doubt if they knew what I was talking about.

"But we have to have someone to attract the boy's attention so that we can apprehend him." pleaded the Chief.

"Well, you go and attract his attention, smart arse....." snapped Andrea.

"But the Chief is a Chief.... we can't risk that..." said a plain clothes man.

"I've got an idea" piped up a grey haired Committee man... "Johnny, if we double your money will you go on."

I made a quick calculation. They're paying me £8 for the noon Show.

I'm being paid £8 at Boilermakers Club.... if these guys double my money to £16, I can pull out of tonight's Club on medical grounds...the Boilermakers people know the reputation of Downhill Club.... they'll know I'm not lying about my health after doing the noon Show.

"I'LL DO IT." I enthused.

The three Strippers came from the same school of accountancy as I did.

"Well, double our money and we'll go on as well." said their spokes-person.

"Hang on a minute" said the Treasurer of the Committee "we can't just throw money away like this.... we'll have to have an Extraordinary Committee Meeting to sanction this."

"When will you have an Extraordinary Committee Meeting to sanction this?" snarled the Chief

"At the next General Committee Meeting... in November..."

The Treasurer's voice trailed off into an embarrassed whisper.

"Right," said the Chief.... "Let's get this Show on the road..."

As the girls began donning their feather boas, the Concert Chairman halted the proceedings.

"Hold it. Hold it... HOLD IT...."

"What now, for Christ's sake." moaned the Chief.

"We seem to have forgotten summat." said the Concert Chairman.

"What've we forgot, Basil?" enquired the President.

"We have forgot the most important thing.... we have forgot that if that arsehole out there starts shooting his gun discriminately, and he hits our Organ Player, we are going to be knackered for an Organist for the rest of the year... what we need to do is turn the Organ round so that it faces the front and Alan will be shielded from the line of fire.... and if Gus sets his Drums up behind Alan we can protect the whole Band, and everything will be honkey dory." He smiled like the cat that just got the cream.

"And what about me.... what if I'm in the line of fire?" I asked.

"Aw howay Johnny man" said the Concert Chairman... "Comics are ten a penny.... Organists like Alan are as rare as rocking horse shit."

So the Organ was swung round to protect the Musicians.

The Concert Chairman went to the side of the Stage (obscured by the curtains of course) and 'one two'd' through the microphone. Loud booing greeted this intrusion into the mobs privacy.

"Ladies and gentlemen... lads and lasses... gizzabirrerorder...howay now... I naa yer a bit uppity cos of the delay but we are now about to start the Show...(boo)... and the first turn on today is a jack the ripper (Stripper) ... the biggest tits in Clubland.... gizza great big welcome to the fannytastic... Jade..."

'Boooooooooooo'

As the curtains swished open the coloured lady followed them across the Stage, tearing off her bra and 'G' rope as she sped left to right. Like a contestant in a relay race she touched Andrea who did the return journey in five seconds, disrobing as she reached the tape... but Marilyn won the race in three seconds flat.

J Harvey Oswald armed with a sub machine gun couldn't have hit her.

This non-display angered the mob even more than the half hour delay.

They were now baying for blood... and I was the donor.

The Concert Chairman screamed for order... The mob, whose last outing was spent knitting around the guillotine in the French revolution, was inconsolable.

"......... Johnny Hammond........."

The Organist played my cue, but the noise that came from the Organ drowned out any semblance of music, mainly because Alan Dorward was kneeling on the Organ bass footboard and with his chin on the lower keys.

Gus, the Percussionist made even more noise as he tried to operate the Bass Drum foot-pedal with his elbows and the High Hat with his forehead.

I was on, although those in the audience who were more than three rows back couldn't see me through the hail of beer mats being hurled in my direction.

I looked at the kid with the gun. A mixture of fear and sympathy showed in his pale blue eyes... His was the only compassionate face in the room.

"Gimme the gun son" I half mockingly pleaded. I'll give it back, I promise.... c'mon kid... my need is greater than yours."

He looked right into my eyes, smiled and shrugged hopelessly.

Just then a shadowy figure dropped from the balcony almost on top of the kid, quickly joined by three more plain clothed Policemen.

They pounced on the young gunman, tore the weapon from his grasp, pushed him face down on the table as they thrust his arms behind his back and handcuffed him.

Then grabbing him by the hair the lawmen dragged the youth screaming from the room.... which had gone strangely silent.

I stood trembling with rage. As the quartet disappeared into the foyer I put the microphone close to my mouth, took a big breath and yelled defiantly; "I hope you're coming back for the rest of the bastards."

Within seconds the Stage was crowded with newly brave Committeemen.

The Concert Chairman snatched the microphone from my hand, and holding his free hand high above his head announced, "Ladies and gentlemen....this Comic what has used foul language on this Stage against the rules of this Committee, is barred from this Club sine die for ever...."

I was manhandled off the Stage and unceremoniously deposited through the Stage door and into the car park. Tears of anger and frustration streamed down my face.

As I reached my car I glanced at the Mercedes next to me and noticed the deep groove running along the car from head to tail light ... and all four were deflated tyres.

I looked at the dry gob of phlegm on my windscreen as I sat in my car and totted up the costs of the day.

'I'd bought three gallons of petrol, been abused and bombarded with beer mats, physically assaulted by the Committee, had my fee withheld and been deserted in my hour of need by the law, had my car spat upon and paid half a crown protection money.

But the plusses were, I'd been expelled from the Downhill Club sine die.... and I swore that if ever... *IF EVER* I was made to go through that experience again, I'd pay the half crown protection money, plus another half crown for those mini Mafiosi to come stand on stage with me.

Clubland's first Victoria Cross

John Paul Jones was an oddity. He was an intellectual who had thrown up a promising career to 'work the Clubs'. I don't know what his previous profession was, but I think it had something to do with being an undertaker. He certainly looked like an undertaker... but there the similarity ended. He had a brilliant academic brain and was a proficient writer, a better than average Musician but somewhere fate had dealt him a bum hand and he took up residence in the North East as a Club Comic.

He had a vitriolic sense of humour, was as adept at ad-libbing as the best of them and it was rumoured he could make docker's cry.

He was not averse to using four letter expletives at a time when the word 'bloody' would have had a Comic ostracised for life.

I never knew how good he was at distance work because as his reputation grew his staying power shrunk to a sardonic greeting and "fuck you". He was not liked among his peers because he could out think and outwit the greatest comics of the day.

Acts would take time off just to go see John work... mostly because he had the habit of rubbing up the wrong way the local Al Capone's and Kray's in the audience, an occupation he seemed to thrive on, even if he had to pay for the honour in blood

So it came about that John Paul Jones was booked for the dreaded Sunday lunchtime Show at the equally dreaded Downhill Social Club within days of my inquisition.

Being a true Pro, John Paul Jones was incensed by the ill treatment meted out to a fellow Entertainer who had the misfortune of not only drawing the short straw to appear at Downhill Social Club but also the opening spot.

John Paul Jones walked on Stage with his masterful gait and immediately berated the mob laid out before him. Fearing a lynching, two members of Committee joined him behind the footlights and tried to forcefully remove him.

"Unhand me, you fucking underground savage" demanded John Paul Jones in his best thespian prose.

"Never mind apologising" said the Concert Chairman, "gerroff now youse".

The crowd were now dragged into the melee and booed the Artiste resoundingly.

"Gerroff ye lanky skinny twat" cried a matronly lady wearing a fur stole in this hundred and eighty degree heat.

"Streets quiet are they?" sneered John Paul Jones at the bitch, then to the audience, "she's either a rejected hooker or a beaver in season."

The two officials tried to manhandle him off Stage but he broke free and holding them at arms length he demanded order... which strangely he got.

"Ladies and gentlemen" he intoned into the microphone. "Before I depart from this place please... PLEASE allow me to say a few words in mitigation.

I would like to say that in all my years as an Entertainer in what is known, euphemistically, as Clubland, I have never had the honour of appearing in such a pleasurable auditorium. I swear on my mother's eyes that this is the finest establishment I have ever appeared in. This is truly an emporium of Entertainment, and a pleasure, nay, an honour for any Entertainer to ply his trade in.

(He stamped his foot) This Stage is not boxwood... it is teak... and these curtains are not sackcloth but the best Arabian velvet money could buy. The Hall laid out before me is furnished in the most salubrious finery one could imagine. You have here on this stage two of the finest...no *THE* finest exponents of their chosen profession I have ever come across...Mr Alan Dorward on the grand Wurlitzer Organ and Gus on percussion." (you could now hear a pin drop)

Yes ladies and gentlemen, the architect who designed this building erected a monument to the working classes.... a Hall fit for the finest audiences in the land, and yet I stand here before you I am at a loss to understand why they opened the doors and let you ignorant bastards in." Legions of Comedians have been credited with appearing in some distant Catholic Club, gaze reverently up at the crucifix above the bar and say; "ah, I see you caught the bastard who stole the television."

I know of only one comedian who would have dared... or had the nerve to improve on that line.... The aforementioned John Paul Jones.

I was with John Paul Jones in North Shields Catholic club on a Christmas morning when he was threatened with immediate expulsion, fee-less, if he repeated the jibe he had made some years ago in the same club.

Hand on heart he promised he would not do a repeat performance this time.

He was introduced, the band played him on and he stepped up to the rim of the stage, wished everyone a merry Christmas then addressing the ten foot crucifix above the bar, cheerfully yelled, "Hey, smile daddyo... it's your birthday."

Last I heard of John Paul Jones he'd gone to Northern Ireland on a one man crusade to cement relations between the two warring factions and he was a huge success...till a few night later as he stood on the kerb outside a club, signing autographs when an armoured vehicle came around a corner and was fired on from a darkened doorway by a terrorist.

The driver lost control of the vehicle which swerved and headed for the crowd on the kerb paying homage to John Paul Jones.

With a Herculean effort John Paul Jones swept the crowd of mainly women and children from the path of the oncoming half-track and took the full force of the impact, losing a third of his scalp in the incident. He lived and was hailed a hero by Catholic and Protestant alike, but he seems to have vanished through the years. I heard that he'd married his nurse and they settled down someplace.

I wish I knew where.

'Cowardice is often the preferential alternative to valour'

Of all the frightening experiences I've had in my career, by far the worst was in a club in Newcastle not long after I'd gone 'solo'.   The venue was one of the smallest I have ever worked, and held a capacity crowd of maybe fifty.

On the tiny dais was an upright piano and a drum kit, and chairs for the other two musicians, one an accordionist and the other a banjo-player. These were the house-band doubling as accompanists to any singers hard up enough to work with them. The piano was so placed that the bass end of the keyboard was flush with the front of the stage.

Immediately below were a row of wall seats.

When I had entered the club earlier that evening I was advised by the compere not to talk to the audience, and furthermore, try not to even look at them during my act.

I drew his attention to the fact that I was an entertainer and one of the things expected of and entertainer is to make some kind of rapport with the audience.

"They're a bit funny in here," the man informed me, hinting that he didn't mean "ha ha" funny, but "who the fuck are you looking at?" funny.

The show started at seven thirty and I was due on stage at eight thirty.

The audience were very quiet, showing scant interest in the entertainment and taking silent umbridge to the fact that the acts made a point of facing the wall while performing.

At this juncture I must explain the type of act I was doing at the time.

I sang a few 'Como' numbers while I sat at the piano and accompanied myself.   This was my comedy spot when, as I mentioned earlier, I played the piano off key and sang accordingly. Before each performance I would place a liberal amount of talcum powder mixed with cigarette ash and butts on the audience end of the piano. A few minutes into the act I would inform the audience that the piano had not been tuned for a while.....and it also hadn't been dusted for a while.....and then I would blow the talcum powder and butts off the end of the keyboard, usually to great guffaws from the crowd.

This never failed…till tonight!

So, I'm on stage and doing very well with this tough audience.

Suddenly the door opened and a mountain of a man entered with his 'doll'.

He wore a blue pin stripe suit, a black shirt and white tie. On his feet were brown and white brogues. He had huge sovereign rings on all his fingers and thumbs. He was heavily tanned and sported a thin black Errol Flynn moustache. His jet black wavy hair was heavily brilliantined and a cheap sickly perfume pervaded the air around him and his paramour who was equally cheap, with dyed soot black hair, a black fur coat, fishnet stockings and stiletto shoes.

As they walked towards me his unsmiling eyes met mine. They were small and black as coal. I was just finishing a Como number on the front stage microphone.

He stopped before me then slowly shifted his attention menacingly to a couple sitting at the ringside table and when the couple hastily rose and vacated their seats, he took the seat immediately beneath me, actually touching the bass end of the piano with his left shoulder. His moll applauded my efforts, and he grudgingly joined in. There was an aura of menace about them, and I noticed that, although I didn't see anyone excuse themselves, the audience was getting mysteriously smaller.

I nodded to the piano player who as previously arranged, rose and left the stage and I took his seat at the keyboard.   I went into my act, and much to my surprise Samson and Delilah were impressed. They laughed at the din coming from me and the instrument and nodded their approval.

As I was announcing that the piano hadn't been tuned for a while the door at the far end of the room opened and four equally terrifying characters came in, went to the bar, ordered drinks, turned and paid homage to the Godfather sitting immediately beneath me.

The mafia duo turned their faces to their subjects and acknowledged their nods...... just as I blew the talcum and ash from the keyboard.   In that instant I realised my folly and tried to inhale the cloud but it was too late.

Suddenly the 'soldiers' at the bar along with the rest of the audience, froze.

Bonny and Clyde looked quizzically at them, and then turned their gaze to me. I was filled with horror. The Godfather's hair was a halo of white dust and this had filtered down onto his eyebrows and moustache and the bull like shoulders.

His companion was equally adorned, the cloud of talc turning her black coiffeur into a skunk-like creation. I felt my arse climb up to my breastbone and, consumed with terror I got to my feet and shouted, "Thank you Ladies and Gentlemen and goodnight." Then hurtling from the stage I crashed blindly through the door, into the street and never stopped running till I was safely on board the last train to Hartlepool.

It was only when I stepped off the train at my local station an hour later that I realised that in my panic I'd left my car outside the Newcastle Club.

Charity Shows… the Agents prerogative.

'United we fall. …Divided at least one of us might make it.'
I got a call from my manager, Doris Boagey. She'd requested my presence at one of the better clubs in Sunderland, 'The Pallion.'
When an artiste bows to an agents 'request', it means that one is giving his or her services GRATIS. It was to be a 'Charity Show' for a young man who had lost both legs in a mining accident in the nearby coalmine at Dawdon Colliery.
Refusal to 'do a Charity' is definitely for the unambitious 'down the bill' entertainer. Such refusal can cost one dearly with one finding one-self cast into the clubland wilderness. I accepted the Gig and joined most of my wannabe peers.
As is the case in all Clubland Charity Shows, the venue was packed wall to wall with heavy imbibers, and high rolling Bingo fanatics. This was not only beneficial to the poor victim that the 'charirty show' was being held. . It was also a huge financial venture for the club who raked in a colossal take from beer sales and Bingo, plus a tidy sum from the raffle... and the half crown cover charge at the door.   It also benefited the agent who put on the show inasmuch as he (or she) would be given carte blanche to all bookings for the next twelve months.
Of course, bar staff had to be paid, as did the musicians. The only genuine charitable selfless souls at the event were the artistes, who not only gave their services free, but had to pay their own fares to and from the club, purchase their own beverages and smilingly give whatever coppers were left in their pockets for the collection for the said victim at the close of proceedings.
Because the cream of clubland artistes was booked for the evening the doors opened unusually early and all the seats were taken long before Showtime.
Tonight's bill consisted of 'Sunderland's Perry Como' Ricky Price. Every town in the country had at least one Perry Como...and/or Al Jolson, Bing Crosby and whoever ruled the airwaves of the day.
Indeed I was Hartlepool's Perry Como, but as I was on foreign soil, the local Perry Como laid claim to tonight's honour.
Raymond Hill was the local Gigli; Mabel Bew was Hartlepool's Jo Stafford,
Murray Macshane was a superb Elvis Presley who accompanied himself on a miniscule Mouth Organ....both at the same time. Tony Minchella was the present North East Clubland's Star Comedian. I was, just for that night, Johnny 'Songs at the Piano' Hammond and bringing up the rear were a German contortionist act, Larna and Verna.   I admired their courage above all on the Show that night, because Sunderland had suffered greater than most north east towns from the attentions of the Luftwaffe, and where a sober Geordie will simply shrug off the horrors of war, a drunken Geordie never forgets.
In the crowded dressing room all the artistes were going through their band call with the musicians. The house-band consisted of Billy Miller on the piano. Maurice, doubling on accordion and tenor saxophone, and Bert on percussion.
Billy Miller, who was blind from birth, was not only a brilliant musician, but a truly talented accompanist to boot... a phenomenon in clubland. However, the rest of the instrumental line up was not conducive to the needs of a seasoned singer.
Jimmy Cook was the concert chairman who had upgraded himself and taken charge of the night's proceedings as compere. Jimmy Cook was in no way on a par with Terry Wogan or any of the Masters of Ceremony one sees fronting today's Television Variety Shows.
Lights - music - curtains.
The overture by the house-band was to herald in a nightmare that has haunted me and my fellow entertainers for the past fifty odd years of our careers.

The night hotted up when, half way through Murray McShanes act, a dart whistled through the air and embedded itself in his guitar, causing him to swallow the mini mouthorgan gripped (till then) in his teeth. Murray staggered choking from the stage. Second act on was Ray Hill. He lasted ten minutes, most of the time competing with a drunk standing in front of the stage balancing a beer bottle on his forehead to great encouragement from the merry throng. Jimmy Cook introduced Mabel Bew several times, before someone reported seeing her minutes earlier boarding a bus heading for Hartlepool.

Tony Minchella went on drunker than the audience, forgot his gags, told the audience to piss off ', dropped his pants and showed his arse to the horrified throng before being ushered off by the compere.

Lana and Verna went on and fared no better than Ray Hill, Murray Macshane or the now comatose comic.

Larna was the male part of this speciality contortionist act, twisting himself into some unbelievable shapes, culminating in him sliding down into a twelve inch wide tube. He was supposed to slide into the top of the tube and wriggle his way out of the other end, but the heat in the club caused him to get the cramps and after much heaving, huffing and puffing he lost consciousness, fell sideways still in the tube and had to be rolled, ceremoniously off the stage past the cheering jeering mob to a waiting ambulance which took him to the nearest fire station where he was cut free.

Jimmy Cook came on and announced that there would be an interval in which time they would play seven houses of Bingo.

In the middle of the first house of Bingo, a furious Ray Hill, incensed by the abuse, walked on stage and ruined everyone's concentration by singing an aria from La Bohemme. This caused Ray to be dragged, still singing, from the Stage and hurled into the street.

During the altercation, Billy Miller, the blind pianist asked me if I was going to perform my comedy piano routine. I answered in the affirmative and he asked me to get a chair and place it against the wall so he'd know exactly where to sit when I requested his stool at the keyboard.

This I did, then joined the rest of my peers in the bar, but not before I sprinkled a match box lid full of talcum powder on the audience end of the keyboard.

Unfortunately, during the interval a late arrival, searching for a seat and finding none noted a spare chair placed strategically by the wall at the bass end of the piano. Climbing onto the stage he commandeered the chair and rejoined his friends in the well of the room.

After the Bingo Jimmy Cook stepped up to the microphone and begged for order "as these turns is 'doing this show for nowt, and them noisy bastards what's shouting and bawling and 'hoying' darts is spoiling a frigging great night for anybody what's trying to hear...... now c'mon you twats ..... please.... give order."

Jimmy introduced me as Hartlepool's Perry Como, adding, "but he's not a patch on Sunderland's Perry Como what'll be closing the show after Johnny gets off."

As he handed me the microphone I called him an arsehole, and went into my act.

After ten minutes of total indifference I decided they were now ready for comedy. Turning to their beloved blind pianist I said "move over Billy and I'll show you how to play the piano." This irreverence to their beloved maestro brought on a huge wave of abuse.

"Gerroff, you big headed bastard."

(this from the President of the ladies bowling section.)

Billy rose from the piano stool and turning to his left he attempted to sit on the missing chair. He fell backwards, badly gashing his bald head in the process.

Accompanied by showers of expletives and missiles I dashed from the Stage. A man stood up from the front table, took the microphone and holding his hand high in the air demanding silence, admitted that it was he who had inadvertently removed the chair. As the man was bigger than anyone else in the room, his admission was accepted with a modicum of good nature.

I was led back onto the stage, passing the profusely bleeding Billy Miller being led by a heavily built matron from the ladies rugby section, who on passing me on the way to the dressing room punched me in the chest and called me a twat.

I went into the act playing the piano off key and singing my song in an entirely different key. This was greeted with friendly jeering and booing. I informed the audience that the piano hadn't been tuned for a while, then, blowing the pyramid of talcum powder from the keyboard in a huge cloud I tagged the gag with... "It hasn't been dusted for a while either."

At this point an ancient crone rose from her seat at the side of the stage, and leaning heavily on two walking sticks she mounted the three steps to the platform, dragged her skeletal frame over to where I sat, took the microphone and screeched into it like a strangled vulture, "Ladies and gentlemen everybody knows I've been the cleaner in this club for the past thirty years and this bastard is trying to get me the sack and lose me little bit of social security."

Once again I was berated by the mob and showered with beer mats.

I decided that it was time to call it a day, and headed for the sanctuary of the dressing room. Billy Miller sat forlornly, gazing with unseeing eyes through the window attended by lady rugby prop who, in the absence of first aid facilities had

stemmed the flow of blood by placing a large sanitary towel on the wound and securing it by attaching the string loops around blind Billy's ears.

I put my arm around my old friend's shoulder and whispered softly in his ear; "Billy, if there was ever in your life there was a good time to be blind.... this is it."

Meanwhile, back on stage Sunderland's Perry Como tried to perform Perry's "Ave Maria" accompanied by an accordionist /saxophonist and drummer, but it didn't come out the way the composer intended it and Ricky broke Murray McShanes survival record by one minute and thirty seven seconds, bringing the night's festivities to a premature close.

Jimmy Cook was I believe, the longest serving concert secretary at the Pallion Club in Sunderland giving 35 years of undying loyalty. I liked the Pallion Club better than any other club on the circuit, and the aforementioned charity show was a one off and not par for the course in this warm and friendly club. But after so many appearances there I felt that I had outlived my welcome, and so when I next returned to 'the Pallion' it was a decade from my last catastrophic appearance.

I was welcomed like the prodigal son by all my old friends…and my popularity was such that had they had a fatted calf, they would have sacrificed it in my honour. But as fatted calf's were out of season I was feted with a pint of Federation ale and a cheese and onion sandwich. The old blind pianist Billy Miller recognised my voice and greeted me with a hug. The musical line up was more or less the same, Billy Miller on Piano, Maurice Taylor, Accordion and Bertie Muckles on Drums. I don't know what happened to the Saxophonist. As we all stood at the bar reminiscing with Billy and a few of the guys I enquired as to whether Jimmy Cook was around.

"Well" said Billy, "he's not still on the committee. He was voted out after that catastrophic charity show twelve years ago, but he's still a member of the club."

The steward intervened to tell me that Jimmy Cook was indeed in the club at that very instant. "He's up in the dressing room with the football physio" he said.

I remembered that the Pallion were very proud of their football team, and had a physiotherapist second to none. It transpired that Jimmy Cook had injured his back while helping move beer barrels in the club cellar, and was in so much pain that the physio had offered his services.

I went up the stairs and pushed the dressing room door open. The sight that greeted me was straight out of a Neil Simon comedy.

Jimmy Cook was bent over the end of a table with his head on a pillow, his trousers round his ankles. The physiotherapist was standing behind him with his hands pressed against Jimmy Cook's lumbar region, and every time he bore down, he made a loud grunt while Jimmy Cook groaned 'oh' and 'hey' and 'ahh's in unison.

I stood in the doorway for a few seconds taking in the hilarious scene, and then walking up to the table I laid my head on the pillow, nose to nose with the patient and said, "I'll tell you something Cookie, you'll do anything to get back on the committee."

The physiotherapist, roaring with laughter collapsed on top of his patient and Jimmy Cook's agonised scream could be heard six streets away.

Mooney's mountain!

Rotund Irish comedian Pat Mooney was booked to appear at a club in Sunderland, which was a 'No-Go Kamikaze gig' to all but a midget's hand-full of the hardiest of club comics. Pat Mooney had been a huge star in the Emerald Isle for many years and bursting with confidence and ignoring darkly whimpered warnings from his peers who had once, and only once bravely ventured into this clubland version of Jurassic Park, he booked steerage. However, his dreams of a showbusiness Shangri la and streets paved with gold were soon shattered like broken glass.

The agent first booked Pat into a few of the better clubs in the English South and Midlands and he'd done exceptionally well. Pat was making a big name for himself and when he arrived in my neck of the woods he headed straight for the miniscule offices of Doris Boagey Entertainments and (almost literally) signed his life away.

But he was, at this point, still a happy and utterly... some would say, over confident man. What he didn't know was that agents sell their acts to other agents and vice versa and Doris Boagey, who booked some of the better clubs in the North East, had sold him to one of the many backstreet agents for this particular Gig. I think however that had the affable Boagey's, Doris and Tommy known the outcome of Mooney's baptism of fire, they would have added a rider in the contract that guaranteed, at the very least, funeral expenses.

The club in this instance had suffered a double tragedy inside a fortnight.

The troubles in Northern Ireland were at their height at this time and the soldier son of one of their members had been seriously injured in a particularly vicious attack on his armoured vehicle. One of the best pal's of the aforementioned hero was also a son of members of this particular club and a couple of days after he returned to his unit in Londonderry, he was himself seriously injured in an attack. The whole area was in shock, but life goes on and it was only a couple of days after the second incident that the unfortunate Pat Mooney from the Emerald Isle unknowingly and unwittingly found himself booked in this very cauldron as tonight's comedian.

I am a Geordie... a son of the North East. I'm a club comic and I'm a good Comic, one of the best...and I'd worked this particular club once, but there isn't enough money in the World Bank to get me to take a return booking there. And, even under the aforementioned circumstances, the fact that Mooney was an Irishman was irrelevant... the baddest man on the planet, Mike Tyson would have suffered the same trauma. In this joint they didn't discriminate...they hated everyone.

The only redeeming feature in the comics favour was that the stage was eight feet high... a formidable obstacle for an aggressive hoard of drunks, and the dressing room was only three steps away from the centre stage microphone. This wasn't purely accidental, either. The architect who drew the plans of the club had once been a club comic and had retired immediately after he'd appeared in the area.

The show opened with a beautiful young female singer who, in the middle of her first song broke into tears at the sight of several morons sitting in the front seats feverishly masturbating and hurtled straight from the stage to the car park, leaving her street clothes where they lay in the dressing room, never again to return.

After complaints and threats from the committee, the lads adjusted their clothing and settled back for the star 'Turn'.

Standing in the wings attired in his emerald green silk stage suit and his green Derby hat tilted at a rakish angle, the unsuspecting comic caught the last line of his introduction,

".... ALL THE WAY FROM NORTHERN IRELAND.."

Pat Mooney marched into clubland history.

All hell broke loose, but a pro to his fingertips, Pat launched himself onto his act, doing a nifty Irish jig to the beat of the music. He was still jigging when a heavy glass ashtray nearly shattered his shinbone. Changing tempo to a waltz and sinking to his knees in agony, Pat looked out at the mob. Three rows back a gang of shaven headed goons were congratulating one yob on the accuracy of his aim. Mooney rose to his feet, his Celtic blood boiling and picking up the missile he flung it back whence it came. The perpetrator was a better pitcher than he was a catcher. The ashtray caught the perpetrator under the chin and a fraction above his Adams apple.

The yob's tongue shot out like a viper's and he pitched backwards over a table and disappeared. For a moment Mooney thought he had gone deaf, so sudden and profound was the silence. The mob, screaming sectarian abuse, launched a concerted attack on the stage. Mooney reached the dressing room a fraction before the organist and drummer. Slamming and locking the door, the three of them grabbed the heavy address system console and used it as a barricade to keep the lynch mob at bay. Straining to hold the fortress, Mooney noticed a strong smell permeating from the ashen-faced drummer who was and sobbing tears of terror. The noise of the assault outside was deafening, drowned out only by the sound of the trio's heart beats. Then as suddenly as it had started all was silence…. and more silence. Then, from outside of the barricade they heard the sound of muffled voices. More silence as the three prisoners gasped for breath. After another huddled conference from the other side of the door came a gentle knock. Then a voice…

A calm soothing friendly voice: "Hello?"

It was the Concert Chairman's voice.

"Hello? …. Boys?"

The voice seemed to be mocking.

"Hello? … Pat? … Pat Mooney? …. Pat, are you in there?"

Pat thought out loud; "Am I in here? …. Am I? …. Is the man an eedjit or something? …Are we in here? …Is he a lunatic? …. We're on the second floor…. in a room with no window and only one door… and that stupid bastard asks me if I'm in here? …."

"Pat", cooed the voice outside the door "this is Raymond…. You remember me…. we met when you came in… Hello… this is the concert chairman…Raymond speaking… open the door Pat."

"Are ye mad?" croaked Pat." For the love of the Blessed Virgin Mary man… you must be joking!"

"No!"

The official's voice was calmly reassuring "its all right Pat… I've got them back in their seats. …They wont hurt you… they were only having a bit of fun… you know what lads is like, Pat …they won't hurt you…they'll do as I tell them"

Pat was racking his brains trying to put a face to Raymond…then it all too slowly came back to him. Raymond was in his late eighties and struggling to be 4ft 6" tall and four stones in weight.

Raymond pleaded: "You have my word on it Pat, I won't let them kill you…just open the door, son."

Mooney looked at his two friends. The organist was grey in pallor, his red hair had turned wispy white and he was in deep shock. The drummer sobbed loudly, and smelled even worse. "We want the Police." Pat stammered. "…

"We want the police…" The musicians echoed.

"Get the police…" Pat cried…" we won't open the door to nobody but the police… what the hell did I do to deserve this… now I'm telling you Raymond, we want the police."

"Police? The POLICE…what the hell do you want the police for…. everything's honky dory now, son…. open the door."

"I'll not," screamed Mooney "I want the police to get me out of here."

"Out of here?" the Concert Secretary's voice sounded incredulous...

"Yes you bloody eejit" shouted Pat.... "Out of here.... I want to go home."

"Home? HOME? What the hell do you mean 'you want to go home'", Raymond yelled, "You still have another forty minutes to do!"

Seeing Stars.

Clubland started to really come into it's own in the Sixties. The old Nissan hut clubs, appropiately nicknamed 'the Blood tubs' and 'Abattoir's' were demolished and modern two and three story buildings seemed to spring up overnight, each more plush than the last one. Competition was fierce.

In a small mining village in Northumberland, there was born one of the finest clubs in all of North East clubland.

To save anyone any embarrassment we'll call it Low-Main Social Club.

The club moved out of the average workingmen's club sphere and started booking stars with a capital 'S'. Indeed the first gig I ever did at Low Main was as chief support in a five-act bill topped by the great Goon, Harry Seacombe. My return booking was with one of the greatest popular singers in the world, Matt Munro.... an artist once described by Frank Sinatra as one of his all time favourite singers. Seacombe and Monroe were just two of the high level acts to work this oasis in a desert of pit heaps and as it's popularity spread like a forest fire Low Main became the Number One showplace of North East clubland.

Soon, the club blossomed into a mini Las Vegas attraction boasting the most up to date facilities, the finest concert room in the North East. Followed by a haut cuisine restaurant complete with the essential Egon Ronay seal of approval hanging above the door. Yet at the height of its fame it was run by a committee no different from 99.9% of the rest of the clubs in the North East. And so well did this Club of Clubs do that at the AGM the committee were informed by their accountants that they had made so much profit over the past two years that they would have to spend, spend, spend, or pay a vast fortune to the Inland Revenue.

But how to off-load such a massive amount of money?

They thought of extending the building in all directions but were informed that there was no land left. They couldn't build outwards because every inch of their land had been used to improve the building. They couldn't build upwards because planning permission had been refused several times. They racked their brains to come up with a viable proposition. Then the concert chairman came up with a diamond of an idea.

"We have gained the reputation of being the most successful Workingmen's Club in Britain..." crowed the entertainment boss. "Partly because of our Eegon Rooney (Egon Ronay) diploma, but mainly because of the 'Stars' what we've been booking on our concert nights. So, me Bonney lads, why don't we go overboard and put on the Clubland Show of all Clubland Shows?"

"Like what like?" asked the Committee in unison?

"Like... er.... Bing Crosby or Gigli...

"Gigli's dead isn't he? Isn't Gigli dead.... aye, I'm sure I read somewhere that Gigli's dead.... So Gigli's counted out ashen faced!"

".........Well, who's the biggest Star in the world right now?"

"Sammy Davis Junior."

"Right.... we'll get Sammy Davis Junior... and some great support turns...and dancing girls.... we'll put on a show that will be the envy of the entertainment world from
 Las Vegas to the London Palladium."

"...Or even the Sunderland Empire." Enthused the steward.

"Great" said the President, "but how do we get Sammy Davis Junior... I mean he's not on the books of Doris Boagey or any of the club agents around here, is he? So howay lads, put yer thinkin' caps on. How do we go about getting Sammy...and how much would he want to come here anyway?"

"Money's no object, is it?" said the Treasurer. "We have enough to put the Clubland Royal Command Show on, and still have enough left for the bairns Christmas party and a day trip to

Whitley Bay for the old age pensioners."

The concert secretary raised his hand. "Have I ever let us down lads?"

A resounding "NO" echoed round the hallowed walls of the committee room.

"Did I not get turns like Anita Harris, Jess Conrad, Bobby Thompson, and the great Harry Secombe, what we hope to have back for our next Leek show?"

"Aye he did" nodded his peers.

"Right then" beamed the concert secretary "I'll now ring Bill Reeves at the Beverley Artistes Agency in South Shields and ask him to get Sammy Davis junior...cos if nobody else can get Sam, that nobody is Bill Reeves"

He picked up the phone and called the North East's biggest Club Agency.

"Hello... can I speak to Bill please ...ah, Hello Bill, Basil Robson from Low Main here... what? Oh aye I'm fine, and yerself? Fine bonny lad... mind ye, that Lynne Perry was great mind...the dogs bollicks...great, a great singer... the Comic was a bit crap like... well he was a Londoner wasn't he.... nah... I believe you've got Bobby Thompson for our pie, peas and pigeon supper...we're delighted, I mean everybody knows little Bobby is God in here.... who? Tony Christie...sixth of December.... thanks Bill, it's in the book. Tony Christie's a sure fire sell out... aye, nae problem... now listen Bill, Bonney lad.... we've come into a few quid.... a lot of few quids actually, and we don't know what the hell to do with it... I'm talking about mega bucks here mind young un.... and we thought of putting on something extra special... now don't fall on your arse when I ask yer, but how much is Sammy Davis Junior?

"Hello... hello...H-E-L-L-O B-I-L-L... he's hung up."

He dialled again. "Bill? Was we cut off or summat? .... Eh? .... Drunk ...me? No, course not you cheeky bugger...it's only half past ten in the morning.... the bars don't open till eleven... no howay man, I'm serious.... let us explain........."

And he put the story of their good fortune and their illustrious intentions to the Mr Bill Reeves of Beverley Artistes.

Later that day Bill Reeves called back to say that the Sammy Davis office in Los Angeles were in consultation, but regardless of how much money the committee could come up with, the fee for Sammy and his entourage would be astronomical.

"We don't want his tourage," said the President of the club.... "We only want Sammy."

After a lot of wrangling the concert secretary conceded defeat.

"Right, Bill... thanks a lot.... no, not to worry... look, we have to get rid of this money.... who's the next biggest stars of the day what might come to our Club? THE BIGGEST? Who?"

He clamped his hand over the mouthpiece and addressed his Committee. "What about Abba?"

"Abba?" mumbled the men around the table... "Who the fuck is Abba...What does he do?" Said the concert chairman.

"They're a group, aren't they?" queried the President.

"They're not only a group" snapped the Concert Secretary... "They're the biggest thing in the world right now... when they work in Las Vegas they use Sammy Davis as a warm-up-man... alright Bill...now, will you listen to me.... money's no object.... they can pick it up... in cash on the night.... pound and ten shilling notes if they like.... direct.... aye, I dae understand... aye... well you can talk to them about your commission.... that's up to you... right.... no, we're not kidding Bill, didn't we put Harry Secombe on.?...By the way we want Harry back for the leek Show....and Mattie Monroe... aye, why aye.... do it bonny lad.... I'll be in all day...alright Bill... tarrar youngun."

He hung up to a round of applause.

"We've got them."

Word got round the village and the surrounding clubland that " ABBA" were booked at Low Main Club. It wasn't going to be cheap, but nothing was too much for "ABBA".

And nothing but the best was good enough for Low Main club.

Two days later a call was made from ABBA's London representatives and a price for the show was mentioned, agreed and accepted.

A team of the mega group's representatives would be calling on Low Main in the non-too distant future. Three days later another call was made to the club to say that representatives of the ABBA consortium would be visiting on the following Thursday and would the members of the committee make arrangement for them to be collected from Newcastle airport and limousined to Low Main Club?'

Two o'clock on the dot on a cold dismal rainy day a white Rolls Royce Silver Cloud swung into the crowded, potholed village street and whispered to a halt at the steps of the Club. A ten-man ashen faced ashen faced reception Committee stood in a regimental line to greet the two British and three Swedish representatives of the 'Greatest turns in the World'... and Bill Reeves from Beverely Artistes Agency, with a weather eye open for International Workingmen's Club representation.

The car door opened and an elderly white haired man dressed in an expensive silver blue mohair suit stepped out and immediately sank up to his knees in a water filled pot-hole. The morning suited club blue ruffled shirted reception committee each took an involuntary step backwards. The man stepped forward, shook his feet and said something in a foreign tongue to the rest of his colleagues who changed direction and alighted from the far side of the car. Tommy Baxter, the president of the committee stepped forward and unfurled a huge brightly coloured golfing umbrella then, keeping the umbrella to himself he turned leaving the guests to their own devices and led them around the limo to the kerb where both groups with water running down their faces stood facing each other for several seconds in silence.

Then Tommy Baxter stepped forward and offered his hand to the man in the dripping massively expensive Italian waterlogged shoes.

"Sorry about that, your Highness" he cringed, taking the man's hand as it hung limply at his side and shaking it vigorously.

A large man dressed in an immaculate Saville Row suit spoke in a polished Oxford accent. "Good day gentlemen... I am David Winstable...should we get inside out of the rain?"... then with the welcoming party and their dripping guests safely in the foyer he said: "This is my son Winstone... we are the British representatives of ABBA. This is ABBA's Swedish director..." and he presented the rest of his entourage, interspersing his English with comments in Swedish, which brought forth several harrumphs and tut tuts from the Europeans.

Tommy Baxter, realising he was still standing under the umbrella offered a '"woops... sorry about that", unfurled the brolly and placing it against the wall turned and did the honours introducing the reception committee; "This is Basil Robson, Concert Secretary... the man what got youse lads here today, God love him.

A round of appreciative applause from the reception committee fizzled to a solitary clap from the club steward.

This lad is Freddy Allinson, our 'onourary treasurer.... and I'll tell you lads.... your fee for your ABBA's put the shits up him for a while... but you have now't to worry about the money... Freddy is straight as a die. Then sidestepping to face the second man he said; "This is Alan Moorhouse, Secretary of Committee and the lad responsible for making us what we are today."

A solitary three round clap from the steward.

David Winstable wiping water from his face hissed a snide "Really."

Tommy went on along the line. "Harry Waterstone,... Games and leisure activities... y'know, Bingo, indoor bowling... darts 'andicap... all that lot.".... Next man; "Ronnie Lazenby... Steward... " Tommy put a loving arm around the shoulders of his next charge. "This is Hans... I can never announce his second name,... anyway, he's the cook and chef in our Aemon Rooney restaurant".

As each man was introduced he stepped forward, snapped to attention and clicked his heels, German military style, apart from Winston Eccles who gave a sweeping low bow which would have done credit to Beau Brummell, and finished off with a curtsey.

The man in the water filled shoes squelched loudly as he led his team as Tommy paved the way into the club.

"These is the steps" Tommy stamped his feet to emphasize his remark.

"This is the foyer" he proudly announced.

His colleagues beamed, while the guests were collectively unimpressed.

"That's the doorman's box.... where the doorman sits.... Syd Beaumont.... he's the doorman.... twenty three years he's been the doorman...and thirty years in the ould club, before we built this new one, he used to be the Treasurer......as a measure of his honesty and dedication, he's never had a holiday in his life...these day's most treasurers retire to Whitley Bay and have their holidays in the Bahamas after three months in the job" He turned to the present Treasurer; "no offence Freddy".

Tommy led them into an exquisitely decorated restaurant.

"This is the restaurant.... Eegon Rooney stuck that plaque up there above the door, said he'd seen worse in London and Paris... we're very proud of our restaurant.... you can get anything in here from steak to fish and chips to a meat and two veg Sunday dinner any day of the week....except Sunday... when Hans has a day off ."

By the way lads, Hans 'ere is a Norwegian like you lads."

He beamed at the entourage.

"We're from Sweden." The man in the silver blue suit corrected him in impeccable English.

"Why, same thing.... well nearly..... just up the road and over the lights, like, laughed Tommy. His colleagues grinned.

David Winstable asked where the Theatre was situated.

"We haven't got a Theatre" piped up Ronnie Lazenby. "We used to have a Picture House at the bottom of the village, but they turned it into a Bingo Hall then they pulled it down and made a 'Mister Mace serve yeself shop....y'know... like a grocery shop but you pay when you've got your rations on the way out."

"Well, where will the concert be held then?" asked the head Swede.

"Why, in the Concert Room ye daft bugger." said Basil Robson.

"Exactly," David Winstable blanched, "may we see the Concert Hall PLEASE?"

"Well we're getting to that... we just thought you'd like to have a tour of the club, like.... y'know, the games room.... the bowling alley... the lounge where we put the women when we have a Stag Night."

"No" said the lead Swede, "we haff long journey and are tired.... and we haff to get back to London Adelphe where ABBA will be playing the night before their concert here."

"So, you don't fancy a pint and a bite to eat...like a bowl of soup and a stotty cake?" asked Basil.

"Thank you no"... said David Winstable.

"Right then" Tommy was a little huffed... "Follow me then."

They all obliged, as the President led the entourage back through the lounge to a door on the right which he took the steward several seconds to open from a bunch of keys dangling on a chain from his belt. Opening the double doors wide, he stepped in and waited for the rest to enter. When the last one was safely in the room, he stepped into a small box by the door, flicked a switch and flooded the room with a soft pink light.

"Gentlemen" he intoned, "our pride and joy.... the Concert Room."

The visitors looked aghast. By Club standards it was a very large room, tastefully furnished with two hundred and fifty seats sweeping down to a stage which measured some fifty feet across, on which stood an Organ covered with a dustsheet, a Drum Kit similarly attired and several rows of highly stacked chairs and a Bingo machine.

"Sorry about the chairs Gentlemen," Tommy apologised, "but these are spares we've brought in for the ABBA Concert and the way the tickets are going, we still won't have enough."

"Tickets?" enquired a tall Swede who had been quietly exploring the room.

"Already you are selling tickets?"

"Why aye" said Basil. "You don't get the ABBA`s in Low Main every night of the week, bonny lad."

"No" sniffed the man and went back into his shell.

The leader spoke. "And where will the 'Show' be?" he enquired quizzically.

"Here." said Tommy...."where d'ya think.... this is the Concert Room... this is where we have our concerts..... this is the concert room, these is the seats, that's the Stage, the Dressing Room is behind the curtain, and there, on the 'big' stage is where the ABBA`s will perform."

"But"... the leader was dumfounded... "but you offered so much money... and we are flattered.... but where... well, where will the Orchestra sit?"

Freddy Allinson, the Treasurer dived into the fray.

"What Orchestra?"

"The Orchestra...the Orchestra who will play for ABBA.... where are you going to put them?" asked the head man, whose shoes squelched as he moved uncomfortably from one foot to the other.

"Hang on a bit, bonny lads," said Tommy, holding both hands high in the air.   "We never said now`t about booking any Orchestra. We asked for The ABBA`s, and you said we could have The ABBA`s for two million quid, and far as we're concerned, that's what we're paying for."

There was an embarrassed silence, then, coughing several times, David Winstable spoke up.

"Excuse me Gentlemen... but the fee... er money that you offered was just for ABBA? The four singers? the… as you put it.. The ABBA's?"

"Aye.... why aye.... what did you expect like?"

"You see," said Tommy, "we don't need any orchestra nor now`t like that. We've got the best backing in the North East in Alan Fox on the organ and Bobby Driscoll on the drums. These two have backed the best.... Bobby Thompson.... Tony Christie...Larry Mason… he's big on Tyne Tees, Larry Mason…The Dinning Sisters and the Sacriston Road Show... so, you see we don't need an orchestra.... we offered two million for the ABBA`s and The ABBA`s is all we want...... take it or leave it."

Now The ABBA team were treading water.

"What about security?" piped up the Swedish member in the waterlogged shoes.

"What security?" asked Tommy.

One of the Swedes made to speak but fell silent as David Winstable cut him short.

"Gentlemen, I don't think you understand the enormity of the task you're taking on. In these days of international terrorism, world stars are under threat every minute of the day. ABBA is no exception. Should some terrorist organisation decide to strike, only the greatest security could thwart them."

The steward emitted a low laugh. "Terrorist's? Here in Low Main? Don't be so friggin' gormless.... "

"Nae problem." Harry Waterstone spoke for the first time. "Nae problem at all bonny lads." he spoke in a rich Northumbrian brogue.   "Now, ah dinna knaa aboot them clubs in Garmany an' Holland where yae lads come from, but we divvant have nae trouble around here… especially from terrorists. We've nivva had one fight in this club since it opened.... and it's been open a lang time, arl tell yez... right lads?"

The Committeemen sang out in the affirmative.

"An another thing"... Harry went on, "naebody, but naebody could get past little Syd Beaumont.... not if they weren't bona fide members."

"Syd?" chimed the visitors.

"Syd Beaumont," repeated Harry. "he's the best bloody doorman in clubland.... an ex boxer... mind, he's gannen on for eighty odd now, but if Syd Beaumont says nae body gets in..... nae body gets in."

"And what about outside" snapped David Winstable..." before they reach the club.... that's when they're most vulnerable." .... and before anyone could answer.... "and where is the helicopter going to land? .....not in the car park. If the figures you believe are going to turn out the car park is going to be packed... so where......"

"Helicopter?" shouted Basil the steward. "What fucking helicopter? Sorry about the language lads but hang on here...first we book The ABBA's... then we get an orchestra.... how many is there in this orchestra we're paying for?"

"Sixty eight!"

SIXTY EIGHT... Bloody hell! Sixty eight musicians we didn't order.... and I suppose they won't be paying to get in...then we need security.... little Syd Beaumont what's got an impeccable record for keeping rowdies and assholes out, isn't good enough...oh no... Then we need a helicopter pad for a helicopter..." he put his hands up, "Alright, they'll not get in the car park, they can't land in the field...too muddy and clarty for them, and I agree, ...so right,..... what about Mister Mace?"

"Mace" said the man in the squelchy shoes.

"Mister Mace," echoed Basil... "the new grocery shop.... Mister Mace... a single storey shop... they've got a flat roof.... plenty of space for a helicopter to land.... and it's right out the back by the dressing room door... they could shin down a ladder and......."

David Winstable brought the proceedings to an abrupt halt.

Turning to his son who'd been taking notes since he alighted from the Rolls, he asked, "Have you got all this down Winstone?"

"Yes daddy" replied the effeminate young man.

"Right!" David Winstable rubbed his hands together. "I think that about clears everything gentlemen. We have a few little hiccups to iron out but I'm sure..... I'M SURE (he sounded like a man on the verge of a breakdown) I'M SURE we can overcome any difficulties that lie in our way."   The head Swede attempted to speak but David Winstable cut him short.

"Gentlemen" he addressed his own team "I don't think we need to keep these gentlemen any longer.... so, if there's nothing else?"

He scanned the faces of the committeemen.

"Good, then "looking at his watch", he grabbed, first Tommy by the hand, then Basil, and rapidly shook the hands of each and every one of the officials, then turned and ushered his party out of the room, through the foyer, out the door down the steps and into the car...each of them stepping into the flooded pothole before boarding.

As the Committeemen stood glassy eyed on the front steps, David Winstable lowered his window and his soaking hair sticking to his face called through the torrential rain;

"Thank you gentlemen, thank you for your hospitality and I'm sure we can come to a favourable conclusion. You'll hear from us within seven days, I promise. I'm sure we'll meet again and continue our friendship....."

Tommy called cheerfully "Are you sure you'll not have a bite afore you go, lads?

Our Eegon Rooney tripe and onions will keep you going all the way back to Frankfurt."

"Thank you 'no' sir.... we'll dine on the plane. Goodbye! I promise...... seven days."

Then screaming onto the Chauffeur's ear.. "move -move –move" the car took off like a rocket bouncing into water-filled potholes and drenching sightseers, past 'Mister Mace' store where the helicopter would land, left at the bookie shop and disappeared in a flash of lightening and a crash of thunder. Several drenched sightseers stood silently waving an assortment of national flags... including a couple of Nazi swastika's.

Alan Moorhouse, standing alone under the umbrella spoke for the first time since the ABBA team arrived.

"Bunch of toffee-nosed bastards!"

"That's now't" said Basil.... "just as long as we're getting the ABBA's, that's all that counts..... God knows we've spent enough on tickets and posters."

"Aye" the rest of them agreed.

It was only then that they realised they were standing in a monsoon, and dashed back into the shelter of the club.

In the two weeks it took for the ABA office to reply, every ticket had been sold.

On that bright Saturday morning the ten man committee sat with bated breath around the table in the plush committee room. The sun sent warm beams of light through the large windows. It was a day for joyous news.

The Club President, Tommy Baxter, rose at the head of the long highly polished oak table and banged his gavel three times. His team fell silent, smiling faces beaming, flushed with bated breath, as Tommy took the gold plated stiletto paper knife and slit the envelope bearing the long awaited reply from Sweden.

"Dear Gentlemen of the Committee of Low main Workingmen's Club". He almost sang. "I and my colleagues would first like to thank you for your wonderful northern hospitality and a most entertaining visit. We would also like to congratulate you on your splendid club, which is obviously the flagship and pride of the whole of British Clubland. The architect who designed and the people who built it erected a shrine to the enthusiastic and hard working miners of your community. It is the 'epytoomee' (epitome) of what you call with deserved pride, Clubland."

As all the men at the table patted each other proudly and applauded the letter, the sun outside slid behind a cloud, cutting off the warm shafts of light into the room, causing a sudden drop in temperature.

Tommy continued in his sing song voice "....and so it is with the deepest regret that, merely because of lack of space in which to house the huge contingent of Stars, Musicians, Security, and props-men, it is with aching hearts that we must sadly decline your offer."

Tommy's voice dropped several syllables as he droned on and on, but the nine men seated before him had suddenly gone deaf....

Before the usual Saturday night 'Big Show', Andy Rollins, the Concert Chairman, walked slowly up the three steps to the stage, and, adjusting the microphone, called out the customary test piece, "One Two...Evening all.... Testing One Two.. get yer Bingo books now...One Two" punctuating each call in unison by tapping the microphone head with his forefinger nail. He took a red and white spotted handkerchief from his rear trouser pocket and wiped the sweat from his forehead.

"Ladies and Gentlemen... lads and lasses... members' and guests..."

The grinning expectant audience leaned forward straining to grasp each word.

"......it is with a heavy heart that I stand here before you tonight, the harbinger of bad news." A stony silence swept around the room. "Some time ago we contacted the people what handle that great group, the ABBA's, and we made them an offer they couldn't refuse....... but they have. We brought them over here at our own expense from Iceland and gave them the hospitality what is customary in this club, from members and committee alike..... and this morning we gets a letter from them in Düsseldorf to say that although the money had now't to do with it, and after we've sold every single ticket.... they are sorry....(his voice went up three octaves) Sorry...They are frigging sorry,..... but their 'Turns' will not be coming after all."

He began to resemble Hitler, ranting to the Nazi legions gathered beneath the balcony of the Reich- Chancellery.

"Well!" he screamed. "all the money what you've paid will be given back..... but I'll tell you one thing.... *them ABBA's will never get another booking in this club again"*

This is a true story as related to me by the director of Beverly Artistes Agency, Bill Reeve.

Little big time!

One of the best Night Clubs in the North East of England was Sunderland's,
'La Strada'.

It was the life's work of one Mr Sandford Gouldie. I worked the club several times, and it was the kind of venue that brought out the very best in each and every entertainer in clubland.

The place was always immaculate; the audience were the best in the country, the entertainment first class and the cuisine second to none.

However old age and changing attitudes to entertainment made Sandford Gouldie decide to sell up and retire.

The club, under new management rapidly went into decline.

Like all Night Clubs it became a place for continued boozing after the pubs and Workingmen's Clubs closed for the night. In fact, it became an extension of the Workingmen's club circuit.

I was doing a week for Beverley Artistes Agency in the North East, and as the club was now one of their venues you could guarantee that one night of your tour would be at the 'La Strada'

I was booked to do the last gig of my tour on the Saturday night.

The worst time to work any venue in the north east was on a Sunday noon stag show, or a Saturday night. The reason is that the Saturday night punters don't have to get up for work the next morning so they can get blown out of their minds..... and these were the people who now adorned the room that was once the crème de crème of nightclubs. I made my way to the 'La Strada' for eight o'clock. The shows there always started around eight thirty and went on till after midnight, and usually took in five or six club acts, the final act being a 'Star attraction' closing the show.

As I was hanging up my stage suit I was approached by the manager who asked me if I'd compere the show as the regular compere was in a home for stressed out Masters of Ceremony.

I asked for a couple of minutes to think it over. This because, if I did a spot (usually an hour) I'd be able to leave as soon as I'd done my penance... whereas a compere is there from the start to the finish.

I went out and took a look at the nights punters. Two tables ringside were occupied by a couple of dozen females of varying ages...a Hen Party.   Several other tables were taken by tee shirted, holey kneed jeans wearing shaven headed characters.

Upstairs, the restaurant the dining tables flanking the balcony were fully occupied by a bunch of suited businessmen whose main aim, it appeared was to wine and dine themselves into obscurity, but not before they made it with the hens tabled directly below, seated around the Cabaret floor.

Occasionally one or more of these suits would hang dangerously over the balcony and yell inane remarks, which would immediately draw abusive answers from the partying maidens.

"I'll Compere." I said, to the obvious joy of the manager.

"Who's on?" I enquired to Brian, keyboard man with the Vance Clayton Trio who were the backing house band.

"There's you," said the Musical director, " Bobby Pattinson, the comic...

Her" he nodded towards the attractive vocalist over whose musical arrangements and ample breasts he and the remaining two musicians were slavering..."Norman Collier, the Rooster, ... Roy Rama and Julie.... the knife thrower and fire eater... and top of the bill is Second City Sound, the group from Birmingham."

The door opened and Bobby Pattinson entered. Bobby, a friend of mine for many years standing and one of the North East's top comedians give us all a friendly 'Hi, lads… who's on?" and I passed on the information gleaned from Brian minutes before.

"I'm the Compere" I informed him.

Bobby said I was 'round the bend as I'd be here all night, but I gave him a 'I know what I'm doing' wink.

At eight thirty the Vance Claytons took the stand for a fifteen minute set.

Eight forty five Brian introduced me, and I opened with an 'up tempo' number which was received by the audience with total indifference.

I introduced the beautiful vocalist who had the boys at her feet and the girls at her throat. After a thirty minute set in which the interest in the girl was replaced by the desire for more of the local brew, the girl called it a day, bowed gracefully to the boys on the balcony and gave the finger to the hens crowing ringside, and, passing me in the wings snarled, "Frigging slags", spun on her heels at my bidding, drifted like a vapour centre stage and curtsied to the mob before making her way to the sanctity of the dressing room.

"Try a few gags Johnny" suggested the manager.

"I'm not here as an act" I reminded him... "I'm just the Compere."

"Try a few gags anyway" suggested Bobby Pattinson as he peeked nervously through the dressing room window at the ever increasing mob.

I went out and tried a few gags. Actually I tried one gag, but a glob of phlegm plopping onto my Tony Curtis quiff sent me hurtling in the direction of the restaurant stairway.... to be halted by a large bouncer who informed me that I do the entertaining and he do the 'hoying out' (ejecting). Taking a napkin from a passing tray I removed the snot from my head, strode back to the microphone and announced ...."ladies and gentlemen... please welcome one of the country's top comedians, Bobby Pattinson."

Apparently Bobby's stature as 'one of the country's top comedians' cut no ice with the heaving mob. He died the death of a million cuts. He did however get some satisfaction of making the mob sit through his full forty five minute routine. While Bobby was being drawn and quartered, Humberside funny man Norman Collier pushed his way through the baying mob and into the dressing room. His face was a deathly pallor. He dropped his props on the floor and asked me "who the fuck is that out there?" and without waiting for a reply informed me that "they're murdering the poor bastard".

I told him that it was Pattinson out there and if anyone could handle this mob, Pattinson can... just as the door burst open and the comic staggered in and vomited into the washbasin.

A fight started outside the dressing room door, and it transpired that three of the bouncers had to be shipped off to the local infirmary. Cutting the security in half did little for the entertainer's confidence.

I suggested that, while re-enforcements were sent for we should have a break to let the punters work off some of their energy on the dance floor.

10.30 pm. The manager strode onto the cabaret floor and informed the audience that 'if there was any more trouble from the patrons in the bal...' seconds later he turned and walked slowly from the microphone, his hair matted with onions, mash and cold gravy...... saved me the indignity of introducing the next act.

"Here's Norman Collier." The manager snarled as he sloped of to 'clean up'.

The consummate pro, Norman strolled onto the floor, and within seconds had the place rolling in laughter. Bobby Pattinson and I stared in disbelief.

However, in every consummate pro there is a consummate ham, and Norman Collier is no exception. Forgetting the old show biz adage, "Leave them wanting more," as is his wont he decided to push his luck and stay on, despite the ominous clanging of warning bells coming from the louts in the balcony. Collier went into his famous "farmyard Rooster" routine. As he slid his jacket over his shoulders, the sleeves flapping like a cockerel's wings, he bent himself almost double as his beak searched for scraps of food in his imaginary chicken coop. It was a wishbone which landed at his feet first.... followed by a wingbone, a legbone, a half eaten piece of breast and finally a parsons nose...then the other diners added, as their contributions, fish, chips, steak, cold coffee.... till the great old comic headed back to the coop and the washbasin.

The manager, now cleaned up came in and suggested we cancel the rest of the evenings cabaret, but the next act was by now in full tribal dress and rarin' to go.   Roy Rama and Julie took this kind of mob in their stride.

"We'll do the knife throwing act first...that'll get the bastards," said Roy, bedecked in full Eastern Dress, Aladdin shoes, baggy silk trousers, turban and scimitar.

In minutes a large revolving circular board was erected on stage, and a nod to the percussionist for a roll on the drums saw me striding out to face the foe.

Maybe they had drunk themselves sober, run out of ammunition or just realised that we were trying to entertain them, but several of the audience turned on their colleagues and demanded order...and in what seemed a lifetime, their request was granted.

Lights....cue Indian music.

Voice off intro.... "Ladies and Gentlemen... Roy Rama and Julie."

Applause.

Julie traipsed out in her see through baggy trousers and her amply filled sequinned bra. She placed herself on the 'wheel'.

Enter Roy Rama. He minced around the rim of the cabaret floor displaying a frightening display of razor sharp daggers and shiny steel tomahawks.

Then, striding up to his partner, secured to the huge circular disc he began to spin it faster and faster to the encouragement of the mob.

Stepping six paces back he eyed his target.

Drumroll!

Silence.

"Whoosh."   The blade embedded itself a fraction of an inch from the girls arm.

An "Ooohah" from the crowd.

"Whoosh."   This time the blade landed between the ladies legs, uncomfortably close to the crotch of the baggy trousers.

'Oooheehahh' squealed the audience, and from a wag to his large pal hanging over the balcony "Good job it wasn't you, Ralphy."

Laughter.

"Whoosh."   Went another knife. Then an axe.. then, from the balcony restaurant, a fish knife which scraped Julies leg... followed by a steak knife... then a butter knife.. followed by a fork which hit the spinning disc and bounced, boinging into the audience.

Julie dropped from the wheel, did a cartwheel, bowed gracefully and backed from the cabaret floor and into the dressing room. Roy bowed to the audience as though nothing untoward had taken place. He made his way to the back of the stage where he opened a bejewelled case and took out several long fire eater's-wands.

Again he circled the floor inviting the audience to inspect them. Checking for space, and noting that the cabaret floor was indeed tiny, Rama lit the wands and performed his fire eating act. Taking a small mouth-full of meths from a bottle, Roy stepped back and spat a three foot flame towards the audience. Then walking to the opposite side of the stage he took another sip and spat a four foot jet which stopped perilously close to the ringside tables. The girls 'screamed' in false alarm. At this juncture a heckler leaned over the balcony, a broken cigarette dangling from his lips and encouraged by his drunken followers, slurred "hey, pal... hey you, Sabu, gizzalight will yer?"

Roy clasped his hands to his chest, bowed in obedience and said "Yes, Sahib."

Then taking a massive gulp from the bottle he held the flaming stick up towards the balcony puffed out his chest and sent a huge jet of flame roaring upwards. There was a muffled scream, followed by a surge of activity as the soot covered survivors headed for the stairs, bent on decapitating the act.

Before the flame had died, Roy was back in the dressing room, offering solace to his partner. Soon afterwards came a battering at the dressing room door amid threats of "Howay lads, let's lynch the black bastard".

While Norman and I manned the barricades Roy called to us in a thick Lancashire accent: "just gimme two minute's lads" ....followed by, "Ok fellas, open up."

As Norma and I stepped back, several burly men fell headlong into the dressing room, looking like a shift of miners straight from the coalface.

One who'd been in the direct line of fire wore a blackened shirt, the wire framework of a bow tie and rimless spectacles, the melted lenses of which hung down the man's cheeks like the eyes of a dejected bloodhound. But they halted in their tracks and backed up to the wall as Roy stood in front of them with a massive 15foot python draped around his neck.

He stepped forward and asked if he could be of assistance.

The evacuation scene that followed would have done justice to the Keystone Cops.

Throughout the following five hours a fleet of ambulances transported dozens of stampede trampled victims to hospitals within a twenty-mile radius of the club.

In the melee the 'top of the bill act, the famous group "Second City Sound" arrived from a previous Gig, looked around the deserted room, retraced their steps and boarded their coach for Birmingham.

Little Big Man!

Ned Kelly is a Geordie club comic with a gimmick...after several (intended) introductions he walks onto the stage naked but pair of red socks and patent leather shoes. His rapidly aging body is a montage of tattoos, from the tops of his socks to his scrag bearded chin... and, proud though he obviously is of his décor, even he would never claim that his tattoo is not even on the same planet as Rembrandt. Ned, the kindest of men only employed skin graffitist because the artist is almost blind and 'needs the money' and he is also the only tattooist in the world who has a 'buy one get the rest free' deal running.

Without malicious intent, I must say that Ned Kelly is not an Adonis. He is no Rock Hudson. Even after Rock was stricken down by the ravages of HIV which completely destroyed his body and handsome face, he was inhered happy in the knowledge that he was even then better looking than Ned Kelly.

Ned, a God fearing clean living mortal achieved the same effect as Hudson without any help from the ravages of vice.

He stands around 5ft 7", tips the scales without even mounting them, is semi bald, wears wire rimmed 'grandma glasses', doesn't have strong white teeth like Robert Redford and whatever shape of body he was born with disappeared while his mother hurled abuse and threatened to sue the midwife for breach of contract.

The plusses are that he's a funny, funny man. He is deservedly accepted in the funny man profession as the funny mans funny man. No funny man ever achieved a more deserved accolade. To describe his act as adult is tantamount to describing the plague was a touch of acne.

He doesn't appear on television, and I don't mean you won't see him on 'Watch with mother', 'Teletubby's' or 'The Epilogue'. An American observer said of Ned... this guy puts Roy 'Chubby' Brown in the same category as Billy Graham.

Yet Ned Kelly has always been up there as the head of the Workingmen's Club headliners. His name on any show bill guarantees a full house. And they always ask him back.

He is an instant crowd puller in the Spanish Resort of Benidorm. If a Spanish barkeeper put a notice up in his bar offering free food and drink, and the next door club owner put up another poster featuring Ned Kelly the barkeeper could put up the shutters.

For more seasons than I can remember Ned Kelly has been one of the five biggest attractions alongside the Sun, Sand, Sangria and Senorita's... and not necessarily in that order.

He arranged floodlit shows on the Benidorm beach so his fans could watch him and have sex at the same time. In fact alongside Ned Kelly, sex becomes secondary... still exciting but not nearly as much fun.

One of Ned's greatest assets is that he is a beautiful man. He is not beautiful as in 'beautiful...he looks like Charles Bronson on a bad hair day...but he is one of the kindest and best loved of people. And more importantly in the comedian business, his ad lib comedy is legendary. I have never heard anyone in or out of the business say a bad word about him. More so, I've never heard Ned say a wrong word about his peers, in or out of the business. A devout family man, he has a gorgeous wife, a fine family and is the prototype 'granddad'. His second greatest love is his pigeons. He is Club-land's Mike Tyson, without Tyson's natural good looks... Ned is rough, tough and irresistible.

In his line of endeavour he has no peers. Who else would have an entrance as bold and daring as Ned Kelly? And boldness and daring is the key to his staying power as a Club comic over the past 40 years. He is fearless in a more than often fearful business. Nothing fazes him. Like when he got a call one Sunday morning from the Doris Bogey Agency 'to get to a waterfront amphitheatre in the toughest area in Tyneside on the double', he enquired as to the urgency of the request. "The comic we had booked there has just walked into the club, looked at the lynch mob and rang for an ambulance."

"So what's new?" said Ned.

"Well" said Doris Bogey "there are only three comics who will work the club...and the other worked for me last night and this morning they emigrated."

"I'm on my way" said Kelly.

Fifteen minutes later Clubland's 'Don Quixote' stepped out of his car and into the maelstrom that was every other comedian's nemesis and announced himself.

The place was a beehive of nervous energy. On the stage a stripper who had long since passed her sell by date was creaking through her Shirley Temple routine oblivious of the verbal abuse spewed at her from the baying mob. As Ned stood at the bar biting the metal stoppers from Newcastle Ale bottles with his gums and guzzling the contents the concert secretary homed in on him.

"Watcheeor Ned, Bonny lad" said the official in the customary Geordie greeting.

"Tommy!" Ned nodded "What's gannen on?"

"Leek show." said Tommy. "Hard bastards in this morning. We had a comic from Newcastle booked, but he took one look at these bastards, grabbed his chest and crawled back to his car....and I don't blame him. I don't know how you fella's do it. They scared the shit out of me and I just had to go on and introduce this gargoyle. (He nodded towards the stripper with the divet armpits). The ones to watch are them six in the front. They're from Gateshead, and they're out for trouble. If they give you a hard time, just come off. Is there anything you want, Ned?"

"Aye" said the funnyman, easing away from the bar. "Me money... "

Tommy gave a weak smile. "Don't worry about your money, son, it's safe in my pocket." He tapped his trouser pocket.

Ned stepped forward a pace, slid his hand into the official's trouser pocket and fished out the cash. Counting it, he slipped it into his own trouser pocket saying it was even safer now and headed for the dressing room.

Loud boos and the clatter of flying ashtrays told him the stripper had finished her set.

As the concert chairman was announcing the change of comic, Kelly, naked as a jay bird tilted his fourth bottle of Newcastle Brown ale and emptied it in ona couple of gulps.

"Howay now lads" yelled the compere dodging pieces of pie and beer-mats, as he struggled to be heard over the renewed and more venomous booing.

"Howay me bonny lads... gizabirrerorder... for the great NED KELLYeeeeeee".

Comedians with years of working suchlike iniquitous dens acquire a third sense.... an ability to confront the mob on a 90/10 basis. The trick is to attack them before they can attack you.

So today, Ned strode onto the stage naked but for his red patent leather shoes and carrying his stage suit on a hanger.

No one laughed.

He addressed the biggest of the six thugs sitting at the first table. The man was stretched out on his chair with his feet on the stage.

"You in Show Business, pal?" Ned smiled.

The place suddenly went eerily quiet.

"You what?" snarled the poor man's Maffiosi.

Looking directly into the man's eyes Ned repeated the question.

"You...you deaf bastard... are you in Show Business?"

The smile froze on the big mans face. "No. Why?"

Ned swung his right foot, sweeping the guys feet from the dais.

"Well get you're fucking feet off my stage."

The expression of shock on the thugs face suddenly changed to a mask of rage.

Someone near the bar laughed out loud, and then realising he was in a majority of one, coughed nervously and retreated into a dark corner.

The thug leaned forward and looked up into the comics face. "You're dead, pal!"

Ned's look of disdain swept around the six men at the table. When he spoke there was not a trace of fear in his voice.

"You assholes don't frighten us."

The guy snarled; "whaddaya mean 'us'. You're on your own."

"Not really." said the comic. "There's six of you and there's seven of us."

The room was now chillingly silent.

The ringleader snarled. "Bollocks."

Sneering, Ned came back with the old chestnut; "I'm not interested in what keeps your ears apart, you ugly bastard.... I said there's six of you... and there's seven of us". And with that he slid a silver, snub-nosed .38 revolver from his jacket pocket and said, "There's six in this.... and me..and the difference between you assholes and me is that I'm willing to prove it... are you?"

Then stepping back a pace he took the microphone from its stand and free from further hindrance went into his hour long routine, bringing the house down.

At the end of his set, now fully clothed he stepped to the front of the stage and held his hands high. The applause died.

"Hold on bit lads... it's not over yet..."and looking down at the now solitary thug he said; "Ten minutes tough guy... in the car park... and you can bring your coffin bearers with you."

Ten minutes later he strode out of the door, climbed into his car, waved to the several men standing expectantly at the windows and drove off... and at the next lay-by, checking the rear view mirror that he was alone, he leaned back pulling his shirt out his pants and wiped away the sweat. Talking to himself in the looking glass he said: "One of these times son... one of these times you're going to meet someone who's as crazy as you... then dropping his grandsons toy pistol into the glove he patted the pocket bearing his easy earned payroll, smiled to himself and headed for home.

Although Ned was in the higher echelon of club acts and possessed a lightning quick brain for all things comedic, he was not exactly Albert Einstein from the eyebrows up. On stage he could stand for two hours reeling off brilliant one liner's and 'well rehearsed add libs' with the best of them.... but back on terra firma he couldn't string more than two syllables together at one time.

He was the ultimate master of the faux pas.

In this field alone he reigned supreme. I could write a book on Ned Kelly's maloprisms. When someone once informed Ned that the doorman at his club had died that very morning, Kelly replied, "I could have told you that a fortnight ago."

When the great Tommy Cooper took ill midway through his week at the upmarket Fiesta Club on Tees-side, the Management, who had every seat sold out weeks before the event, went into freefall. Every Agent was alerted, every name, act in the area was approached, but knowing the strength of the great cod magician, no one, to a man would even consider risking his career by acting as Cooper's stand in.

Well, no one but Ned Kelly.

Ned was at the time appearing at a stevedores club in Middlesbrough, a ten minute drive from the Bailey Club.

"Can you stand in for Tommy Cooper?" asked the management.

"No problem" answered the hard man of comedy.

"Be at the Fiesta by eleven o'clock?" said the relieved booker.

"I'm on me way" said the bearded one.

He finished his spot at the stevedores club with a standing ovation from the area's hard men and arrived at 10.30 outside the Fiesta Nightclub. A queue stretched from the neon lit front of the Club back into the darkness as far as the eye could see.

"Pull up here, Tommy" he said to Tommy Carthart, his anthropoid driver.

The car pulled up at the kerb feet from the Nightclub entrance. Kelly collected his stage suit from the rear of the car and followed by his minder made his way to the head of the queue. The very large dinner suited doorman with a nose shaped like blind cobblers thumb held up a restraining hand.

"Sorry sir, but as you can see there's a queue."

"Aye, I can see that, watcher think I'm blind or something like?" Ned shoved his face into that of the doorman.

"Well maybe you'll go to the back of the queue sir" said the doorman, pressing his nose harder against the comedian's nose.

"No, ah'll not... yer see pal, I'm booked here tonight." said Kelly.

"Wrong" said the man, "Tommy Cooper's on here ... that's why there's a queue a fortnight long, and you're at the back of it."

"Wrong, yerself" said Ned... "cos ah just had a phone call from the your boss about twenty minutes ago to ask me if I'll come here and fill in cos Tommy Cooper has just took sick and he'll not be coming any more for the rest of the week, see, smart arse."

Within seconds the word had passed along the queue and in an instant literally hundreds of Tommy Cooper's most ardent fans did an about turn and disappeared into the inky darkness. Ned and Tommy and the doorman stood silently staring into the empty street. The doorman said something into his walkie-talkie and in seconds the deeply shocked manager joined them. Ned explained the predicament to the swooning boss, who asked why Kelly hadn't gone round the back and come in the stage door. The Club Comic said he didn't think. The manager, himself more than a little short on mathematical expertise informed him that Ned had just lost him four thirds of his audience, but to come in.

Ned shrugged and entered.

Neds minder, Tommy was about to enter when the doorman clamped a hand on his shoulder and said, "FIVE QUID".

Kelly wheeled around to face the bruiser.

"He doesn't pay, he's with me."

"I don't give a fuck who he's with, he pays FIVE QUID".

Ned tried a new tack. "Look Pal, he doesn't pay cos he's my choreographer."

"He's your what?"

"My choreographer" said the Comic.

"What the hell's a choreographer?" asked the doorman.

Ned donned his best Einstein pose and replied "Choreographer.. never heard of a choreographer... it means he drives the car for me!"

I once rang Ned with the news that a well-known and loved entertainer had just died.

"Was it the big 'C'?"

"No" I answered. "He died of motor neurone disease."

"Aw well, I don't have that problem," he said "Tommy's still me choreographer!"

Ned once tried his hand at being a club-booking agent.

"So, who have you got on your books?" I asked.

"I just got a great new group called 'Fleetwood Mac." he boasted.

I knew Fleetwood Mac from a few gigs we'd worked when they were just starting their climb to international fame in the business.

"Fleetwood... that's a fishing town near Blackpool, isn't it?" I played ignorant.

"That's right" said Ned... "These four lads were on the trawlers. But they packed in the fishin', got a couple of guitars and some drums, changed their name to the town what they came from and started a little band, and now they're working for me, like."

I was instrumental in getting Ned set up with work in Benidorm.

Struggling for work but to proud to admit it he once rang me to tell me he was booked the following week for three months in the most expensive hotel in Dubai. "It's great bread." He confided. "Five grand a night, bed and breakfast and all me beer and fags."

Warmly congratulating him I told him he deserved the success and said. "Most of the guys nowadays are having to work for a pittance in Benidorm."

There was a long pause as he swam round the baited hook then clamping the barb securely between his naked gums he said, "Who's booking that like?"

I said "It's an agent friend of mine in Manchester…"

After another pause he asked what kind of money this guy fella 'Benny Dorm' was paying.

I said, "No, the agents name is …… and it's no good to you Ned… he wants someone to start next week and it's only eighty pounds a night… pay your own flights, digs, food and fags."

He said "Oh…" and hung up.

Minutes later my phone rang. It was Ned. "Johnny, it's me again….can you ring your mate and book me in for a couple of weeks in Benidorm starting next week?"

I had him hooked.

"But what about the three month gig in Dubai?" I said.

Obviously geography is not his Forte because he took a deep breath and said;

"Who the hell wants to freeze his arse off in Dubai when you can lie on the sands in Benidorm."

That's what makes Ned Kelly so loveable…. he's deep down, a little innocent kid… and who doesn't just love kids?

And he did make the move (as aforementioned) to Benidorm, and made the gig well and truly his own.

The Big Time

I was now divorced and living in Bootle, Merseyside, with my girl friend Jeannie but because I was an outsider I found it hard to get work in 'the homeland of comedians'. No one my side of the footlights wanted to know me.

We'd go to the clubs to eye up the competition, but outside of Ken Dodd I wasn't impressed. In desperation and unbeknown to me Jeannie rang around the Liverpool club agents but all she got was "ring us again sometime!"

Then Jeannie read in the Liverpool Echo that the Mike Hughes Office were holding a 'new Talent' contest in Melling Road Social Club in Aintree, almost on the world famous Grand National racecourse in Liverpool.

She suggested that this could be a way into Liverpool clubland because Mike Hughes was the main agent in Britain and had on his books some of the biggest names in the industry, like Freddy Star, Russ and The Black Abbots. Gerry and the Pacemakers; The Merseybeats... Dustin Gee, Tom O'Connor and many more. All headliners.

However, my feathers were ruffled because after 30 years 'in the business' I deemed myself too much of a pro to audition in a workingmen's club... and I certainly wasn't going in for an amateur talent competition.

But I was not working and what cash we did have was being sent to my ex and the brood in the North East, and I was living gratis on the hospitality of Jeannie's widowed mum. And more importantly, we needed cash to start a new life. So after several verbal batterings from Jeannie I relented. The following evening I turned up at Melling Road Social club.

The place was packed to the rafters and I spent some anxious minutes trying to pluck up courage and enter my name as a contestant...And when I did I gave a false name to the adjudicating panel.

The compere informed me that ten acts were auditioning and I would be third act on.

Act's 1 and 2 were dreadful and in the North East clubs they'd have been lynched, but the Liverpool audiences were several rungs up from the clubs I'd been weaned on.

I was introduced as Johnny Marks, Marks being my mother's maiden name.

Fortunately, this being a Mike Hughes show the agency had installed a first class sound system and the backing musicians were the best I'd encountered in a club in years. I also noted there was an ancient upright piano on the stage.

After victim number two had stolen another curtain call I saw the compere heading towards me. I was sorely tempted to run out of the back door, but resisted the temptation when I noticed the back door was chained and padlocked.

In the crowded dressing room I went over my act with the musicians, and then, fumbling in my music case I took out a small carton of talcum powder and asked the compere to sneak on stage and raise the piano lid and sprinkle a liberal amount of powder on the keyboard... and not to forget to close the keyboard lid before exiting.

The musicians wished me luck and took up their posts on stage and the compere, straightening my bow tie said, "you'll be okay, Ace, just give us about fifteen minutes"...and stepped in front of the microphone and demanded 'the best of order', and introduced me as "your next act... a kid who's come all the way from Newcastle to entertain us tonight" (And throwing in a Cilla Black impersonation which raised the mood of the audience and my confidence) said: "So give a lorrer lorrer order for the fantastic... I hope...ha ha har... Johnny Marks."

Cue Music! Curtains! I looked at my watch. It said, 8.45.

I opened with an up-tempo Perry Como song, at the end of which I got a roar of approval and a standing ovation from every part of the room. I went into the comedy and stood them on their heads. I took a bow and strolled over to the piano. I thanked the audience and announced that I'd like to finish with a self-accompanied song at the piano. I sat at the keyboard and pretended that the lid was locked. My mind hurtled back over the decades to the Old Howard Vaudeville Theatre and pictured old

Mike Sachs doing his hilarious struggle trying to raise the lid. It was pure Laurel and Hardy with pinch of Chaplin thrown in. I finally raised the lid to roars of laughter, struck a note and, turning to the band asked the sax player to give me a 'B' Flat. He blew a 'B' Flat…I hit a 'G'… I repeated impatiently "No, a 'B' Flat… gimme a 'B' Flat. Each time he blew the same note. "Look" I said in false irritation…"Gimme a 'B'… I'll flatten the bloody thing myself." The place erupted. Striking several dreadful chords I explained to the audience that the piano hadn't been tuned for a while… then taking a deep breath I blew the talcum powder out into the audience. "I't hasn't been dusted for a while, either!" I cried.

Fortunately the piano was out of tune anyway so I sang the song in one key and played the piano in several different keys.

They wouldn't let me off.

Acts 4 to 10 departed while I was still on stage.

After my final bow a young man came up, shook my hand, said: "An hour… you did a bloody hour!" as people came up and congratulated me. I got so many handshakes and backslaps I felt like I'd scored the final goal in the World Cup.

Then the young guy handed me a business card and asked me to be at the

Mike Hughes office at ten o'clock the next day.

Back home I told Jeannie and her Mum that I 'did okay!" and told them of tomorrows appointment.

I was drinking my third Cappuccino in a small café round the corner from the Hughes headquarters in the world famous Liver Building at 9 am.

At 10.30 I reported to the Commissionaire and was ushered into a large office to be greeted warmly greeted by a white haired immaculately dressed man who introduced himself as Tony Birmingham. It turned out that Tony was Mike Hughes main man. Over coffee and biscuits Tony chatted amiably about the fact that the office was looking for acts for a new television talent show.

His talent scout had phoned Tony the previous night and enthused over me.

Mr Birmingham asked me to sign an already named and company signed three-year management contract there and then, which I did. Before the ink had dried my new manager of five minutes told me that I'd be on a Trade Show at a club in Birkenhead three days hence. It was another audition, this time for the second series of the fantastically successful Granada Television's "New Faces Show". Then he shook my hand, welcomed me to the Mike Huges Organisation and said, "Glad to have you Mr Marks." I blushed and said, "Well actually its Hammond… my name is Hammond… Johnny Hammond!" He smiled and said "I know, I saw you in the Dolce Vita in Newcastle a few years ago when you shared top billing with Tony Hancock…you won't believe this but we tried to buy you from Beverley Artistes office years ago but they wouldn't part with you… When my assistant, David rang me at home last night after the Melling Road show I asked him what you did… as soon as he mentioned the piano act I knew. I'll tell you something, Johnny… you'll never need change your name again.

The 'New Faces' auditions were at the Port Sunlight British Legion club.

There were several acts on and every one of them was hoping to take that first shaky step on the ladder of stardom, the same ladder which I'd been struggling up sliding back down for the past thirty years.

To me, even today I think there's no such thing as the stairway to stardom. It's not even a ladder, it's a greasy pole…a lottery draw and reaching the top is no guarantee of staying there. And if you ever do reach the top of the mountain savour the experience. It will last a fraction of the time it took to get there.

Every one of the acts gave their all that night… except one. I'd been down that road so many times it seemed just another gig me.

And being selected for a spot on the TV show left me with a feeling of deja vu.

But it was nice to know that at least for a while I'd be able to repay Jeannie and her mum for propping me up and whipping me into shape.

Albert Stevenson, the Producer of the 'New Faces Show' congratulated me and said I'd be appearing on the 'Nationally Televised' show in two weeks time.

I dashed back to tell Jeannie and she lay awake all night thinking we'd at last won the lottery. I lay beside her knowing that I'd bought the winning ticket the first time I clapped eyes on her.

Two weeks later I turned up at the Granada studios, Birmingham with my new manager, Tony Birmingham. Of the two of us you'd think he was doing the show. He kept nipping to the toilet, to the bar and back to the toilet… and checking my heart rate and my state of health. Tony couldn't understand why I was so calm and nonchalant about this, his idea of the greatest day of my life. My mind slipped back to the times when stepping ashore in one piece in Murmansk, or back in Scapa Flow after living on a razors edge for what seemed like an eternity was an incredible achievement. I told him if he wanted to see fear he should stand beside me when I work those clubs in Sunderland, Gateshead, Middlesbrough or Hartlepool… and for that matter most of those Workingmen's Clubs south of the Scottish Border.

All the time I was with the Mike Hughes management Tony had tried to get me to rehearse an act but I had never rehearsed in my life. I was, and still am strictly an 'ad lib' comedian. This, for two reasons. I think faster on my feet… and I can't read. Oh, I can scrape through a typed sketch… and in seconds forget every word.

I have the concentration of a goldfish swimming in a bowl. By the time I get half way round I've forgotten where I've been….or where I'm going.

This came about in the early days of my career in 'the clubs'. If you went on stage with a well-rehearsed and polished act and started to die after the first minute, you couldn't carry on with the rest of the script.

With an ad-lib act you study your audience the second you walk into the room and look around for an Ernie Bilko, or a King Kong or an Adolf Hitler. And if, or more to the point 'when' it doesn't happen for you and you find you and your audience on opposite sides of a ten foot wall you dig deep into your bag of tricks and, somewhere in there is a point of contact.

Every comic will have at one time had some 'Quasimodo' come into the dressing room before the show and lisp "…if you want to use me in your act I don't mind. I'm sitting at the table right in front".

However, we never used anybody in the audience with an affliction… he gets the sympathy and we get thrown out of the club.

The first lesson a club act learns is to speed read his audience… and never take the audience for granted. I've worked in dives and stood them on their heads, and alternately I worked the London Park Lane Hotel and they nailed me to the wall.

I rocked them in the MGM Grand Hotel in Las Vegas and deep freezed in Llandudno Junction (un) Social Club in North Wales. And the place was packed to the door… but it still resembled a five hundred-character oil painting. Had they have heckled or booed I'd have murdered them, but there was complete silence. I even quipped, "It's not the silence that puts me off. it's the smell of embalming fluid drifting through the room."

I remember Icons like David Jason and Eric Morecambe staring in disbelief when I told them I didn't have an act, 'apart from "good evening" and "Thanks for having me!" I believe that dead audiences arrive at the venue in that state.

It's written in the Bible that Jesus Christ made a man rise from the dead. And I'm not being irreverent when I say that was okay for J.C…but he never worked some of the clubs I worked. If in the middle of your execution you get some drunken slob heckling you don't have time to pull your script out of your jacket pocket and come up with a put-down.

Once you let the audience know you're in charge its plain sailing.

On the first New Faces heat I won them over with my piano act…a similar off key piano act that Les Dawson did to great acclaim *many years later*.

I'd start the set with my ad lib comedy, and once I got them, which I invariably did, I'd finish them off by playing the piano off key and singing a nice popular love song in an entirely different key. Later I incorporated a 'stooge drummer' into the act.

It never failed… and if it did it's because the audience had a line of hearses waiting in the car park to return them to their mausoleums till the next Showtime.

It was more difficult for Les Dawson…he was an excellent pianist who had to work hard at making it sound bad.

I didn't have that problem. I really played like that.

Three weeks after I won my first 'New Faces Heat' I was on the final of that series of the Show.

On that Show there were four young boys called "Our Kid" from the tough Scotland Road area of Liverpool and the news-sheets were laying very good odds on the kids to win hands down. Some scribes even had the kids down to steal the mantle of the Beatles…But I think they were smoking a different kind of shit to the rest of the junkies. And "Our Kid" they were good… very GOOD! But to relating them to Lennon, McCartney, Harrison and Starr was tantamount to voting Saddam Hussein the new head of the Family Planning Association. In the studios I tried to make friends with them and although the kids were great their manager treated me like I was something he'd just stepped in.

This time Tony Birmingham stayed in the V.I.P.Lounge with his fingers, and everything else crossed while I went before the cameras.

I figured that this time I'd do a few gags first then finish with my ''If' in 'F' act.

Comedy act. This had come about purely by accident some years previously when I used the pop group 'Bread' hit song, "If" in my club act. In the clubs most acts carried their own sound systems, and singers also used an echo chamber for added effect. I was no exception.

One night in a back street joint in Wolverhampton I closed my set with the great romantic hit. It laid the audience in the aisles.

Just as I was taking my final bow, a giant Irishman stepped up to the stage and requested I should sing the song again.. "y'know, dat 'If' ting with the wobbly sound, because me woife and mother in law had been in the 'bog' and missed it."

I said I couldn't do it again as it was unprofessional.

An ominous black cloud spread over his face, his thick black bushy eyebrows came down and almost covered his misaligned nose and I deciphered that if I didn't want to spend the rest of my days in traction, I should grant this one request.

In a panic I clumsily switched on the Echo machine and to my horror the tape wizzed a couple of times and snapped with a 'ping'. I tried to explain the technicality to Paddy KONG but he wouldn't listen… and he kept grinding his knuckles into my feet while he talked.

So I turned to the organist and asked him to give me an arpeggio, and then to the audience I explained that, as the echo tape was broken I'd have to pretend.

It came out like this.

"If if if a pic pic picture paints a thou thou thou thousand words then why why why why why why cant I I I paint you ou ou ou oo oo oo".

At this point I said to the howling screaming audience, "I I I I think think think I'LL Piss Piss Piss…. Off off off…right right right now now now."

This was pure adlib and it had the whole audience on their feet. As we say in the business with more than a little exaggeration, it tore the roof in. Even the County Down anthropoid loved it. And, simple as that, I had a new act.

I decided I'd do this on the 'New Faces' final show tonight.

Unfortunately, when you're appearing on Television, the Producer, Director, Orchestra leader, floor manager and the whole sound and camera crew have a script on which is typed every word, comma, apostrophe, full stop, breath, smile, twitch, scratch of the crotch and whatever idiosyncrasy the artiste in front of the camera did at rehearsals...*AND AT REHEARSALS I SANG THE SONG STRAIGHT AND SCRIPT PERFECT.* This is because, during rehearsals the crew, who make up a large part of the audience, will also react to something new on the night.

To add to the confusion the Johnny Patrick orchestra was following the proceedings on monitor's two studios away. And worse still, during the run through on the afternoon in front of the orchestra, I had the musicians in fits of laughter when I asked them if they'd heard about the French Horn players wife who divorced her husband for cruelty because every time her husband kissed her he shoved his fist up her arse.

(If the reader never saw a French horn player performing, this gag is deader than a Do Do)

So... here I am, on live television, laying the audience in the aisles with the gags, when I come to my closing set, 'If' in 'F'. As the orchestra struck up right on cue in Studio 'C' I asked (in studio 'A') if I could have an echo effect. This innocent ad-lib completely threw the entire studio crew into confusion.

The request had the producer Albert Stephenson demanding from the prompt girl if she had inserted 'anything about an echo'. The floor manager was also rifling through his script to find the line. The more I demanded an echo effect, the more they tore at their scripts.

In Studio 'C' the maestro, Johnny Patrick, while holding his musicians on an extended lead cue and screaming through his intercom, "echo...? ECHO? What the fuck is he talking about? There's nothing here about an echo!"

The audience are now in on the gag and they are roaring with laughter. The studio panel, sat completely perplexed. The compere, Derek Hobson is trying to keep the show rolling and wetting himself at the same time while up in the control room someone is giving the kiss of life to the producer.

"If If If If a pic pic pic picture............"

I was told later that (apart from the panic stricken Johnny Patrick) the orchestra were in fits and now playing wonderfully from memory. And when it came to the eighth bar and a long drawn out mournful note emitted from the speaker behind me I turned and shouted, "That'll be that poor French Horn Player," I was told later that the lead trombone laughed so hard that his dentures slipped out of the corner of his mouth and stuck in his cheek causing him the change in a split second into a gravely pittsicato.

Miraculously we all finished in perfect unison.... And we never missed a beat and finished the ten-minute spot 'on the dot'. However, the control room was a frenzy of screaming people tearing scripts to shreds and hurling them like confetti, the floor manager lay against the front audience rail with a mild coronary and Johnny Patrick vowed if it the last thing he did on this earth he was going to tear my windpipe out.

In the studio the panel of four judges resembled the three monkeys 'See no evil, hear no evil (twice) and speak no evil. But the audience roared and screamed their approval, and against all odds I was immediately forgiven and awarded 'First Prize'.

After the fiasco the now recuperated and beaming Albert Stephenson embraced me and said in all his years in the industry he had never seen anything like it.

But it could have my undoing. In the corridor Johnny Patrick had to be restrained from attacking me...and no matter what I did from now on, I could never improve on that nights showing.

And to add insult to injury the following week Tony Birmingham rang to say I was to appear the following week at Liverpool's tough Scotland Road Club as Star guest.

On arriving alone at the Club I was horrified to see the outside of the club decorated with huge posters hailing "Our Kid" as future winners of the forthcoming 'New Faces Show'. As I entered the club I was informed that the group I had just wiped the floor with were in fact the offspring of the club members sitting in the front row, and were the darling's of Liverpool. However, typical of all Scousers they gave me a great welcome, and when I finished my act with 'If in 'F' all was forgiven.

Next day Tony Birmingham rang to say I was to appear on the "New Faces All Winners Show" at the Granada studios in four weeks time.

Tony Birmingham told me that the only act we really had to worry about was a young cockney kid called Jim "Nick Nick" Davidson.

A month later Tony Birmingham and I went to the Birmingham Granada studios.

From the auditorium I watched young Jim Davidson during rehearsals and wondered how he'd won his heat. He was a loveable cheeky cockney teenager but was so raw and devoid of talent that I figured it was probably the fact that he was so young that the audience had taken him to their hearts and when his likeable Manager, Wally Dent introduced us Jim we I gelled immediately. I found him terribly shy, lacking in confidence but with a captivating sense of fun. He had also been told that the only one he had to worry about with this old codger named Johnny Hammond. He later told me after he'd seen my win my (If –If- If) heat he'd told his manager he didn't want to appear within a continent of me. But we were both to receive a shock.

As we spent the long boring rehearsal time together Jim came out of his shell and I decided that he was indeed a force to be reckoned with.

Shortly before we were due on air Jim came up to me and said he was sick with nerves and could I, the oldest pro on the show, suggest something.

I said, "Go to the bar and get a brandy.... not whiskey, not rum, not gin but Brandy... a large one….no, make it a double… even a treble."

He was back in minutes saying that the brandy hadn't made an iota of difference.

I said "Brandy? I didn't say Brandy… what the hell… not… BRANDY … nor Gin.. nor Rum .. Brandy's the worst you can have. Whiskey is what you want... and don't have anything with it. Take it NEAT. …Neat Whiskey… a double."

Minutes later he was back, his face sweating profusely and redder than a beetroot...

"The whisk-iskey wasn't working either," he spluttered slurring like an old sailor.

"No, no" I said in my pseudo American 'Ernie Bilko take', "what are you trying to do son? You got to listen to me… Whiskey is worse than Brandy… I told you...(I cupped his face). hang on, I'll come with you" and I marched him off to the VIP lounge and got him a large Gin…. The effect I wanted was immediate… I almost had to carry him back to the dressing room.

Fifteen minutes later I went before the cameras. Once again I tore the audience up... as did, I must say, every other act on the show apart from Jim "Nick, Nick" Davidson...

Compere Derek Hobson introduced the trembling wreck and, sweating like a pig he staggered, drunkenly onto the set and completely destroyed the audience.

No one...not even "The Singing Angel" and Miss Mary Bagley combined could have followed Jim Davidson in his hour of glory. He was brilliant.

Even I cheered him. I cursed him, but I loved him.

And more than anything I cursed myself for my chicanery. Sober nobody could have lived with me that night… but drunk, Jim Davidson was the main man… and a hands knees and both feet down winner…I often wonder how he would have fared had I not plied him with enough drink to sink a ship.

But I also felt proud that, unbeknown to the rest of the world I'd played a big part in launching this young man who was destined to become one of our most successful comedians…and drunks! And it was all my doing.

Some weeks later Tony Birmingham rang to tell me that I was to appear, once again at the Granada Studios, this time for the "New Faces All Winners Gala Show".

Jim Davidson, now my great pal, was appearing as were all the other past winners including ventriloquist Roger de Courcey & his cheeky doll Nooky Bear….Marti Caine and myself.

Rehearsals were on the Wednesday and the Show was to go out live on the Saturday. The first thing that struck me was the set. A huge Gold Star was laid out so that the two bottom points were actually on the floor and the single point at the top of the Star was raised three feet off the ground.

There were several printed cards with names of the contestants laid on the Star…but in the centre was a card which read, "Roger deCourcey."

Immediately we started to question the positions. Especially when we found out that Roger and Nooky wouldn't be coming to rehearsals and would just turn up for the live broadcast. We realised that Roger deCourcey and Nooky were to be pronounced

The winners, and though we all railed against this, we were informed that it didn't really matter who won because we were now all 'stars'.

We accepted that but were still miffed on the big night.

Breaking all Showbusiness rules that an artiste should never interfere with another acts props I borrowed a small safety pin and while Roger was in the bar I pinned Nookey's lips together… but I made the mistake of telling Jim Davidson. He was ecstatic, and told everyone… who in turn told DeCourcey. Who laughingly waved a warning finger, slowly doubling it into a fist, at me but took it no further.

The Show went down great. As expected Roger deCourcey and Nooky Bear won, and we all crowded round them both and, tongue in cheek congratulated them, warmly.

Jim Davidson came third and I came fifth, it didn't matter… fifth place was as good as second and second was just as bad as last.

After the Show we were all invited to a top restaurant for a wrap party by Granada.

After a sumptuous Champagne Dinner the producer, Albert Stevenson called Roger deCourcey and Nooky, as outright winners to the rostrum and presented him with a silver statuette of the little busker logo of the New Faces Show. It was in a way, the British equivalent of the 'Oscar'. I sat with my great pal Marti Caine on my left and a paralytic drunken Jack Parnell on my right. Roger went into a long patronising speech about the honour it was to accept this statuette on behalf of him-self and his wonderful peers.

At this, Jack Parnell snapped back into consciousness, stood up and slurred loudly, "Sit down you asshole, they're all getting one"

I still have mine. A reminder of a great period when we all thought the world was our oyster… and for many of us it was, just briefly, a breathtaking time. Some of us quietly disappeared… some, like super talented Marti Caine died right at the pinnacle of fame, and some are still going, sadly, long, long, long after their sell by date.

Jim Davidson and I had become good friends. He was our best man when Jeannie and I tied the knot.

Some years later when I had slid from second top rung of the showbiz ladder to below pavement level and things had taken a frightening turn, Jim Davidson saved us from starvation and obscurity by brining out a latent talent I never knew I had.

He booked me as his writer for the successful shows he had running through the seventies, eighties and nineties.

Back in the early nineties I was once again struggling as clubland was gasping its last breath. Once again Jim Davidson stepped in and saved the day when he told the BBC that he wanted

me as one of only two writers for his " Jim Davidson's Generation Game."

S.A.S. shows always had the best sound system, greatest backing musicians and the finest talent in the entertainment world.

In my 54 years in show business some of the best work I ever did was with Jim Davidson in the early days. I was flattered that he had a huge respect for my progressive years in the business. We always had exceptionally great nights at Hereford, home of the S.A.S. Regiment, and after one show, a friend's of Jim. Later to become Jim's bodyguard, a top SAS man nicknamed " Nish" Bruce led me into the bar and I was feted by several male and female members of the SAS.

Nish said "Johnny, we've voted you our all time favourite comic." Jim smiled and said "So what….. he's mine too…that's why he's down here on my show…only the best for the best!" Nish would often visit us, just out of the blue and would ring from different parts of the World. Jeannie and I even made his Christmas card list.

Then a few short years ago he was travelling home from Europe in a small plane piloted by his girlfriend when without warning, and without a parachute, he opened the door of the plane and stepped out into oblivion.

Whatever demons tortured his soul, I always found him a jovial, friendly and real man's man…not like John Wayne or Errol Flynn….Just a mate!

"It was Mount Rushmore. Washington, Jefferson, Lincoln...

Like concrete, man!

I was now a 'sort of' mini celebrity and the gigs were coming in fast and furious. But I was spending more and more time on the road and away from the lovely home Jeannie, my daughter Helen and I were striving for. I hated the travelling and the digs… it may have been an adventure to the other guys but I had spend the past twenty six years struggling and slumming around the Workingmen's club circuit and the extra cash and novelty of working to audiences who were coming to see me, as averse to the past when they came for the beer, Bingo and the breaking of the comedians heart didn't make up for the loneliness I felt night after night. Jeannie and I hadn't been married for long when the big chance came and we grabbed it with both hands, but showbusiness is a fickle friend and soon, although I was moving in higher circles I was beginning to pine for the old days when Jeannie and I were 'doing the clubs' together… I suddenly started yearning for 'the hungry years' not knowing that they'd come sooner that any of us could envisage. Prior to the 'good times' Jeannie and I had worked together… not as a double act but mostly the only two acts on the bill. She was a great singer in the Dusty Springfield mould and, like Dusty she always worked and looked like a million dollars on and off the stage.

Unlike my first marriage, which shouldn't have happened, both for my ex wife or myself, our lives together was one idyll after another, and apart from the sudden change in our fortunes it meant that Jeannie and Helen were as alone as before I'd come along. Jeannie had had a promising career in showbusiness but the second she walked into her very own home she ploughed into it all the enthusiasm she'd put into her career. To this day I have never heard her complain of her sacrifice. And I repeat she was good. One of Clubland's greatest success stories was, and after resurgence, still is, Tony Christie…he was for many years the main man in clubland. He was never out of work and there were many times when the strain on his vocal chords would put his career in doubt. Tony often needed a support act to ease the strain and when the need was greatest he wouldn't hesitate to offer first choice to Jeannie (who worked under the name of Lee Christian.) I used to get Jealous of her and Christie and once taxed him about his interest. He said, "The only reason I plump for Jeannie is because she oozes class, looks like a million dollars on stage, enhances our show and is, first and foremost the best band singer in the business. And that's all I'm interested in."

I worked several times with Tony Christie and the PenMen, and more girls and women hurled their knickers at him than ever hurled them at Tom Jones…

And to this day, in the year 2007 Tony Christie is still touring and laying them in the aisles. Back to Jeannie…apart from the fact that she was a first class act she was also a very funny lady. And when we finally got together our peers nicknamed us as Clubland's 'Burns and Allen' … and that's the highest accolade anyone needs in showbusiness.

When I was at the height of my success I got a call from the Birmingham Granada studios to do a guest spot on the ever-popular New Faces Show. But when I arrived I was greeted by a cheering mob, mainly of teenage girls and mature women being held behind metal barriers. Flattered I stepped from my car to acknowledge the accolade that immediately went from a howling hoard to a silent throng. I turned beetroot red and made for the studio entrance. At the doors the immaculately attired Commissionaire told me that I'd have to wait in my car because a very special guest was about to make a visit. I walked back to my car silently followed by a thousand eyes who were wondering as much as to who I was as I wondered who they thought I was. I climbed into my car and waited for the great coming.

After a short time a limousine pulled up within feet to the studio doors. The liveried chauffeur climbed out and marched round to the rear passenger door and salututed as his charge emerged amidst much screaming and fainting from the crowd gathered behind the barricades, and out into the brilliant sunlight, which appeared to have been switched on at that very moment was the then most desirable male in the world.

Omar Sharif made the short dash from car to studios and vanished amid deafening screams and a thousand flashing camera bulbs.

I was allowed into the studios and half an hour later I finished filming my short set and went with the shows compere, the amiable Irishman Derek Hobson into the V.I.P lounge where I was greeted by the producer Albert Stephenson, the director Johnny Pullen and OMAR SHARIF. There were no introductions, just friendly banter. Then Omar put his hand on my shoulder and said, "We just watched you on the monitor. You're a very funny man… but would you explain for me the gag about…" and he recalled a gag I'd just done on screen. I thanked him for his kind remarks and retold the gag in more detail.

Joined by the rest of entourage he roared with laughter. A few minutes later I excused myself and leaving the lounge I dashed along the corridor down to reception and rang Jeannie.

After some small-talk I asked her to try to guess who I was in the V.I.P lounge with.

She stumbled over such luminaries as Robert Redford? (No!) Paul Newman? (No)

Frank Sinatra? (No).. oh Jesus… (No)… "who, for God's sake… Laurel and Hardy? Tell me, you swine or I'll hang up!"

"Only Omar Sharif."

"LIAR."

"As God is my judge… Omar Sharif and he says he just watched my recording and he loved…….."

"Never mind your spot… Tell him… tell him…tell him I'm his greatest fan …Invite him… ask if he'd like to come up to dinner…you don't have to be here…"

And just then I heard that familiar voice in my unoccupied ear.

Omar and his entourage were leaving… he looked at me, smiled said, "Hey, you're a funny man… it was nice to meet you…." (then he looked quizzically at the phone I had just stuck under his nose) "Goodbye, er…"

"It's my wife, Jeannie… I was just telling her…."

"Omar Sharrif smiled, leaned towards the phone and cooed, "Goodbye, Jeannie!" And he was gone.

"Did you hear him?" I yelled… did you … Jeannie? Jeannie?" But the line was dead.

I arrived in my Southport home just after midnight… The lights were out but in the glow of the fire I could see Jeannie… she didn't speak… she just sat there… looking at the phone still gripped in her hand.

I had recently done a hugely successful tour of Australia. My final Gig this time was in Rooty Hill RSL Club, on the outskirts of Sidney. I was chief support to Georgie Jessell, an old Vaudevillian Icon in American Comedy and a hero of George Burns, Jack Benny, Bob Hope, Dean Martin and a thousand superstars of that ilk.

Maybe some of Georgie's class rubbed off on me, because at the end of the show I shared in the standing ovation from the capacity crowd and wallowed in the five curtain calls, which fazed me because until then I'd never had so much as a hint of one curtain call…. possible because most of the joints I worked didn't have curtains.

Bryan Fehon, the Australian Agent, who was in the audience that night said he'd never seen a 'pom' comedian do as well as I did and he promised that I'd be back within six months.

I felt that I was on the verge of international stardom, especially when Mr Jessell took my card and promised to see what he could do regarding work in the States.

It was a promise, God bless him he religiously kept.

In Sydney I was staying in a luxury flat in Bondi Junction a few miles out of the city.

Brian Fehon had picked me up at Sydney airport and on the way back to that beautiful city he casually said, "Did you ever know a Pom… a piano player by the name of Malcolm Francis?

" I said I did, he was the piano player in a dreadful club in Redcar, but I hadn't seen him in years. "They just disappeared…"

It turns out that Malcolm and his family, sick of the smog and grime of Teesside had upped stakes, taken the ten pound Emigration ticket trip to Australia and now Mal was the leader of one of the finest big bands in Sydney…and was in fact running the house band in one of plushest RSL clubs down under… the 'Bondi Junction RSL Club', just a few hundred yards from the famous Bondi Beach.

The week I headlined at the club was one of the best in my whole career.

The Aussies will say RSL (Returned Services League) Clubs are the Australian equivalent to the British Workingmen's Clubs.

THERE IS NO COMPARRISON.

I flew out from Sydney on the Monday, arrived home twenty-seven hours later and on the Wednesday I was booked by my Manager, Tony Birmingham to appear, heavily jet-lagged at a Club in Mid Wales. I was the only 'Turn' on the show as the Welsh girl singer, had suddenly been taken ill with flu. From the very start I had the impression that to a man (and woman) the audience hated me, a feeling strengthened by the fact that when I walked into the dressing room the other occupants immediately switched from English to their native language.

The Organist (accompanist) was a crone who played the Organ in the local Chapel. She looked at my music with disdain and at me with contempt.

Needless to say, I died. I blame this on my opening gag relating to the newspaper reports on the anti English feelings in the area followed by the burning down of British holiday homes. "Good evening ladies and gentlemen...it's great to be here in this friendliest of friendly places... like the T.V. commercial says, "Come home to a real fire…. buy a cottage in Wales." I lasted maybe twenty minutes, eighteen of these in dreadful silence. However, when I said I was about to leave the stage I received a thunderous, but sarcastic ovation.

I mentioned to the several committeemen who'd come into the dressing room to speed up my departure that seventy two hours prior to this engagement I had shared the stage in the finest club in Sydney, Australia with one of the biggest names in American Show Business, and had indeed, taken five curtain calls.

The concert chairman sniffed loftily and remarked that the Australians must be easily pleased. My fee was dropped onto the dressing room table and I was dismissed without so much as a goodnight.

I shrugged the incident off with a 'some you win, some you lose' attitude.

Two weeks later I got a call from a friend who owned a nightclub in North Wales and who had intended to come along and see me on the night, but fortunately for him, had been unable to make it. However, he did manage to get to the club the following week and he'd heard about my professional demise.

He decided to stay and watch tonight's Act... 'another bloody Englishman' named Clive Webb. Clive Webb was one of Clubland's zaniest Comedy Magicians. Many of his peers think Webb was mentally certifiable, but he is the funniest of funny men in the right environment. This particular mid Wales Social Club, however, was not it.

Ray, my Club owner friend gave a word for word of that night's scenario.

Webb had, as usual arrived at the Club some hours before Showtime in order to assemble his myriad of props, including arm and leg irons, assorted bottomless boxes, thunder-flashes and a full sized working guillotine.

He also went round the still empty room placing small explosive thunder-flashes under several tables and chairs. The Show started badly when the young lady support act, a singer from Yorkshire was asked to change her sequinned mini dress with something 'more acceptable to our God fearing members'.

Webb should have read in that the kind of audience he was about to play to.

In a word, they were 'Chapel'.

The girl's choice of songs didn't help the Show along either. 'Blanket on the ground' was greeted with an icy cold silence and 'Who's in the Spring onion patch with Sally?' was interpreted as a slur on the Committee President's wife of the same name, who had just been divorced from her spouse, for an indiscretion with the local greengrocer.

Clive was busy slapping on the motley and rehearsing his patter. He was totally unaware as to the mood of the audience as the young vocalist, who had cut her repertoire drastically, stormed off the stage, grabbed her street clothes and vanished into the night.

As a member of the club's committee, the local undertaker had been relegated to the post of compere and his approach to the task ahead was on a par with that of his chosen vocation. A tall, gaunt, grey-haired unsmiling man, he bore an uncanny resemblance to the butler in the American soap, "The Adams Family."

This was not the setting for a devil may care comedy magician to ply his trade. It didn't help that the compere suffered from stage fright and elected to announce the artiste from the well of the concert room.

Nor did his introduction do anything to ingratiate Webb to the waiting throng.

"My friends that was a girl singer..... I'm told.... lets hope her performance is not indicative of the rest of tonight's expensive entertainment.....please give your customary welcome to an *English* comedy magician what goes by the ridiculous name of Crazy Clive Webb. Thank you."

There was a loud burst of silence as Webb leaped onto the stage in a black cloak and skull mask. "Thank you Lurch...say hello to Queen Victoria when you lie down tonight...there's an old saying in Show Business, 'there's nothing like a good introduction'...and that was nothing like a good introduction."

This was met by a sharp intake of breath.

Pulling a large knife from under his cape, he proceeded to hack off his left hand.

Seven of the ten people sitting at the front tables winced, stood up and turned their chairs backwards to the stage.

"Don't worry, I'm 'armless' said Webb pulling the severed blood soaked member from his sleeve and dropping it at the feet of the ringside guests.

Silence.

This is a small town... the speeding signs are back to back. (Nothing). The mayor and the village idiot are the same fella. (Icy silence).... And the local hooker is still a virgin." (Rumbling of voices and scraping of chairs on the wooden floor.)

"And now, you city slickers, can I have a volunteer to join me up here on the stage."

No one moved. He was slowly drowning in quicksand.

"They say that when someone dies in this town they don't bury them... they stand them up in bus shelters. (To compere)....looks like you've had an epidemic lately."

Scowls and loud 'harrumphs'.

"Can we have a volunteer, PLEASE?"

Silence.

Turning to the miniscule corpse seated on the organ bench, he strode across and said, "Ah, Morticia..... You'll do," and scooping the screeching writhing woman up in his arms he carried her kicking to the guillotine where he pinioned her arms and head in the contraption. As she knelt, struggling at her bonds, Webb stepped behind her, and pretending to unzip his trouser fly he announced boldly, "This is my favourite part of the act."

Suddenly the audience came to life. Incensed, they demanded that the old lady be released immediately.

"Silence" Hollered the Magician.

Taking a disc with a small handle attached to it, he began to count, "Ten, ..nine,.. eight.. seven..." The audience were now on their feet, shouting and waving their fists.

"Three.. two... one... ZERO".

As he turned the handle, all around the room explosive charges went of, causing people to clap their hands over their ears and dive for cover. Then returning to the task at hand he gripped the lever on the guillotine, announcing, "When the blade falls, there'll be a hand over there another hand over there, a head over here, and,"   sweeping his hand over the wall behind him, "shit all over here."

The old lady's 'no o o o o' was cut off in a dead faint as the blade fell.

The crowd began to move towards him like a plague of locusts.

"Back, back I say" cried Webb in a pseudo Shakespearean voice. "Back, or I'll blow you all to kingdom come."

He took from the table a small dynamite plunger.

"Ten... nine... eight..."

The audience stopped dead in their tracks and as Webb continued the countdown, they began to retreat, a step back with each number.

At this juncture an old man was shuffling past the stage carrying a tray containing four pints of ale and four gin and tonics. As he shuffled past a metal dust bin, strategically placed on the edge of the stage the magician screamed "ZERO" and pushed down the plunger.

There was an ear-splitting crash as the bin exploded causing people in the front row to recoil and fall from their seats. The old man flung the drinks high into the air, grabbed his chest and fell backwards, twitching and gasping. A cloud of acrid smoke filled the room.

Three very large men dashed forth and leaped onto the Stage, and as two of them wrestled the artiste down into the dressing room, the third gallantly freed the organist from her bonds.

Webb was roughly manhandled for several minutes, ordered to get his 'damned paraphernalia off our stage... and get out before we set fire to it....... AND YOU.'

An ambulance arrived in minutes and the old man was carried on a stretcher into the car-park, accompanied by the organist. An hour later, as Clive finished his packing, he asked the two remaining committeemen, ' who's going to pay me?'

They informed him that as he had almost decimated the club and it's members, simulated the rape of the organist "what plays in our Chapel every Sunday..... and nearly killed Dai Jones, who was celebrating his eighty seventh birthday", his fee was being confiscated "to pay for the damage you done."

The van now loaded Webb went backstage and toiled for a few minutes in semi darkness. Then sticking his head through the curtains and calling to the two guardians seated at the back of the room, he bade them goodnight, and left Mid Wales, never to return."

The following Sunday, the concert chairman walked out onto the stage and in his native tongue, informed the audience that he would like, on behalf of the committee, and the booking agent, to apologise for the disgusting fiasco of the previous week.

"That girl and her bawdy songs was a disgrace to all GOD fearing persons" he said. "But that demon what came into our midst, with his obscenities and his violence to our lady organist, Miss Blodwen Evans, and the near fatality to Dai Jones, who, thank the Good Lord, has fully recovered, amen, was the Devil incarnate. So, from now on, we are going to vet every act what comes across our border.   But tonight, we have two great *WELSH* artistes.... a mezzo-soprano from Carmarthen what sang in the 1956 Eisteddfod and a wonderful Duo from the Rhondda what you has probably seen singing on the wireless."

The applause from the partisan crowd was deafening. The concert chairman afforded himself a smile. Holding up his hands for order, he said in a voice trembling with passion, "But before the show begins, my friends, we are going to play our customary five houses of Bingo. So eyes down....(pause) and your first number is......"

As he stooped and flicked the switch on the machine, there was a blinding flash, an ear splitting roar accompanied by a cloud of soot and acrid smoke which enveloped the room, and ninety little numbered balls ricocheted off the walls....

Above the din, the compere's voice was heard to bellow.... "THE BASTARD".

The first time I ever saw Clive Webb was when we were booked together at a better than average club in Newcastle on Tyne called 'Throckley Union Jack Club'

It was one of those clubs that had gone to great expense and trouble to emulate the new Bailey Cabaret Clubs that were mushrooming up all over the North East. And like the Cabaret clubs, Throckley had done away with the flat-capped concert chairman type of master of ceremonies and hired a 'proper' compere.

His name was Joe and when the club committee gave him Carte Blanche over the running of the concert room they didn't realise that they were creating a monster of Frankenstein proportions. In the short time that Joe was 'in charge' he acquired such titles as 'Himmler', 'Eichman', 'Attila the Hun', 'Hitler', and even 'Arthur Scargill.'

Joe, a stocky bull-necked gorilla who was always immaculately turned out in dark blue suit, patent leather shoes and dark blue silk bow-tie, was loved by the audience and admired by his employers, the club committee.

He was equally hated by the artistes who objected profusely at his totalitarian attitude.

He would march into the dressing room and inform the 'turns': "My name is Joe... I'm the compere in charge of the entertainment. If I think you are okay you won't have any problems... if I think you're crap, which most of you are, your feet won't touch the ground till you hit the car-park. You please the audience and that in turn pleases me. No half way measures. If you do anything that I don't like, I walk up and dismiss you, up there on the stage... in front of all them people. Easy as that.   Understood?   Good"

And he'd turn on his heel and goose-step out to charm the waiting, expectant throng.

Naturally his attitude didn't endear him to the seasoned artistes, many of them veterans of such salubrious venues as Hartlepool Owton Manor Club, Sunderland 's Downhill Social Club, Gateshead's Central Workingmen's Club, Swansea Dockers Club and the Moston Democratic Miners club with it's nailed up dressing room window, a precaution against potential suicides. Faced with such a megalomaniac asshole as Joe some of these stalwarts would just collect their belongings and desert the ship before the anchor was out of the water. Others would adhere to his wishes and try that little bit harder to please the audience, and in doing please Joe, collect their wages and on reaching the winning post would climb into their cars, flick on the interior light, open their diaries and cross out the name of Throckley Union Jack Club with a deep sigh and one satisfied stroke of the pen. Because Joe was not one to bend even one iota, sometimes things didn't go the way he would have wished, occasionally to his discomfort. Like the night Liverpool's miniature comedy strong man who performed under the name Tony Brutus touched one of Joe's rawest nerves by reading a book whilst Joe was pointing out the do's and don'ts of his regime. Joe foolhardily trespassed where men several times younger, taller and heavier feared to tread. As Brutus ignored the ranting's of the King of this Castle, Joe foolishly lost his cool and lashing out knocked the book from the mini Marciano's grasp and sent it flying across the dressing room. The other artistes, a shaven headed five piece group from Glasgow's Gorbals district who were working the clubs with the sole intention of making enough cash to afford Group plastic surgery, knowing of Tony's reputation reversed into the corridor leading to the car park, closing the door gently behind them.

Minutes later Mr Brutus opened the door and informed the group that they could 'come back in now.' The sight that greeted the band went down that night into the annals of club-land lore. Joe was hanging, still immaculately attired, from the clothes rack some 6 feet up the wall. He showed no sign of distress. He just hung there with his chin resting on his silk shirted chest. He was fast asleep.

It was almost a year after that night that I found myself in the Throckley Union Jack club with the gloriously funny but mentally deranged Mr Clive Webb. As I walked into the dressing room Clive turned to greet me. "Hi, I'm Clive Webb." And he

thrust a friendly hand in my direction. I took the hand and was still shaking it while he left the room, entered the toilet and closed the door behind him. I placed the hand on the dressing room table. Seconds later he came out carrying a toilet roll which he unrolled at arms length. On each leaf was a photograph of all the members of the present day's government. "Just to shows the assholes who they voted for" he said, earnestly.

I was already beginning to warm to him when Joe stormed in with the admission; "I'm Joe, the compere and I'm a bastard!"

Clive replied; "Oh, I'm sorry to hear that.. but I could be the same...My mum told me that my dad was some American airmen."

This sort of threw the illegitimate compere a curve, and he sort of spluttered for a while. But after taking a deep breath he regained his composure and went into his speech to the Reichstag, during which time Clive trawled through his props trunk and donning a long leather coat and a German steel helmet said; "Don't worry Herr Kommandant.. your secrets are safe mitt us!'

Anyway, somehow Joe got the message across to me and I acquiesced.

As Joe left the room in some distress a tall thin young man passed him in the corridor. Clive introduced him as Brian, his new props assistant. Clive reeled off several props that had to be laid out on stage... including the Guillotine.....' oh, and don't forget to go to the bar and ask the barman for a Newcastle Brown Ale label.' And placing a 'prop' beer bottle (made of brown sugar) on a small table he told his new assistant to fetch the label back and glue it to the 'prop' bottle. Then Clive climbed up onto the dressing room table and went into a deep slumber.

I went into the concert room which was slowly filling up. I watched Brian setting up the props. Then I saw him beg a label from the barman and make his way to the stage. He licked the label and was sticking it onto the prop bottle when the whole thing disintegrated in his hands. He turned and went into the dressing room, I assumed for another 'prop' bottle and then I got into conversation with a couple of 'fans' at the bar.

7.30 the room was packed.

7.45 Joe came on stage and sang a song, handed a couple of bouquets out to celebrating couples, told a few of cheeky gags, introduced the three piece house band and at 8 pm on the dot he introduced me.

I did over an hour to one of the most appreciative audiences I'd ever played to in North East clubland. I caught sight of Joe standing in the wings, willing me to say or do something un-towards, but I played it by the book and after taking a couple of curtain calls, I left the stage to rousing applause.

The Bingo took up most of the next hour, then after a short break Joe introduced Clive Webb. I was glad to see the funny guy take control immediately.

The crowd loved him and he loved them. Even his little 'bombs' exploding alternately under tables brought forth 'oohs' and 'ahs' accompanied by laughter and applause. He hacked off his hand with great aplomb. It was at this point that his new props man sidled onto the back stage and apologising to Clive slipped a Newcastle Brown Ale bottle on the table at his elbow, before getting on all fours and making his exit. Even Brian got a round of applause. Everything went great till Clive secured a giggling volunteer into the Guillotine. As the crowd rocked with laughter, Clive reached the line; "……… and when the blade falls there'll be a hand over there, a hand over here, a head over there… and SHIT…" It was the word 'SHIT' that Joe had been waiting for. And even though the crowd howled at the expletive Joe strode onto the stage, grabbed the microphone and yelled at the comic, "That's it. No one uses that language on my stage... YOU ARE OUT…" And as the audience thinking this was part of the act roared their approval, the mad magician took the (GENUINE) Newcastle Brown Ale bottle, raised it high in the air and, reciting the line he'd used dozens of times as he wielded the prop bottle he yelled, "NO..YOU'RE OUT and brought the bottle crashing down.

The effect was instant. Joe went up on his toes, did a little circle, looked at the ceiling dripping with his own blood and fell prostrate at the feet of the still cheering mob.

They were probably still cheering as Clive and his new props man drove at brake-neck speed towards the M6 motorway.

Hail, Caesar!.

If Clive Webb is a nut, he has a doppelganger in Geordie Guitar/Vocal Comedian, Johnny Caesar.

Caesar was the first guy to have a mobile phone in his car... before mobile phones were invented. Actually he fitted an ordinary phone to the dash of his Triumph Herald and rigged a bell push to the right hand side of his seat. Whenever he had a passenger in his car the phone would ring and, begging the passengers pardon, he would clinch a deal with some big impresario from London, Paris or New York to fix him up with a Gig at the London Palladium, Radio City Theatre, New York or Caesars (a relative y'know) Palace, in Vegas..... These calls usually came in while he was on his way to work some cesspit in Sunderland, Middlesbrough or Hartlepool.

Another of his brainwaves was the Metal Detector, where he would show off his prowess as a treasure hunter to an open mouthed disbeliever by finding wallets stuffed with bank notes in the corner of some field adjacent to his house.

"Metal banknotes?"

"Er, aye, it's the little metal strips wot attracts to signal."

So it came as no surprise when I looked out of my window one sunny Sunday morning to see a figure clad in a wet suit... complete with flippers, snorkel and oxygen tanks strapped to his back.

"Oh no, it's Johnny Caesar" said my wife in panic.... "Get rid of him."

It turned out that Caesar had decided to retire from Show Business and become a deep sea diver, having recently watched Jacques Cousteau (Jacks Custard...his words) on the telly, and realised that there really was sunken treasure waiting to be scooped from the sea bed.... and it was a damn sight safer than working the Clubs.

"So what's happening?" I asked.

"Well" said the great adventurer "I need a bit of underwater practice, and I thought maybe you'd help me.... like coming to the park, rowing the coble and checking my time and movements."

"The park?" I inquired, incredulously.

"Aye" Caesar enthused. "It belongs to the public... the lake isn't too deep, there's no danger, and you can get a coble for five bob an hour."

I asked him if he was really serious, and if he expected me to walk through the streets on a summer's afternoon with him dressed like the monster of the deep.

"No" he said, earnestly.... "that's why I came to you.... you've got a van... I can ride in the back... and I'll pay for the boat.... all you have to do is drive me there, and row the boat."

Realising that it was a waste of time arguing, I donned my coat, got the van out of the garage, loaded the cargo and drove to the local park. Unfortunately, cars are not allowed through the park gates so we had to leave the van at the entrance and walk the few hundred yards to the lake.

This on a bank holiday Sunday in a heat wave when the park lake was full of tiny tots with nets and jam jars decimating the underwater wildlife. On seeing the crowds, I went back to the van and retrieved an old hat which I put on, pulling the brim low over my face.

I hired the tiny coble and rowed around to some overhanging bushes where I could take aboard my passenger. Within minutes we were in the centre of the lake. I told Caesar that I didn't think it was deep enough for underwater exploration, as even out here in mid lake, tiny kids were milling, knee deep round the boat.

Seating himself on the gunwales of the craft with his back to the shore he adjusted his snorkel and eyepiece, then, giving me the thumbs up he fell backwards into the lake with a loud clanging and a thud as the air bottles and the back of his skull made contact with the concrete bottom of the lake. Staggering to his feet he grabbed his head with both hands and rubbing it furiously he knelt down till the water came up to his thighs, slid forward and with a whish of his flippers he drifted off while children screeched in terror, causing their parents to dash into the water, some throwing rocks and several of them kicking out at our intrepid adventurer and cursing him loudly.

In the balmy heat of the day I could hear his belt buckle and the naked blade of the Shark knife strapped to his leg scrape the bottom of the lake. For my part, I sat in the bottom of my tub with just my eyes and the top of my head visible, embarrassed and furious that this maniac had gotten me into such a situation.

After an age, his form appeared rounding the little man made island. He waved and gave me a thumb's up and headed back to the boat while several men on the grassy bank threw large pebbles and waved their fists at him. On reaching the vessel he pulled himself up so that his elbows rested on the gunwales of the coble. He had the rusted frame of a long lost pushchair around his right arm and a wheel-less child's tricycle hanging from his air bottles.

A little silver fish wriggled furiously in the mound of frogspawn sliding slowly down his shoulders, and a deflated condom flapped from the flagpole of his snorkel. Freeing his right hand, he slid up his mud clouded eyepiece, removed the breathing tube from his mouth, and looking ecstatically into my beet-red face he gasped,

"Oh, I wouldn't have missed that for all the tea in China.... I tell you Johnny, it's a different world down there."

This is Clubland

Veteran Yorkshire comedian Jimmy Marshall was booked to do a show in a workingmen's club in South Wales. He was greeted by the concert chairman with,

"This isn't really a comedian's club, boyo..... I don't know why they book comics here in the first place.... comics die on their arses in here see, yet they send them week after week.....
You see, it's more of a Bingo club.... and it's the kids what puts comics off see.... what with the little ones screaming and running up and down the room, I tell you boyo, I wouldn't be a comic in here for a big clock."

In ordinary circumstances, the role of the club comic is stressful enough, but in circumstances such as the one Jimmy found himself in that night, it was totally soul destroying. However, always the ultimate pro....and being short of readies, Jimmy bit the bullet. At least there were two 'turns' on.....himself and a girl singer.

While Jimmy was contemplating whether money was really that important, the girl was going through her band call with the house musicians, while the concert chairman sat on a low stool behind her looking up her skirt.

Minutes later, Jimmy listened with knotted stomach as the girl went into her act.

She was fighting a very one sided battle.... she on one side.... two hundred and fifty morons of assorted ages, sex and stages of insobriety, on the other side. It was open to conjecture who made the most noise. The mob, the girl, and the organist and drummer were doing an impeccable impression of the H bomb exploding over Hiroshima.

Jimmy, a very large man at the best of times, started to shake like a huge jelly. He prayed that the girl singer would finally subdue the noisy throng, but his hopes diminished when the girl stopped in mid note and hollered into the microphone,

"If you don't get these frigging kids off my stage, I'll throw the little bastards through the window." An equal amount of abuse was returned from several parts of the room, mainly for the tots.

Then there was a crash as the door burst open and the girl gathered her meagre belongings, flung the exit door open and left, calling back over her shoulder

"They're all yours pal..."

Loud booing followed the vocalist's departure.

This turned to even louder cheers when the concert chairman took the stage and announced with great eloquence "...that screaming cow will never get back in this club again."

Jimmy was looking for a bolthole when the chairman informed the audience that, despite his protests to the agent, the booker had sent yet another comic, "but give him a chance anyway. Here he is. Billy Martin..."

As Jimmy, resplendent in midnight blue mohair suit, white shirt, red bow and patent leather shoes reached for the microphone, the concert chairman snatched it from out of his reach and informed the audience that the Bingo books were now on sale at the front of the stage.

The comedian endured at least thirty five minutes of mayhem and abuse and indifference before he staggered back to the sanctuary of the dressing room where he vomited his last meal into the wash basin, wiped his mouth, locked the dressing room door, grabbed his street clothes which he stuffed into his case, stepped gingerly onto the small dressing table, shoved open the window high upon the wall, pushed his belongings out into the night and straining, forced himself through the tiny aperture and hung by his fingertips while he stretched his toes downwards trying to make contact with terra firma.

When his fingers could no longer sustain the weight of his eighteen stone frame, he took a deep breath, released his hold.... and dropped the twenty odd feet into the canal. Although the water was only waist deep, the current pitched the big man forward and carried him, struggling and gasping for breath, downstream. He had only travelled about twenty yards, at an estimated ten knots when he suddenly struck a sandbank.

Above the noise of rushing water he heard voices above coming from a footbridge directly above him. As he looked upwards, he was drenched even more as three men stood on a small bridge and urinated on his upturned face.

"Hey........." was all the comic could muster.

"Bloody 'ell" shouted one of the men from above "There's a fella down there."

"Where?" slurred his companion, still pissing on the hapless entertainer.

"There" said the first man pointing between his feet.

The trio made their way down the canal bank and dragged the half drowned, evil smelling victim from the sludge. Then the reeling quartet staggered back into the club from which Jimmy had minutes before escaped.

An elderly couple passing the strange quartet in the foyer stopped and stared.

"Who the 'ells that, Dai?" asked the woman.

"That's the bloody comedian, innit" replied her spouse.

"Oh well I don't know, God bless him" she tittered.... "They'll do anything for a laugh."

One of Clubland's biggest attractions during the fifties to the seventies were 'Yorkshire's Pride,' the international clog dancing champions, Roland Roy and Jackie Toaduff. Jimmy Marshall told me about the time he 'did' a Sunday noon show in a club in Sheffield. As the girl singer was running through her dots (music) with the musicians, Jimmy studied the wall-to-wall, floor to ceiling 10x8" photo's that decorated the dressing room walls.

Everybody who was anybody in clubland had proudly autographed his or her picture and bequeathed it to the club's hall of fame. Jimmy was awakened from his reverie by a heavy hand on his shoulder.

"Jimmy Marshal, is it?" enquired the concert chairman.

"Aye," replied Jimmy in his best steel town dialect.

"Comic are you.... I say, are you't comic then?"

"Yeah, Yorkshire born and bred." replied Jimmy, hoping to ingratiate himself while still scanning the picture gallery.

"If you do well today. I say if you do well 'ere today we'll have your picture up there... duly signed of course," pouted the concert chairman, immaculately attired and large check trousers, donkey jacket, mauve shirt with a canary yellow frilled front and red and blue polka-dotted bow tie. His sparse hair with a centre parting ran down from the crown of his head like a herringbone.

"By gum, you've had some turns in here, haven't you" said Jimmy, patronisingly.

"Good turns? *GOOD TURNS?* We've only had the biggest.... I say only the biggest stars in clubland on that there stage, young man.... and lets pray to God that thy picture will be up the before long hence."

Jimmy noticed a postcard sized snapshot in the centre of all the autographed ten by eight glossies. Slipping his glasses on he peered closer. He recognised the man in the centre of the snap as his old friend Howard Jones, a great Welsh dance band singer who had appeared for many years with the illustrious Joe Loss Orchestra.

The photograph had been taken while the Joe Loss orchestra was on coast to coast tour of USA.

Howard was flanked by two icons in the world of Show Business outside of The Sands Hotel in Las Vegas. On his left was the great Tony Bennett and on his right was no other than the worlds greatest ever 'Tarzan' Johnny Weissmuller.

Jimmy drew the concert chairman's attention to the snap. "Isn't that Howard Jones?" he queried.

The official almost burst with pride.

"That is mister 'oward Jones, if you don't mind young man.... I say, mister 'oward Jones...

you may have, perhaps seen him singing on the wireless with the great Joseph Locke and his Orchestra. And that star... that Superstar what you're talking about appeared on that stage what you're about to stand on this very day."

He grabbed Jimmy by the arms with both hands.

"Be proud lad.... be proud.... saviour the honour. Do you know, that lad... that great Welsh singer appeared in this club one Sunday noon, and a week later they had him on the British Legion down the road on a Pigeon and Leek show pie and peas supper.... now what do you think of that?"

'Not much' thought Jimmy to himself.... he'd appeared at the Legion down the road and he had to admit, on good night's he'd worked better places.

"Gerraway" Jimmy chided.

"Every turn on them photographs is a star in his, or her, own right. A star the lot of them.... and did you notice, every picture is signed to 'Yours truly, Basil'...that's me.... Basil Fairburn. Stars the lot of them."

Jimmy was bursting with mischief.

"I don't seem to recognise the two people with Howard, there... are they turns, then?"

The Concert Chairman took two involuntary steps backwards, and almost had a coronary.

"Turns. TURNS????? Bloody 'ell man, have you been on another planet?... don't you know who they are?"

Jimmy could hardly contain himself. "No" he stuttered "Who are they?"

Basil, beside himself with pride pointed first at Tony Bennett then to Johnny Weissmuller"

The one on the left is Roland Roy, 'tuther one is his partner, Jackie Toaduff....the best bloody clog dancers in the club-land!"

The great old trouper Jimmy Marshall died of a heart attack on 7 September. 1996.

Sheffield Steel.

Like the North East, every county in the country has its share of nightmare Clubs. Sheffield is no exception. I was booked to 'do a double' a couple of years ago in the City of Steel. I avoid doubles like the plague, but this was a very well paid double, so, against my better judgement I took it.

The first venue was Firth Park Social Club. Like Sunderland's Pallion Club, it is one of the better clubs in the City. I'm being modest when I say I murdered them. I just didn't want to come off. Reluctantly I took one more curtain call and headed for the late spot at a club, which has for generations struck fear into the hearts of comedians.

'The Dial House Club' is not a comedians club, even on a good night, but a commitment is a commitment so swallow your pride, hide your prejudices and hope for the best. What I did to the audience in Firth Park, the mob in 'The Dial House Club' did to me ...in spades.

However, satisfied that I gave as well as I got, I took a bow and left the stage to be   met by three elderly gentlemen of committee.

After they'd grudgingly paid me they informed me that in their opinion I was not very good.

Incensed, I opened my brief case and took out brochures of shows I'd done at the London Palladium.

They were not impressed.

I also showed them brochures from some of the top venues on the international scene where I had, not once, but several times, performed.

They were even less impressed.

Then, to top it off, I took from an envelope a 10x8" glossy of Perry Como, signed, "To Johnny, Salute, Perry".

Thrusting it into the hands of the spokesman, I snarled, "That's the calibre of act that I've worked with."

The three of them studied the picture, looked at each other, and shrugged. Then the moron holding the photo said, "Well, he didn't do very well in here, either."

I couldn't believe my ears.

"It's Perry Como, for Christsake." I almost screamed.

The one in the middle studied the picture for a full minute, screwed his face and studied the ceiling then, with almost childlike innocence said, "Well, I can't remember his stage name but I think he comes from Cleckheaton."

The following night I did a Show in a Steel-worker's staff club, just out of the Sheffield city centre. The audience were so appreciative; I would have gladly done the show for nothing.

For over an hour I laid them in the aisles when, with just ten minutes to go, the door opened and a trio from a Mack Sennett two reeler walked in. A wizened little man in an ill fitting suit and a battered trilby hat was followed by two harridans, one of whom said, on passing the dais on which I was performing, "Oh shit, it's a frigging Comic."

Never one to shy away from a confrontation I greeted them with," Good evening girls..... streets quiet tonight?"

They smiled, obviously taking the slur as a compliment, then the younger of the two began to heckle me. At this juncture let me give warning to any budding club comic reading this. Male hecklers are fair game. Females are a different proposition.

My years in the business has taught me to never try out a put down on a female (or Gay) heckler. However, on this occasion I was fighting to regain my popularity with the audience. So, I accordingly ignored her and let the audience do my fighting for me. No matter how much abuse the punters gave her however, she battled on regardless. In sheer exasperation I appealed to her male companion to shut her up. In a slow, faltering Sheffield drawl, the man replied; "I've been trying to shut her up for seven years, flower."

"Oh" I said, "Is she your wife?"

"Aye"..........he paused. "Actually she's my second wife."

"That figures" I stabbed, "She wouldn't be my first choice either."

As the audience roared their approval, the lady stood up and with a display of footwork that would have dazzled Muhammad Ali she punched me in the chest sending me and the drummer crashing through the back curtains into the Dressing Room.

Gays are another no no in the smart comedians 'put down' book.

I went to a nightclub in Birmingham some years ago with some friend's including my favourite comic of the day, the incomparable Larry Grayson.

There was a young wannabe comedian on the stage struggling against the tide for laughs. He spotted Larry and called out "Ooh, hello ducky... where's your pearls?" And Grayson, now in the spotlight completed the hams deflation with,

"Pearls?" with Corduroy? Oh you bloody philistine".

That brought the only laughter and applause during the novices 25 minute set.

Chubby

Before Roy "Chubby" Brown became the most controversial comedian on this mortal coil he served his apprenticeship in pubs and clubs in the dirty choking industrial steel town of his birth, Grangetown, Middlesbrough. Comedians would say, "During the riots for better living conditions the mobs in the area did thirty quids (£30.00) worth of improvements."

Chubby started his career as a semi pro drummer in a forgettable group, scraping a 'few bob' doubling as a labourer in the local steelplant. When they rapidly ran out of gig's 'the band' folded and like hundreds of thousands of other non-directional kids in the post war era, Roy went back to the streets, ran the gamut of petty crime,

and once again resorted to basic animal instincts. He and his 'mates' hung around the bars and dance halls and workingmen's clubs. And closed the nights proceeding in an orgy of violence and destruction. He'll readily admit that he was a nonentity among nonentities. A time served thug who stamped his seal on his peers by stamping first on their heads and later, miraculously, on their funny bones.

He said later; "We'd go out looking for trouble, which was never further away than the next street corner!" But something happened one night in a downgraded club as, pint of beer in hand he leaned against the bar and watched a comedian up on stage actually winning a raging battle against the seething hoard of violent drunken hecklers and hookers. It was, in those days, fair game to joining in the jubilation of seeing a struggling deflated entertainer being verbally torn apart by a pack of howling

Morons. It was par for the course…but this victim was different. He seemed immune to the snarling insults and barbs. At one point in his act he was showered with beer mats which he collected mid gag and hurled back at the mob. The mob suddenly cheered the man's stand… and smiling, the comedian picked up a vacant piano stool from the stage, lifted it high and threateningly and yelled, "Fuck the beer mats, lets up the ante!" Suddenly he was 'one of them' and in his favour, he'd always been at the same level as the mob most of his young life. In minutes he had the undivided attention of everyone in the room, and he had them howling with laughter…

In that few seconds, the hybrid Roy Chubby Brown was born.

Years later when we swapped stories about how we started in 'The Business.' Roy said: "It was you who started me…I was in a dreadful club one night, just as a punter and you were that comedian. You were like a lion tamer… I was hypnotised by the way you handled every thug in the room… and unbeknown to you I scanned the local entertainment columns of the papers just to see where you were appearing… and I never missed a show. I learned more from you than I ever learned before or since… and I'll always owe my career to you!"

One of his most hilarious anecdotes about clubland was when he was booked to do a show in a renowned tougher than tough Mineworkers Club a few miles South of Sunderland.

He died the death of a thousand cuts on his first set, and during the interval he rested in the sanctuary of the dressing room.

After an extraordinarily long break, the Concert Chairman came in and seemed surprised that the Comic was still in the Club.

"We thought you'd gone" the official informed Chubby.

"No" he replied, "I have another spot to do."

"Aw, forget it" said the Concert Chairman. "We decided we don't want your second spot cos' you were crap. We have a fella out there demonstrating a new seven thousand pound Organ the Club might buy…. he's playing for dancing right now, so you can go if you like."

"Chubby" asked for his cash, but was informed that the Committee had decided, because they thought Chubby had not come up to the standards set by the Club, they would not be paying him…'not even expenses'.

Affronted, the cuddly grizzly bear walked out on the Stage and made a heartrending speech to the audience pleading that he'd done his spot and demanding fair play.

Unfortunately the audience, to a man, agreed with the decision of the Committee, and to add weight to their decision, they roundly booed and hurled a thousand beer mats at him. Some of them even made derogatory remarks about Chubby's birthright.

In a fury Chubby strode over to the new Organ where with Herculean strength he upended it. The Organ was of the modern type with an oak bench seat attached to the body and, from a 90% angle the Organist shot into the audience like a corpse being buried at sea, demolishing several tables in the process.

Holding the Organ chest high, Chubby screamed the warning, "It's either seventy five pounds for me or seven thousand for a new organ."

An emergency Committee Meeting was arranged while several very large miners displaying their badges of office and gripping clubs made from recently dismembered chairs and stool moved gingerly onto the stage.

The Treasurer stepped forward and offered Chubby his wages.

Holding the instrument even higher, the irate Comic demanded that the Treasurer place the money in his ("Chubby's") pocket. This the Treasurer did, adding that he would like a signature on the chit in his outstretched hand.

With a characteristic lapse of concentration, Chubby gently lowered the instrument back to its rightful place, whereupon eight huge miners leaped like dervishes onto the Comic, thumping and battering him almost senseless..While the weasel of a Treasurer retrieved the seventy five pounds from the funny-man's pocket.

Bent double with pain Chubby was dragged, like the unfortunate Quasimodo through the gauntlet of spitting kicking rabble to the wheel of torture in the Cathedral square in Notre Dame, struck over the head and on the neck by snapped off chair legs and unceremoniously thrown down the stairs and into the club car park.

After what seemed a lifetime, Roy hauled himself painfully to his feet and dragged his broken body to the little van he used as transport. Seated behind the wheel he burst into tears of frustrated rage.

Half an hour later, composed, he got out of the vehicle and looked through the windows of the dark-end, deserted games room.

There were ten snooker tables.

Chubby limped back into the Club, passed the doorman who demanded 10 pence cover charge (which he paid) and made his way into the games room where he filled his pockets with as many snooker balls as he could carry. Then, taking another exit, he made his way back to his van, climbed, tortuously onto it's roof, and looking up at the brightly lit Concert Room, with the sound of "The Dam-Busters March" blaring loudly, he heaved every ball he'd collected through every window in the Club.

The following day, Chubby's then Agent, Brian Findlay informed the Comedian by phone that the Club's Committee had rung in to say they were not satisfied with his client's performance last night, and they were sorry to inform the Agent that a return booking would not be Entertained in the foreseeable future, "And he'd not be getting any money either!"

A couple of weeks later I was doing a week in the Tees-side area for the Brian Findlay Agency. I was booked to do the early spot at a Middlesbrough Club with Tony Christie. I was through by 9.pm and Brian came in and handed me a cheque for £100.

Accepting cheques from North East Agents is a no-no at the best of times. Some have been known to bounce. To emphasise the point, I knew of one Agent in the North East who used give out tennis racquets with his cheques. And on another occasion when I was grudgingly paid in ten pound notes, the cash bounced. Brian Findlay was an enigma…. A straight and honest agent. I accepted the cheque confident that it would not rebound. I asked Brian what other Acts he had on in the immediate vicinity that night and he told me that Chubby was doing a 'special' at the beautiful Ladle Hotel a couple of miles down the road.

I had just, the previous week performed at the Ladle Hotel with great success, and, happy in the knowledge that Chubby would be working in a top class Cabaret room with a first class audience, I made my way to the Venue, where the Commissionaire greeted me.

"Hello Johnny" said the liveried one, "are you on again tonight?"

I said I was in fact just dropping in to see my friend Chubby Brown who was appearing here tonight.

"Aye" said the man, "I thought it was a funny booking for him, what, with the kind of lavatory material he uses.... especially as this is a dinner come engagement party for the daughter of the Chief Constable of Teesside and the son of a prominent local conservative MP."

I was dumbstruck, especially when a couple of late arrivals opened the doors to the main Hall and out floated the music from the band playing the 'Gay Gordon's.'

I made my way into the room, which was dressed in great splendour. Male guests were in white tie and tails and the ladies were beautifully attired in evening gowns. I tried to relate the image of Chubby Brown, reputedly the country's foulest Comedian with the scene before me.

I made my way through the well-laid tables towards the Dressing Room.

A couple of feet from the dressing room door I was hailed by two ladies who remembered me from my show the previous week.

"Hello" cooed the first lady who wore a high-necked ball gown fastened at the throat by a large cameo brooch. "Are you here again tonight... we thought you were wonderful, didn't we Angela?"

Angela, who was dressed in similar fashion but in different colours with her coiffured blue rinsed hair piled high and crowned with a diamond tiara smiled, fluttered her eyelashes and nodded in agreement.

"Afraid not" I said, "Actually I was doing a show down the road at the Middlesbrough Dock.....er.. (I corrected myself).. The Hilton Hotel so I just dropped in to see an old friend.... well, he's not exactly a friend… who is appearing here tonight in cabaret."

I felt like the disciple denying any relationship to The Lord Jesus.

Excusing myself I pushed the door open and entered the Dressing Room to be greeted by Chubby and his friend George.

"Hey pal" said the big fella and gave me a bear hug. "Posh fucking do here tonight, eh?"

For the first time in my career I had Stage fright for somebody else.

The Compere came in and informed the comedian that he'd be opening the show in a few minutes as the guests had finished dinner and were now on the crackers and cheese-board....

"and (smiled the MC enthusiastically) they're looking forward to a great evening's clean comedy".

I looked around for a washbasin or even a bucket... anything to throw up in.

If Chubby heard the 'Clean comedy' request he pretended not to. Minutes later Chubby stood in the open doorway resplendent in his multi coloured patched suit, calf length trousers, carpet slippers and leather flying helmet…. And under his arm he had a life-size toy fox terrier with two partly filled condoms attached to its tail and swaying back and forth like a pair of testicles.

The Compere, suddenly apprehensive went out to introduce the Comic and as I was about to leave the dressing room I turned and said, euphemistically, "Break a leg, Roy". He thanked me and picked up the plastic dog which he tucked under his arm, its head facing to the rear and its rear to the audience.

I hurried out of the dressing room and made my way to the darkened back of the crowded function room and stood trembling by the exit.

With my heart wedged in my throat as I heard the Compere's introduction:

"My lord and lady mayor... chief constable... the Mayor's son and Chief constables daughter what is celebrating their engagement here tonight, my Lords ladies and gentlemen... it's Cabaret time... and it's with great plea... er... give a big welcome to a great comedian... 'Roy Chubby' ... and dashing back to the sanctity of the dressing room he almost whispered into the radio microphone in his hand...Brown!".

There was, I faintly recall, a fanfare and Chubby danced up to the front microphone and stood with his dog showing its rear and swishing testicles to the crowd.

The roar of applause was suddenly cut short followed by an ominous icy silence

grinning broadly, Chubby set the dog down and in a voice that echoed off the walls he pointed to the still open dressing room door, shouted "Fetch" and with an aim that would have brought pride from the great George Best, he kicked the dog straight through the open Dressing Room door... a feat which brought a ripple of applause from football pundits at the rear of the hall. Then with a broad grin on his face he went into his act with: "Did you hear about the Siamese twins what were joined at the tips of their noses? The first words they ever said was 'Who the fuck are you looking at?'

The warm cosy atmosphere suddenly dipped to 50 Below zero.

The silence was broken by embarrassed coughing from the shell shocked observers... Then one of my two female admirers stood up, banged the table with a champagne bottle and yelled; "How much longer are we to be subjected to this filth?"

The fat funnyman replied with a bone shattering ad lib, "Aw shit.... its bad enough working in this frigging mausoleum ... now I'm being heckled by Minge and Bracket."

I didn't hang around to catch the reaction to the retort ... I turned and crashed through the swing doors...and as I passed the commissionaire he looked grey and drawn as he stuttered, "I know... I know ...I heard it out here...."

Reaching my car I almost tore the door from its hinges, and crouched with my knees pressed hard on the brake and clutch pedals for perhaps half an hour.

With my eyes super glued together I listened to the noisy confusion around the car park and fancied that I heard a gallows being hastily erected. When, after an age the noise subsided I chanced a peek over the doorsill.

The car park was almost deserted.

I lit a cigarette and smoked it slowly and when I noticed several of the hotel lights being switched off I slid out of my car and went, this time through the stage door and slipped into the dressing room.

The scene that met me is still to this day frozen in a pigeon hole at the front of my brain. The six musicians stood silently around the forlorn figure of the comedian who sat on a stool by the washbasin.

George, his 'man Friday' stared into the mirror before him, his ashen-faced reflection staring back in disbelief.

The orchestral sextet were all attired in 'roaring twenties' dinner suits... with lapels like hang gliders. They silently stared at their feet like respectful pallbearers.

Chubby looked like a man who'd just been sentenced to life on Devils Island.

His unbelieving eyes focussed on the bottom of the closed door through tiny dilated pupil's as he slowly shook his helmeted head and garbled, "They were a hard crowd tonight... I don't think they're gonna pay me...I'm sure they don't think they're gonna pay me..." Then he slowly looked up and through the fog recognised a sympathetic face. "Hey Johnny, Jesus I died tonight... did you see them... they didn't give me a chance..." then as an afterthought... "can you lend me a hundred quid? I felt like Judas as I lied and said I didn't have any cash and that I had been paid at my gig by cheque. If there was anyone in the world I would have loaned a

hundred pounds to at that moment it was the defeated fat man grovelling before me.

But I feared that the loan would never have been repaid... not because I didn't trust my friend, but because of the logical assumption that before the night was over he was going to climb onto the steeple of the nearby Middlesbrough Presbyterian Church and fling himself from the spire.

Chubby said he was worried that his wife would decapitate him when he arrived home minus his wages. He also said he'd been thrown out of the last four gigs in a row and had forfeited his fee each time.

I said, "What do you mean the last four Gigs... it's only Tuesday."

He said, "I know. I got tossed out of the gig at the St Peters Catholic club on Saturday, the Stockton on Tees Ladies bowls and Knitting Circle Whist drive and Dinner on Sunday, the 'Our Holy Mother of Jerusalem Tabernacle' last night and this one tonight."

I suggested that he get rid of his present agent and find someone... possibly an Atheist... or at least an Agnostic...

Someone who booked shows at the Dock Workers, Stevedores and Reprieved Murderers Rugby Club... in places a little farther away from home... like Beirut, Belfast or Iraq.

No one in the room smiled at the light-hearted banter.

"I have to get some money from somewhere. I daren't go home without...where can I get some money...?" Chubby groaned.

Just then George, his faithful man companion came up with an earth shattering idea. "I know, Roy... why don't you go back out there and announce that your audio tapes are now on sale."

Chubby had been with George through thick and thin and they were as close as Siamese twins... but no matter, Chubby still punched him in the mouth.

The following night I was doing a gig in the dock area of Middlesbrough and Chubby came to offer his support for my gesture the previous night.

The 'Club' was an old Church, which had been purchased by the former Committee of a Club that had recently been burned to the ground, almost killing the old watchman and his bedridden wife who hadn't been informed of the forthcoming inferno.

In an amazing lack of respect, the former place of worship had recently re-opened as a strip and gambling den cum whorehouse.

In the middle of my act a large Canadian merchant seaman started heckling and making obscene gestures towards me. Chubby went over and I saw him whispering in the sailor's ear. Then suddenly the mans face turned purple, his eyes almost popped out of their sockets and he looked up at the ceiling and began making loud effeminate 'oooooing' noises which ceased only when Chubby released his vice-like grip on the mans testicles.

As the victim sank slowly to his knees my saviour took a number '8' ball from the nearby pool table, pulled the sailors jaw open and shoving the ball into his mouth, stepped back and hit the guy under chin causing the victim to spit multi coloured teeth all over the green baize. Not only did I continue my set unacosted, but, at an appreciative nod to the audience from my benefactor, I left the stage to riotous applause.

But thanks to great management, Chubby became an overnight success and never again had to commit mayhem to members of his audiences.

Some years ago the now famous funny-man was invited to appear on a breakfast time TV chat Show. I made the effort to rise early for the occasion. When he appeared on screen he was wearing, not his trademark leather flying helmet, but a large, snow-white Fedora trilby hat.

Later, I asked Roy the reason for the unusual headwear.

He said that he didn't want "all them cockney bastards to think everybody in the North East wore flat caps."

I pointed out that I never saw anyone from the Boro (Midlesbrough) wearing a Fedora either.

He looked nonplussed but, not being the sharpest knife in the cutlery drawer when it comes to ad-libbing, he couldn't dredge up an answer to my observation.

He told me that when he'd arrived at the studio at 6.30 am he was shown into the VIP lounge and given tea and biscuits.

Chubby went on:, "There was only one other person in the room. He was about six feet six inches tall... and looked very familiar. I gave him the nod as I entered the room and he said somethin' like 'morning'. I thought, 'I know this fella'. Now, where have I seen him before? Have I worked with him? His face is very familiar.... I wonder if he's in Show Business.... who the Hell is he?'

Is he a Club Comedian? Naw, he doesn't look the part... maybe an Agent.... nah, he looks too intelligent..."

Coming from Chubby, this is an earth moving observation.

While Roy was racking his brains trying to put a name to the face the door suddenly opened and a young lady holding a clipboard entered. She strode over to the man seated opposite and said in a loud cheerful voice; "We're ready for you now

MR HESTON."

"Jesus Christ" Beamed Chubby, "it was that fella out of 'Death Wish,'... What's his name???..." Then his face lit up.... "I've got it... that's him, Charles Heston."

I have a framed 'Chubby Brown' letterhead hanging on the wall of my office, which reads:

'If it wasn't for Johnny Hammond there'd be no Chubby Brown.

I've been a massive admirer of his work for over thirty years, and I'll continue to be his greatest fan. His sharp wit, ad-libs and the sketches he's put together makes every act that sees him envious of his talent. I can't think of a time when, even in a serious conversation he wasn't hilarious. What disappoints me is that some of these so-called comedians have missed watching and learning from 'The Master'.... 'The Comedians Comedian'.... 'The comedy writers Comedy Writer'... and saying that, they have missed out seeing the best stand up comedian of our time!" Signed: Roy "Chubby" Brown.

My pride knows no boundaries and I thank him for that.

I was very proud of Roy's claim that I was the most influential force in his climb up the show-business ladder.

He once told me that after he gave up drumming with the group he wandered into a club one night in Redcar. I was the comedian on the show. He said he stared in amazement at the way I controlled an unresponsive audience and at that moment he decided that comedy was going to be his vocation. Apparently he was made of sterner stuff than I was. He made many millions laugh and in return they made him a millionaire several times over. But he never lost the common touch. We are still great friends to this day.

As I write this Roy is in full remission from his throat cancer. With his wealth he could retire to the sunniest climes and most expensive locations in the World. His ambition is to follow

Blackpool
Oct.
94

SOUNDS OF BRITAIN

Roy Brown and friend

Teesside

12.30

The traditional feud between Tyneside and Teesside gets an airing as the Teessiders—the Southerners of the North East Region—take the floor.

Ron Angel and the Blue Anchor folk group set the musical scene. A chauvinistic Teesside audience encourages Middlesbrough comedian Roy Brown and Hartlepool entertainer Johnny Hammond to put the Tyneside Geordies in their place.

Johnny Hammond

The Lindsay-Monaghan Dancers provide the glamour; your Geordie host is Bobby Pattinson.

DESIGNER ASHLEY WILKINSON:
RESEARCHER MALCOLM GERRIE:
DIRECTOR TONY KYSH: PRODUCER HEATHER GING

Tyne Tees Television Production

the path he has trodden all these years.

This big lovable bear of a man is now in remission from his agonising disease… and possibly for the first time in his life he's afraid. Not of the Cancer but of the fact that he may not be able to continue with his career.

He says; "I don't know what else I can do. You know I'm not the sharpest knife in the cutlery drawer, brightest penny in the piggy bank. Without show business I'd be no-one… nothing. I was a bum.

But I started out to be the best. And in my own field I made it. What else can I do? Where else can I go?"

I was uncharacteristically stuck for an answer. So I just looked at my feet.

Here in the year 2006 "Chubby" is competing with younger, cleverer and, maybe not too soon, more acceptable comedians. No man is an island. Not even a huge mound like Roy "Chubby" Brown.

The Enforcer

I worked a Club in Whitley Bay with a guy named Bobby Day.

I thought he was a great young Singer and the five very large guys he'd brought with him thought he was a great young Singer too, which left us in a minority of six... or seven if you counted Bobby.

Sadly it turned out that tonight's venue was a 'Group Club'... they only liked Groups...they wouldn't dance to a Singer, and they couldn't dance to a Comedian. The audience thought Bobby was awful, but five minutes into my set they decided he was the best Entertainer they'd ever seen. Consequently, as is the wont of many Club Committees, they decided they wouldn't pay us.

I went into the Committee Room and remonstrated with the several large officials, but to no avail. I went back into the Concert Room and informed Bobby that we were not getting paid for our pains, and it was hinted to me that if we weren't out of the Club within fifteen minutes, our pains would be increased tenfold.

At this point one of our entourage named Vinney who, I believe, during the War had modelled for wartime air raid shelters, suggested that we, Bobby and myself should accompany him back to the Committee Room where he would make the gentlemen in charge an offer they couldn't refuse.

In the Committee Room Vinney demanded fair play for his friends.

A Committee man who was even larger than our formidable benefactor stood up, stuck his finger under our champion's nose and suggested he "mind his own friggin' business." Vinney reacted to this rudeness by grabbing the offending digit and snapped it like a dry twig.

The Committee man looked at the finger hanging down the back of his hand and collapsed with a thud face down onto the office table. Vinney then asked the remaining six members of Committee if they would like to stick their fingers in his face, and when there was no reply from the trembling sextet, he left the Room, calling over his shoulder that he and 'the boys' would be waiting for us 'as soon as we'd been paid'..... ".. and don't forget the V.A.T.'"

After double checking our wages, plus the Taxman's cut, Bobby and I made our way back to our circle of friends where it was suggested that we should offer King Kong some of our newly acquired wealth as a show of gratitude. The Godfather graciously accepted half of our wages, making it the first time we'd ever paid fifty per cent commission.....but we figured fifty per cent of fifty pounds was better than fifty
 per cent of nothing.

The following weekend the Doris Bogey office booked me for a week in the Newcastle area, the penultimate Show being a Stag function in a back street latrine in Gateshead. I got in touch with Bobby Day who promised that he and the rest of the guys would come in and give me support. The Gateshead Venue was unique in that it was worse than any Club I'd ever appeared in to date, and the three Strippers didn't help the situation by being the ugliest Crufts' rejects on the Stag Circuit.

Five minutes into the offering from the first 'Stripper', an octogenarian schoolgirl named Candy, the demand of the perverts to "get them off" was replaced by a simpering request of "please, put them back on."

I walked on to a wall of abuse, but I'd done more Shows than the hecklers had and I was shooting them down like a battle of Britain pilot. This incensed them, but I didn't worry because big Vinney and the boys would be in any minute now. I got into a slanging match with a huge docker. We went head to toe but I wouldn't give an inch. Goaded on by his drunken pals he threatened to come on stage and decapitate me.

I played the 'you and whose army' card. I was getting into deep water but the thug faltered reasoning that a lone Comedian taking on a mob of drunks must have something up his sleeve..... like a Samurai sword and a hand grenade. Anyway I threw a couple of one liners at the mob.

"Twenty Dockers boasting who had the biggest dick". Put them on the table. Two gays walk in". " Oh look, Bruce… A buffet.

A girl sat on Pinocchio's face and said "tell me a lie"

Dick Turpin is dead…The last coach he tried to rob was full of Newcastle supporters. Newcastle, Rough? On bonfire night the mothers cuddle their nervous kids and say "Don't be frightened….its only gunfire.

The huge Docker continued his slanging match. I retorted hence.

"I thought I told you to stay in the car and bark at strangers?"

"You know… I could get aids in the ear listening to pricks like you"

"I'm not a ventriloquist. Why am I standing up here talking to this fucking dummy?"

"I'm trying to do a job up here…You wouldn't like it if I came round your house and switched your mothers red light off"

The Docker was spitting blood. I looked him right in the eye, the one in the middle of his head. A great sage once said, "The difference between a bucket of shit and a heckler, is a bucket". I digress!

Just when the mob were about to throw caution to the wind, the old doorman came up to the front of the Stage and hollered, "Hoy, bonny lad.. a fella called Big Vinney just rang to say him and the lads wouldn't be able to make it today......"

I quickly reversed into the Dressing Room, opened the window and throwing my street clothes out slid down the drainpipe.

"There he is" screamed a voice from above. But when the adrenalin is moving a desperate man can perform miracles. I tore the car door open, switched on and left the on coming mob in a cloud of exhaust fumes.

YOU'RE A STAR

I was asked to attend a 'shop window' in Leicester. (A shop window is a trade Show where Acts from all over the country show off their Act to visiting Agents, hoping to get more work.)

The small Stage was cluttered with the instruments and props of several Bands. The floor immediately in front of the Stage was also cluttered with instruments and props, from Arial rigs to Magician's boxes and bric-a-brac. Two small tables were pushed together and set before the Stage. On these were clipboards containing sheets of A 4 paper, ash trays, several plastic cups, assorted pots of tea and coffee, packets of crisps and a couple of bottles of lemonade.

This is where the Agents would sit.

The bar area was crowded with assorted Bookers, Secretaries, Club Committeemen and a smattering of big name Club Acts. I was one of these.

The Show had started at 10.am. It was now 2.30pm and several Bands, Singers, Magicians, Contortionists and Comedians who had performed, almost unnoticed had packed and left. More and more hopefuls immediately took up their places.

The air was acrid with cigar and cigarette smoke, and the noise was ear splitting. As each Act finished their short spot, a ripple of applause would emanate from the bar area. I spotted an old familiar face.

Pushing my way through the crowd I hailed him.

"Hi Abe.... Abe Rosen... nice to see you." I pumped his hand.

He beamed and said, "Stop with the handshake.. Don't tell me. It's..."

"Johnny" I said, "Johnny Hammond... City Varieties, Leeds. Comedy.. Piano Act."

The old Jew recoiled,

"Johnny... what're you doing here" It wasn't a question.

"I just came to watch these guys who have so much work, auditioning for the fun of it. How're you doing Abe?"

"How'm I doing "(He tapped his head with his knuckles) knock on wood I should be doing so good. Johnny, where you been? ...how's your partner... great little Singer... woiked for Kenny Earl....."

"Abe" I shrugged, "I didn't have a partner... you're thinking about Malcolm Vaughn... he was partners with Kenny Earl... Kenny is a big Agent now........."

Abe blanched at the faux pas.

"Who cares about who's an Agent.? So tell me about Malcolm, what's he doing since the Act split?"

"Last time I saw him was in Wolverhampton... he's gone solo...."

"Naw" said Abe ... "so," (loud enough for his peers to take in every word) "all the time I'm trying to get hold of you but you moved.... I checked the Stage but you're not in there anymore... Bernard...(DELFONT)..Nobody knew where you'd gone....... I have so much woik, you wouldn't believe..."

He chomped on the butt of a large Havana cigar as he spoke. As I let go of his scrawny mitt, he threw his arms around my neck and kissed me on the cheek, the cigar butt warming my ear.

Abe Rosen was now in his eighties. He had travelled the globe with his partner in a Comedy Double Act. This when the Acts had names like, 'Up and Down' and 'Under and Over'. Abe was 'Rosenberg and Bloom.'

They'd exhausted all the Vaudeville houses in America and branched out on a European tour. In England when the War had started Abe and Al tried to get into the forces. Unsuccessful they went onto the Variety Circuit, did a few ENSA Shows then they retired into the Agency Business.

Abe would go out hustling for work and Al ran the office. After a while they couldn't pay the rent so they had cards printed with the number of the payphone in the callbox outside Euston station.

Five o'clock one summer's afternoon during the blitz just as Al was about to close Business for the day the phone box suffered a direct hit. A few days later an old Pro   bumped into Abe in a cafe in Soho.

"Hey Abe, I been trying to get you for a week but the lines dead." said the old Pro.

"So is Al... did you hear, the office got bombed Saturday......Nazi bastards.

Next week try the box by the canal... those bastards............."

Abe soldiered on for a few years as 'Abe Rosenberg and whoever' he could find to work with him.

He went back to the States after the war then came back around '49, did some work in the provinces... managed a couple of acts, then with the dearth of the theatres in the late sixties he moved to an attic in Soho booking whoever, whenever and wherever.

In his sixties he'd met and married a chanteuse, the daughter of a London Agent and when the old man passed on, Abe took over the business, changed his name to Abe Rosen, and did OK till the theatres finally became Bingo halls and car parks. He moved downmarket to cheap London clubs and pubs, and finally branched out into the newly lucrative Workingmen's club scene in the provinces.

He kept the office in Soho, believing, correctly that an office in the city exuded more class than an office in Barnsley.

Abe was famous for the line delivered to one pro who'd had a problem contacting the agent. Abe called out loud enough for all and sundry to hear; "Did you try my new York office?"

The old club act gasped, "You've got an office in New York?"

"No" said Abe, "I got a new office in York."

Abe was a shrewd agent and manager. He'd brought a lot of good Northern acts to the capital and many of them owed the old vaudevillian for taking them from the clubs and setting them up in the big time, but alas, in the nineties, our business was dying faster than Freddy Starr's gags, and agents were finding it as tough as the out of work acts.

But the old show business pride was still there. Each one of us was as low as the next guy.... but the smell of show business bullshit was as pungent as ever.

"Johnny," Abe spoke in earnest, always within earshot of several of his peers.

"When I moved office to the West End a lot of papers went missing. I couldn't find you. Lots of times, like when I need you for Des O'Connor, or Cilla Black, or Max...Max Bygraves said just a couple weeks ago, 'whatever happened to Johnny Hammond? I wanted to use him on my series... I could have used him on my Australian tour... get me Johnny if you can Abe.... they don't make them like Johnny any more'. That's what Max said. Did I ever lie to you? So I rang around, but no one knows where you are. I have so much woik for a good funny man... but where are you? I'm ringing around all the time. 'Johnny Hammond?' they'd say.... 'I hoid he'd moved West... left the Business.

He took me by the shoulders and gently shook me. "Look Johnny... woik I got for you... here, take my new card...(he held his card aloft for all to see) when you're in town again, call me... I got so much woik you wouldn't believe ... "

He turned and his face lit up as he saw another 'Star' from the past.

"Eli...Eli Woods.... from out of the woodwoik they're coming..." and he was gone. I mingled with the opposition for a while.

I listened to the crap from acts who pretended there was no recession.... guys who boasted they were working eighteen nights a week for fees that would have attracted Sinatra out of retirement even again. Up to my knees in bullshit the smell was getting unbearable so I left. Six months later I was working for the famous Johnny Laycock office in London who had taken me on a 'seven night, guarantee four' tour. This meant that I was working Sunday, resting Monday, Tuesday and Wednesday, "but Thursday, Friday and Saturday should be okay... Times are bad but we can always book acts of your status."

I decided to take a stroll around the city. Again I saw the Palace, Madame Tussauds the old Windmill ... the Palladium, the rest of the sights and ended up in Soho.

Strolling past a few clip and strip joints I glanced at an unpolished brass plaque outside a dingy Victorian block of offices and there, leaping out at me, was the name 'Abe Rosen. Theatrical Agency & Management.'

More interesting was the rider, 'Penthouse suite'.

I rummaged through my wallet, dug out his card.   Right enough. 'Abe Rosen, blah blah blah.... Penthouse suite.'

I went through the swing doors, caught the escalator to the, second floor, then the ancient lift to the seventh floor, then a narrow staircase up three flights to a floor with three doors. One had a glass panel which read in faded gold lettering, 'Abe Rosen The trical Ma-g-m--t'.

I knocked and entered. The room was dingier than the dingy building. A threadbare casting couch stood on a threadbare rug. On an uneven coffee table were piles of musty back dated copies of "The STAGE" and the American equivalent,"VARIETY".

there were six chairs, all fashioned by different craftsmen.

The walls were floor to ceiling with faded black and white publicity photos of long dead and dying entertainers.

Every autographed picture thanked 'Abe Rosen the best Manager in the world'.

It was almost unbelievable that Abe had booked these Icons of show business.

The likes of Al Jolson, Frank Sinatra insisted on coming back time and again... but only for Abe.... 'Nobody else but Abe'.   Dean Martin, Gracie Fields, Laurel and Hardy, Sammy Davis Jnr, Jimmy James Gang, Perry Como and Gigli all smiled graciously from their respective frames and the signatures all praised Abe for his efforts.... albeit in the same handwriting.

At a cluttered oak desk sat a scarecrow of a woman dressed in a heavy ankle length plaid skirt, high-necked blouse fastened at the throat by a large cameo brooch.

What was left of her thin hair was piled high on her head in a bun. On her beak were perched a pair of pince-nez wire framed glasses.

"Can I help you?" she shrieked like the Witch from the Wizard of Oz..

I handed her the card and informed her that Mr Rosen had suggested I call on him next time I'm in town.

She studied me for a long minute, then struggled to her feet, turned to the door behind her high backed chair, knocked, and without waiting for an answer walked into the inner sanctum, leaving the door wide enough ajar for me to hear the following conversation:

"Mr Rosen. There's a Mister Johnny Hammond in reception. He said you asked him to get in touch next time he's in town. "In a croaky whisper loud enough to be heard across Soho, he said "Tell him to fuck off."

The croan reversed out of the office, closing the creaking door behind her, then sitting back on her perch, returned my card, smiled charmingly and said, *"Mr Rosen sends his regards and says to please to forward your vacant dates. Goodbye."*

...and as an afterthought..."have a nice day!"

The last time I saw Abe was at a Clubland Trade Show in Leeds. He was walking through the Jewish quarter with Rachel, his Yenta (wife) when a pervert stepped in front of them, whipped open his dirty mackintosh and exposed himself to them both.

Without batting an eyelid Rachel looked down at the goon's raincoat, stepped back, surveyed the scene then said,   "You call that a lining?"

I have always been American comedy orientated. Especially Jewish American comedy.

There was a story going round the grapevine that Abe tripped on the sidewalk and laid in a semi conscious state. As a small crowd gathered a lady removed her coat and slid it under the old agents head, and asked him; "Are you comfortable?"

Right on cue Abe shrugged his shoulders and like the true vaudevillian he was replied; "I make a living!"

With lines like that how could he fail?.

Shangri la-South Lodge

As The Bailey Organisation became a Mecca of entertainment, North East club-land
began to realise that they had two options… sink or swim. The smaller, poorer clubs learned
to survive by booking those acts that couldn't compete with the horde of class acts who
worked under the Bailey banner.

The slightly better organised clubs began to emulate the Cabaret clubs, and in so doing they
themselves became richer and more habitable. And as with the club competition, 'pro digs'
began to mushroom in every town, large and small.

The bigger the towns the better the clubs. The better the entertainers the more choosey
the acts who became mini headliners. Sunderland in those days lacked the high class hotels
needed to accommodate the legions of artistes drawn to the area in the boom years. And
anyway, from the old Variety theatre day's artistes always preferred the homely camaraderie
of 'pro digs'.

Mrs Naseby and her outrageously gay son, Derek suddenly realised that they had an oasis in
this miniature Nevada Desert of Sunderland.   Located in Roker directly overlooking the sea
and almost adjacent to the Sunderland Football Stadium, it was a comfortable stroll over the
Wear bridge to the Town centre and a beehive of, on the lower scale, clubs, good bad and
indifferent to top class Cabaret clubs either owned by the Bailey's or privately owned, like the
classy "La Strada" owned by the entrepreneur, Sanford Gouldie.

The Naseby's soon realised their huge Victorian abode was a potential goldmine. They
erected a large sign in the beautiful manicured front garden announcing that this was a
"SOUTH LODGE" pro dig to the Stars.

There were never, before or since, pro digs of the magnitude of South Lodge.

It was a 'home from home' with first class hotel service and comfort.

The 'boarders' were afforded the best possible care, the finest cuisine, large, airy tastefully
furnished rooms and a happy, 'everybody muck in' atmosphere not found in the Hilton type
accommodations.

Every act playing the North East club scene who was anybody in the business stayed at 'South
Lodge', and it was the only residence that maintained its five star attraction
till the bubble finally burst.   Stars of the day like Dorothy Squires, who was married
to Roger Moore; Pat Phoenix fated as Elsie Tanner, the true star of Coronation Street's;
American super-star singers, Guy Mitchell, P.J. Proby, Solomon King,
 Billy Eckstein; Billy Daniels. The rapidly shooting British stars Tony Christie and Ken Dodd
rubbed shoulders with up and coming club acts who were just a couple of rungs from the very
pinnacle of national and international success.

Mrs Naseby treated every guest as one of her family. Derek flirted outrageously with the
men and was 'one of the girls' to all the females, regardless of stature. No one was treated
any better than anyone else.   There were no 'Stars' in this star studded establishment…and
everybody benefited by the experience. Every minute spent there was an education. Every
night was a party. Every act was treated like a star and every star was treated like an act.

I remember when the giant American singer, Solomon King booked in for the first (but not
the last) time. He was one of the early 'headliners' to appear on the club scene and acted
like one. He informed Mrs Naseby that he always had four eggs, extra helpings of bacon,
and two pints of milk with each meal. She informed him that if he wished he could have four
chickens to supply his eggs, a sow and a boar to ensure the freshest of pork and a herd of
Jersey cows in his room. "You get what you pay for." He settled for the wholesome meals
laid before the rest of us.

However it was not the superstars who made South Lodge the happy crazy merry-go-round it
became. It was the true, died in the wool show-business characters.

Danny O'Hara was a great favourite at 'the Lodge', as it became affectionately known.
Danny was a wobbly fat red-faced jovial Dublin Irish vocal/comedian.
He worked seven nights a week, fifty-two weeks a year. And he and his wife Patsy were always as poor as church mice. The reason being that they were perpetual givers. If someone came up with a hard luck story, the O'Hara's would always lend two shoulders to cry on...
"And a few quid to tied you over." And they were not takers.
I remember one guy trying in vain to repay Danny £10 he'd borrowed on their last tour.
Danny pushed the two fivers back into the man's hand and said, "Just give me it when you've got it!"
You always knew when Danny and Patsy O'Hara were in residence. Right in the centre of the line of flash automobiles outside of 'the Lodge' would be O'Hara's bubble car.
Most nights great thinkers among the guests would wrack their brains and wear out boxes of pencils trying to work out how 18stone O'Hara, the more than petite Patsy, their three kids and a boatload of baggage could fit into that 4x4ft armchair on wheels.
A man of Danny's physical stature was never the healthiest of people. After one bout of illness he went to see the doctor. After the examination O'Hara was ordered to get into a regime of more exercise, less drink... "And stop smoking all those cigarettes...if you have to smoke, get yourself a pipe." Danny promised he would take seriously, the advice the quack offered. He told Patsy of his new resolution and said he would forsake the car and walk all the way round to the next street and purchase a pipe. At the tobacconists he studied a large display of pipes and plumped for a monster with a curved black and brown stem and a yellow bowl the size of a baritone saxophone... "Loik that Sherlock Houses, the ould detective used to smoke." The man behind the counter enquired as to the fat mans choice of tobacco.
"Show us some!" boomed Danny.
He examined several brands laid out for his perusal and plumped for a thick wedge of 'Blackjack' which resembled a four inch block of polished oak.
"Ah now, that's a man's baccy" smiled the tobacconist. .
He'd start with the pipe... as soon as he'd seen of the 60 full strength cigarettes in his pockets.
Back home in Doncaster Danny decided to drop into his local club to show his pals his new pipe and down a few pints to his celebrate new life of sobriety.
He boarded a Number 10 City bus and took his seat immediately behind the driver.
On the bus he spotted several members of pipe smokers and informing them that he was a new recruit he flashed his new acquisition. The smokers just looked out of the windows and puffed away.
Danny decided to join them, and gripping the 'Sherlock' in his dentures he withdrew his 'baccy' from his waistcoat pocket but matter how much he tore, twisted and stamped on the wad he made no impression whatever. A small heavily wheezing man seated behind offered the sweating Irishman a small penknife. Danny thanked him and cutting the slab in half spent the next several minutes forcing the chunk into the bowl of his pipe.
Several boxes of matches later he was finally stoked up and settled back in his seat to enjoy his new found vocation. Breathing out to empty his lungs he clamped his teeth around the pipe stem and sucked as hard and long as he could.
Felling giddy at the effort he removed the pipe from his lips and lowly inhaled a cloud of lung-searing Blackjack. Then, he heard a Low Mainched whistling in his ears and felt hot tears run down his cheeks. Looking up he was amazed to see the backs of FOUR uniformed men driving the bus, each one floating alternately around the cab. Then he felt a hand pushing his shoulder and a voice speaking in a singsong Deli dialect asking for his 'fare pleeease'.
Danny looked up at the reeling quadruple black faces under whiter than white turbans and searching for a receptacle found and vomited into the deep black well of the conductor's cash

bag.

Back at South Lodge some months later Danny was showing off his 'new' car to several of his peers he had herded out of the lounge into the small car and caravan park on a spare lot at the rear of the Lodge.

Danny boasted that the 'new' car was a twelve years old Morris Mini Minor., but we all silently thought he lied about its age.

"One owner!" beamed O'Hara.

"Saint Peter?" asked Tony Christie.

"Aye, could be…" admitted the Irishman… "His names on the logbook."

Several people accepted Danny's invitation to 'give it a go', in the water filled pot-holed car park much to the annoyance of a brand new pair of honeymooners in a small caravan at the end of the yard.

As the faded curtains were tightly closed and the van swayed rhythmically we gathered that the newlyweds were consummating the marriage for the umpteenth time that morning.

I stood with my then girlfriend, Jeannie and one of our best friends, the famous Dwarf, Kenny Baker, who would sometime in the future be world famous as 'R' 2 'D' 2 in the Disney Star Wars movies.

O'Hara asked Jeannie if she'd like to have a drive of his new car.

"I'd love to Danny but I can't drive." said my fiancé.

"There's nothing to it" said Kenny (who incidentally tore around the World's High-ways and byways in a huge American monstrosity). "here, you get behind the wheel… I'll show you how."

Never one to turn her back on a challenge Jeannie jumped behind the wheel of the already ticking over mini, while Kenny climbed into the passenger seat. After the minimum of instructions Kenny said; "Right…. Push the clutch in… no. that's the brake… the clutch… that one there… no not that. That's the accelerator for Gods sake… the clutch… this one near me… right down. No. Right down to the floor.. right, hold it there.. we're going to reverse… just take it nice and easy.. now, gently press the accelerator… NO! Gently… Jesus Christ woman.. gently… now gently drop the…….."

There was a roar and a whoosh as the car few backwards across the yard and crashed into the honeymoon caravan, propelling it at least six feet from its moorings.

As Jeannie clasped her hands over her eyes, and Kenny was climbing down from the glove shelf, the naked groom, with a roar threw the caravan door open and, not realising the steps were six feet away, stepped out into space, did a complete summersault and landed flat on his back in a pool of muddy water.

It was several years after we were married that I convinced Jeannie that she should bite the bullet and get behind a wheel again. After one weeks tuition she passed her driving test with flying honours.

The last time I saw Danny he was a far from healthy man and though he had lost a lot of weight he had retained his wonderful sense of humour.

He told me that he, like thousands of his peers was now working less and less, and was struggling to make a living. Comedians of our era had become dinosaurs and the only acts making money were those who'd invested in Karaoke machines, Guitar vocalists and girl singers… and every one for a pittance.

Like most observers, Patsy decided she was as good a singer as most of the girls on today's circuit. She wasn't. She wasn't even as good as the bad girl singers on the circuit, but what she lacked in talent she made up for in spunk.

She changed her name to 'Debby', got a stage outfit and some dots (musical arrangements) and went out on the club circuit. The pundits added "Dangerous" to her adopted Christian name and after a short but courageous career she rapidly became Patsy O'Hara again.

Danny, always a comedy force to be reckoned with took a pipe smokers deep breath and dived headlong back into the fray. Hence our final show together.

Our respective agents had secured a week in Wales for the Gareth Thomas Agency in neath. The jovial booker turned up to see the show a couple of times, both of which were hugely successful. On the final gig we were doing a tiny venue in the Rhonda Valley. As I recall it were a cricket club, and a hot and humid summer's night.

My wife Jeannie opened the show to great acclaim. Between acts she and her old friend Patsy O'Hara shared old memories. During the 'Bingo' I sat in the small bar with Danny who was not in the best of health. He'd been suffering stomach cramps for some time, which he'd concealed from Patsy. He showed me some medication one of his friend's had recommended. They were black and green capsules.

To give them time to work Danny suggested I go on next. I was delighted (and professional enough not to want to follow a comedian of O'Hara's calibre)

I had a great set, but it was uncomfortably hot. However they were an excellent audience and I finished my spot to great acclaim.

Back in the dressing room Danny was looking decidedly uncomfortable. His face had taken on a grey pallor and his still ample stomach rumbled noisily.

However, always the consummate professional Danny lived up to everyone's expectations. Although physically he didn't resemble the old 'loved by all his peers' Danny, professionally he was even better. He sweated profusely. In fact during his spot a member of the audience stepped up onto the stage, begged Danny's forgiveness and drawing a red velvet curtain he revealed a small window. As the interloper opened the aperture a cool breeze wafted into the room affording the man a round of appreciative applause.

Danny finished his set as usual with a wonderful rendition of Danny Boy.

The audience sat silently enthralled when, on the final high note Danny's eyes almost popped out of his head, his stomach rumbled like a role of thunder and clicking his heels tightly together he slowly turned and walked tight legged towards the dressing room.. Leaving two thin dark brown trails behind him…while the putrid stench was wafted into the auditorium on the breeze, which had suddenly turned into a Force 7 gale, starting the greatest disorganised retreat since the wartime evacuation of Dunkirk.

Several times since that fateful night I caught glimpses of the great Irish comic

Starring on the popular Television show "The Comedians", and everyone in Clubland was delighted that he had finally made it.

He can still be seen regularly on the repeats from the grand old show.

A few short yeas ago I got a call from a friend. "Did you hear old Danny O'Hara died?" I didn't remember 'old' Danny O'Hara. To me and all who knew him he was always young and fresh…. Apart from the night at the Nelson Cricket club in the Valley.

His ghost is always popping up in the most unexpected places…when, using my free pass I sit directly behind the driver on a bus… when I see some-one drive by in an ancient but greatly loved ramshackle bubble car… or on one of those hot humid nights when I drag myself out of bed and open the window and suddenly I'm sitting in the front row of some Welsh club enthralled as the fat funnyman suddenly stops mid note through a wonderful rendition of 'Danny Boy!"

I wonder if Patsy still has "Sherlock Houses" pipe.

Pro-digs.. a showbusiness phenomenon

'Old' Marge Jeffrey's pro-digs in the ancient fishing port of Hull in the county of Humberside were a smaller version of the aforementioned 'South Lodge'. Everyone who was anyone in 'The Business' lodged with Marge and Bob Jeffrey's while gigging on the East Coast.

It was spotlessly clean, beautifully furnished and the meals were 'haute cuisine'. When Marge laid before you her Humberside cod and chips you needed two plates...

One for the chips and butties, and a much larger one for the cod. It was said that Marge's fish was so huge and fresh she supplied her diners with a club to beat the monster to death. Many argued that the fish was not cod but was in fact Barracuda, Porpoise, Shark (great white) or Orca (Killer whale).

One lived and dined magnificently at Marge Jeffrey's and as Long John Silver himself would have said: "and you may lay to that, Jim lad".

However, Marge and Bob was not a luvvie dovey couple. It was said that because of some marital tiff many a long season ago they stayed married in name only.

It was even whispered that they berthed on different decks...and although the Jeffrey home was shipshape and Bristol fashion there was however an ever present chill wind blowing across the place from bow to stern, from port to starboard.

While Marge dined with the boarders, seated at the head of the table in a throne like high backed chair, the arms of which were two Dolphins carved in teak, Bob was the chief cook and bottle washer, serving, pouring and clearing. He even took his meals alone in his allotted berth at a small table in the galley.

To say that 'old Marge' ruled the roost would be an understatement.

She was in full command and don't you dare question her rank.

Breakfast was at 09.00 (seated). Late risers would cower under the commodore's stare, tug the forelock and whisper an apology. In all the years I messed with the Jeffrey's I never knew a boarder be late for victuals more than once.

There was no lunch. It took Bob most of the day to sweep, dust, vacuum, black-lead and polish the hearth and fill the coal scuttle from the bunker.

During this period boarders would be expected to stay in their quarters, or more favourably file down the street to the Hull docker's club and weigh up the pro's and cons of berthing with the old sea dog... or cat as the case may be.

Dinner was at 1700 hours (seated). This lasted anything up to an hour during which time the diners would be regaled with tales of the 'Stars' who had berthed here... and how Marge was, herself once an artiste of some prominence. Her greatest achievement was that she once appeared on ' Hughie Green's Opportunity Knocks' rigged out as an old sailor smoking a clay pipe and relating comic anecdotes of her cruise of discovery as first mate to the great navigator, Captain Cook who hailed from Whitby, just up the coast. She finished her act doing the hornpipe. She didn't win... in fact she didn't even get a mention in the local paper for her efforts.

It is believed that as Hughie announced. "...And now folks, a great novelty act folks from salty old Humberside, folks... We hope you'll vote for her, folks... and if you can't remember her name folks, just put 'Popeye', we'll know whom you're talking about. Folks!"

After dinner all the guests (who were to a man. and woman) club entertainers, would excuse themselves, collect their stage suits, dresses and props and head off to whatever fate the good club members would afford them.

Decks cleared Marge would settle down for her nightly ritual of several hours of scrabble, while old Bob will have cleared and swabbed the deck, washed dried and put away the crockery, cut dozens of tiny quarters of cheese and cucumber sandwiches, carefully curling the crusts and fill the name labelled thermos flasks for the weary acts returning back aboard after the 23.00 hours finale. Then, and only then was old Bob allowed his nightly, weekly, monthly and yearly ritual of watching the   news after which, on the orders of his formidable spouse he would settle on his old rocking chair and drop off to sleep and dream of far off good times.

After all of the acts were aboard and wined and suppered the television would be switched off, often in the middle of an exciting or heart rending or nail biting scene and 'volunteers' would be inveigled into a boring final sixty minutes of scrabble with the good hostess. And on the dot of 01.00 hours, old Marge would call a halt to all activities and order each and everyone to their berths. The last ritual of the evening would be for someone close at hand to waken old Bob from his slumber.

The last time I ever shared the hospitality of old Marge and Bob was the night, at the end of a gut wrenchingly boring game of scrabble during which time we all sniffed at the curled up sandwiches and put them to one side, and as the guests were making their final move, I, being the nearest, tapped old Bob on the shoulder and said; "Bob… Bob… c'mon old lad, it's one o'clock."   And for the first time since the ritual began in 1943 during an air raid on the port, old Bob didn't respond.

In fact he was dead.

The local GP was summoned and he duly arrived dressed in Homburg hat and pyjama's, partly concealed beneath and ankle length black overcoat and carrying his little black bag . He examined the corpse, then biting his biro pen and screwing his eyes, he turned to Marge (who was busily scooping her Scrabble blocks into a little bag) and said; "How long has he been like this?"

Marge looked at the ships wheel clock on the mantelpiece and said; "Since half past seven… Why?"

Putting his stethoscope back into his little bag he said… "Could be the heat I suppose. Rigor mortis. Probably been dead since just after the 7 o'clock news…"

And dropping the business card of the duty undertaker on the table, he picked up a sandwich, sniffed it, took a bite and bade us all a pleasant night…

….and that's not all

Jeannie and I were booked for a week in the North East. The call to South Lodge to hopefully reserve our regular suite was apologetically turned down. Sunderland FC was playing at home to Liverpool and every room in Sunderland had been booked up weeks previously.

A couple of hours later I got a call to say that, although South Lodge was still fully booked, the lodge Hostess, Mrs Naseby heard there was a room at another pro digs a couple of streets away. And she'd taken the liberty of reserving it for us.

We thanked her.

When we turned up at he digs a very old lady answered the bell.

She stood around four feet tall. She was wearing boots. Not ladies button at the ankle boots. Large army issue hob nailed boots. She was also wearing an American leather and sheepskin-flying jacket which reached almost to her ankles.

A monogrammed 'T' shirt and a mini skirt finished off the ensemble. Her head was shaven all round apart from the short fringe cut straight across the eyes.

"Are you my coachman?" she asked in a little girl voice. Before either Jeannie or I could answer an attractive woman in her late thirties appeared behind the old lady and, taking her by the arms ushered her back along the hallway and pushed her into a room, noisily locking and padlocking the door with several keys before rejoining us where she apologised for ' mam… she's not right you know, but she's harmless and you have to amuse her. But really, she's all

right.!" Then, "Are you the couple from the Naseby's then? Derek rang and booked you in…come in, come in, and don't
mind me mam… or the boys."
'The boys' I said. 'I, er… the…er… the boys?'
"No, the boys are all right, high spirited and get up to all kinds of mischief, but they're quite harmless. Oh, by the way, I'm Paula… the, the landlady…. Please, come in…" and over her shoulder "Richard… Richard… where the hell is…."
The door behind her opened maybe three inches and what at first appeared to be the old ladies sister peered at us, and then slowly made an entrance. It was Richard. He stood maybe five feet tall and was dressed in loud check trousers and a woolly sweater around each cuff of which were several wristwatches. He was also wearing huge, long eared Bugs Bunny slippers. His head was also shaved apart from the jagged eye level short fringe over the forehead. He gave us a gap toothed smile and said 'Hi.'
"This is my husband, Richard, "said Paula with an expression which read, 'believe it or not'. "And you are Joan and Jimmy?"
"Jeannie and Johnny" I corrected, "… this is Jeannie and I'm… "
"Johnny" interrupted my partner…. "It's nice…. You have a nice place here…"
"We only moved in maybe six months ago." Paula said. " We… used to own a pub in Darlington till my husband died suddenly…. and Richard came to work for me… then, when his dad died in Australia… who owned one of the biggest sheep spreads in Australia… and then he died left him…Richard… an absolute fortune…"
'Ah ah!" Jeannie mumbled.
Paula caught the reaction and faltered for a moment. "Well Richard was lonely and I was on my own… of course we didn't get married straight away… matter of fact he took the job down here at the mental hospital… he'd been in mental hospitals for years… not as an inmate…I mean not as a patient of course" she smiled " he was a hairdresser before that… in York… then when we came down here Derek Naisby got him a job as the lunatic asylum's… or rather the home's barber… he's the barber down at the home… and I look after the hotel… but Richard helps out at weekends."
Jeannie gave her now customary 'ah ha'
" And when this place came on the market…. Richard is a friend of Derek Naisby. And he said maybe Richard would like to go into the hotel… small hotel business…" Paula stepped aside and said, "Richard. Will you take Jennie's and Josephs cases to number five?"
"Jeannie and Johnny" Jeannie said impatiently. Richard stepped forward and took our two suitcases. As he turned and walked up the stairs we noted he had little white woolly rabbit tails on the heels of his slippers. Paula followed our gaze, laughed and said, "Oh, he's crazy…. Mad I mean…mad about… well, he loves rabbits…"
I couldn't resist. "Who's the old lady who answered the door?"
"That's Richards mother, Adele…. She's a patient in the home where Richard works."
"Oh" said Jeannie, "Is he into psychiatry then?"
Paula laughed a giggly girly laugh. "Oh God, no… He's the Barber…"
"Oh, of course", said Jeannie…" You can see the like….!"
"He's not a proper barber of course, he didn't even finish his apprenticeship…but one of the inmates stabbed the last poor barber with his own scissors and Richard filled in the vacancy. He only knows one style and, it doesn't matter, men women or children, they all get a Richard special…. even his mam!"
If Richard was a little strange, his kids were homicidal. But they had ambitions. Dean was 14 and his IQ went through the top of the thermometer…and had aspirations to become a scientist, and failing that, an explosives expert in the S.A.S or a hit man for the Mafia. Elvis was 11 and wanted to be a bus driver or an ice-cream man and if he couldn't aspire to those

dizzy heights he'd settle for being an airline pilot in the Royal Air force and drop an atom bomb on an island full of people or a school. They were forever putting the lives of the guests, their parents, the house and themselves in deadly danger. As a precaution Paula had a direct line to the police, fire and ambulance services. Many years later we heard she also carried a short samurai sword with her twenty-four hours a day.

But they ingenuity came to the fore and almost ended the dynasty one Sunday after dinner. Richard and Paula were asleep on the couch in front of the television, and their hands were joined together in a grip of undying love. The boys had been reading an American crime magazine and were engrossed in an article about, 'Old Smokey', the electric chair in Sing Sing prison. After consuming and digesting all the information on the art of 'frying' condemned human beings, Dean had a brainwave. He and Elvis tippy-toed to the prostrate forms of their beloved parents.

Dean whispered to his baby brother to take his mummy's left hand in his right hand...
then he gently took his fathers right hand in his left hand, and with his free hand he shoved a Yale key into the electric plug on the wall. Suddenly the couch hummed and vibrated like 'the Sing Sing hot seat'. The human daisy chain jerked bolt upright doing a group impersonation of the fight promoter Don King on his worst hair day. Their open mouths frozen in a silent scream and little sparks danced between their fathers upper and lower gold dentures. If the television set had not at that very moment imploded cutting off the electric current, only God knows what the alternative outcome would have been.

On the Wednesday of that week we awoke to a wonderland of thick lush snow and tinkling icicles. After breakfast I looked out of the living room window at the form of Richard leaning, half naked under the bonnet of his ancient car. He was dressed in his favourite bunny slippers, pyjama bottoms and a 'T' shirt. There was a three-inch layer of snow from his waist right up the back of his shaven head. Paula said he'd been out there at least two hours trying, in vain to start his car. I put on some heavy clothing and, grabbing a coat from the rack by the front door I made my way down the slippery path. On reaching the shivering wretch I threw the coat over his shoulders, and asked if there was anything I could do to help.

With chattering teeth he said that the battery was flat and that he was trying to get the car started, but he felt he was fighting a losing battle. I suggested giving him a tow and maybe that would do the trick. I manoeuvred his creaking carcass into the drivers seat of his car, cleared the snow from all the windows and starting my car I reversed up to his vehicle, got out, hitched my tow rope around his front fender and instructed him to signal with a couple of toots on the horn and a flash of his main beam when his car sprung into life. Then dashing back into my car I threw it into gear. I Towed him from Roker, onto the Sunderland promenade, through Cleadon, South Shields, Gateshead, Newcastle and Whitley Bay, constantly listening for his signal and keeping a weather eye out for a flash of his lights. None came.

I decided to take the scenic route the eighteen miles back to Sunderland. Once on the trunk road I could get up a decent speed and hopefully resuscitate the old banger. nothing.

I looked constantly through my rear view mirror and was surprised to see Richard crouching over the wheel, a manic grin on his face, eyes wide open, his lips vibrating
sending a spray of spittle over the inside of the windscreen. He was obviously emulating Sir Malcolm Campbell tearing across the salt flats in Utah, USA in his successful challenge at the World Land-Speed record.

I flashed my tail lights and he grinned back at me, took his hands off the wheel and doubling them into fists shook them wildly above his head. After fifty-five minutes of towing, honking the horn and waving and driving recklessly over red lights, we finally chugged to a halt directly over the damp snow free launching pad I'd earlier launched him from.

I got out and was about to tap on his window when realised it was wound down to the last

174

cog. I realise that he'd endured the whole tour with the windows wide open to the elements. His naturally black eyebrows were stiff white bars of frozen cotton wool.

Tears had streamed down his face and froze into shimmering shards like miniature stalactites. And the wind from the speeding car had blown his fringe forward and it had frozen stiff like the frozen peak of Norman Wisdoms cap, and his lips were bluer than Paul Newman's eyes.

"No good?" I said.

"Afraid not." He said, adding," but I really enjoyed that!"

I suggested I take a peek under the bonnet. He stooped under the steering wheel and pulled the bonnet release handle. I lifted the bonnet, pushed and shoved at things mechanical, tugged at several pieces of wire and cable then my eyes fell on two thick leads, one positive and one negative dangling over an empty shelf. Feeling my hackles rise I called to him to join me. I put my hand on the back of his neck and pushed his head forward.

"Where's the battery?" I asked.

"It's flat," he said.

"It's not there" I said, stabbing my finger at the empty space. "For Christ sake!" I yelled in his face." It's not there!"

"I know" he said in all childish innocence, "I have it on a charge in the kitchen."

An hour later Jeannie and I were ensconced in South Lodge. The delightfully gay Derek Naisby kindly rigged a camp bed in the attic and brought us a tiny two bar electric fire… and he even climbed on a table and spread a sheet over the hole in the roof. I thanked him and he gave me a kiss.

Jeannie thanked him and he shook her hand, and I asked him to phone the agent and say we had a very bad cold and so we wouldn't be working tonight.

Then we went to bed for two days.

and Worse,…
a Stalag in Moss-side

My Manager Doris Boagey rang to tell me she'd fixed me a week with the Bunny Lewis office in Manchester. Bunny Lewis was an outrageous transvestite. He was also an outrageously funny Comedian, when outrageous Comedians were being ostracised by every censor and homophobe the length and breadth of the country.

Bunny was in fact one of a group of Mancunian Comics who had shocked their way into the hearts of almost everyone in the city limits and beyond. His co-conspirators were Jackie Carlton, Nick London, Johnny Goon Tweed, Pancho Villa and the outrageously outrageous, Al Showman.

There was the time when the Group were dragged before the court for allegedly performing a lewd Show. So many punters turned up for the trial that Bunny later said that if they'd have done his bidding and sold tickets for the trial they'd have broken all judicial box office records. As Lewis stood in the dock, the counsel for the prosecution asked him what his occupation was.

"Drag Act" cooed the Comedian.

"Huh, er, um "spluttered the Judge, scratching his wig, "What did he say?"

Counsel turned to the Judge. "He said he's a Drag Act, m'lud."

"Drag Act? DRAG ACT???? What in heavens name is a drag act?" His worship puffed.

"I believe m'lud, a drag Act is a man who performs in female clothes."

"Female clothes?" gasped his Worship.

"Yes m'lud" sighed counsel. "He works in wigs and gowns."

Bunny, never one to miss a cue turned to the Judge, then to the Counsel benches, and brought the house down with, "And who are you girls working for?"

I called at his office home, met him for the first time, resisted his advances, and was delighted when he said he had great digs for me.

"Have you ever been to Manchester before, Darling?" he purred, stroking my hair.

"No" I replied.

"Oh, well, you'll love Moss-side.... it's the heartland of Manchester and you'll love the landlady. She's a German bird... blonde with big tits. She'll love you too. It's the best cock lodge in the country." he cooed.

He scribbled the name and address of the digs and I caught a taxi to Moss Side, bent on starting the week with a bang.

The taxi driver sensing that I was a 'foreigner' decided to take the scenic route.

We passed the Moss-Side Bowling, Yachting and Country Club. Then we dropped into the local hostelry, "The Flying Bottle" for lunch. It was a quaint Olde Worlde Tavern. I asked the landlord why there was so much sawdust on the floor and he replied, "That was furniture before last night's fight."

Nearing our destination the driver put out his right hand to turn a corner and someone stole his watch.

When I alighted from the taxi, I noticed that the driver and I were the only coloured guys in the street. There were African's, Asians, Rastafarians, Pakistani's and Indians, and a smattering of Chinese, and, I swear, an Inuit building a Kayak in his front garden." (Okay, maybe not an Inuit, but when I'm on a roll...)

I made my way up the path to the door and rang the bell.

Frau Schlessenger, the landlady, was all that Bunny Lewis had described.

She was indeed, German, and big tits, which Bunny, possibly out of jealousy had not done justice. They were massive. In fact everything about Frau Schlessenger was German. Her blonde hair was parted down the middle and done in bangs over each ear, like a Luftwaffe pilots earphones.

She'd had her face lifted so many times she had a dimple in her forehead and a Van Dyke beard. She seemed to have muscles on her eyebrows.

Below where her waistline used to be she wore a short blue skirt revealing massive thighs wrapped in rust coloured stockings and Jack Boots. Not kinky boots like most girls were wearing at the time but Jack Boots...Wermacht issue Jack Boots with the stout leather thongs to pull them on with.

"Ja?" she snarled, standing to attention, arms by her sides.

"I think I've got..."

"You iss Joachim Hemmundt, Ja?"

"Yes, no, it's Johnny but I..."

She snatched the small suitcase from my hand. "Frauline Lewis reng me to say you vuss on vay.... Com mitt, Schnell" she ordered, loudly clicking her heels a she stepped aside letting me pass, then slamming the door behind me.

"Make right."

"Pardon?"

"Make right... go into zimmer on right. Ve vill hef tea. You like tea, Ja?"

She dropped my suitcase in the hallway and passed me in the narrow passage, pushing her huge breasts into my face.

"You are handsome man. Frauline Lewis is telling me you are very fit. You not to do ze fock in here, do you hear? Bringing back fraulines iss verboten. Ja! To do ze fock hier iss verboten."

"Ja...er yes, of course, no. I don't... I'm married.... not long... actually...I..."

"Bullshiesen...." She put her ham shank hands on my shoulders and sat me at the table. "I don't believe zat you not screw while you are from home. All heren is fock at dis time." She poured tea from a large silver teapot, placing the cup before me.

"You rauchen, ja?"

"Pardon?"

"Rauchen…mitt cigarette? Smoke?"

"Yes please, thank you." My tongue was beginning to stick to the roof of my mouth.

"Vell?" she held out her hand.

"Oh" I stammered, and took out my cigarettes, and offered her one.

She opened a box of matches which were handy and removing one, lifted her ample leg and ignited the match on the sole of her jack-boot. After lighting her cigarette she removed mine, put it in her mouth and did a Lilli Marlene, shoving the weed back between my lips. As we talked I tapped the ash into the receptacle on the table.

Each time I did this, Frau Schlessenger paused in her conversation and squinted.

The fourth time I tapped the ash from my cigarette, she squinted, sighed and said in that low guttural tongue, "Entschuldegen ze bitte, but you iss tapping your feg ash in der focking sugar basin."

She suddenly leaned towards me and put her hands between my open legs. As I held my breath she grabbed the seat of my chair and pulled me rapidly towards her, then checking around her for spies she put her lips to my ear and hissed...."You vill be careful in Moss-side... Lots of people disappear around here. I am note zat you don't heff Volkswagen... unt I must tell you zat you vill not get texi-cab after nine o'clock at night."

I said, surprised, "The taxi's don't run after nine o'clock at night?"

She furtively checked again for eavesdroppers and whispered, "They daren't run efter nine o'clock at night."

I was terrified as I said; "Well, how long will it take me to walk from the Del Sol club back to here?"

She shrugged nonchalantly, raised a bushy Rudolf Hess eyebrow and said solemnly "I don't know... nobody he's ever made it."

Then she lifted her leg, placed her boot to my crotch and slid my chair back to its original position.

Emitting an agitated sigh, she went on; "Und der is people who vill rob you.

Today, I am at Indian market. I see man is selling cigarette lighters, '24 cigarette lighters for £2'. Vell, I am alvays losing mine cigarette lighters…. Show business people is thieving schwein…. so I give this Indian man £2 and ask him for ze 24 cigarette lighters und….und… he gives me a box of matches. I say ver is mine cigarette lighters?"

He points to box matches. "Der dey are".

"I say. 'Dese are matches.'"

He says, "Vat are you vanting them for?"

"I say "To light mien fucking cigarettes....

The man shrugged, 'SO?".

"Indians iss robbing bastards…. Dey iss coming hier into our country und the first thing zey do is to be rob us…"

Suddenly leaping to attention she ordered, "com mitt… schnell… rouse rouse"…and grabbing my case she goose stepped out of the room and up the stairs to a huge bedroom in which there were six iron army camp-beds. Each bed was immaculately made up with the occupants clothing regimentally laid out.

"Der tidy zimmer makes for happy family" she said proudly.

She noted I was looking at a picture of an SS Officer on the wall above the dressing table.'

He was young blonde and handsome with a small 'hot cross bun' scar on his cheek.

"Mine Son, Fritz...nice boy...nicest boy in the wermacht... he vas given the Iron Cross by the Fuhrer...Herr Hitler himself... I sink Herr Himmler put in the word... ya? I am believe he is somewhere in Russia... I don't hear from him for a while... I got a postcard made from sole of shoe... it vos post in Stalingrad in 1944... I miss him... some night I try to imagine vot he look like now." She looked dewy eyed at the picture and gently kissed it. "Here he is 22 years aged here." She tapped the fingers on her right hand on the table..."Mien Gott... now he is 68...zo..." And she shrugged.

She led me to the bed in the corner, turned and bounced her ample arse on it causing the springs to chime like a village chapel on Christmas Eve. "Dis iss your zimmer and hier iss your bed. Maybe iss small but in time ve vill manage, huh" and she threw her head back and her laughter shook the rafters. And with a bow and a click of her heels she reversed out of the room slamming the door behind her. But even before she left I was agonising how to tunnel my escape back to Bunny Lewis's office.

All the boarders were given strict orders never to go into the kitchen after she had retired. In fact, there was a notice on the kitchen door, which read, "Achtung! Entre Verboten." Some heroic wag had scribbled skull and crossbones above the message.

As this was Pro digs, 99.9% of the boarders were Show Business people, and it so transpired that during my stay, we also had rooming with us one of the best bands of the day, the brilliant Birmingham group,'Second City Sound.' Today they'd be the biggest things around, but in those days there were more bands than solo acts.

Not only were the band brilliant, but also they were very brave. They broke every rule in Frau Schlessenger's book. The single ones would bring 'Birds' back to spend the night, playing a form of Russian roulette. They'd pass six of them around... and one of them had VD.

They also brought back fish and chips, making sure all windows were wide open and cigarettes were smoked afterwards to kill the smell. So it was that one night, one member of the band fancied some chip butties, but to make the sandwich, he needed a couple of slices of bread.

Ignoring all our pleas he blacked his face with soot, dropped on his belley and, Commando style crawled gingerely along the dark passage, groping his way through the blackness of the kitchen till he found the bread bin. Here he purloined a couple of slices and made his way back into the living room. He was just about to spread the butter when the door burst open and Hausfrau Kampkommandantshturmfuhrer Schlessenger stood silhouetted in the doorway. She was a formidable sight, in dark green canvas camouflage pyjamas held up by a thick black leather belt with a silver SS buckle, her blonde tresses flowing almost to the floor... her unfettered breasts seemed to hang to her pubic region.

She stood, legs apart, then clicking the heels of her jackboots like an Oberleutnant of the SS she screamed, "Achtung! der rules has been broken. I know that vun of you schwein hess been raiding the pantry.... the alarm vent off vile I am trying to get a sleep...stend up undt take two pace forward der guilty schwinehundt... schnell!"

Fearing for his life the culprit flicked the slice of bread away from him, and as it sailed towards the drummer, he lashed out and sent it in the direction of the bass player, who ducked letting it fly over his head towards the keyboard man, who slapped it back to land at the feet of the Kommandant.

"Right.... everybody out... schnell, schnell...rous, rous."

Minutes later twelve of us were lined up in the front garden where the landlady interrogated us for the best part of fifteen minutes.

I, like everyone else couldn't believe that we'd allowed this to happen, but like me my fellow 'deutsch gefangenen (prisoners of war) stood frozen with cold and fear
before this formidable foe. Unable to get a confession, she marched us back indoors where she informed us that, until the culprit owned up, no one, 'but no vun' will get fried bread for the next three breakfasts."
She was always proud to relate her family's military background. She said her long dead husband was an unorthodox Jew... he was in the SS. It appeared that every member of her family had fought in either the Eastern, Northern, Southern or Western front.
She didn't appreciate my humour when I said, "Your family couldn't get on with anybody, could they?"
We would crowd in the front bay window as she stood in the middle of the street screaming at the multi-coloured kids in the neighbourhood.
"You vill stop immediate mit the footbol outside mine zimmer.... vy don't you get back to your own focking country, you black schwine?"
The kids would return the vitriol. Snapping their heels together and giving the Nazi salute they would yell back in their thick Mancunian dialect. "Zieg Heil, you Teutonic twat."
But Frau Schlessenger's greatest enemy was the skeletal four feet three inch tall Irish lady who lived next door. They had feuded from the first day they met. Every Sunday they would bawl at each other over the back garden fence, while the immediate populace would bring chairs and settees into their gardens to watch, yelling encouragement to each contestant.
"Get out from our country.... go back to Irelundt you IRA whore." Frau Schlessenger hollered.
"Piss off, you Nazi cowbag" Mrs Bridget Finnerty would screech, and to get a little leverage into her ire, she'd stand on her tippy toes and hang by her substantial hawklike talons to the top of the five foot garden fence.
Hostilities came to an end one freezing winters day when, in the middle of a particularly heavy verbal panzer barrage, Frau Schlessenger thundered up the three flights of stairs to the attic bathroom where she kept the tub topped up with water in case of a fire.
As the little Fenian battler clung to the fence hurling Celtic abuse, the massive Teuton smashed the thick layer of ice with her fist, scooped up a huge bucket full of water, and standing on the fire escape directly above the old lady, tipped the frozen contents over her. The effect was instantaneous.
"Whoy don't ye get back to your feck . . ."
'Whoosh!'
We all heared the sharp intake of breath from fifty yards. Suddenly the little old lady stiffened and dentures clattering like a pair of castanets she began to vibrate like a four feet three inch tuning fork, then leaving her talons embedded in the fence she fell slowly backwards, her skeletal body making a soft plop as it hit the snow covered lawn..
She was collected by her large son, Paedre who bent down and gripping his mother by the ankles raised her to waist level and bore her at an angle of 45 degrees into the kitchen where he held her in that position in front of the roaring fire till she melted.
The following day the widow Finnerty erected a 'For Sale' notice in her front garden and within days she and Paedre had sailed from Liverpool to the Emerald Isle.
My last Gig of the run for the Bunny Lewis Agency was at the infamous 'Del sol' Club standing like a deserted fortress on a derelict bombsite on the edge of Moss-side.
I arrived at the Club at 9.pm. The Agent had informed me that I didn't need to get there till nine because they were having a sportsmen's evening.
Actually the correct terminology was 'A Boxing Writers Dinner'.
I knocked on the heavy cast iron door.
A small hatch opened and a gargoil growled "Yeahwaddayawan?"

"Johnny Hammond..... Comedian." I said.

An Adams family rattling of chains and sliding of bolts preceded the opening of the door. The huge Rasta headed black man waved me in and pointed to a door at the top of a narrow staircase. As I passed him the doorman picked up a phone and announced me.

By the time I reached the top of the stairs the door opened and a small slim man in a canary yellow suit and pink ruffled shirt and a heavily made up face greeted me.

"Ah Johnny.... lovely to meet you darling.... my name is Raymond, though the boys call me Queenie..." He tilted his head to one side, causing a bell shaped ear ring to tinkle a merry little tune.

"All the boys and girls are here.... I believe you know one of them..... Randy Ralph Turner?"

I did in fact know Ralph. He was a Saxophonist and Comedian, and he hailed from my neck of the woods. Later he became one of the big names in clubland when he dyed his skin a leathery brown, grew a Zapata moustache and changed his name to Pancho Villa. He looked like a saddlebag with eyes.

"Follow me, sweet lips" cooed Raymond as he minced across the tiny Cabaret floor, past the three camp musicians who lasciviously looked me up and down. I followed Raymond into the tiny curtained off 'dressing room'. It was packed with five Comedians and six Strippers in assorted costumes from Nuns to schoolgirls.

"Boyth...

boyth and girlth" Raymond lisped, clapping hands to command attention, "Thith ith Johnny, our other Comedian... Johnny, thith ith......" and he reeled off a list of names, placing a hand on the shoulder of each individual as he named them.

I didn't hear the names, as I was too engrossed with the sight of the Strippers.

None of them would have reached the quarterfinals at Crufts. Raymond passed little chits of paper to each Comedian.

Slipping the piece of paper into my hand and squeezing it he whispered "Johnny" thith ith your girl,"

I looked at my slip, then at 'my girl' then back to the nametag 'Druchella.'

In my mind I accepted that of all the nom de plumes in the curtained off dressing room, mine certainly was a 'Druchella'. She was a Titan. Standing five feet ten in her huge bare feet, she had shoulders like an Olympic weight lifter. Her breasts made Frau Schlessenger's mammeries look counter sunk. She stood on two tree trunk legs, yet her midriff was honed into an egg timer. She had a jaw line that made Desperate Dan look effeminate, but her most redeeming feature was her pubic region. The Afro Cuban mass of thick black hair appeared to have been back combed and coiffured by some London crimper and Druchella, obviously proud of her crop had dusted it with tiny glittering Stars. She then concealed the whole mass with a multi coloured 'G' rope... (As averse to the 'G' Strings the other girls wore.)

Ralph Turner greeted me warmly and I asked him what kind of show it was.

He said it was a stag show. As I had been working the Moss Theatre circuit for so long I was obviously out of touch. I really didn't know what a Stag Show was.

"Just go out there, do a couple of 'Fuck gags', introduce your girl and get off."

"Say a couple of what?

"Do a couple of fuck gags."

"I can't do that. I can't go in front of an audience and say the 'F' word... I'm a Pro."

"Well" snarled Al Showman, shoving his face into mine. "You could go out there and do your nice act, and maybe do a bomb.... but then we'll have to follow you and maybe we won't do a bomb, and then we'll be so upset, we'll drop you out of the fucking window.... Mister Superstar."

I looked pleadingly to Ralph. He shrugged, reiterating Al's remarks.

"Look Johnny... these drunken bastards don't want to hear a funny man... they only came to see pussy.... try to be funny and they'll kill you.... and if you try too hard and you are funny, we'll kill you."

I needed time to think, but being a coward and no longer a 'Theatre front cloth man', I decided, just for tonight I'd run with the pack.

As this was a Boxing Writers Dinner the audience was purely pugilistic, from handsome new fighters to gnarled shaven headed punch-drunk old pugs, most of them with enough vegetation on either side of their heads to open a garden centre.

There were also several famous Boxing Writers, ringside Television and Radio commentators including Peter Wilson and the present British Heavyweight Champion of the day, Henry Cooper.

The show started with Raymond who sang a cheeky little song, and sat on some old pug's knee and kissed him. As he stood up to take a bow the old fighter sunk his fist into the little mans solar plexus and he had to be taken home in a taxi.

Ralph took over as Compere. He 'fucked and blinded' and abused the punters for five minutes, ducked a couple of beer glasses and introduced his girl.

She went on and did a three minute strip. Ralph went back onto the floor, took the girl off and introduced the next Comedian, Jackie Carlton who did more or less the same as Ralph but with decidedly more vitriol, then introduced his girl, who did exactly the same as the first stripper but did it as a topless-fishnet stockinged Mother Superior. Jackie then took the girl off and introduced Al Showman who walked on with a huge inflated balloon tied to his erect penis. Someone threw a stool, so Al cut short his Act and introduced his girl, who gave a repeat performance of the previous strippers, but this time as a fourteen stones, forty-seven years old schoolgirl.

By the time I went on I had vomited my undigested sauerkraut into the washbasin. I don't remember what comedy I did but I introduced my girl thus, "Now Ladies and Gentlemen, here's the next lady on the show who can boast that she is in the Guinness book of records as the only human being ever to come fourth, five years running at Crufts… the beautiful Druchella." As she passed me, my girl dug me painfully in to chest and called me a twat. I was too stressed out to bring her off Stage, so Ralph filled in for me.

My peers congratulated me warmly and suggested that I should take up stag as a new vocation. But I detected a hint of sarcasm in their remarks. During the thirty minute interval, in which time most of the audience drank themselves sober and drunk again, Druchella came into the dressing blanket and informed all and sundry that she had 'started,' and did anyone have a 'thingy.'

In all innocence I apologised and said I didn't smoke. She replied that if I hadn't been going back on stage, she'd have "knocked my sarcastic teeth down my frigging throat." One of her friends then gave her what I thought was a large cigarette, but what was in fact a new fangled sanitary aid.

I'd heard of sanitary towels of course, but in those days they were things that ladies didn't flash around. Druchella thanked her friend, saying that she owed her one, lifted her foot onto the small table, buried the 'thingy' into the star spangled forest, withdrew the cardboard shell and flicked it across the small space where it bounced off the back of Ralph Turners head and landed into the ash tray.   I was just about to applaud when I thought better of it.

On the other side of the curtain it was mayhem. Old pugilists were relating past battles they'd fought and demonstrated their favourite knock out punch on anyone within striking distance. However, not all of the audience were drunk and the sober ones were at first pleading, then demanding order... and furthermore, 'would the gentlemen please stop throwing wine glasses at the wall.'

Ralph went out to face the foe and got some semblance of order. He took this opportunity to put on his girl, who started the same ball rolling all over again. I hadn't noticed that my peers had been plying me with booze, till I started seeing three of everything.

The next forty-five minutes passed in a drunken smoke filled haze for me. I remember Al introducing me, and I remember a shaven headed flat nosed man stepping onto the floor and dancing with me.

I also vaguely remember garbling the words, "the franstaticest gorgeous tart I ever seen. Dru…Fucking..Chella".

Then I was sitting on the floor with my back to the piano. I also remember a wine glass smashing against the bass player's instrument... and yet another one hitting the wall to my left. I heard a distant plea from a dinner-jacketed man yelling for order and "please gentlemen, stop throwing glasses... someone's going to get...."

A Champagne bottle sailed through the air and a smashed into a thousand pieces.

Completely unfazed, Druchella drove them wild.

"Get them off.... off off off... let's see IT."

This was followed by a snowstorm of ten-shilling notes and a fusillade of flying half crowns. Druchella looked over to Al Showman, who had taken over the mantel as Compere while Ralph grunted in a dark corner with the second stripper sitting astride him.

"OK get it off" ordered Al.

Druchella obliged, first getting some old boxer to untie the silken strings holding the G-string together. The band struck up for the umpteenth time with 'The Stripper'.

In the audience the Good sat transfixed, the Bad went berserk flinging wine glasses at the chandelier while the Ugly continued hitting each other.

The room seemed to throb as the lady revealed her pubic star-studded thatch.

"More... more...more..." yelled the sex crazed mob.

Druchella went into overdrive, sliding the 'G' string slowly, tantalisingly up and down between her ample thighs finally withdrawing it all the way. As the crowd roared she began to swing the G-string round and around above her head. Several more wine glasses exploded against the four walls. At the front table, two gentlemen sat staring unbelievably at the spectacle unfolding before them, then one of them clapped his hand to his face, removed it, stared at the streak of blood, and turned horror stricken to his friend, who recoiled, leaped to his feet and screamed, ***"stop the show, Harry's been slashed."***

But no one heard or cared as the Druchella walked around the throng, swishing the silken cord, (and the Tampax,) round and around in ever increasing circles, writing a perfect 'Z' on the ceiling with the dexterity of a latter day Zorro.

It took thirty years and near starvation to get me back on the Stag circuit again.

If I can make it there I'll make it anywhere!

'Resting' is a phrase used by thespians of the legitimate theatre. It means an act is out of work at present.   Most artistes in the legitimate theatre spend more time resting than they do working.

There's a story about a character actor who had been resting for years. Couldn't even get a one-on part anywhere, despite a daily, weekly, monthly and yearly round of agent's offices, auditions and job centres.

A sympathetic friend suggested he should seek alternative employment... maybe take a job as a traffic warden. "What, are you mad? Me... give up Show Business?" cried the Pro, clasping a clenched fist to the forehead.... "Never!"

Club acts don't have that problem. There are so many clubs the length and breadth of the country that all one needs is a trusty car, a national road map and the ability to take anything that's thrown at them... so long as it's connected with show business

During a bad recession in the sixties when, thanks to industrial strikes, clubs were having a lean time I took a job for three weeks as a compere at the Fiesta Cabaret Club in Tees-side. It was a venue I had previously worked as chief support to some of the hyper showbiz names, British and American.

Conceding that one has to put bread and butter on the table and clothe his kids, I swallowed my pride and accepted the lowly position and a vast cut in wages.

Fortunately for me the club was just seven miles from my front door in Hartlepool.

I made my way to the club for the show's band call on a Sunday afternoon, around five o'clock.

As I swung into the car park, a Benny Hill look-alike attendant leapt from his stool by the gate and standing directly in my path, arms akimbo he flagged me down. It was a sweltering humid day, but he was kitted out in the uniform of all car park attendants...yellow plastic peaked cap, John Lennon glasses, fluorescent ankle length plastic raincoat and Wellington boots, and dangling from a piece of string around his neck was his whistle.   I lowered the window and explained that I was the new compere reporting for duty.

"Park over there by the wall." He said, pointing to the far side of the car park.

"No" I replied. "I'm the compere.... I'm on the show.... I'm one of the turns... I need to park over there by the stage door."

"No you don't, mister."   He said still in front of the car but now with his hands on both hips and his right foot resting on the front bumper.   I dropped the car into reverse, revved the engine and let out the clutch.   The man fell to his knees. I dropped her into first and zoomed round him, and skidded up to the stage door. There were already several cars parked there. I grabbed my Stage clothes and went into the club.

The star of the show was a fiesty young singer who was hurtling up the ladder of fame. Her name was Kylie Maxwell and she had both feet firmly placed on the penultimate rung. One small step to stardom for Kylie.... But for this week at least 'Several near crashes into ignominy.' Her support was an excellent South African Piano playing comedian called Ray DeCosta.

He was the kind of competition mega stars avoided like the plague. So brilliant was this multi talented artiste that only Icons like Sinatra, Perry Como, Tony Bennett and Matt Munro could afford the gamble.

Inside, I made my way to the staff dressing room, hung my stage suit on the hanger in my wardrobe, checked the schedule and making my way to the Stars Dressing Room, I tapped on the door.

After a minute the door opened and a small man in a badly fitting wig and blue blazer glowered.

"Yes, what is it?" he asked.

"Er, hello. I'm Johnny Hammond.... the Compere... I just thought I'd introduce myself to Miss Maxwell."

"Very well" said the little man, "thank you." and closed the door in my face.

I felt that I knew him. Then it struck me. He'd been one of the county's top band leaders during and immediately after the War. He was George Nelson.. Lately, he'd become the manager of the aforementioned beautiful Kylie Maxwell, and had steered her to the dizzy heights of stardom. However, in his band leading days he was known to all and sundry as an arrogant, conceited and rude asshole. When he took on the manager's mantel, his reputation preceded him. He was still an arrogant, conceited, rude asshole. He stood around five feet seven and walked like a sawn off

John Wayne. His toupee was brilliantined to a patent leather shine. He wore a thin pencil moustache and his voice was a rasping croak. He insisted on being addressed by all and sundry as MISTER Nelson...... although his first preference was 'Sir'.

Suddenly the door opened and he demanded,

"You still here?"

For the first time in my life I was stuck for an answer.

"Is the Manager in yet?" he snapped   "tell him I want to see him.....NOW".

An apparition appeared behind him in the doorway. The smile she gave me saved her mentor's life.

"Is it Johnny, did I hear you say?" then to her Manager, "George, move aside and let Mr er.. come on in Johnny."

I almost trampled the runt underfoot. I took the proffered seat as Miss Maxwell lifted the intercom from the wall,

"Is this thing working?" Her voice trilled like Disney's 'Snow White'.

"It is, but there's only the house-band and us here at present."

I noted that my voice had dropped a full octave and I had taken on an Anglo American drawl. Before I could settle in my chair, Bobby cooed; "Johnny, I wonder if you'd give a call to my MD (Musical director). He's next door, Tell him, if you would, I'd like to see him."

I suddenly realised I was in love with her. I backed out of her presence, bowing, closed the door gently, went along the corridor and tapped on the MD's door. It was slightly ajar, and silently swung open at my knock.

A fat bald man in his vest and underpants stood with his back to me. Through the mirror I could see he was injecting his arm with a hypodermic needle. I was just going to back away when he looked in the mirror and saw me. He whipped the needle out of his arm and dropped the syringe into his dressing table drawer. We looked at each other for a long minute then he stammered...

"It's medical.." he said in a beautifully cultured voice. "I'm er.... come in, come in."

'Maybe he's diabetic'. I thought. "Er, I'm, er, I'm Johnny Hammond. I'm the Compere... I was just in Miss Maxwell... I mean I was just, Miss Maxwell asked me to ask would you go see her as soon as you finish sticking...as soon as you put your needles. I mean your trousers, trousers on"

Then I offered him my hand.

The man took my arm, pulled me to him, put his lips to my ear and said in a hushed voice,

"Is that little twat with her?"

"Yes." I replied, then "do you mean, Mr Nelson?"

"Mister Asshole... that's who I mean.... watch him.... he's a little cunt.... he'll have you out of work for just looking at her... ah yes, he'll be in there... little bastard...... I haven't been too good lately, Paddy.... you are Irish?"...and without waiting for a reply he went on. "...that's why I.....you know..." and he nodded towards the drawer.....

"It's just between us... Ok Paddy? Just go back and tell her I'll be there in a minute.... and stand on that little bastard's foot, do that and you and I will be friends. Good fellow."

I backed out into the corridor just as a tall, sharply dressed young man came in through the stage door. He was carrying a couple of leather suit bags and an expensive leather briefcase.

"Hi" he said..... "You on the Show?   I'm Ray DeCosta, who the fuck is that out there? The man is certifiable..... I had to park right at the back of the car park....guys a fucking nut.... you're not the boss, uh?"

"No, I'm the Compere" I offered my hand.

Ray DeCosta dropped his briefcase and gave me one of those handshakes, which immediately bond you to a man.

"I've got to see the boss man about that fucking psycho out there...is he like that every performance.... if he tries that on tomorrow night I'll run over the crazy bastard and that's the truth, ... I don't suppose there's any chance of a gargle,... er... what did you say your name was?"

"Johnny."

"Shit, I'm sorry about that, but that prick.... man, he's something else."

DeCosta had an international brogue. A basso South African with a tinge of Australian, leaning heavily on an American dialect.

"I think you'll find drinks in your room." I said.

It was courtesy of the house to furnish all the dressing rooms with bouquets of flowers and several bottles of hooch, soft drinks and expensive chocolates.

As Ray opened the door and entered the dressing room he stopped it closing with his foot and gave me a hiss...

"Hey Johnny, have you met her yet?"

"Kylie, yes, I just...."

"Is he with her?"

"Who, Mr Nelson?"

"Yeah you've met him...." It was a statement. He changed the subject

"What about band call?" .

"Anytime you're ready," I said.

He picked up a bottle of Scotch."Wanna slug?"

"Thanks, not yet, thanks" I said... "maybe after the Show."

"Ah, forget that," he laughed. "Do me a favour sport; don't come in after the show... know what I mean?"

I didn't but I figured maybe he may be entertaining in private.

"OK!" I said, "I'll go see the band... anytime you're ready.

I made my way onto the cabaret floor. Joe Boston was one of the top keyboard men in the North East...before and since. When Ray and I went into the cabaret room the trio was having a swing session. The musicians and I were old friends. We exchanged pleasantries; I introduced Ray and then went back to my dressing room and curled up for a couple of hours. I started the show proper at eight thirty, made everybody welcome, passed out a few bouquets and sang a few birthday requests.

Sunday, nine o'clock Ray DeCosta went on and tore the roof in. After one hour and fifteen minutes the boss man came down and asked me to rearrange the schedule. After DeCosta finally left the floor amid wild applause I looked into the wings and a furious George Nelson demanded to know why Ray had been allowed to milk this, Bobby's audience. I replied that this was the way it worked in the sticks.

10.55.. Kylie's small fat MD made his way across the darkened stage to the mini

185

white piano, centre floor. He spread the star's music on the piano and took his seat.
Backstage, Mr Nelson told me, at the last minute to make sure that both he and Bobby had their own spotlights.
I grabbed the house phone, called the lighting console and relayed his request.
11. O'clock. 'Lights... Music.... Curtains'
"Ladies and gentlemen," I drawled in my best pseudo American accent,
"The Management proudly welcome you to the beautiful Fiesta, the county's finest Night Club...you've already had a sample of the calibre of Entertainers presented at the Fiesta and now it's Star Cabaret time (Drums roll)...."Ladies and Gentlemen..... Miss Kylie... Maxwellllll."
A pin spot cupped the beautiful face as she slinked to the front microphone.
The music throbbed.
"Tonight, tonight, won't be just any night, tonight there will be..."
CRASH!
The sound was deafening. The voice faltered then carried on...."er,no morning star.."
A commotion behind the beautiful apparition caused her to turn. The fat accompanist was on his feet, ranting and throwing sheets of music over his head.
Miss Maxwell half turned and swayed in disbelief.
"That's it!" the accompanist cried. "That is it... I don't wish to know...it' not you, Darling girl." He pointed a finger at the trembling girl, then slowly, he brought the finger round and aimed it at the small man, standing in his own spotlight, resplendent on white tie and tails, and the baton frozen in mid air... "I don't want to know you, you insignificant little bastard."
With that he kicked the Piano stool aside and disappeared into the wings. At this moment I was in my dressing room having just removed my bow tie. I heard the interruption over the intercom, and at first thought it was a radio taxi that had come in on our wavelength. Then I heard another crash as the MD slammed the stage door behind him as he vanished into the night... but not before I heard his voice in the car park yell," Get out my way, you fucking gargoyle."
I dashed out of my dressing room just in time to see George Nelson and a couple of stage hands escorting the prostrate Star back into her dressing room.
Then the Manager grabbed my by the arm and told me to 'get out there and calm them down.'
Clipping on my bow-tie I rushed into the wings, and was brought to a halt by the voice of Ray DeCosta. He was sitting at the piano, joking into the microphone that all
was well 'the poor old guy just had a bit of a brainstorm... it happens to the best of us.....' etc. In seconds he had the audience eating out of his hand.
On Monday Miss Maxwell informed the management of the club that she was too ill to perform that night. However, the management informed Mister Nelson that if the star didn't turn out for that night's show she would be sued. After a hasty conference the star and her manager relented and being the professional she is, did the Monday night show, and wowed her audience.
6.00 p.m. Tuesday I pulled into the car park, steered round the car park attendant and raced to the Stage door with him in hot pursuit, slamming the door behind me and almost removing his fingers. I was learning.
I tapped on the Star's door, and shouted my congratulations for her previous showing.
"Thank you darling," she called back through the closed portal.
I felt faint with passion. I tapped on Ray DeCosta's door, but he wasn't in yet. I went out onto the Stage and was greeted by Joe Boston, who had taken over for the rest of the Show as Miss Maxwell's MD.
But the show once again was a sell-out hit.

Wednesday I made it to stage door before the car park attendant made it out of his sentry box. Once again I tended my congratulations through Kylie's door and received a grateful 'thank you darling' back.

I went onto the floor and was met halfway by Joe Boston. He looked worried, and taking me by the arm he said, "Johnny, Les (the Drummer) had a problem with a wisdom tooth and can't make it, BUT..... (Before I had a chance to faint) I've got a dep (deputy) Drummer. He's great... I mean GREAT...... BUT...er..that's him."

He pointed towards the rostrum.

Behind Les's huge Drum Kit was a guy who resembled something from the Muppet Show. He sported a huge red Afro hairstyle decorated with little flowers and tiny jingling bells and a full beard. He wore a dark blue John Lennon glasses, a multi coloured caftan, adorned with rows of beads, gold chains and trinkets, and an Indian belt with a massive silver buckle.

His jeans were shabby and torn at the knees and on his feet he wore 'Jesus' sandals.

Joe explained, that the man had recently returned from backing Ray Charles in LA and afterwards moved to San Francisco, where he had spent a couple of years in a Hippy commune of Flower children, and despite his appearance, this guy was a darling and the best drummer he'd ever had the dubious pleasure of working with.

Joe introduced us. His name was ZAK, and when I offered my hand in friendship, he slapped it black and blue, then put his bony arms round me, dragged me to him in a bear hug and kissed me on the forehead. When he stepped back he held up two fingers in a reverse 'V' sign and said; "Peace little brother".

I was flattered and greatly amused. His entire vocabulary was, 'Man', ' hey', 'yo', 'mother fucker', 'chill out', 'baby', 'cool' and 'wicked, man'. He had a small pouch tied round his neck with a leather thong, which held the elixir of life.....his 'shit'. Some of his 'shit' he smoked, some he snorted up his nose through a rolled up banknote, and some he injected into his multi coloured arm with a syringe similar to the one used by Miss Maxwell's recently departed MD. Joe's concern was that Mr Nelson would not wish his Star to be seen on the same planet, let alone the same show as Zak.

We agreed that if we arranged with the house electrician to brighten the lights on the Star and her mentor, and dim the spots on the band, maybe Nelson would be too occupied with his own image to notice the Musicians. It was a long shot, as Mr Nelson insisted on conducting the three piece Band with a Maestro's baton.

However, Drummers of Zak's calibre were thin on the ground, and Miss Maxwell deserved only the best. We decided to keep shtum.

Tuesday 9.pm. In front of a full capacity house that were all fans of Kylie Maxwell, Ray DeCosta excelled himself. Not only did he wow them but he switched his Act midstream, centring it around 'this swinging cat on traps'. Ray enthused so much about Zak's talent; "This is the greatest Drummer I ever saw in my life, ladies and gentlemen," that he had the audience stand and applaud the Percussionist's virtuosity.

Kylie Maxwell went on at 11 o'clock and just stood before her adoring fans and milked them for all she was worth...... and this was before she'd sung a note. When she did sing, her trained ear told her that there was something different here ...... some added ingredient that brought out a quality in her work that even she didn't know existed. She didn't know what it was, but it came from behind and made the soft down on her neck rise.

"Tonight, tonight, won't be just any night, tonight there will be no morning star......"

The beat of the music was intense and she felt an exciting tingle in her spine.

"Tonight, tonight I'll see my love to... "

Suddenly the vibrancy left the music. Suddenly the sound was thin...Suddenly there was a crash of Drums and Cymbals that were out of sync with the bass and keyboard.

"Whoa." A Low Mainched growl broke the magical spell.

"Whoa, man.... what the fuck's going down here man... I can't take this shit man.... the Chick doan' need this shit.... she's cool... she's cool.... (to Kylie) your'e wicked baby, y'know… like wild, man...... so what's with the prick with the stick..... Yeah man, you man... split... like don't you read me….I said split mother fucker."

Zak was aiming his venom at the small bewigged man in the white tie and tails waving 'that goddam stick' at him. There was pandemonium. Kylie collapsed in a heap. George Nelson ran in an arc, first to his client, then AT the man now standing tall on his Drums stool. They started fencing with their respective weapons... Nelson with his baton, Zak with a large knobbed tympani stick. The audience sat in stunned silence. Two stagehands dashed on and scooped up the fallen Star. Another two grabbed the foaming conductor, dragging him, kicking and screaming from the Stage. As he vanished into the wings, a beaming Ray DeCosta appeared Stage left and almost dived onto the piano, and within seconds he and Zak had the audience leaping about like a tribe of Comanche during a drought.

Thursday's Show was cancelled because of unforeseen circumstances.

Friday morning the Clubs solicitors called on Miss Maxwell and her Manager and gave a solemn promise that there would never again be a repetition of last nights fiasco...... and what's more, the Club would pay for the Star's non appearances on both the Monday and Thursday nights.

FRIDAY. 11.p.m. 'Tonight, tonight, won't be just any night.'

WHOOSH!!!!!

Miss Maxwell exceeded her wildest expectations. Even Ray DeCosta stood in the wings and applauded her. She proved that she was every inch the icon her legion of fans sworn allegiance to. They wouldn't let her go. She was showered with rose petals and toasted in the best champagne. The penultimate performance turned out to be the greatest of her career. None deserved it more than she. A Star was re-born.

SATURDAY.

Around noon the morning sun slipped behind a cloud and in minutes the sky turned an ominous grey/black. Minutes later the skies opened and we had the worst rainstorm in the North East in living memory. I made my way to the Club with great difficulty. The windscreen wipers strained to keep the lashing rain at bay. The road to Tees-side was littered with cars that didn't make it.

I pulled into the car park around about six o'clock and my headlights picked out the hazy figure of the car park attendant.

He was a sorry sight. The heavy rain bounced of his yellow plastic cap and the shoulders of his ankle length raincoat. He held his open arms high in the air, and I shuddered as I imagined torrents of rain gushing down his sleeves and swishing round his armpits. He toot tooted on his whistle but the lashing rain had waterlogged the instrument so that every time he blew, little jets of water shot up his nose.

As he was just a foot into the car-park I couldn't get round him. He swept his arm in a Shakespearian arc, directing me to the far left side of the car park. I flashed my lights, blew the horn and indicated that I wanted to get to the Stage door. With his left hand held palm first at me, his right hand swept round in a full circle, the right forefinger aimed at the far corner of the park.

I flashed my lights again, cursing him. He came to my side of the car and banged on the window.

I wiped the mist from the inside of the glass and yelled that it was me...... 'the Compere.... I want to get to the Stage door.'

"Eh?" he shouted back above the crash of thunder.

I lowered the window a fraction of an inch. He put his face to the glass.

"I'm the Compere" I almost pleaded. "I'm with the Show..... for GOD's sake, you've seen me all week... don't you recog......"

"Over there, in a straight line."   He dropped on one knee and aimed like a bowman is the chosen direction. Water spilled from his pockets and rain bounced of the peak of his cap and flicked across my face. He 'toot tooted' again, stepped back a fraction and sneezed. I grabbed the opportunity with both hands, threw the car into first gear, dropped out the clutch and lurched forward. There was a bump-bump, followed by a scream. I ignored his cries and for the last time raced for the sanctuary of the Stage door.

Through the rear view mirror I saw him take off after me, then turn as fresh lights appeared in the gateway. I opened my door, unfolded my umbrella and dashed into the dry sanctuary of the Club.

Ray Maxwell was standing in the corridor fumbling with his key.

"Hi, Johnny" he smiled. "Did you have any trouble with Benny Hill out there?"   And before I could answer.... " I feel sorry for the poor crazy bastard..... Shit man, what makes anybody take a Godforsaken job like that.... I mean, they don't print the kind of money I'd need to take on something like that....... poor bastard....... do you know, I'm sure I ran over his feet."

"Me too" I said, guilt ridden.

Ray said he'd drop the poor guy something for his pains and disappeared into his room and closed the door. I tapped on Miss Maxwell's door. I was surprised that she opened it herself. "Good evening, Kylie" I smiled.... "You were magnificent last night.... I mean, you've been great every night, considering... but last night..."

There was the flushing of a toilet, and then George Nelson appeared behind her in his underpants.

"Oh, for Petes sake, shut the bloody door, darling" he growled.

"Thank you Johnny, see you later." Kylie smiled fluttering her long curly lashes.

"Break a leg, this is your crowd.... they've come through hell and high water......"   I said, my heart aching just at the sight of this beautiful apparition."

She smiled again....

"Thank you Johnny," and closed the door. I checked the Band. It was the original line up. Great. I went to my Dressing Room, towelled my wet hair, poured a large Scotch into a tumbler, switched the television on and cursed as the picture suddenly

flickered and died as a particularly heavy crash of lightning lit the sky. Another stiff scotch and I checked the time. Eight fifteen. I dressed into my Stage suit, checked the bouquets and bowers of fragrant flowers. Most of them were from assorted fan Clubs stretching from Devon to Aberdeen and East to West.

Each card swore the sender's undying love and devotion to the adorable Kylie Maxwell. Tonight Ray DeCosta worked harder for his audience than at any other time during this catastrophic week. The people warmed to him, but they had come to pay homage to the Star... and the warmth afforded the brilliant Ray DeCosta was more of respect and admiration than adoration.

The fact that a lot of these people had travelled long distances, had queued in one of the worst rainstorms to hit the area in eons, and were now sitting in uncomfortable soggy clothes, their expensive hair do's wrecked, was proof of the influence this great Star had on her adoring disciples. For almost two hours the Diva before them fought against fatigue and the staccato ear shattering hailstorm that from time threatened to demolish the building.

Time after time her great talent brought them to their feet, screaming encore after encore till their fatigue was as burdening as hers. The heavy atmosphere of humidity, drink and ecstasy hung like an opium cloud around the room.

At last Kylie had to take a final bow. The Stage was littered with every variety of flowers, men and women alike stretched out to touch their heroine.

One man at ringside, drunk with wine and passion reached down and removed the Singers silver slipper, filled it with expensive champagne and tried to drink the nectar, not realising that the shoe was toeless, and he reeled as the liquid poured down the front of his tuxedo. A wave. A bow. An adoring word, a kiss, and she was gone, but yet she was again brought back for 'just one more time'.

"Ladies and gentlemen......... no..... friends...dearest darling friends.... you may have read in the papers of some of the horrendous things that have befallen me during my week at this beautiful Club... It has been at times a nightmare, but you, my dear darling fans have turned that nightmare into the most unbelievable dream of my career..."

She milked them dry

"Sing it again......" they pleaded..... A thousand voices speaking as one.... "Sing it again...... Sing 'The Song'

As the Band struck up and arpeggio, the room fell silent, broken only by the spontaneous crash of lightening and the ominous rumble of thunder. There was an eerie silence, broken occasionally by a heart-rending sob from the darkness.

An arpeggio.... A tinkle of fairy bells. "With a song in my heart… I behold you adorable face, Just a song at the…

There was a thunderous crash.... not from the sky, but from the wings, as the Stage emergency door burst open and the rain saturated car park attendant strode, like the Beast from a Thousand Fathoms a river of water trailing behind him to the centre of the Stage. There was a horrified intake of breath from the auditorium. Bobby's voice trailed to a silent whisper, followed immediately by the drone of the music as it died like a set of punctured bagpipes. She looked, not at the interloper, but straight into the well of the room, an expression of Deja Vu darkening her beautiful tear stained face.

The car park attendant took his yellow plastic cap from his head, raised it high in the air and flung it with a loud splat at the fallen idols feet.

"That does it," he screamed in a maniacal falsetto. "That fuckin' does it. I'm standing out there since five o' fucking clock without a bite to eat or a drink across me lips.... wavin' and shoutin' and tooting this useless fuckin' whistle, (beep beep), water pissing down me back and up me nose.... and not one bastard taking a blind bit of notice of me.... I might as well not be there.... and you bastards, breaking your piggin' necks to come in and listen to this screaming cow for ten fuckin' hours, running over me feet with your flash cars and your charabancs, not giving a bollocks for me or nobody but your frigging selves... well, bollocks and fuck the lot of you..."

At this point two doormen dashed onto the Stage and hustled the wretch back from whence he came. Kylie had turned and glided in a trance phantom like into the arms of her mentor who locked them both in their dressing room. The owner of the club dashed backstage and tried to rescue something of what had promised to be the greatest of great nights.Grabbing me by the lapels he pleaded:"Do something.... for GOD's Sake... Dooooo something."

Looking over the owners shoulder my heart seemed to rise as I saw Ray DeCosta emerge from his dressing room... but my heart sank down to my patent leather shoes as he smiled, blew me a kiss and gave a John Wayne cavalry salute before disappearing through the Stage door. Forsaking my bow tie I dragged myself to the front of the stage and above the screams of 'Kylie.... Kylie' I pleaded for order.

"Please ladies and gentlemen" I begged.

"Boooo."

"Please, ladies and gentlemen...." I pleaded... "If we could have just one more round of applause, I'm sure we can get Kylie Maxwell to come back just one more time." And from the darkness of the balcony bar, a mocking, drunken voice yelled back;

"Screw Kylie Maxwell, bring the fuckin' car park attendant back".

True confessions.

Some of the most entertaining times I've had were spent talking to old pro's about their worst or funniest experiences. Many of them, unlike the young lady in the previous story who threatened to sue if her real name was mentioned, would rather die than admit they have ever had anything less than spectacular nights, and have never, EVER died.

These 'artistes' are, according to stars like the late Tommy Cooper and many more, "as rare as rocking horse shit."

But it was Bob Monkhouse who said "Anybody who hasn't died in this business hasn't lived. I'm not calling them liars… I just think they're strangers to the truth.

Cilla Black loves to tell the story of when she was appearing in Pantomime in her home town of Liverpool. "It was a matinee" said Cilla "and full of little scousers".

Plagued by the antics of the 'wicked witch' I called for help from the audience. "How can I ever get rid of the wicked witch?" I pleaded? There was a short pause, then a six year old piped up from the 'Gods' 'Sing her a song Cilla!'

But then Cilla Black, like all of the aforementioned is a dyed in the wool pro.

Icons like Monkhouse, and Tommy Cooper, Morecambe and Wise, Chubby Brown and the rest were more than pleased to be included in this book…. indeed they insisted on inclusion. However, the young lady was entitled to exercise her prerogative, but I think she'd have been deemed a greater pro than even she believes she is had she joined the rest of her peers in this light-hearted wander down memory lane…. Or maybe she, like the guy who walked on water 2000 years ago really is as great as she believes. And in her favour let me say she was an exceptional quantity. No-one could fault her… she was just in the right place at the wrong time. Icons before and after her shone like

beacons at the fabulous Fiesta club. We all had our bad breaks but 99.9% of the pro's who had a lesser than great time at the establishment got back up, dusted themselves off and did it better next time. These are the ones this book is about.

The Originals

As a comedian I'm often asked the age-old question, 'where do you get all your gags from?' In most cases they come from the last successful comic whose act I just sat through. It's also been my experience that they originate from the bars of pubs and workingmen's clubs… from the ordinary working (or not) imbibers and bonafide members. 'Terry Joyce' was a fine example. Joycey was an ordinary member of the Iona club in the North East. He is now a highly sought after comedy impressionist in his own right. Incidentally he has just appeared in my good friend Mike McCarthy's latest feature film, Six Bend Trap, but like the aforementioned Terry Laffin, and hundreds like him, Terry Joyce was, and is, a natural comedian. His stories of the hard climb up the ladder of fame are paramount.

One of my favourites was witnessed recently by the Geordie funny-man.

We were watching the match between Sunderland and Newcastle on the television set above the bar. Naturally the place was crowded. Newcastle were one goal ahead and the excitement was at fever pitch and many hundreds of pounds changed hands between the rival supporters. Five minutes to go and the crowd were on their feet as their hero's battled for the cup when the bar was plunged into darkness. For several minutes there was an eerie silence and through the inky blackness all that could be seen were the floating tips of glowing cigarette ends. Then there was an explosion of noise as the cheated supporters from each camp vented their spleens by screaming abuse and throwing chairs and tables to the accompanying 'oohs and ows and grunts and groans' as the missiles found their targets.

After an age the lights suddenly and magically came back on.

As the melee subsided the eager fans turned their attention back to the dying minutes of the match. Suddenly every face froze as they stared up at the space, ten feet up on a shelf where just a few minutes previously stood the 27" illuminated tube.

Both camps stared in disbelief as all eyes focussed on a medium sized potato crisp box on which were chalked the words **"CRIME WATCH UPDATE".**

It was a Friday night some years ago when, in the early hours of the morning the sleeping steward of a Workingmen's Social club in Grangetown, Middlebrough his wife awakened.

"Bart" she whispered.

"Mm, eh, what?"

"Bart… shhh… listen… there's somebody downstairs."

They held their breaths.

Bump… scrape…. crash…. There was definitely someone downstairs. Bart knowing that cowardice was the better part of valour told his wife to follow his actions and dived under the duvet where he slept with one eye open till morning when they made a thorough investigation of the premises. They concluded that there had indeed been a break-in, and contacted the police. The posse of lawmen were thwarted by the fact that nothing was missing from the bar shelves, the cash registers, cigarette or gaming machines. A non too thorough search of the bar cellar revealed nothing was amiss… and the conclusion was the fact that all that was missing were twenty four new type plastic beer crates from the back yard of the stewards quarters.

"It was probably kids, stealing something for the blaze on bonfire night" said the plain clothes detective constable.

"Kids" said the uniformed sergeant "would not break into a club to steal beer crates". They'd climb over the wall, open the back door and carry them out that way…. They would not break into the club itself, leave a veritable goldmine of booze, cigarettes and cash from the tills and the one armed bandits at 3 o'clock in the morning. Then steal fireproof plastic beer crates for bonfire night, which, by the way was three months ago…"

The DC blanched, turned away, hunched his shoulders, sank his dentures into his knuckle and winced.

After refreshments of cold pork pies and Grolsh lager, the crime squad decided to leave the case on the 'unsolved' files, along with those on three murders and the burning down of the local fish and chip shop, for the time being and make their way back to the station.

It was at this point that the two cleaners, having finished mopping the floors, made their way onto the concert stage, and as one dusted the drums and the bingo equipment her colleague whipped the dustsheet cover from the neatly arranged twenty four fireproof plastic beer crates which now occupied the exact spot where last night had stood with pride a brand new multi keyboard two thousand five hundred pound Hammond organ.

The Incomparable Danny Duggan!

One summer in the late 1960's I received a phone call from the secretary of the Working-men's Labour social club in Eston, Middlesbrough. The caller said that they, the club, were playing host to the first paraplegic workingmen's clubs Olympic games to be held in the north east of the country. There were fifty-two invalid competitors taking on the crème de crème of the workingmen's clubs in the area. The events included a five a side football match, archery, discus and javelin throwing, weightlifting and circuit racing, plus a question and answer sports quiz.

Apart from their obvious disabilities, the paraplegic teams were honed to perfection and were to a man, fine athletes.

In contrast the teams dredged up by the Club and Institute Union were a motley run of the mill pot bellied members of the surrounding Labour, Liberal, Conservative, Dockers, Steelworkers and I.C.I clubs whose closest proximity to any team sporting event was as observers seated in groups around the clubs 'games room' large screen television on a Saturday afternoon. To a man they had volunteered just for the fun 'and the free victuals and beer' put on by the clubs 'ladies sections'.

The days events would close with a concert by local club acts, the proceeds of the ticket sales would go to the Paraplegic Society Fund.

The man on the other end of the telephone line requested that I get half a dozen acts to perform at the social buffet evening, GRATIS.

As entertainers are always the first to give their services free to any and every charity event I didn't have too much trouble making up a well balanced show. I got Larry Mason, who was a star turn on Tyne Tees Television. I also acquired the services of Mabel Bew, Jackie Barton, and the hilarious Terry Laffin. Tees-side's favourite comedians Sep Jones and Timmy Taylor and the top comedy duo of the day, Durkin and James also volunteered their services. The Joe Boston Trio from the fabulous Fiesta Club would be the backing band. The only dark cloud on the horizon was the choice of Master of Ceremonies for the evening, Danny Duggan.

Danny was a slob. Not just the ordinary, run of the mill slob.

When Danny Duggan was elected 'chief slob of the North' they threw the mould away. Duggan was the ultimate slob. He had all the qualifications. He was ignorant, inarticulate, a pig among pigs and an undesirable moron. Somehow, and it's still a mystery even today, 55 years after the event, he was given the position of compere for the evening.

The games started at one o'clock in the afternoon and by two o'clock the paraplegics won every single event of the competition. They whitewashed the local five a side football team. In the archery they missed, by one meagre point the record for the event in the paraplegic Guinness book of Records. The weightlifting was also a whitewash when the event was cancelled when two club contenders were taken to the local hospital in the same ambulance, one with a trapped nerve and the other with a triple hernia. The local discus throwers were disqualified for replacing their disc with a silver plated saucer from the kitchen. The Javelin throwing event went to the Paraplegics with a score of 98 to two... and the watchers even argued about the award to the Workers...and it was awarded to them because one of the competing team suffered a punctured tyre thanks to a badly aimed shot from Dickey Waterford, the octogenarian doorkeeper of Redcar Pensioners team.

The circuit racing was called off because the locals had been training for the beer drinking championship since dawn in the clubs bar and could not stand let alone run.

But in all the day was voted a good natured event and a huge success. All the three hundred tickets were sold out at 5 shillings a head and the lady volunteers buffet meal swelled the coffers even further.

The variety show started at 8 o'clock when Danny Duggan stepped through the curtains attired in black dinner jacket, jeans, ginger coloured sand shoes and a Norman Wisdom cap. He eyed the seven rows of competitor's wheelchairs and stunned everyone into silence with his opening remark; "Christ man, it's like the frigging starting grid at Brands Hatch down here." This was followed by embarrassed coughing when he announced that the day had realised "a gross take of a hundred and thirty quid".... but when the cost of the grub and drinks for the organisers is took out the poor unfortunate people in their buggies might as well have

stayed at home." At this point the double act of Durkin & James stepped forward and whispered in Duggan's ear that he was now living on borrowed time and maybe he meant that the proceeds had come to over seven hundred pounds and a cheque of that figure would be presently presented to the guests. Duggan regained his composure (and his future good health) by stating that he was only kidding and the money was in the safe ready to be collected at the end of the evening. However, his every announcement was aimed at 'these poor unfortunate buggers in them wheelchairs wot needs all the help we can give 'em.' He then introduced the "first turn... what can't be up to much cos he's working for nowt tonight... ha ha. Only kidding, kiddo!" There was an icy silence, interspersed with the customary coughs and harrumphs and threatening growls from the back of the hall. When he introduced Sep Jones. The old comic, on passing Duggan on the stage cast aspersions on his birthright, and the dubious occupation of his mother and sisters'.

Back in the dressing room we suggested to Duggan that it may be better if each artiste introduced each other. Duggan lodged an objection but relented when Terry Laffin suggested we should throw 'the scruffy bastard out of the window'.

From then on the mood and atmosphere rose by a mile and stayed on that plane till the finale in the early hours of the following morning.

Duggan was however allowed to make the closing address with the dire warning that this could be his last night on earth, and even at best he may next year be appearing as a member of the competition. We even prompted his every word... and he stuck to it like a seasoned pro... till, after presenting the cheque for 'Seven hundred and forty seven pounds, seventeen shillings and three pence' he let the side and himself down, sealing his fate by announcing; "Thank you, thank you all.. each and everyone of you'se has been a credit to me... and now, just before we ask you all to stand for the National Anthem... apart from the poor buggers what can't stand, I think we should have a few words *FROM THE HEAD CRIPPLE.*"

Then there was Ernie
I had an S.O.S call from a club in Blackpool asking if I was working that very night. I said I was not and the voice at the other end of the phone almost begged me to stand in for to-nights comedian who had shied off and sent a 'sick note' to prove he was not capable of fulfilling his obligation. We agreed a fee and I threw my stage gear into the boot of the car and headed for the gig.

I arrived at the club with seconds to spare. In the dressing room I bade good evening to the backing musicians who I knew from my many appearances at the venue, and introduced myself to a good looking young man who was connecting a battery transformer to a cable in the rear waistband of his trousers. We shook hands and he slipped into his star spangled jacket, pulled a fine cable up though the collar and inserted an earpiece into his right ear, explaining that this was a new American sound system he'd just acquired. Just then the club compere entered the room. He greeted me then, looking at the contraption in the young man's ear he leaned forward and screamed... *'ARE YOU READY THEN LAD?'*

The 'lad' controlling the urge to punch the official, said he was and the MC went out and seated himself in his control box on the side of the stage. He started the night's proceedings thus; "Good evening I said good evening ladies and gentlemen.... We 'ave a grand I say we 'ave a grand show for you tonight... a slight change in't programme of course but these things seeee, I say these things 'appen... apen they do out on our control... but first turn on't show tonight is a young fella... oh by the way, Florrie McCallister, I say, is Florrie.. oh there you are Florrie.. well, its Florrie McCallisters eighty seventh.... I say, it's her ninety seventh birthday tonight and it couldn't 'appen to a grander... I say it couldn't 'appen to a grander lass.. so lets all wish Florrie many..I say many 'appy returns.... I say, see theee Syd, give us a touch of 'appy birthday to the lovely Florrie McCallister.."

Syd on the organ struck up and three people at Florrie McCallisters table, all older than their guest struggled through the first couple of lines of 'appy birthday' to the skeletal little crow hunched up in her wheelchair. Ms McCallister obviously had been kept in the dark about her birthday because she joined in the singing to herself and even afforded herself a rousing round of applause.

Minutes later the young guitar vocalist was 'on'. He wasn't received well by the sparse crowd... and worse still, this time it wasn't the crowds fault. But the kid persevered and came off to moderate applause, his face as he entered the dressing room showing his disappointment, but the 'excuse' from the MC added to the young man's misery. "Now ladies and gentlemen, I think you should give that young man a round of applause, not for his singing or the way he played his banjo. I think he sounds like that cos he's wearing an 'earing aid.'

My introduction was even worse. It went like this; "Well ladies and gentlemen, its comedy time now and the turn what we have coming on now is not the turn what were booked for tonight's show and what you probably saw hanging on the board behind the doorman's desk. No, this lad is another turn, a last minute substitute... the turn what were booked for tonight has unfortunately been rushed to the infirmary with a touch of Gonorrhoea.

"Death, where is thy sting......."

I was booked to do a Saturday evening show in a Liberal workingmen's club on an overspill estate in Middlesbrough on a sticky hot summer's night some years ago.
If the graffiti scarred exterior was off putting, the interior was frightening. The door leading into the concert room had been completely torn from its hinges and rested against a wall. Several of the ten windows stretching the length of the room were broken and boarded up. The tables were screwed to the floor (an ominous sign but not a rarity). The dressing room door had a bottom panel broken, probably by a boot, and the top panel was splintered, possibly by a fist. I imagined some Artiste cowering in the barricaded dressing room while a mob, bent on a lynching tried to break the door down.
The only part of the dressing room wall that wasn't covered in obscene graffiti, was a pencil sketch of Andy Capp in a yellow square eighteen inches by twelve where once in some bygone era had hung a mirror. The cracked wash basin was choked with discarded cigarette butts, and there was a dark putrid smelling stain on the rotting canvassed floor beneath it where water had run through an aperture which once housed a 'U' bend.
A three legged chair and a tiny table made up the entire suite of furniture.
I hung my suit on a nail and went out into the concert room.
On the stage was a drum kit and a huge, expensive state of the art electric organ. Propped against the back wall of the stage were also a dozen chairs, some old packing cases and a thirty foot step ladder.
A strong smell of urine permeated from a dark patch of mould on the wall behind the drum kit. I looked up to the ceiling for any sign of stage lights. There were none, but a bright sun sent two shafts of light through the windows. Maybe I could work the floor, at least I would be seen.
A tall man with heavily Brylcreemed hair approached me. The 'Concert Chairman' (Compere). He was dressed in an ancient black dinner jacket, with lapels like hang gliders, a lemon, frilly fronted shirt, blue velvet bow tie, checked Bruin Bear baggy trousers and brown cowboy boots.
"You the Turn?" he squinted through the smoke from the cigarette burning his lip.
"Yeah" I answered. "What's that smell?"
"Fight in the bog (toilet) last New Years.... smashed the trough off the wall, and the piss is seeping through the plaster. It's cos its summer.... it doesn't smell so bad in the winter. Do you sing?"
"Yeah!" I replied, "just a song on and a song off.... depends how I'm doing really. Why?"
"No, I'll tell you why," said the man... "see the fella at the bar... the one sitting on the foot rail with the carnation in his jacket spilling beer into his shoe?
"Yeah!"
"He's the organist, and his daughter Sharon got married today and he's pissed...so if you can get by with just your gags, well I'd do that if I was you."
He looked over my shoulder and his face brightened.
"Oh, thank fuck, here's the tart singer."
He nodded towards the door. A very attractive blonde, maybe eighteen years old swished into the room. She resembled a rose in a garden of weeds and wore a three quarter length silver fox fur coat. Over her arm she had a plastic dress cover and in her hand she carried a leather music case. She walked straight past my friend and I, went into the dressing room, and without missing a step did an immediate 'U'turn,out of the dressing room, head high, down the room, out of the door-less portal and
vanished in the direction of the car park.
The man in the lemon shirt silently followed her departure and said; "She's pissed off...aw

fuck… they always do that… every week..I fancied giving her one as well! "

I gave him ten out of ten for ambition. "Yeah?"

Customers were now coming in, most of the men in shirt sleeves or string vests, one very obese lady wore a pinny (apron) and her ample bare arms still bore the traces of flour from a hastily made loaf of bread which she had sectioned into the sandwiches, wrapped in silver foil which she placed before her on the small table.

"Right!" said the luckless rapist. "Ah, here's Barney."

I looked in the direction of his nod. A very short, very fat man in a badly fitting jet black wig limped falteringly down the room. He was attired in a full dinner suit, complete with black waistcoat over a white shirt and yellow bow tie.

Several drum sticks and a couple of Tympani hammers protruded from the top pocket of his silk lapelled jacket. His left arm hung limply at his side, causing him to walk with an even more stunted gait.

On his left hand he had a shiny brown leather glove.

"He's the Drummer…funny really cos he's only got one arm, steel one, from the elbow down and he had two steel hip joints fitted.

Then he laughed; "He's probably worth a fortune in scrap value."

After allowing himself a loud guffaw he went on; "Do you Sing Tony Christie...?

He can play anything Tony Christie ever did... you sing any Tony Christie and he'll follow you, you'll have no problems with Barney."

I wasn't worried about Barney and I wasn't worried about the man with the carnation who now lay at the feet of several imbibers at the bar. I was worried about me.

My colleague continued,

"Problem is you picked a bad night to come here, cos Stan the organ player's daughter Sharon got married today."

"Yes" I said, "you told me."

"Aye," the man volunteered, "But I didn't tell you that she'd married Mickey Lee...... he's a tatter..... gyppo…. a pikey.... they're all gypsies... there's about twenty of them.... evil bastards... cut yer throat as soon as look at you and they hate Stan's lot.... ... Stan's lad, Ralphy stuck a knife in one of them Lee's about three year ago.... stuck it in his neck...he got seven years....GBH.... and then Mickey Lee shoves Sharon up the stick, so, they got hitched today and they're all coming in tonight, both outfits....it'll be like the Battle of the Little Big Horn in here tonight. See what I mean about you picked a bad night...I mean comics...phew... I mean, even a good night in here is a bad night for a comic"

He wiped his brow,

The door opened at the far end of the room and Eddie Flanagan walked in.

Eddie Flannigan was a Liverpool comedian. It's said that all Liverpudlians are comedians, and Eddie was the role model. I would stick my neck out and say,

Ken Dodd excepted, Eddie Flannigan was the funniest man ever to come out of Merseyside.

Eddie stood in the doorway for a second getting his bearings... then he spotted me and waved.

As he approached he said, "Hello Johnny...Jesus, what's that smell?"

"Fight in the gent's.... New years eve.." And I went through the concert chairman's descriptive routine.

"Aw, hey lad" said Eddie in that lovely Scouse sing song twang, "I just walked out of a better cesspit than this..."

"That's the organist, lying under the bar" I said, "And the fella with the sticks in his jacket pocket is the drummer, he's got a metallic arm and aluminium hips."

Eddie tilted his head to get a better look at the keyboard man, as I went on:

"His daughter married an entire gypsy tribe this afternoon...out of spite because her brother peeled the chief peg makers Adams apple. They're all coming in, Custer's seventh cavalry and the entire Sioux nations. The Concert Chairman said this place is going to be the battle of the Little Big horn reincarnate."

Eddie shuddered and looked around him, wiping a dewdrop of sweat from his nose.

"I've seen some shithole's in my time....." he said.

At this point a large man wearing a cheap ginger wig with grey sideburns, complaining about the heat, walked over and, hitting the bars on the emergency doors, flung them open revealing the car park littered with old prams and pushchairs, discarded washing machines, fridges and tubeless television sets.

Eddie, stared at the garbage and turning to me, said, "I don't think much of the games room either."

Half an hour later, Flanagan and I were propping up the bar at the Scotch Corner Hotel. £300 lighter but several stones heavier in wisdom.

My favourite Eddie Flanagan story was about the night he was booked to do a Show in one of Liverpool's biggest hotels. As all the rooms were block booked, the Artistes were asked to use the kitchen as a dressing room.

Eddie said: "All through the evening, during the meal, the chef would come into the kitchen, stir something, taste it, take a swig out of a bottle of cooking wine and go out again.... calling over his shoulder, "They're on the soup now." A few minutes later he would come back into the kitchen, repeat the ritual and depart with, "They're just starting on the main course."

Time dragged by, and none of the six acts could leave because it meant walking through the main dining room. At ten fifteen the chef, now rather glassy eyed came in, stirred, tasted, swigged, wiped his nose on a hand-towel and slurred, "They're onto the dessert now.... hic!"

Then at a quarter to eleven... "They on the coffee and cheese-board.. hic.. so they (belch) won't be long now, eh... noooo, they won't be.. er............"

Ten minutes later he was back. As there was nothing to stir or taste he concentrated on the wine." They're just on the speeches now... woooaant be... er.. hic... long now, kids. eh?"

We must have gotten through a carton of cigarettes between us. The next time the chef came in he was noticeably zigzagging around the room...he took a shot of claret, walked to the corner of the kitchen, lifted his apron, noisily pulled down his zip, took out his penis and pissed noisily into the mop bucket. Then shaking his dick, he fumbled for a full minute to replace it, pulling so hard on his zip that he staggered backwards falling onto the table, and with a "whoops" he headed once again for the door, where he stopped, spun on his heel, and facing us, slurred;

"Hey, listen, don't let the Manager come in and catch you smoking... he's a stickler for hygiene."

I could write a book on Eddie Flanagan alone, but there are other great club acts trying to get in. There would be a riot in Merseyside if I didn't mention Eddie's better half, Irene. She was as scouse as Eddie was funny, and loyal to the core.

It was blatantly obvious that Irene was the inspiration behind the Flannigan phenomonon. Had they gotten together as a pro double Act they would have ousted Burns and Allen from their pinnacle in the show business World.

Here's a small sample of Flanagan and Flanagan normality.

Eddie: "Hi dere Queen. What you been doin' terday, girl."

Irene: "Aw, not much Eddie lad. I took the kids to the museum."

Eddie: "Oh, dat's nice."

Irene: "Not really, Ace.... It wuz crammed wit ould fashioned stuff."

Eddie: "Oul fashioned stuff? Like what like, Queen?"

Irene: "Well, dere wuz nuttin' new in the place...ould photos and skeletons, so help me God, Eddie."

Eddie: "Skeletons?"

Irene: "Honest to God ace... there was even had the skull of a leg in dere."

Eddie once broke his dentures and this affected his act drastically. So he went to the Bootle dentists, Parks and Jones for a fitting. Mr Jones took an impression and told Eddie he'd call him as soon as the dentures were ready. Eddie asked him to gee it up as he was losing work. Three days later Eddie got a call to pick up the new set.

However, because it had been a rush job, the top set didn't fit snugly and they caused Eddie to loudly whistle every 'S'. Irene decided to take her spouse back for a re-fit. Never one for protocol, Irene, dragging Eddie behind her entered the surgery, barged straight past the receptionist, up the stairs and walked into Mr Jones room unannounced. Pushing her husband forward for the dentist's examination, she demanded; "Scuse me lad, but are you the fella that does the impressions?"

During a particularly bad winter too many years ago the great funny man succumbed to pneumonia. A few days later I was doing a Charity Show for the hospital where Eddie died. The nursing sister who had been with him said;

"He was a great Comic right to the very end. As I helped wheel him into the Theatre he tugged at my sleeve. I leaned over to ask what he wanted and he raised his hand shakily, slowly swept it round the room, smiled and said; "Its nuthin' like the brochure, is it?"

Then he died.

Shakespeare couldn't have written a closing line like that.

But if none could surpass the natural comedy of Eddie Flannigan, one came very close to it. His name was Jackie Hamilton. Jackie is that rare breed of human being who can upstage the great Ken Dodd merely by saying, "Hya lad."

Not funny? It is when Jackie Hamilton says it.

He got the part as an extra in a war epic being filmed in North Wales. Actually Jackie only heard about the gig on the last day of shooting, or if he had heard about it before he ignored it because he had 'a few bob for a gargle' (the price of a pint) and it was only when he started putting the bite on his mates for a loan (a dangerous occupation in Liverpool) that someone whispered that there was a couple of quid to be made for one day only as a thespian. Jackie was stowed away aboard the film company bus, and on alighting gave his name to the effeminate young man in charge of the films extra's.

He was hustled off to the wardrobe department and rigged out in an old too small army blouse and a too large khaki beret which sat like a cushion on his head. Then he and a couple of dozen of his fellow 'prisoners' were marched a mile to a large compound comprising of several long huts and four sentry towers manned by armed guards. They were cheerily greeted by a young lady carrying a clip-board who informed them that when a siren sounded they were all to stagger out of their huts and line up in front of the camp Kommandant and several men in German uniforms holding the leashes of snarling vicious looking Rottweilers. They were then sent off to the huts to await the klaxton call. Jackie noticed for the first time that every one of his unfortunate comrades looked like genuine captives who hadn't eaten in months. Jackie, with his four chins, ruddy complexion and docker's beer belly stood out like Rose in a garden of weeds. One of his friends, knowing that this was Hamilton's first stab at the movie business whispered to his fat friend that, at the roll call he should make sure that he's in the front line and as close to the camera as possible. This would ensure him a place on the casting register for any future saga's that may pop up. Suddenly, on cue the camp klaxon summoned the several dozen starving beings to the roll call. Jackie did his best to copy the fainting staggering gait of his fellow unfortunates. And being obviously bigger and better nourished he ended up directly in front of and a mere several inches from **camera 1**. The German sergeant screamed out the names of the pitiful throng before him and, when Hamilton's name was called his reply "Over here pal" reached the ear of the director high up on a sentry tower.' "CUT" he yelled through a battery operated megaphone. Then leaning on the rail he espied, among all his emaciated charges the rotund Mr Hamilton. Aiming his megaphone directly at the casting director he shouted, "Victoria…. this is supposed to be a Nazi prisoner of war camp… these men haven't had a bite across their lips for weeks…so how come we now have Oliver Hardy letting the team down?" And before Victoria could summon up an answer Jackie took one pace forward, gave the Nazi outstretched arm salute and spoke the only bit of German he ever learned in his national service days he bawled out. "Entshuldigenzee bitte pal, but I was only captured this morning."

In an instant his movie career was over.

An irreverent kind of a comic he was one asked to leave the stage of a Catholic club in Huyton when he split the 'congregation' asunder with the following biblical tale according to saint Jackie; "So, Saint Peter let's the cat outa the bag when he let's it slip to Jesus that him and the rest of the lads was throwing a sportsmen's dinner party for J.C cos the twelve of them had took to him like a duck to water. When Jesus and Peter turn up at the club about half nine the party's in full swing. The other eleven are already well gone with the bevvy, and they're singing all the scouse song's, like 'Maggie May' to a four piece Beatles look alike group from Toxteth…y'know, gittars and that like and a kid with a big hooter like Ringo's on the drums. Anyway the MC takes Peter and J.C up onto the stage and sits them down on the top table with Jesus in the middle cos he's the guest speaker and old Peter is on his right cos he's Jesus's chief mucker.

Well, they have the soup and the main course followed by the peaches and ice-cream and the cheese board then they put the comic on… but no stripper cos 'the you know who'is…'You know who'…

Anyway, they have a crackin' night and by half ten they're all pissed outa their skulls…and while Luke and John are up doing their party piece, 'Pal of my childhood days' Jesus is getting a bit worried cos it's his party and nobody's put their hand in their pockets yet, and he's a bit short because his ould fella what helps him out now and then is only a carpenter or maybe even only a joiner, and in them days joiners was ten a penny and weren't making that much unless they was working on the docks and it was taking the ould fella all his time to feed hisself, so Jesus leans over to Peter and he says; "Listen ace, I'd like to thank you and the lads like for this gesture and all that but you know I don't have any bread… I mean me dads only a joiner, and things are a bit tight down at the shop right now… in the last few days he's had to lay-off a couple of lads, and there's a chance that if things don't pick up he'll have to flog the donkey."

Peter looks him straight in the eye and says, "Relax Jeez,..don't worry about the bill, it's your function so keep shtum… it's a freebee for you…"

Well, when he hears this Jesus is made up… and he says, "Well, who's coughing up for this lot then Pete?" and Saint Peter said, "Well, I don't really know lad, but words out on the street that Judas has just come into a few bob."

From that minute on every agent booking Catholic clubs in Merseyside was asked to omit Jackie Hamilton from their list of comics.

Liverpool has bred some of the great Comics through the ages… Arthur Askey;

Ted Ray, Rob Wilton, and the greatest living comedian of them all, Ken Dodd. They still breed Comedians there in Liverpool, but none like the aforementioned, Eddie Flannigan and Jackie Hamilton.

And not all the funniest scousers are on the casting director's pay-role.

I got a call from my casting agent that there was a part for me in the Liverpool sit- com, 'The Liver-birds.' The part was a police panda car driver. It was a walk on with a couple of lines.

The scene was on location in a run down part of Liverpool….and a rough area to boot. The script called for the demolishing of a couple of terraced houses.

Actually the location guys found four, the remainder of a clearance lot. One of the doomed premises, number 5 was occupied by a recluse, played by one of the characters in the show. The story line had it that he'd been born in the house, spent all his life in the house and intended to end his days there. The council had other plans and a stalemate occurred. The 'Props people had boarded up number 5 and, painted across the front door was the warning in bold lettering , **"We Will Not Be Moved."**

What the DSS had forgotten to inform the Film Company however was that next door to the 'set' house number 7 there lived a genuine recluse, a rebel who had steadfastly stuck to his guns and defied all attempts to dislodge him. The tug of war had gone on for so long that the council had more or less washed their hands of the whole affair and decided to wait till the man finally expired. This was partly due to the fact that, in true Liverpool form the whole neighbourhood had given their backing to the persecuted 'victim', and had been so vociferous in his defence that it was decided the situation could get ugly if the council tried to forcibly remove the man. In the meantime, the mans friends (every citizen within a two mile radius) would keep the rebel fed and watered by shoving hot dogs, burgers, fish and chips and cans of lager through the enlarged letterbox.

Rehearsals went on without serious incident, apart from one morning when I was walking towards the 'set' with my 'sergeant' when we were attacked by gangs of kids shouting 'pigs' and pelted with stones. I escaped but the 'sarge' ducked the wrong way and was felled by a half building brick. Rehearsals were suspended while he was taken off to the infirmary and casting found a stand in lawman.

Although the scene seemed pretty straight forward there were several tricky shots and lines which necessitated re-writes and we were running over schedule.

On the last day we all worked extremely hard and late in the afternoon the director was satisfied that we were as good as we'd ever get. And as we were losing light this had to be a 'take'.

"ACTION". The limousine carrying the bailiffs swung into the street and stopped outside the target house followed by the Panda car driven by me accompanied by my new sergeant. The camera's zoomed in as the occupants alighted. I slid out of the 'prop' Panda car to a storm of abuse from the extras and we walked gingerly to the graffiti covered front door of number 5. The Bailiff stepped between the two large police escorts, and raising his arm crashed his fist heavily in the door.

'Cut to living room window as face appears from behind torn curtains'.
The Bailiff took an official form from his assistant and as the crowd went silent, the official tilted his head back and as he opened his mouth to read out the eviction notice there was a crash as the upstairs window on NUMBER 7 opened and an unshaven old man wearing an army balaclava leaned out, spat at the entourage and to a thunderous cheer of the non Equity members of the sightseeing crowd, screamed, "I'M NOT MOVING .... SO FUCK OFF OR I'LL PUT THE LAW ON YOU....."

The director, in tears yelled 'cut' and the scene was re-shot several days later in a closed set.

I worked with Laurence Olivier in Blackpool. It was in a production called 'lost empires.' It was about the old Empire theatres. Oh yes Larry and me go back a long way. He spoke to me once he said "get the hell out of my way."

I was Bet Lynch's cousin Arthur in Coronation St. I had one line. I had to walk into the Rovers Return and go up to the bar and say to Bet Lynch. "Don't you know me I'm your cousin Arthur?" The producers said to me beforehand "You must be very very careful with this line not to say cousin Albert." The actor who had played Albert Tatlock had died a few years earlier and the cast of the street thought it was unlucky to say Albert on set. His ghost was still in the studios. A bit like saying Macbeth if you were working on stage. So they told me to be very very careful with the line. You couldn't say his name. Not many people know this but they never rehearse on Coronation Street. That was the case at the time anyway. They read their lines and then out they come. So I came out and walked up to the bar, which was full, and Julie Goodyear playing Bet Lynch said "Can I help you?" and I said "Don't you know me I'm your cousin Albert." They asked me to leave but they couldn't find anyone else to do it so I came back again.

That's Entertainment ?

Sir Basil Summersby got a Sunday noon Gig in Byker bottom Club Newcastle. Byker, has some fine clubs. The aforementioned was not one of them.

And 'Sir Basil Summersby' was his stage name.

'Dixie' Summers had been a run of the mill singer for many years, doing the grinding round of the Workingmen's Social club circuit the length and breadth of the country. However, a starving Agent and the name change also changed the fortunes of Dixie Summers for good. The owner of a fine tenor voice, marred only by the worst vibrato in the business, he started getting better paid and better attended Venues.

Inevitably Radio and Television followed his launch.

Unfortunately, moving into this medium was followed by a sharp drop in bookings and after a meteoric rise to the lowest register of the showbusiness heights, he just as rapidly plummeted back to earth with a bone shattering thud.

However, thanks to his sole appearance on the box, he was now more marketable as a club act than when he was Fred 'Dixie' Summers, 'Haverton Hill's Mario Lanza'.

But as all things come full circle, Sir Basil was rapidly approaching the end of the lucrative line of engagements.

The Byker Venue was the buffer which was about to derail the gravy train.

Lesser Pro's would have wilted, or even submitted.... but Fred 'Dixie' Summers had walked these mean cobbled streets before. Nothing fazed him.

The consummate Pro' he took the Byker Gig in his stride.

It was a Sunday Noon Strip Show.....the worst kind, with Sir Basil giving some credence and class to three Strippers who wouldn't have reached the first fifty places at CRUFTS.

After two of the 'Dancers' exotique' had ground the mob into a non screaming, non yelling non masturbating cauldron of indifference, Sir Basil was thrown to the wolves.

He strode onto the Stage, resplendent in full evening dress, top hat, cloak (bearing the Knights regalia) and silver topped cane, and did an unforgettable impression of a man drowning in treacle.

Then, on the very verge of capitulation, trying to make himself heard over the rattle of dominoes and beer glasses, he announced: "And now Gentlemen, I shall now sing you an aria I performed just seven days ago at the Dordoigne in gay Paree.".....then peering down through the flat caps, tattoos and choking cigarette smoke, he enquired,   "Do we have any Parisian's in the hall this morning?"

JOHNNY MORE, star of dozens of top class cabarets and television shows worldwide and arguably the best comedy impressionist to grace any stage was being liberally dissected by the mob in a Gateshead workingmen's club.

He ended with his piece de resistance, the finest impersonation ever seen of the great George Burns. The mob were greatly unimpressed.

Removing the silver hairpiece, the cigar and the horn rimmed glasses, he replaced them with a snap brim trilby hat and, with a cigarette dangling from the corner of his mouth, in a perfect take off of Humphrey Bogart, he lisped:

"Of all the shit holes in all the towns in all the world, I had to walk into this one."

A Club in Hartlepool was undergoing extensive renovations. New bars being fitted on the windows etc. On the third day of work, several men began to stagger around the immediate site in a drunken manner, this when the bar was tightly shuttered and padlocked. However, after making intensive investigations the foreman discovered that a gas pipe had been fractured and reported the fact to one of the minions of the Committee.

Should he call out the gas board immediately?

The official held up his hand restraining the foreman and informed him that this was an internal club matter, but he would bring the matter up at the next General Meeting of the Committee... two months hence.... in November.

I walked a million miles.. for this?

Des Lane was Durham's Al Jolson.... and so long as he stuck to the county boundary and sang quietly out of earshot of the original, Des could continue making a fair living doing the clubs. You'll gather by that remark that Des was not the world's greatest Al Jolson impersonator but he was as good as the other seventy eight thousand Al Jolson impersonators in the county. Des did have one thing the others didn't have.... he not only sounded nothing like the original but did at least he bear an uncanny resemblance to the great man... and had even cultured the Al Jolson mannerisms down to a fine art and on stage.

However he was remarkably like Jolson on one of Al's off nights.

Frankie Walpole sounded more like Jolson than Des, but Frankie didn't dress the part.

He wore grey flannel trousers and a red polo necked sweater and although he blacked up, he didn't go to the expense of black curly wig. He had a black face, thick shiny white lips but this was topped of by a mass of fiery red hair.

Terry Blenkinsopp, Redcar's Al Jolson blacked up and wore the black wig.... but he was blonde and gay, sang in a mezzo soprano and his carefully coiffured locks hung down to his waist completely ruining the illusion.

Robbie Gilchrist blacked up, wore the wig and calf length black trousers and white socks, but he could only sing when he removed his top and bottom dentures, so he was well in the fore of non runners.

Gert Frobische had been a prisoner of war incarcerated in Easington Colliery, when he saw his first Jolson movie in the camp's cinema and was hooked.... but he was German and when he'd been shot down by a Spitfire over Hartlepool bay he'd lost both arms and an eye... Blacked up he knelt down when he sang 'Mammy' but when it came to the line **'the sun shines east, the sun shines west'** he could only nod in each geographical direction. His accent didn't ingratiate him to the partisan Geordie audiences either.

But Des Lane sounded like a Jolson. Not necessarily Al, but he sounded like, maybe a distant relative of the Greatest Entertainer in the World. (That was another handicap Des laboured under.) He wore the burnt cork makeup, the tight jacket with the white shirt and black bow tie. He wore the obligatory calf length black trousers with the white socks and the patent leather shoes. There was no way you could mistake Des Lane for Mario Lanza, especially when he went down on one knee.

Then Des pulled a first which put all the others Jolson wannabee's in the shade.

He saved the fare and went all the way to America to meet his idol. As proof he brought back a snapshot of him shaking hands with the great man and now Des was using the authentic Jolson makeup. Out went the burnt cork. The real Al kicked that into touch when he spoke those immortal words, "California here I come".

Black greasepaint was now the big thing in the minstrel business and what was good enough for Jolie, was good enough for Des Lane. Now Des looked more like Jolson than Jolson. His face shone like a highly polished nine pin bowling ball in the glare of the single flex 40 watt bulb that lit up three feet of the Stage. Des had carefully read the instruction on application. He also discovered that the only way to remove the goo was with wads of cotton wool, soaked in undiluted Turpentine.

The night Des and I shared the bill in the Easington Miners Welfare club in County Durham, Des stole the show. However, I must take some credit for his success, because if I hadn't died so badly, he wouldn't have looked so good. He came off stage to rapturous applause, having taken three curtain calls.

Back in the tiny dressing room Des threw me that old 'follow that' smile, then settled down to remove his makeup. He must have used a full gallon of undiluted Turpentine and a removal van load of cotton wool. When he'd completed his task he scooped up the waste from the washbasin and deposited it into the toilet bowl at the very instant that the house drummer dashed offstage, obviously taken short. Thrusting Des out of his path, he dived into the cubicle, slamming the door behind him.

We could hear him stamping his feet and grinding his teeth as he noisily unbuckled his belt, tore at his zip and fell backwards onto the seat without a second to spare. There was a loud rasping whoosh and several pained 'oohahh' as he disgorged a five course Tandori meal. Then silence. The stench permeated the tiny dressing room and we tried to dress and evacuate at the earliest possible moment.

In the cubicle all was silent satisfaction. Then came the sound of rustling as the percussionist tore open a cigarette packet. Then more fumbling, the slide of the tray of the matchbox opening and closing. The rasp of the match head on sandpaper.... the gentle 'Ah' as the man filled his lungs with smoke and eased backward and dropped the still ignited match between his legs into the bowlful of Turpentine soaked cotton wool.

The explosion, catapulted the blazing drummer upwards and forwards, ripping the door from its hinges as he pitched headlong into the dressing room wall. After the ambulance and firemen bore the charred remains of the musician from the premises, the committee held an emergency meeting and decided that, as we had not both done our allocated two spots, and as how we'd deprived the club, not only of a toilet, but also of the only acceptable drummer within a fifteen mile radius, it was the decision of committee that we, Des and I, should forfeit any monies due and that we were both barred from the Club 'sine die'.

Lightning does stike twice

Three years later having served my penance I was re-engaged at the same club with a young, rather robust lady singer who, although already summoned to the stage, stuck her head round the door and asked the concert chairman to give her another couple of minutes grace as she urgently needed to pee.

Her request was granted. However, since the prior catastrophe, the toilet had not been rebuilt....'in case we have another Jolson Singer'.

Being a true Pro, the vocalist decided to emulate her male counterparts and urinate in the washbasin. So, with her knickers around her ankles she hoisted herself onto the pedestal and was in mid flow when the whole contraption collapsed under her weight, sending her crashing to the floor and inflicting a thousand lacerations to her nether regions from the razor sharp porcelain splinters.

Her screams brought forth an army of helpers. An ambulance was hailed and the paramedics, deciding bandaging such a vast area of injury was an impractabilty, covered the injured parts with large dollops of anti biotic cream, pressed a thick pad of gauze onto the concoction, and covered this with a mountainous wad of cotton wool.

As the operation took almost half and hour, it was decided, in true show business tradition that the show must go on. So, during the dressing of the ladies private parts I was introduced back on stage. Unfortunately, the only way out to the ambulance was through the concert room, and while I was in the middle eight of 'Bridge over troubled water', the dressing room door opened and the two stretcher bearers appeared carrying the stricken victim, who, because of the geographic location of her wounds was placed on the stretcher in a kneeling position, the mount Everest wad cotton wool reaching almost to the ceiling, while a grey blanket had been draped over upper body, completely covering her head.

While this was the second such catastrophe in as many appearances at the club, I decided, if not for my own well-being, then for that of my Peers, I should erase the venue from my engagement diary forever.

THE WRITER

I was working on the very successful series of "Stand Up Jim Davidson" shows for Thames TV. The first few series I was the only writer on the series and they were some of the happiest times of my writing career. The producer was one of the top in his field of endeavour, David Bell and under the direction of the highly respected Royston Mayo, and the general consensus of opinion was that the show was arguably the best stuff Jim ever did on Television...before or since. With such a salubrious team the powers that be would accept nothing less.

One of the favourite characters on the show was the late Bob Todd. It was said that if the show had been an Olympic event for boozing, Bob Todd would have had a wardrobe full of Gold medals. It was rumoured that he once belched at a funeral and turned it into a Mardi gras. Todd was one of those phenomenon's, a naturally funny man.

I remember him coming into the VIP lounge in a very bad temper. Someone or something had upset him. He started to rant and rave as we all sat around watching him... then he said something silly, and as soon as the spell was broken he changed in a flash and had us rolling on the floor.

Tommy Cooper was in the pub with the cast and crew one day and we were watching Margaret Thatcher on the television talking about apathy.

Tommy said, "That's the problem with the world. There's too much apathy. It's a pity no one can find a cure for it."

Quick as a flash Bob Todd said, "But I did."

"You did what?" said Cooper.

Todd put on his serious face and replied, "I found a cure for apathy...but nobody gives a fuck." As in movies, most of the best stuff is left on the cutting room floor... so it is with Comedy... the best lines are cut to be related with great appreciation in some remote noisy smoke filled bar.

While I was working on the "Stand Up Jim Davidson" Show I was billeted in London's Regents Park Hotel, and each day a studio car would pick me up at 9.30 a.m. take me to work and when the show was 'in the can' another car would bring me back. After the final show we had a wrap party and I was ringing for a staff car when Bob came out of the VIP lounge the epitome of sobriety wearing his none the worse for wear persona and asked where who I was phoning. I said I was trying, in vain to get a studio car back to London. Bob said he'd give me a lift. He went down to the car park and I went back to say goodbye to Jim, Royston and the rest of the crew.

I made my way down the car park and was looking around for Bob when he whistled from the far side of the car park and waved. I threaded across between the parked cars to where he was sitting behind the wheel of a Rolls Royce convertible. I climbed in beside him and he decided to pour praise on my writing ability.

Just as I was getting really engrossed in the conversation one of the high priests of Thames Television arrived escorted by a liveried chauffeur and a security man, and demanded to know: "What the hell are you doing in my car?"

Leaving Bob to do the explaining I baled out and hurtled back into the Studio.

Another time, again at Thames, Jim Davidson, the cast and crew went next door to 'The Gardner's' pub for their break, leaving me in the office doing a re-write on a couple of sketches. Work completed, I made my way to the pub, just as a black cab pulled up at the kerb. As I approached the cab door opened and a huge man backed out of the taxi. It was the inimitable Tommy Cooper. As he paid the driver he said 'would you like a good tip. The driver said "Yes sir". Tommy turned and as he walked away he said "keep away from married women" and burst into laughter, but not nearly as loud as the Cabbie, who went into convulsions, calling after the big man.. "Gawd, you're a diamond guv... a bleeding diamond."

As Tommy walked behind me.. I held the door open for him and he thanked me and stepped into the foyer.

At that instant the public phone in the entrance vestibule rang. Tommy turned, took the phone from its cradle and shouted into the mouthpiece,

"'ello...'ang on" He shoved the handset into my hand and pushing the door open, stepped outside, looked up at the board bearing the name of the pub then stepped back in taking the phone from me.

"Yes it is.. who?... WHO?.... speak up, I can't ... 'ang on a minute" then turning to me he asked, "What's your name again?"

"Johnny Hammond" I replied.

Tommy spoke back into the phone..

"'ang on a minute... here he is".

He handed the receiver to me and made his way to the bar where he joined Jim, Bob Todd, Royston Mayo, Frank Ifield and Benny Hill.

"Hello" I called into the mouthpiece over the din from the bar."

"Hi, Les?"

"Who?"

"Les... is that Les?"

"No, this is Johnny Hammond."

"Who?"

"Johnny Hammond."

"No," said the caller "I want Les... is Les there?"

"Who the hell's Les?" I asked.

"Les... the barman." He said,

"Hang on a minute" and I hailed the barman.

The bartender waved, lifted his little flap door and came over, taking the phone with a cheerful "thanks pal."

Feeling stupid I walked up to the group at the bar. Before I had chance to speak Tommy reached up and took his battered trilby from his head, pressed it to his heart and donning his famous sad expression, put a huge hand on my shoulder and said, "I hope it wasn't bad news."

Bob Monkhouse tells the funniest ever Tommy Cooper story. I hope Bob won't mind my borrowing it from one his hilarious books.

He writes, 'Once with West End streets at a standstill due to poll tax demonstrations, Tommy persuaded me to travel with him on the Underground. I argued that the other passengers would recognise him even if they failed to spot me.

' Bob, its London mate. Anywhere else we may get bothered, but I've lived all my adult life in this city and I'll tell you something you ought to know already. Only taxi drivers recognise you. No other bugger looks at you and taxi drivers only clock you in case you do a runner.'

Even Tommy with his great lumpy face and lurching height went unnoticed as we bought our tickets and rode the escalator down to a crowded platform.

'Being this tall I have to be careful on the Underground' he confided as we boarded our train... He looked round cautiously,

"I hate strap hanging... there's a lot of gay midgets on this line."

Boarding the train they found seats and settled down for the journey.

At the second station a foul smelling tramp boarded the train carrying a filthy, distemper ridden mongrel and as he moved down the train he'd push the slavering hound in passengers faces snarling, "Money, gimme money..." as he held out a

stained plastic cup demanding donations. Terrified commuters dropped coins into the receptacle.

The bum arrived at our seat and loomed over us. 'Money for food' he growled.

Tommy looked up from our conversation and seemed to notice the beggar for the first time. "Y'what?" Tommy asked.

"Need money" the beggar growled.

"What for?" said Tommy.

The man screamed in the giant funnyman's face. "I'm hungry."

Tommy screamed back, 'Well, eat your Fucking dog'.

Next stop the terrified tramp dismounted.'

In my last season at the Jersey Sunshine Hotel I was sharing the Bill with two of my favourite people, Janette and Ian Tough, the 'Krankies'.

As the hotel was full of paying guests, we rented a small house across the road from the venue. There were six acts staying and it fell to the miniscule Janette to do the cooking. The Krankies and I were the only Workingmen's Club acts on the Show. The others were 'legit' players from Theatre and Television, and they looked down on our lowly status.

One guy in particular, a dyed in the wool thespian, rubbed us the wrong way from day one. He moaned about everything from the small sleeping quarters, the tiny portable T.V., which belonged to me, the dreadful working class holiday makers who made up the audiences....... you name it.

I used to goad him into action but he always backed off from a real confrontation. On the last day of the show, a Sunday, Janette was preparing dinner. As she walked to the kitchen carrying a large pan of newly peeled potatoes the boor stopped her in her tracks and said: 'I hope you haven't left any eyes in those potatoes... I can't stand potatoes with eyes left in them.'

Janette blanched, raised the pan high in the air, and in her cheeky 'wee Jimmy voice' said: "Here, take a closer look" and emptied the contents over the thespians head.

Jeanette loves to tell about the time a member of the audience kept pestering her to come back to his room. Ian knew about it, and, knowing his wife's talent for deflating these pests, left it up to the 'wee one'.

On that night's show as she did her 'wee Jimmy' act walking round the audience and stopping at a table she asked the guests if they'd 'seen me mam?'

An immaculately attired business man leaned over and whispered that he'd like to spend the night with her.......'if she could get rid of her dad'. She gave the man a knowing smile and wended her way through the crowded tables where she stopped at the regular pest.

"Tonight" she whispered in the guy's ear.

The man beamed and nodded.

"What's the number of your room?" she teased.

The man fumbled in his pocket and fished out his key.

Jeanette rolled her eyes, took the key and whispered "Twelve fifteen." and carried on with the act.

Making her way through the tables she came up to the horny business man. Plonking herself on his knee she ruffled his hair, kissed him on the cheek and as the audience roared she slipped the key she'd just been given into the hand of the guy now bristling with expectation. "Twelve thirty" she said. "Don't let me down."

Next morning at breakfast the business man came into reception sporting one of the worst black eyes she'd ever seen. "We never saw the other guy... but it was believed he'd caught the first boat back to the mainland."

NAME DROPPING HELPS.

I was doing some shows in Newcastle when I was invited along to the Grand Theatre to see the pantomime, 'Cinderella' by a great Geordie Entertainer, Leah Bell, who was playing the female lead. Backstage after the show she introduced me to the man playing 'Buttons.'
"This is one of our top Comedians, Johnny Hammond" Leah said as she introduced me to a smallish shy quietly friendly man who was just making a name for himself in situation comedy on Television.
"David Jason" he said and offered his hand.
"Oh, hi" I said, "I've seen...er... how are you?"
He smiled knowing what I'd seen and when and said; "Fine. You?"
"Yeah, great.... how are you enjoying the North East?"
"Yes, fine, they're very nice people..y'know, friendly...great audiences."
Leah exchanged knowing glances with me, grinned and said, "David hasn't worked the 'Clubs' yet."
I understood what Leah meant and hoped Mr Jason would never come that far down the ladder. After the Show I strolled back to his Hotel with him, partly because he seemed a nice guy, secondly I'd enjoyed him immensely on the Television Show "Sharp Intake of Breath", although I didn't mention it as yet because I didn't like to sound like a starry eyed pain in the ass. The other reason was that, Newcastle around ten thirty on a Saturday night is not the kind of place where one takes a leisurely stroll alone.
We went to the bar in the Swallow Hotel, David bought the drinks and we settled down for a chat.
David asked me about my job as a club comic. I explained the layout of the job, and said it's a different kind of showbiz to the one he knows. He told me that on a Wednesday evening during the interval of Cinderella at the Grand they put on a local act. He said that last Wednesday during the interval he'd strode into the wings and there was a scruffy little man, dressed in flat cap, over-large red sweater, baggy trousers and large boots, obviously waiting to go on stage.
David introduced himself. The little man asked that after he came off would David give him an autograph. He also asked what the audience were like.
David told him they were great and that the little man shouldn't worry as they were there mainly for the Pantomime.
Just then the Theatre Manager walked on stage resplendent in dinner jacket, greeted the audience and said he was about to introduce the extra Wednesday night artiste.
David said, "I was so busy telling the sad little man not to worry that I didn't catch his name, but within seconds of walking on the nondescript little 'Comic' had them rolling in the aisles.
"They wouldn't let him off." said an embarrassed David.
When they could laugh no more the little man thanked the audience and strolled off stage.
"He came up to me, shook my hand and said; 'Yer right bonny lad... they're a canny crowd'" and with the audience yelling for more, the miniscule nonentity said, "By the way Dennis, my name's Bobby Thompson."
David said; "I couldn't believe that there I was telling the North's greatest comedy genius 'not to worry, just go on and do your best.' Later, in the wings we swapped autographs.... And I never saw him again!"
We live and learn.
Leah Bell was invited to a Christmas party not far from the Theatre and invited David and I along. She gave me a slip of paper with an address 32 Scotswood Road.
David went back to the Swallow Hotel, changed and we met up in the bar. We had mare than a couple of drinks then headed off to the party.

Unfortunately I'd mislaid the address.

It took us a while to find the street, which incidentally had a party in every house. Racking my memory I decided it was number 23. During the search we visited several noisy Newcastle pubs so we were fairly well tipsy by the time we found

23, Scotswood Road. The place was heaving and the din from the music made us even headier. After a hectic couple of hours in which we consumed most of the party's liquor, some very large, very drunk men came over to the couch that we were sprawled on, each holding a bottle of whiskey and asked us who we were.

David slurred that we were friends of Leah Bell....

The next few minutes are now a painful blur, but I remembered doing several cartwheels before ending up on the snow covered lawn with a bloody nose and David draped across my feet. We decided to head back to the hotel and passing number 32 we stopped and stared as Leah led a line of Conga Dancers down the path and up the street. As she passed us she gave a wave and wished us a Cherry Crimsess.

Some time later I was appearing in Cabaret at a nightclub in Epping. I got a call at my hotel. It was David Jason. He'd seen the announcement in the Entertainments section of his London paper and wondered would he be able to get in as he'd always wanted to see me work. I asked the owner if there was any chance of finding a seat for the now very, very famous David Jason. The boss was thrilled to have such a Superstar in his establishment. David got the red carpet treatment, which he richly deserved.

He asked me what I was going to do in the act. I said I didn't know yet.

Aghast he said, "Yet? YET? You're on in ten minutes and you don't know what the Hell you're going to do.... have you forgotten it or what?"

I said "No, I never know what I'm going to do till I get on stage... I just come on, say 'good evening' and leave the rest to fate."

He was so visibly shaken, that as the compere was introducing me David went out and stood in the car park, only coming back and peeking round the door at intervals to see how I was doing. When he heard the roar of laughter he meekly sneaked his way back to his seat. I had a great night, David and I were wined and dined, signed autographs by the score and the last time I saw him was when I escorted him to his car. He shook my hand and said; "Thank's Johnny, it was a truly wonderful night, you were great but please, please...don't ever do that to me again."

We wrote to each other and stayed in touch for a while, but now we were travelling in different directions, professionally. He was on the way to the top floor and I was once again heading for the basement.

I haven't met up with David for many years, but I never miss a chance to see him on Television.

You can learn a lot just watching at an icon like him. And it's typical of David that he said the same thing after breathlessly watching 'Little Bobby Thompson' from the wings as 'the interval turn' in Newcastle all those years ago. I still have David's letters to me and his photo's signed personally to me. I could have sold them a thousand times over, but, hungry as we have been occasionally, we've never been THAT hungry.

Touché!

I have always loved practical jokers, but I hate practical jokers who don't like practical jokers. I was booked as chief support to a truly brilliant Liverpool Comedian called Mick Miller. A great patter man, Mick's forte was a re-hashing of "Guzzlers Gin" an act devised by the great wartime American movie comedy star, Red Skelton.

Mick Miller is still doing the rounds and the same old act is as fresh as it was in the 40s when Red Skelton invented it. Also, Mick could drink with the best of them and would down several pints of strong ale before going on stage with no apparent effect. His finale was hilarious in the extreme.

Doing a send up of the children's radio Programme, 'Watch with mother" his props were a "Gordon's Gin" bottle half full with water and an empty half pint glass.

Mick would announce, "Its bath time now kiddies. Let's put some water in the bath should we?" Then holding the glass to the microphone he would noisily half fill the glass with the 'fake Gin'. This he would drink in one gulp.

"Ooh," he'd say amid roars of laughter "that's still a little hot, isn't it kiddies.. Let's put some more wold corter in, eh?"

He would repeat this till he was staggering round the stage much to the hilarity of the audience. It was a brilliant act and nobody could do justice to the old Skelton act better than Mick Miller.

However, Miller was that kind of practical joker who would pull stunts on the rest of the cast, but somehow he always avoided reprisals. I fell a painful victim several times during the week but no matter how I tried I could never come up with a suitable equal to his, sometime cruel stunts.

As chief support, I would always close the first half of the Show. There would be a half hour interval during which time the punters could play a couple of hands of Bingo. After this, Mick's props would be set down front stage and at the compere's announcement Mick would be greeted by great applause. He was usually bolstered up with a few pints of the local brew beforehand.

I was equally happy by the way my act had gone down, even with the partisan Scouse audience.My performance consisted of a few songs, a few gags then I'd close with my Comedy Piano Act (which years later was 'borrowed' by, but performed with brilliance by Les Dawson).

The week had gone down well and, though Mick had ruffled a few feathers backstage by the end of the week all was amicable. On this final night of the show I had a great last spot unhindered by the amiable headliner. Announcing my last number I went over to the grand piano. I noticed straight away that for the first time that week the keyboard lid was not raised. I tried to lift it but it wouldn't move. I felt a slight panic as I tried to prize the lid open but it refused to budge, bringing on a wave of laughter.

I looked appealingly at the audience then my eye caught Mick Miller at the back of the room. He was smiling broadly and dangling the piano lid key above his head. Then slipping the key into his mouth he grinned and headed for the bar.

Thinking quickly I sat on the piano stool and mimed the act. It went down so well I decided in future I would keep it in the act. I laid the audience in the aisles and took a trio of curtain calls before the organist played me off.

Behind a curtain back-stage I noticed a table containing the Star's 'Watch with Mother' props.... a Gordon's Gin bottle filled with water and a half pint glass.

Back in the dressing room I was greeted by the Mayor of Birkenhead. He shook my hand warmly, congratulated me on the act and asked, 'Would I nip into the old folk's home next door and do a fifteen minute spot?'

"Sure, I'd be glad to." I replied.

I did the spot for the old folks and left them happy.

On the way out the Mayor and the club steward took me behind the bar and told me to take my pick of any bottle of spirits I'd like. I chose a bottle of 'Gordon's Gin'.

Back in the club I passed the men's bar and Mick Miller was holding court surrounded by a half dozen howling fans.

I went onto the darkened stage, swapped the water filled gin bottle with the genuine stuff and made my way to the back of the room. Minutes later Mick entered the Cabaret room and unsteadily weaved his way to the dressing room. Looking at me with a grin he said: "How did the Piano Act go?"

"Quietly...but it got laughs....and anyway, I love practical jokes... and the crowd loved it. How're you feeling?" I asked.

He gave me a quizzical look and as I was collecting my suits to leave he said, with more than a touch of false hurt; "Aw, aren't you gonna watch my spot?"

I put my hand on his shoulder, looked him right in the eye and said; "Mick, I wouldn't miss it for the world."

He stopped in his tracks and gave me one of those, 'hello, there's something going on here' looks.

The Compere came in and told Mick he was about to announce him, then he went onto the stage, carried the small table bearing Millers props to the foot-lights and 'one two-ing into the microphone introduced "the Star of the Show...Mick Miller."

Mick murdered the audience for thirty minutes, during which time he had a man at ringside pass him a pint of strong ale which he downed in one gulp. Then he went into his 'Watch with Mother' Act. On cue the organist played the theme tune. 'ting a ting... ting a ting'

"Hello children... are you sitting comfortably? "

A loud sweeping 'Yes' from the expectant audience.

"Its bath time for Big-ears." Mick shouted "Should we bathe Big-ears?"

The audience squealed a falsetto "Ye-e-e-s"

"Right... let's fill the bath, should we?"

"Y-e-e-e-s"

They were already in fits of laughter.

Mick raised the glass to the microphone for effect and poured a three quarter measure of the liquid into the glass.

"Ooh I think I put too much water into the bath, let's take some out" he cooed, and, bottle in one hand, he tilted his head back and emptied the contents of the glass down his throat. The effect was instantaneous.....

Mick gulped, his eyes almost popping out of his head and gasping for air he desperately filled the glass to the brim and once again, downed it. The audience were rolling in the aisles. Mick lurched forward, then backward, clamped his eyes tight shut forcing tears down his face, then shaking his head wildly he half opened his eyes and squinted round the room. His face, which had taken on the shape and colour of a pumpkin, looked like it was going to burst... then he focused on me, standing by the door, smilingly holding a Gordon's Gin bottle full of water above my head.

I don't know what happened after that...but I knew that my practical joke topped anything the brilliant bald headed Scouse could come up with.... I just wheeled round, made my way to the car park and victoriously headed for home.

I recently saw Mick Miller on the new Des O'Connor show. He tore the audience apart with a myriad of side splitting gags. He is still a great comedian...and probably still driving young and old pro's frantic with his practical jokes...

I never got his opinion of that memorable night. Despite many phone calls he never honoured me with an answer. And that year was the first time since we'd met that we didn't get a return Christmas card from the Liverpool funnyman.   And we haven't had one since.

*As the old saying goes...***If you can't stand the heat, stay out of the kitchen....**   Anon.

Fame???

Looking back over my 54 years in the business I'm proud that I progressed from the Workingmen's Club-scene. I went onto what I thought were better things, through Cabaret Clubs, radio and Television, Winning the National Television "New Faces All Winners Show" which took me to countries I had only dreamed of.

Australia, New Zealand, Canada, Germany and Italy... to exciting cities like Singapore and Hong Kong. From the new Crystal Club in New York to the MGM Grand Hotel in Las Vegas...and to the greatest honour afforded to any Entertainer....several dates at the greatest 'Gig' of them all, The LONDON PALLADIUM...

Sharing the boards with Icons like Perry Como, Dean Martin, Sir Lawrence Olivier, Georgie Jessell, Frank Gorshin (The Joker from Batman), Morecambe and Wise, Ken Dodd, Petula Clarke, Matt Munro, Marti Caine, Tony Christie, Les Dawson, Bob Monkhouse, Max Bygraves, Larry Grayson, Bernard Manning and a host of others.

In my career I even worked American Vaudeville in Boston Mass, with Hollywood Star Lilli St Cyr and stole 'Les Dawson's future Piano Act' from the great old Vaudevillian Mike Sachs, many years before Les Dawson was born. This was the Act that carried me through 54 years of non stop adventure.

I made friends with Icons like David Jason, the loveable Sir Norman Wisdom, Harry Secombe and the American hyper star, Jackie Mason.

I had several cameo roles in Coronation St, Emmerdale Farm, and The Liver Birds. I even appeared in a couple of movies, once in Lost Empires with Sir Laurence Olivier, and a 'turkey' featuring the 'New Faces All-Winners' filmed at Elstree Studio's called, 'It'll be alright on the Night'.

On that show we had a tall skinny shy kid named Michael Barrymore. We never knew how he'd won his heat on New Faces. He didn't have an act and he wasn't funny. No matter where they put him on the show he died. But we all liked him because he was brave. Maybe he was hungry because through sheer guts and determination he persevered and became one of the most successful comedy artistes in British Television history.

He was married to Cheryl, but even then we had doubts about his sexuality. His young beautiful wife seemed to keep him on the right track, but the higher he climbed the ladder to stardom, the heavier the burden of his private life. At the time of writing Barrymore is one of the most reviled characters in British show-business. He is finished as far as a career is concerned. But acts like Michael Barrymore and Freddy Starr and Jim Davidson were the yardstick I always used in my many years in show-business as a gauge to measure the degrees of success against the unbearable stress it all brought. Bernard Manning, once commenting on my laid back attitude to the business christened me, 'the Perry Como of comedy'. It was kind of Bernard but he was wrong. I was never in the league of the man who changed my life all those years ago in New York. But then again, Who Was? I like to think that in the tiniest of ways Perry and I had something in common. We each never believed in our own publicity. As long as Perry Como lived he'd have remained an icon... I did what I did for a million reasons... it paid well... fed me and showed me places I could only read about in magazines... and when I felt the first cold draught of impending rejection I got out. I lasted longer than I thought it possible to do and when the time came and I realised that I had become a dinosaur I called it a day. I could have stayed on past my sell by date. But of all the things I owe Jim Davidson for, none of them match up to his belief in, first my talent... then, most importantly my ability as a comedy writer. I kiss him for that.

No one could behave like some of the guys (and girls) I've worked with and remain unaffected by it all. The fabulously talented Michael Barrymore is gone. The once brilliant

Freddy Starr is an embarrassment and a dark unreal shadow of the talent he once was. And in a recent poll throughout the country, the hugely talented Jim Davidson was voted the worst comedian on television. Despite our differences I think the latter statement is the most cruelly inaccurate. No one, by any stretch of the imagination could say that Jim Davidson is a lousy comedian. Nor a mediocre or a bad comedian. He's been at the top too long for that and he's still one of the most talented entertainers in the business. It's my belief that Jim's problem was that he either forgot, or ignored the old show business adage 'Be nice to those you pass on the way up because some-day you're going to pass them again on the way down.'

And I believe he has that dubious honour waiting just round the corner.

I don't agree with those people who relish Jim's discomfort.

Nobody I ever knew in the business did more for me than Jim Davidson.

And even now, regardless of the animosity between us, if there was some way I could repay him, I wouldn't hesitate.

In his autobiography "The Full Monty" when I appeared with Jim on New Faces

Jim was more than his reflections on our past times.

And in his autobiography my great lifelong friend Roy 'Chubby' Brown said, 'If it wasn't for Johnny Hammond, there'd be no Chubby Brown.

And although I can't say that about Jim Davidson and myself, I would categorically say, if it wasn't for Jim Davidson I'd have never still been on the periphery of 'the business'..

Yet in a way I wonder if the semi rapid decline on ones career, as mine was, is better than hurtling through the sky like a shooting star to fizzle out and disappear right at the top. I only wonder...I'll never know now...nor would I want to.

So thanks to Jim Davidson, and no-one else, I became a comedy writer... and have had more than my share of success in that line, mainly in close proximity to Jim in a good percentage of my work.....'The Jim Davidson Show.'... 'Stand up Jim Davidson..' 'Jim Davidson's Generation Game'.....etc, etc.

I treasure the memories of that first time Jim rang me and said "Hi John... how'd you like to do the London Palladium with me?." None of the top agents or managers I paid to get me good work ever asked me questions like that. No one ever rang me and said "I want you to write comedy for me... the contract is on its way." And when I said "But in your position you can pick the cream of comedy writers", he said "I just did!" and put the phone down. Twenty four hours later I was his number one writer. But I hope Jim will forgive me when I say, in the latter years of our partnership he was not the funny loveable kid I met all those years before when we were in fierce competition on the "New Faces Show's".

I wrote a gag against him once when I said I saw a haggard looking lady who looked familiar. I said "Are you the same woman who married Jim Davidson?" She looked sadly into my face and said "After twelve months with Jim Davidson, no one is ever the same again." Maybe there was more than a ring of truth in the statement.

Thanks to Jim I worked the London Palladium several times. It didn't launch my career into orbit, but when you can include 'THE LONDON PALLADIUM' in your CV you're up there with the best of them.

The first show I did at 'the Palladium' was a fund raising even for the survivors of the horrific Zeebrugge Ferry disaster. Jim booked all of his favourite acts to do the show. He produced it himself and it was a great financial success.

On entering the theatre I was assigned a dressing room shared with comedian Mike Reid later to become one of the stars of the cockney sit-com East Enders.

I walked into the dressing room and there was this big man. He was watching horse racing on a tiny television set whilst he shaved. I introduced myself and held out my hand. He completely ignored my gesture. Seconds later the door burst open and in walked my 'mate' Bernard Manning. He greeted me in his usual manner. "Johnny Hammond... me favourite failure….. how are you my son?"

Reid greeted Bernard with a nod which Bernard didn't return.

Bernard asked me if I'd go down and get him a can of Coke. It gave me the opportunity of meeting my peers and getting away from the 'superstar' dripping lather.

Backstage Jim Davidson approached me and asked was I sharing with Bernard. I said I was… and also had the dubious honour of digging with Mike Reid. Jim made some comment like 'some poor bastard has got to share with him.' I felt better that Reids snub was not entirely personal.

Jim asked me to inform Bernard that to-nights audience were made up of several minor Royals and in the Royal Box would be Prince Charles and Princess Diana 'look a like's' and would I ask Bernard to clean up his act and 'watch his language'.

I was not a task I relished, but I collected a couple of cans of Coke and made my way back up to the dressing room. As I entered the room Bernard was sitting before the mini television in his usual state of undress… baggy underpants and string vest. No matter where he works or who is present, Manning has a habit of discarding his shirt and trousers and sitting in his huge underpants and string vest. He was glued to the set and Reid was bending his ear as to his (Reids) station in the business. "I was a big star' he boasted. Over his shoulder Bernard threw back. "I don't know, I was in America that week ..now will you piss off and let me watch the telly."

When I noticed Bernard's countenance light up….. obviously he was on a winner… I relayed Jim's request. The fat Mancunian exploded. I pointed out that I was only delivering the message and Bernard relented and said "skinny cockney Bastard, (referring to Jim) I'll give him 'clean'".

Jim opened the show with a brilliant four minute spot then introduced a new double act, who didn't set the place on fire, although they got a polite round of applause for the capacity crowd. It was Bernard's turn to go on next for six minutes as front cloth man, and although he wasn't whiter than white he was magnificent.

It was a great show and no-one was better than anybody else….

I thought I did well, Jethro did as well as I did, Paddy Green got a standing ovation, Jim held the whole thing together magnificently, but Bernard wowed stole the show. Next day Paddy Green rang and told me to go and get the Daily Mirror. The write up praised all and sundry and said…. 'But the outstanding talents were Zany Irish comedian, Paddy Green, hilarious Cornishman Jethro and the superbly professional Geordie funnyman Johnny Hammond.'

But honoured as I was at being on the great old Theatre, I didn't get that stomach churning buzz I always got from working the hardest clubs in the world. I couldn't get used to all those nice people accepting whatever was laid before them. I didn't have to dig down into my soul to get the laughs. In a way I felt patronised.

Maybe I was.

When the caviar work fizzled out I found myself doing spontaneous Gigs on the Sportsmen's after dinner Circuit, supporting retired Footballers, Rugby Players, Cricketers and Boxers who became ersatz raconteurs , 97% of whom couldn't link two syllables together.

We Comedians were there mainly to save the night when the speakers 'died,' which most of them did. For this we would receive a fraction of the fee paid to the 'Star Speaker'.

On one such Show I was support to a guy who, in my opinion was worth the fees of ten of the other so called speakers put together… Earnie Shavers.

To the uninitiated, Earnie Shavers is a former Professional Boxer. A black American heavyweight with more first round knockouts over some of the biggest names in the Golden years of boxing than any other fighter… ever.

Shavers is accepted throughout the world as the hardest puncher ever... and that includes Joe Louis, Jack Dempsey, Rocky Marciano, Mike Tyson, Muhammad Ali, Larry Holmes, Smokin'

Joe Frazier, uncle Tom Cobley and all.

As a child Earnie Shavers family had fled from the Deep South of America "one step ahead of the Klan".

A good American Football Player he took up Boxing late in his career. It is no exaggeration to say Earnie exploded onto the fight scene. He decimated the opposition with so many first round knockouts he got the reputation of being too lazy to want to go more than one round at per fight. He fought all the top fighters in the World. He was knocking out guys in the first round, who were taking Muhammad Ali the distance.

Earnie Shavers not only went fifteen rounds with "The Greatest" but in the minds of many, Shavers beat Ali. Ali went on record after the fight as saying; "Earnie Shavers hit me so hard he shook up my kin folk back in Africa".

Ken Norton took Ali the distance three times, beating Muhammad in one of their fights and breaking Ali's jaw in the process. Joe Frazier said; "Kenny Norton beat Ali in all his three fights. He was robbed in two of them."

They shoved Earnie Shavers in with Ken Norton and Earnie knocked out Ali's conqueror in less than two minutes of the first round. Earnie fought the invincible Larry Holmes and knocked Holmes down for a seven count in the fifth round. Holmes said afterwards; "Earnie hit me so hard I was unconscious, but when I hit the canvas the noise woke me up. Somehow I got to my feet at the count of seven and beat Earnie later on a cut."

Earnie Shavers said of the fight later; "For seven seconds I was heavyweight Champion of the World."

Back in America Earnie was training a very good young British Light Heavyweight boxer from Liverpool named Kenny Rainford. Kenny invited Earnie to come back to England and train him in his Liverpool gym. Earnie made the trip, fell in love with Kenny's beautiful aunt Sue and decided to stay.

Shavers had been a top after dinner speaker in the States and rapidly became a huge favourite over here. I found myself working with Earnie on a Sportsmen's evening and we immediately hit it off. We've been close friends for the past three years. So it came about that I got a call from the Chairman of a Workingmen's Club in my old home town of Hartlepool, asking could they book Earnie Shavers for their Sportsmen's Dinner.

Earnie said OK and I stated the fee for Earnie as the main speaker and myself as support comedian and a verbal contract was made.

Three days before the function I got a call from the Hartlepool Club saying that tickets hadn't gone too well and could we put the Show back a week. Earnie agreed and so we accepted the new date. Only to be told the day before we were due to appear, that the ticket sales hadn't warranted our long journey from Liverpool to Hartlepool and so they had decided to cancel a second time. This time I relayed to the Concert Secretary of the Club this message from Earnie. "We'll be at your Club at 7.pm tomorrows. Be on the doorstep with either the money OR AN AMBULANCE."

We arrived at the Club to be greeted by a crowd of fight fans. We entered the Concert Room which was packed wall to wall. The Committeeman, a huge obese man and his six piece posse stood sulking at the bar. I pointed out the full house to the Chairman and asked him what the trouble was.

"Youse guy's is making all that money and leaving now`t fer us like." He snarled.

The expression on their faces never changed all through the evening. The dinner went well, the Show went better. However, all of the Committeemen sat at a table at the back of the room and glowered, non stop at us.

Earnie and I signed autographs then just after midnight I went down to the Committee room to collect the cash. Crammed into the tiny broom cupboard of an office were seven very large gentlemen. The 'main man' sat behind his desk with a blank expression.

"Yeah?" he barked at me.

"I've come to collect the money" I said.

"Right" he growled, "'ave you got a proper receipt with today's date on a special letterhead and signed by a solicitor and me?"

"No!"

"Then get one!"

"Where am I going to get something like that at this time of night?" I said.

"I don't care... get one or you don't get paid." he said.

His six large friend's grinned their approval.

"There's no way that I can get that kind of receipt, it's nearly midnight for Christsake."

"Not our problem" said the fat man. I was loosing the plot.

"Look, we did the Show...we want to be paid." The huge face took on a victory smile.

"No receipt, no money."

"Yeah" chorused his backers."

"Wanna bet?" I asked.

"Yup!" smiled the toad.

"You're sure you want to do this?" I asked.

"Oh hey, we're tremblin' 'ere".They were enjoying every minutes of this…but not for much longer.

I made my way back upstairs to the concert room. Earnie was at a table in the centre of the room surrounded by a mob of autograph hunting fans. I pushed my way to the front as Earnie was in the process of signing a red Everlast boxing glove.

"Earnie".

"Yeah Johnny" the fighter beamed in his Uncle Remus voice.

"Earnie, we have a problem."

"What kind of a problem, Johnny" he asked without looking up.

"These guys refuse to pay us." I said. The effect was instantaneous.

"Huh?" he said, standing to his terrifying fighting height.

"I said these............"

Turning to the guy whose glove he was signing he said; "Hold onto my signature friend..... ah'll be right back." and turning to me ordered; "Johnny, lead the way".

Scenting a war several supporters tagged on. I led the way into the small office. The fat man was beaming behind his desk. Two of his henchmen sat on chairs, one leaned against a filing cabinet, a tailor-made cigarette hung from the corner of his mouth. The other three leaned casually against the wall, smirking.

I stepped aside and let Earnie enter.

He addressed the fat guy. "Hello sir" he said, all Southern charm.

"My name is Earnie Shavers. Ahm known as the hardest puncher ever. Johnny tells me you have a little problem."

The Chubby one laid back in his swivel chair which creaked under his vast weight.

"We haven't got a problem," said the official... "You've got the problem."

Earnie turned, and apologising to the expectant gathering in the foyer, removed a small chair that was holding the office door open and let the door gently close. Then, without speaking he started to remove his diamond encrusted watch, slipping it into his trouser pocket, and then he removed his tie and started to slip out of his jacket.

At this instant the magnificent seven lost their lustre. Suddenly realising they were in a bullring with no exit they started to wilt. Earnie turned and taking me by the shoulders moved me so that my back was pressed against the closed door.

"Don't move till this is over" he said, then leaning over the desk he stuck his nose, broken in

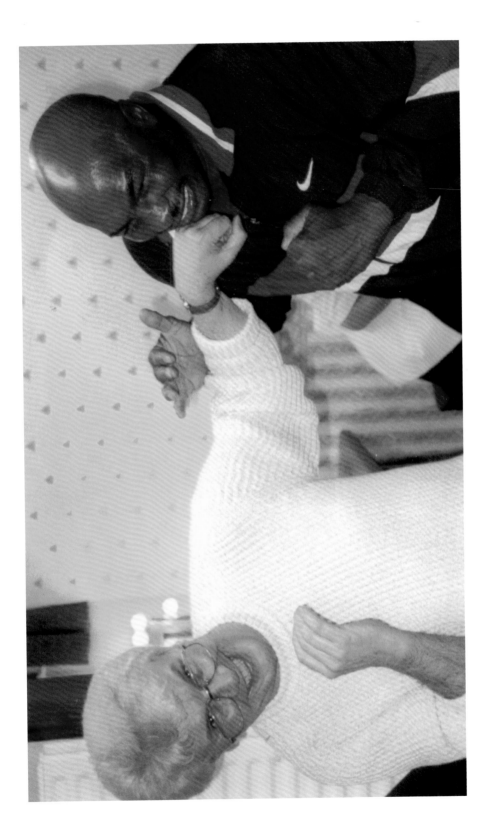

some of the most epic battles in the history of the prize ring into, the officials face and said ominously,

"I don't think I heard you right, sir, did you say I got a problem?.... is that what you said?"

One of the visibly shaken sextet slid along the wall and, his face a grey mask, whispered to me; "er, excuse me Johnny... would you tell Earnie I have a wife and kids?"

I put my hand on the guy's chest and eased him back to the wall.

"We don't have a problem with your wife or kids."

Earnie sat on the corner of the fat mans desk and said, "You see sir, I get paid for hitting people, and if somebody has something belonging to me which they wish to keep, that's up to them... and in truth I don't know what will happen, cos I never had a guy take something belonging to me, and live to spend it. Now, let's have a count down... starting at two!"

Far a massive mountain of fat, the official moved fast... whipping a thick brown envelope out of his pocket and shaking like a leaf in a hurricane, sweat pumping out of every pore and tears of fear streaming down his face, he offered the cash to Earnie, who said, over his shoulder, "My my, look what the man just found in his pocket Johnny.... would you be kind enough to count it.... CAREFULLY?"

Purposely taking my time I counted out the notes onto the desk. Half way through I turned and looked at the six tough guys. They all stood with their backs to the wall and their heels tight against the skirting board, hands clasped in front of them. They looked like a line up of condemned men standing before a firing squad.

All this time Earnie's eyes never left the fat mans face.

"All there, Earnie" I said.

Earnie stood up, looked around the room and addressed the occupants.

"Gentlemen" he said, "the next time you find yo'selves in this position, Saint Peter will be standing where I am right now." and slowly slipping into his jacket he replaced his watch, went along the line of reprieved men and shook their hands, thanked them and bade them 'good-night'.

As we stepped into the foyer fifty or sixty guys gave us a rousing cheer.

I like working with Earnie Shavers. He's the most Entertaining speaker I ever appeared with, a gentle humorous giant of a man, and with Earnie on the Bill I never have to worry about my wages.

Earnie and I had become good friends. We went all over the country together doing these nights. He phoned me one day and he said he had a problem with his car and would I mind driving him to a dinner. "I'm going to see my old friend Marvellous Marvin Hagler." He said "Would you like to come?" So I said "Do the Kennedy's wear black? Would I like to meet Hagler? Course I'd like to come." So I said "I'm on my way."

I drove down to Morton on the Wirral, which is where Earnie lives now. Morton is very much a one horse town. Nobody goes to Morton. They go through Morton but never to Morton. But Earnie lives there with his lady and he's happy so I went down there and he's waiting for me with his beautiful lady Sue. I ask 'Where are we going champ?" and he says "Stoke." And I thought you don't hear that coming from the mouth of a fighter who fought Muhammad Ali much. "Stoke?" So we drive to Stoke and all the way down there he's talking about his good friend Marvin Hagler and he says "Now listen when we get down there let me do the talking." Earnie knew that I was an old show business comedian. He knew I was a talker. I can talk. When I go to the fridge in the evening and the light goes on I can do two hours "Good evening, lamb chop. Hey, sausage haven't seen you for a while"

So he thinks I'm going to go down there and hog the company and you don't do that with Earnie so all the way down he's telling me. "Hey, when we get there, I'll do all the talking. When we get there I'll introduce you to Marvin and then you can shake hands with him and I'll do all the talking." And he's talking about his great friend Marvellous Marvin all the way.

"Me and Marvin this that and the other." So we finally get to Stoke. Earnie goes up to the reception and says to the girl behind the counter. "Hi, I'm Earnie Shavers. Ex Heavyweight contender. I fought Muhammad Ali…" It didn't make the slightest bit of difference. "Well I'm here to see my good friend Marvellous Marvin Hagler." So the girl at reception rang Marvin's wife, Kay, and then she said "Mr Shavers will you take your friends into the lounge and Mr Hagler is on his way." Now at this point I'm flying. I'm off the ground. I'm about to meet Marvin Hagler and Ernie says as we sit down. "Now listen Johnny when he arrives let me do the talking."

"Yes alright Earnie." He was getting on my nerves a bit by this time.

"Alright Earnie." So we sit down and wait. So I'm sat down with my mouth clamped closed and suddenly in he comes. The great Marvellous Marvin Hagler walks in and suddenly Earnie jumps up and runs over to him with his hand out and says "Marvin wonderful to meet you I'm Earnie Shavers." And I thought "He fuckin doesn't even know him." Marvin said. "Earnie the last time I saw you was in 1977. I was three rows from the back."

Ernie, I salute you!

(Earnie Shaver's autobiography, **"Welcome to the Big Times"** is a must for aficionados of the Golden Era of the Greatest fighters in the World.)

Meet 'The Family'.

Among my close friends in the after dinner Business are Barry McGuigan, John Conteh, Sir Henry Cooper, Jim Watt, Brian London, the Brilliant Ken Buchanan, the amiable Frank Bruno, Tommy Docherty, Jack Charlton, and a host of others.

When Earnie Shavers came over to Liverpool he brought with him some Muhammad Ali memorabilia to see how it would sell in Britain. He was working in co with a guy who ran a Muhammad Ali merchandising company in Hackensack, New Jersey.   Steve Jackson, the President of Alico had been a friend of Ali for some years and had bought up almost all of the genuine Ring Worn Muhammad Ali stock.

He was now one of the biggest Muhammad Ali merchandisers in the world. However, Earnie had his fingers in so many big fight Organisations that he was finding it difficult to give his undivided attention to the memorabilia business.

Out of the blue he asked me if I'd like to take over the business... FREE!

To say that I was flattered would be the understatement of the century. Although I was not a rich man I talked it over with my wife and she gave me the green light.

I figured that the after dinner Business was grinding to a halt, partly because of the lack of quality 'speakers'.

I had worked with some of the great raconteurs and they left most of these retired sportsmen in their wake. Also, a few ex Club Agents had moved into the lucrative after dinner field, made up a register of speakers and Comedians and, like Club Agents before them were in a position to make and break a speaker.

Another problem in our field was that Top Class Comedians on the after dinner field found they were putting themselves out of work, mainly because the sporting personalities hated the fact that support Comedians were exposing their mediocrity by milking the audiences and making the 'Stars' look amateurish.

A word in the Agent's ear and a lot of the top Comics were out of work.

So Earnie Shavers gift of a lucrative business carrying the Muhammad Ali flag was manna from heaven. Earnie rang Steve Jackson and told him of his plans I had to phone Mr Jackson at 7pm GMT (2pm New York time). In five minutes I was the new Alico representative in the UK.

Steve sent me brochures. I got a small bank loan and holding my breath dived in at the deep end.

Although I was flattered and excited with the new venture, I was soon to discover that there is a vast difference between Show Business and business Business. In showbusiness the greatest treachery comes from acts stealing others acts material.

I was about to move into the real world of Shiesters, shallow friendships and treachery. BIG TIME.

In a couple of weeks after receiving my first stock I was putting money in the bank and making great headway. I even jumped on a plane and went to visit my new boss in New Jersey and was surprised at the stock Jackson had. He was number one in America, Australia, Japan and Europe.

However I was working blind. For 54 years I'd been a Show Business Entertainer, and I had no a business acumen.

I'd met some academy award winning shyster's in my old line of endeavour but the guys I was now tangling with were real humdingers. First, I was advised by a Solicitor 'friend' that we should start a limited company. I forked out the cash and WE were in business. I bought a top of the range computer, went onto the Internet, had a great Website designed by a young computer wizard in Ireland and although I wasn't making a fortune I was paying the bills. There was a time when I sent a lot of money to America for merchandise from a 'highly respected merchandiser because Steve Jackson couldn't supply me with what I needed. Unlike Steve Jackson, this guy took my cash and vanished. My world collapsed and I was suddenly drowning. However it was my problem and I was trying, unsuccessfully to get out the hole myself. After several weeks of silence from New York I enlisted Earnie's help. He gave me a number to ring in Upstate New York. I rang and the guy at the other end of the line said Earnie had been onto him about my problem. The man gave me a number to ring in LA 'in thirty minutes from now... no sooner!'

In 30 minutes I rang the number in Los Angeles and I'd swear that the man who answered was Humphrey Bogart. He said 'as I was a friend of Earnie' he'd 'see what he could do'. He asked me for the guy's phone number in the Bronx. I gave it to him but warned him that I'd run out of avenues to follow, saying I feared he didn't live there anymore. 'Sam Spade' said, 'if he's alive, we'll find him'

He said if I didn't hear from the bandit in seven days to call him back in L.A.

I had little hope because I was convinced the bandit and my last dime had vanished from the face of the earth....

The Bogart sound alike said 'ya gotta have faith friend'..and to give my regards to Earnie. Exactly five days from the call my merchandise arrived. No messages... no receipts...no apologies or explanations... just the merchandise... plus several expensive pieces I hadn't ordered.

I rang Earnie and thanked him. The old fighter chuckled on the phone and said; "Johnny, you jes' spoke to the main man....Welcome to the Big Time."

I thanked Earnie and said 'should I ring 'the main man in LA' and thank him.

Earnie said not to worry, "someday he may need a favour from you.... Just stay clear of the phone."

Another time I had a guy in London owed me cash for merchandise he'd taken from me. 'I said pay me or the return of merchandise'.

He ignored my pleas and demands for 9 months.

Earnie knew I had this problem and asked me had I got the guys number. I gave it to him. In his soothing 'bass drum' voice he said "I'll appeal to his sense of fairness and his good nature". and twenty four hours later my merchandise arrived by (very special) delivery, nine months late.

Earnie is my friend.... *AND DON'T YOU FORGET IT!*

In the late nineties I was doing a fair amount of after dinner work. Most of the speakers were sports-men, but I worked with speakers from all walks of life.

I took a last minute gig at a Chinese restaurant in Chester. The original comedian had pulled out for some reason known only to him. I turned up at the allotted time and was surrounded by the most nerve shattering mob I've ever had in fifty four years of nerve shattering audiences. The guest speaker was an elderly man with a broken nose. He had several very large and very menacing gentlemen surveying his every move. The master of ceremonies introduced us thus. "Er, this is our comedian for the night, Johnny Hammond."

The man smiled, stepped forward and shook my hand warmly. "Hello Johnny..." he said in a very gentle cockney drawl. "I heard a lot about you. You're a very popular man and I'm looking forward to a great night."

The MC said "Johnny, this is Mister Frankie Fraser!".

To which the man added.. "'Mad' Frankie Fraser..... but you just call me Frankie."

I was surprised at the infamous old gangster's stature. Small and insignificant....sort of like a hand-grenade, and apparently just as dangerous. He was however courteous and friendly.

I had a great reception because Frankie loved my gags...and every-time he roared with laughter, his disciples joined in. He loved my story about Ronnie Kray's funeral which was pulled by a horse drawn hearse, "led by 'Shergar'".

That threw the old gangster into convulsions of laughter which ignited the rest of the 'mobsters' like a forest fire.

In the course of our evening I happened to say that I was a great friend of Earnie Shavers. Frankie had naturally heard about Earnie and he asked me if I could get 'Mr Shavers' to drop a line to his best friend, the infamous God-Father, Reggie Kray.

Next day I rang Earnie and he and I agreed to not only write to Reg but to send some Muhammad Ali memorabilia.

The following Saturday morning at precisely 9.50 the phone rang and a voice, in a soft cockney said "Good morning…could I speak to Mister Johnny Hammond please?"

I said 'Yes, you're speaking to him' and he said "Ah, hello Johnny, my name is Reg Kray and I'd like to thank you and Earnie Shavers for your kindness towards me." When I got over the shock I asked was there anything else we could do for him and he asked if my family would mind if he started up a correspondence with me. I said I'd love that, and for the last two years of his life we were in regular contact. I told Steve Jackson at Alico in New Jersey about Britain's ex-public enemy number One and Steve hopped on the wagon and became an occasional supplier to Reg.

I was also a friend and benefactor to a British boxer, a former Champion of the World in a lighter division and I occasionally got him work on the after dinner circuit.

Though he was never going to set the World alight as an after dinner speaker, it kept him in the fickle public eye. I happened to mention that I had the Alico franchise.

A few days later Steve Jackson rang from New Jersey and said a guy had been ringing him regarding getting merchandise direct from the New Jersey store.

Steve said 'says he's a friend of yours', but with friends like that I'd never need enemies. He was trying to muscle in on my patch.

From then on, although relations were a little strained we still did the occasional gigs together. One night I took him along to a dinner in Wales and when I dropped him off at his front door he thanked me profusely for the work and on parting he shook my hand, kissed me on the cheek and said "You're a great friend, Johnny, and I love you."

The following day I came back from town and there was a message on my answer machine. I pressed the button and a gruff cockney voice said; "Johnny Hammond? My name is (and he mentioned the name of an old Kray gang member). I'm a friend of ….. and he wants to take over that company you've got with Muhammad Ali. Now listen carefully, you cunt… if my friend doesn't get this Muhammad Ali contract, you are fucking dead mate.. you and your wife, Jeannie, and the rest of your family." And he went on to name my daughter and her two boys….. and after a few more death threats and a warning that 'I had better get in touch with him he hung up'.

So I rang the number he'd left and he said more or less what he's said on the tape.

I asked him who he was and he said "I'm the brains behind the mobs in London."

I said "Well I'll tell you something pal, you're no John Gotti."

(The late American Capo di Capi).

He exploded "Waddya fucking mean by that?"

I said; "You ring me up and threaten me and my family… and you leave your name and number on the answer machine…. What kind of a fucking gangster are you?"

He gave an embarrassed grunt and put the phone down.

Then I rang the guy who'd kissed me, Judas like, on the cheek and swore his love for me and asked him if he'd just had a thug try to lean on me. There was a short pause and a few 'er's and 'ah's then he said, "Yeah I did… I'm a boxer… I should have that contract."

I let him ramble of for another minute then I stopped him and told him to listen carefully while I played back the TWO messages that I'd just recorded. The scumbag nearly fainted, and then started pleading when I told him I was now on my way to the police station with the

226

tape, which I had the good sense to re-record several times.

To this day the police have one copy of the tape. My bank has another copy and three of my sons have a copy each. I rang a friend in Belfast who is a part time partner of mine and relayed the tape to him. And just for short measure I also mentioned the problem to Earnie. A couple of days later the 'brains behind the mobs in London' rang back and apologised, saying he was 'just trying to do a friend a favour.'

Then, on the Friday of the same week I got a call at 8.50 am. The now familiar voice said "Hello Johnny… Reg Kray here…. I heard on the grapevine that you had a problem phone call of late. I was worried about you. So how is the problem going with this geezer in London?"

I was amazed because I hadn't mentioned it to Reg.

I said "It's okay now Reg, the guy rang and apologised." And I was even more amazed when he said calmly…. "Yeah, I thought he would, and I'm happy about that. Please tell your lady wife and the rest of your family not to worry. You're okay now…. Oh, and thank you for the signed Muhammad Ali boxing glove. I'll ring you Sunday.. God Bless you." And he was gone.

A couple of days later I got another letter from Wayland Prison on Norfolk, thanking me, and Earnie for our kindness. It was signed "God Bless, Reg Kray… and in brackets he wrote; ('From now on your problems are my problems'.)

Earnie and I kept in touch with Reg and his wife Roberta right up till a few days before he died. I still keep in touch with Frankie Fraser. He did the crime and, after 43 years behind bars, he more than did his time.

And the Judas who betrayed me? He still crawls into bed at night with several large tubular garden chimes hanging behind his front door.

Sort of an early warning system.

I remembered 'Mad' Frankie Fraser telling me not to worry about threatening phone calls. Unsmilingly he said; "The time you've really got to worry is when you open your eyes at three o'clock in the morning and see four fella's standing at the foot of your bed."

It was only then that I saw the significance of the minefield of garden chimes.

Maybe in the past, Judas had rubbed four large and determined nocturnal characters the wrong way.

Some time later I mentioned to Earnie Shavers, the name of the guy who'd threatened me and my family. Earnie was a great friend of this well known former Kray soldier in 'The Firm'. Earnie said "He isn't the type of guy to try to put the frighteners on a couple of pensioners…. And if ever he finds out that your tormentor used his

(the alleged caller's) name to take frighten a couple of pensioners, he'll find himself floating face down in the Thames."Sheisters!

I was approached by a business-man who was, I believe, on the board of a great children's Charity in the North of England. There was a big Sportsmen's evening coming off and I was asked to supply at the lowest possible fee, some

Muhammad Ali memorabilia for an auction being held to help a local children's hospital.

I put in four items at a small profit to my company and sat in the audience and watched the bids go through the roof. One piece alone, a beautiful framed 16x20 picture of the famous Ali-Frazier, "Rumble in the Jungle" went to a young Liverpool footballer for £4100. A pair of trunks signed by Muhammad Ali went for £2250. A signed, framed boxing glove went for £2000 and a pair of Joe Frazier's signed trunks fetched £1250, bringing £9650.

I made a fair profit and the un-named charity scooped the pool.

I was delighted and amazed that I had helped raise such a sum for a good cause.

It was only later that I discovered that half of the money was going to a retiring former official of the local football team in appreciation for services rendered. The man in charge of the

Charity later shook my hand and said it was a wonderful gesture on my part.

A few days later the same official rang me and asked could I supply him with more merchandise at the same price. I delivered the stock, picked up the cash and after shaking my hand, as an afterthought, he asked me what I thought of the new personalised registration plate on his limo.

I've never been impressed by the ego boosting status symbol and told him so.

He asked me to guess how much it cost.

"No idea" I said.

"£20, 000" he beamed.

I froze and suggested that he should have done what the rest of the audience had done at his function.

"What's that?" he asked.

"You should have kept the old number plates and gave the much needed to the kids."

He blanched, spun on his heel, told me to 'Fuck off' and I never saw him again.

I was learning the hard way.

I am not suggesting that the official had done anything untoward... but when the same guy who congratulates you for the fine gesture you made blows £20, 000 on a trinket while others break their asses for sick children I think it makes one loose faith in human nature. Shiesters?

I was so pleased with one after dinner organiser and speaker, a man who'd acquired great wealth in the football memorabilia Business and who had once played football for a major club, for hiring me to be the Comedian on a fund raising dinner that after the Show I took him to my car and presented him with a pair of boxing gloves signed by my friend, Marvellous Marvin Hagler.

A young newspaper photographer was touched by the gesture that he offered to get me some Manchester United memorabilia to add to my Charity stock, which he did and for which he accepted the minimum payment. A couple of weeks later I got a phone call from the ex Manchester City guy who'd accepted my gift of the signed boxing gloves, accusing me of 'working his patch and losing him money.

He threatened that should I continue treading on his toes he'd make sure I never worked the Manchester after dinner Circuit again.

I told him to go forth and multiply, but not in those same words. A few days later I got a call from a Manchester booking Agent cancelling all my work in the area.

True to his word the recipient of the boxing gloves, which incidentally would fetch around a couple of thousand pounds a pair did make sure that I have never worked the Manchester Circuit again.

It was right then that I got the urge to get back into Show-business... where the only crime committed by my Peers was to steal the gags that I'd stolen from other comedians.

The first after dinner I did was with Tommy Docherty. Tommy and I are great friends but he steals gags off people. Tommy and all of these speakers are the same. They nick your gags. But I was with Tommy for 3 nights. One night in Sheffield. Which was a great night. The comedian always goes on last to give them something in case the main speaker isn't very good and to be honest 99% of these speakers aren't very good so you have to give them a real good last part of the show. The comedian is there to save the show in case it goes wrong. So I'm doing three nights with Tommy doc. The night in Sheffield had gone down well but the next night is in Preston. So Tommy went on and he did about 7 or 8 gags I'd done the night before so suddenly I'm an ad lib comedian because I couldn't do the gags he'd just done. But that suited me because I'm an ad lib comedian anyway. I like to pick people out of the audience. So anyway I'm up there doing my thing when this girl walks past who is selling raffle tickets. Gorgeous girl. Topless as well and I don't mean she was flat chested and she

came towards me and I said – an old chestnut now – "If you were my daughter I'd still be bathing you." The audience loved it. Now I think Tommy Docherty used to have a hole in his pocket and a little pencil and he used to dip it on his tongue and write the gags down on his leg. The following night we were in Wolverhampton. The Wanderers club. Lovely club and it was packed with about 2000 people. Great place and they had three speakers and a comedian. So before Tommy there were these two professional speakers and they really milked the audience. They were good. Professional speakers. Tommy's good but he is just an ex sportsmen so when it was his turn to get up and speak he felt like he had to do something to follow these guys. A leper on the Hughie Green show couldn't have followed these guys. Cause we were in a multi cultural city like Wolverhampton they had 4 West Indian girls, topless, with little grass skirts on. So when I came in and saw them I thought "I'll leave the bathing gag out." I didn't want to offend anyone you know. So Tommy went on after these two who had brought the house down and he's doing terrible. His tongue is stuck to the rood of his mouth and he's looking for a way out. I can see that he's desperate for something so this black girl walks towards him and she's beautiful and I looked at this face and I knew what he was going to do. And I thought 'No.' So she walks towards him and he says "see you?" and she turns and says "Who me?" and he says "Aye…if you were my daughter I'd still be bathing yer." And she said
"If you were my dad I'd wash yer." And this other black girl was very offended so she shouted at him "What did you say?"
and Tommy a little flustered and still desperate for something said "You look like you need a bath." I went "Oh dear. I've got to follow this." And slid down in my seat.

I'd pulled out of the writing by then. I was struggling to make a living out of the writing so I carried on with these speakers dinners. The next one I did was with Barry McGuigan. Dear Barry. Whenever he comes to stay here I get the cot out for him. He's only a little fella you know. I love Barry. Barry came along. It was just around the time of his problems with Barney Eastwood. So he got up this night and he was the worst speaker I'd ever heard. Naturally everybody loved him because it was Barry but he was a terrible speaker back then because like anything else it takes time and practice and these guys are sportsmen not entertainers. But he was talking about his troubles with Barney Eastwood. Now if you pay to see someone and hear them speak you don't pay to hear about their problems and there was Barry going on about his. They don't want to know about the one million pound you could have had when they've saved up for six weeks to pay the £25 to get in. I loved him to death but his speech was dreadful. So when he'd finished we had a chat together for a while and he said. "You're a great comedian."
"I said I used to write for television I can write you some gags to help you out." so Barry said "' Aye that'd be great." I told him how much it was going to cost and he said no problem. I wrote a 45 minute speech for him and from then on he went on to be a very average speaker on the circuit to one of the best and he still is. So I must have been doing something right. Then I started writing for other boxers who were on the circuit. John Conteh, Ernie Shavers, Brian London. I love boxers. I always got on great with them; they all have their own stories. Ernie is one of the most entertaining ex fighters because he talks about the mafia and Don King and all types of things like that and I get on with him great. I always get on with fighters well. They are great people.
They are living by their name and its easy money. Whether they are good speakers or not people will pay to see them because of who they are. George Best who I loved to bits and worked with a lot, was never a great speaker because he was always drunk. But everyone forgave him because of who he was. They just wanted to shake hands and see him up there. Jack Charlton and Tommy Docherty are an exception to the rule. They are knockout speakers.

But most are very average. They try to be funny but it doesn't work. Suddenly they go from a footballer to Chubby Brown. If it wasn't for Bill Shankly there would never have been after dinner speaking. He was the first of them who could make a crowd laugh. The famous Shankly gag being about the goalie that lets a goal in through his legs "I should have kept my knees together." Says the goalkeeper. "No," says Shanks "It was you mother who should have kept her knees together. " Aye but I'm good in the air" the keeper replies. "Aye so was Douglas Bader." Shankly started it all and then the others started telling stories and trying to be funny. I saw them all and saved more than one. The main stories came from Shankly and Clough. I met Shankly many times and he was a lovely man.

The best speakers in the football world are the managers. Some of the footballers earn ten times more than the comedians. They just throw scraps to the comedians. I know many great comedians who are not working because of the footballers.

Ken Buchanan is funny but he doesn't mean to be funny. I was his agent for a while, when I had sporting icons, and he always called me Jimmy. I honestly think he thought that was my name. Kenny is a lovely man but I think I would have made more money booking Adolph Hitler for bamitzvah's. Like a lot of boxers Kenny will do things for nothing. Footballers go out there to get the money first and then give everybody a good time later. Boxers go out there to please everybody for next to nothing. A lot of them are generous to a fault that's why they end up with no money.

Ken Buchanan was going down to Cardiff once for a Howard Winstone charity night. Kenny was going down there and he was doing a book signing and he was going to get paid for his book signing. I said "How much are you doing appearance for?"

"Oh, I'm doing it for nothing."

I said "You can't do it for nothing." Like I said boxers give their money away. So anyway he goes down there for nothing and he pays his own train fair. They pay for his hotel. He went down there and the weather was dreadful. It was sheeting down with rain and he phoned me from the train. "Is that you Jimmy?" he shouted over the noise of the train.

"No, Ken, this is Johnny."

"Who?"

"Johnny, your agent."

"Oh aye sure…I've been trying to get in touch with Paul."

"Who's Paul?" I said

"Paul your partner."

"You mean Philllip."

"Aye that's right Paul." He says

So he's on a train going from Glasgow down to Cardiff and he's telling me there's no heating on the train, it's slow because they're mending the tracks. So it's taken him about 7 hours to get somewhere near Cardiff and its freezing. "I've never been so fuckin cold in all my life." He's saying "There's nay coffee either. All they've got is a fuckin glass of lemonade and it's got fuckin ice on top of it." And he keeps saying "Och, I'm sorry…" To the rest of the people on the train when he swears and I can hear them all saying "Don't worry champ. We agree with yer. It's fuckin' disgraceful." Talk about making life hard for yourself. So he goes down there and loves the show and everyone loves him. He'd just been inducted into the boxing hall of fame a few months before that so he was feeling happy and confident and he went down very well like he did at the hall of fame. But when he got back he rang me about three days later.

"Is that Jimmy?"

"No it's Johnny."

"Aye that's right…Ouch, it was fuckin freezing on that journey, Jimmy. Terrible journey it was and now I've got the flu."

I said "Well the main thing is you made a few quid…Did you make a few quid, Ken?"

"Aye." He said

"Good, well that's the main thing." I said

"I made it but then I gave it back." He said.

They paid him and he put it all back into the charity. It cost him to go down there and he gave what he made back to the charity. Like I say, next time I'll ring the local rabbi and tell him Hitler's available for children's parties. I'll probably make more money.

In my life's work I don't know of anyone who gives so freely to Charity as Entertainer's, and Club Entertainers in particular. But I know of a few big name Sportsmen who not only give their services free but usually refuse even expenses. 'BIG' Jack Charlton is one, Tommy Docherty is another. In the fight game I can rely on Barry McGuigan, John Conteh, Jim Watt, Nazeem 'NAZ' Ahmed, Earnie Shavers and Brian London to name but a few.

I got a call from a Charity organiser asking could I put on a Show for the Chester Hospital, and could I get the speakers as cheaply as possible. I phoned Tommy Docherty and he said "I'll be there". I said I'd at least get him expenses and Tommy poo pooed the idea. To add a little balance to the event I rang the great old boxer friend of mine, the former British and Empire Heavyweight Champion, Brian London.

"How much?" he asked.

"Free Chinese dinner and all the orange juice you can drink." I said.

"It's for the Chester Hospital".

"I'll be there" said the old battler.

The function was held at the gorgeous 'Slow Boat' Chinese restaurant in Chester. The never unending dinner finally did end and the well wined and dined all male audience settled down in anticipation of some great sporting reminiscences.

I opened the Show as Comedy/Compere and was roaring along at a pace to the appreciative throng when a very large drunk sitting at the front table with an entourage of similar very large men, shouted, "Hey pal, can I ask you a question?"

"Sure" I said.

"What do you do for a living?" he chuckled to encouragement from the rest of his group of primates.

My mind hurtled back through hundreds of situations like this on the dreaded 'Club' Circuit;

"I get clients for your sister"

The crowd roared their approval while the heckler, suitably chastened slid deep down into his chair. I took my bow to loud applause and introduced 'a man who fought some of the greatest boxers in the world including five world champions... one of them being The Greatest of all time, Muhammad Ali……… Gentlemen please give a great welcome to the former British and European Heavyweight Champion...

Brian London"

Almost every man in the room stood and gave a rousing round applause to the loveable old Warhorse.

I said almost every man... the only one who didn't get to his feet was the giant heckler, who sat with his arms tightly folded glaring from me to Brian for at least ten minutes into Brian's speech... then, at a little egging on from his pals he eased up in his seat, stuck his arm into the air and shouted; "Hey, Mister Champion.... can I ask you a question?"

The room suddenly went ominously quiet.

"Yes sir," said Brian... "waddya wanna know?"

The man stood up to his full six feet seven, rocked unsteadily on his feet and asked,

"When is Tommy Docherty getting up?"

An icy chill wafted round the room as Brian said amiably,

"I don't know..... but you won't see him."

"Oh," said the big man "Why not?"

Brian stirred into the man's face and rocked the audience with, "Cos you'll be laid unconscious in the Fucking car-park." And to add emphasis to his threat he walked round the table and headed for the drunk who looked around for support from his friends who were sheepishly examining their shoes.

It was at this point the guy decided to sit back down, but in rising he'd shoved his chair to one side, and as the old battler approached, the man staggered backward falling head over heels across the table sending his whole entourage into a sprawling heap. Brian, his face a picture of childish innocence mockingly turned to the now roaring audience and yelled; "I wish Ali had been as easy as that!"

Many years ago Brian challenged former World Champion, Ingmar Johansson for the European title. Johansson had previously knocked out the great Floyd Patterson to become the Heavyweight Champion of the World. He lost it back to Patterson in their return fight. Johansson accepted the challenge from London with disdain, repeatedly announcing that he had been World Champion and should not be fighting a 'bum' like London.

"I haff sister in Sweden who could beat this bum" yelled the Swede loud and often to the news hacks. During the fight he boxed London's head off. Coasting through the last round Ingmar contemptuously stuck his chin out and Brian, a known deadly puncher nearly tore Johansson's head off. He was unconscious before he hit the canvas and as he laid half in and half out of the ring, London leaned over the top rope and for all the radio listening crowds around the world to hear, he shouted; "You should have brought your fuckin' sister."

When Brian London took the World Title fight with Floyd Patterson it was classed as such a mismatch, so much so that the British Boxing Board of Control ordered London to call it off. Facing a huge fine Brian went ahead with the challenge and he nearly pulled it off.

On his arrival in America he was interviewed on a coast to coast radio link by the great American broadcasting pundit Howard Cossell. Although the interview was going out live the Radio station decided first on a dummy run.

"Hello, this is Howard Cossell speaking to you from New York. We have here today the British and European Heavyweight Champion, Brian London who has come over to fight our great American Heavyweight Champion of the World, Floyd Patterson."

"Brian, Welcome to America."

"Thank you 'oward... nice to be here."

"Brian, this fight has been condemned by your own British Boxing Board, and we here in the States agree with them that it's a one sided affair."

"Oh Aye?"

"Yes Brian.. it appears that you're a patsy... you come over here to fight our great Floyd Patterson, and ...."

"Wot's that mean, like, 'a Patsy', 'oward."

"Well, it means that you come over here for an easy night... coupla rounds, take a dive, grab the money and run."

"Go fuck yourself"

At this point the Producer of the radio station jumped in.

"No, no, Mr London, that's not Howard's opinion, it's the general consensus of opinion here in America."

"Oh, I see... aye, ok, sorry about that... can we do it again?"

So the station switches on live coast to coast.

"Hello America.. We have here tonight the British Heavyweight Champion........"

As Cossell droned on Brian listened intently.

"…..a patsy…. America thinks you've come to lie down, take the money and run."

Brian, with a cheeky twinkle in his eye said; "Oh, is that wot you think 'oward"

Patronising, Cossell said; "No Brian, that's the general consensus of opinion of the American people."

All those surrounding Brian leaned forward to catch his every word… and then every face bar one froze as London said loud and clear, "Well, 'oward, you tell them consensus people of America to go fuck themselves."

And just to prove them wrong, in the seventh round Brian, who was doing exceptionally well caught Floyd with a London haymaker as he came forward. Patterson shuddered and fell into the Englishman's arms, and to the consternation of the watching world, held the World Champion up, even enquiring,

"Floyd, Floyd, are you alright Floyd?"

Brian's corner, which consisted of his Dad, Jack London who once held the same titles as Brian now held, his brother Jack, a good light heavyweight and his seconds, screamed at Brian, "Let him fall…. for Christsake let him fall….." just as the bell rang to end the round. London thrilled the crowd with his bravery and his true fighting heart, but he lost in the eleventh round. Back home he was browbeaten on radio by a lady from the "Anti Boxing Lobby".

"Don't you realise you could be killed… or you could kill the other human being" he was asked. And like he'd stunned Patterson in that seventh round, he now stunned the listening BBC audience the length and breadth of the country with his reply.

"It's imperial to me what you say… it's us what does the fighting and I know we're only prawns in the game."

Okay, so Brian London was no Shakespeare, but he was one hell of a fighter and he still is one hell of a nice guy and Johansson was wrong… Brian London is not a bum.. he is one of the few hyper rich fighters from the Golden age of pugilism. He's highly prized on the After Dinner Circuit, he's as famous in Blackpool as the Tower and he lives in a magnificent house on Blackpool's 'Nob Hill' with his wife Beryl, and every time he passes his local bank it's the Manager who tugs his forelock. Most people thought Brian was from Blackpool but he wasn't, he was a Hartlepool lad. I've known Brian for ages, since he was a boy, and I always followed boxing. There have been some great fighters up there in Hartlepool. Knockout fighters. Just a shame I can't remember any. But I got quite pally with them, whoever they were. They used to fight in this place called the stadium, in Hartlepool. It was the backyard of the engineers club, the working men's club. They had a decent sized backyard and that's were they put the ring and that's the first place I saw Brian. I think the first time I saw him he got knocked out by an unbeaten fighter. It was the cleaning lady from the club. Sheila I think she was called. Nothing changed. Every time I saw Brian he got knocked out. He was on the canvas more times than Rembrandt.

I have many great boxers on my "Greatest list." Brian London is one of them.

And he's as immovable in Blackpool as my Grandad Hammonds 'knock the milk bottles down to win' were.

Looking back on my life in Clubland, it wasn't nearly as bad as I've painted it, but I'm a comedian, and that's the way I see it. There were more highs than lows. In its favour I can say in all honesty, Clubland was a great training ground and I sympathise with the kids who don't have that medium to show off and cultivate their Talents any more. Today these kids appear on a talent show on a Monday and by Wednesday their touring the world. They're being screwed by unscrupulous shiesters, feted for a couple of months then, when they're burned out they're tossed onto the scrap heap to be replaced by another untalented wannabee.

I remember an old comedy magician Murray Smith, a hyper talented artiste who ended his days being howled down by druggies in lousy fun pubs, fodder for the brainless morons who couldn't link two phrases together.... Yet he never lost his sense of humour. He told me he was wandering along the promenade in Blackpool when he noticed an old fashioned Punch and Judy show on the rain swept beach.

Making his way do the tiny tent he noticed the name of the artiste painted on the rear flap. Murray waited to the interval and popped into the claustrophobic space.

The old pro's embraced, and the maestro offered the old magician a flask lid of tea and a tiny cheese sandwich. As the two old troupers were recalling old and happier times a tiny cherubic face appeared through the 'stage door'. Begging his old friends pardon, Murray turned and informed the freckle faced boy that "no one is allowed backstage."

I kept in contact with Murray right up to his overdue demise. He was, at the end a sorry sight. Unable to tread the boards any more he told me he'd tried to end it all several times. Trying one more time he contacted his antique mentor, Abe Rosen.

"So Murray, how much would you want to woik a nice club in Benidorm?"

"My air ticket, a bed and three meals a day?"

"Ah, I'm sorry my old friend... the gig doesn't stretch to that."

Last time I saw Murray was when I was nearing the end of my career. I was doing a back street flea pit in Sheffield, Murray's home town. I called in to see him. By now he was a recluse living in squalid conditions. We talked of the good old days, which were really bad old days but not nearly as bad as they had become to acts like us. But, as had become the norm he left the stage to the sound of his own footsteps.

As he walked me to my car he said, "You see Johnny, there's no business left. There's no place for the new kids to learn the trade. Seventeen years old television producers are coming out of college with a diploma for fitting fucking light bulbs. They know nothing about entertainment." He sighed a long, sad sigh.

"Life goes by too fast nowadays, love." He said sadly.

Then just one more time he was back in the spotlight, front stage, and he rocked me with; "One minute you've got a diary full of gigs, a case full of glossy ten by eights and the world's your lobster...next minute you're sitting on the back of a Sunshine coach going to Scarborough with a fucking balloon in your hand. If there's one thing I hate I'll be glad when I'm fed up... that's what I wish!"

I automatically came up with a better line, but the old pro was dying and I didn't want to upstage him. He'd been a headliner for as long as he could remember... now it didn't matter... if he could dredge up a line like that who was I to try to top it?

Weeks later every act that'd ever trod the boards turned up for Murray's big day.

He looked great in his casket, and for the first time in years he was really asleep.

In his stage suit and monster bow tie he looked like he was auditioning for the Palladium. His toupee was placed at a jaunty angle... like he'd said to the undertaker, 'make me look nonchalant ...like Murray say's "fuck you, Abe Rosen... I'm alright... I'm warm, clean, I'm independent and I'll never die again...and my Equity dues are paid right up to the minute."

I used to keep in touch with what's left of the old Acts... but now before I ring a familiar number I think of Murray Smith and check the "Stage" Obituary column.

I rang Norman (Collier) out of the blue a few days ago... I had to, I needed to talk to someone who was around when Steelworks Clubs and Miners Clubs, Dockers Clubs, good rooms and Entertainers and audiences were mushrooming like fields of mushrooms...When *'the bread'* came second to the applause...When new acts were seasoned pro's and really did become stars when they'd learned their trade and paid their due's. Ask me! You can't start lower than piano player in a dockside brothel.

I was one of the lucky ones. I was as good as the best and I struggled right up to the penultimate rung of the ladder. I never aimed any higher. And I stayed there just as long as they'd have me. I knew when to get on and when to get off. You have to learn the art of dying first...make it look like part of the act and the rest follows on like night follows day. That's the trick.

It wasn't easy and the climb was hard but the view from the top was exhilarating.... Not an eternity but long enough to let them see you made it.

'The Business' as I knew it has been dead for years... but I'm catching up... and there are still a handful of the 'old pro's' left. And when I do hear from them they go straight into their act... and it's just as funny as it was.... Well, it's familiar.

Example. I got a call a couple of days ago from one of the funniest guys I shared the boards with. He's still ambitious, but 'resting' at present. The format was the same as when his young bride would ring me to herald the great man's presence.

"Hello, is that Johnny?... Lucy Collier here... Norman wants to speak to you."   And she hung up. No problem. It's part of the schtick.

So, as is customary, after a 'pregnant pause' (timing is important) I did the expected thing and rang back.

Norman Collier answered. "Hi Johnny."

I said, "Norman, Lucy just rang and said you wanted to speak to me!"

Norman: "Huh Huh!"

Me: "Then she hung up."

The 'old Rooster' broke into his maniacal laugh and said; "I know, we're saving on phone calls.

(Pause for laughs). A further pause while he reached centre stage, Then he drifted into rehearsal mode. "I don't take so much work now." (Which means nobody's offering.)

"So, how is it with you Johnny?"

"I'm still alive."

He paused... "How do you know that?"

I played it straight. "I can tell when I wake up in the morning. If I don't wake up I stay where I am till the resurrection!"

Norman laughed loudly, "I do it the easy way. Every Friday I check "The Stage" Obituaries to see if I'm featured....If my names not on the call sheet I play a game of golf."

(I hear Lucy putting a cup of tea on the phone table... Norman thanks her and I hear the definitive sound of a kiss.)

He continues; "I try to keep fit. I jog every morning for the paper, rain hail or shine."

"You jog to the paper shop every morning?" I asked.

He laughs, "No, not to the paper shop, I have it delivered...I jog into the hall..."

"Why don't you get a dog?"

"I have a dog but I can't trust him. During the newsboy's strike I gave him a £1. and sent him to the corner shop for the Daily Mail. After two hours he still didn't come back so I went looking for him. I found him with a bitch who works nights as a hooker. They were hooked up like only dogs can. I told him I'd never seen him do anything like that before. And he said, "I've never had any money before!"

I could feel a long set coming on and I was paying for the call. "How's Lucy" I asked, because he knew he now had me eating out of his hand.

"You didn't hear? It was touch and go for a while." He intoned morosely.

"It sounds serious!" I said in mock concern.

"You didn't hear. She fell off the mountain bike."

"Lucy fell off the mountain bike? She's eighty years old... what the hell's she doing riding a mountain bike at 80?"

"Oh no" he said "I was riding the mountain bike."

I was netted

"So what happened to Lucy?"

"She fell off the crossbar. So how old are you now Johnny?"

"I'm as old as the day is long. And this has been a very short day. I just heard you're older than Bob Monkhouse....." I said

"The only thing in the Business older than Bob Monkhouse is Jim Bowens Act... He died you know."

"Who died?" I asked

"Jim Bowen."

"When?" I enquired

"All last summer in Blackpool. He said they were a terrible audience."

"Then why did they keep coming back for more?"

"God knows...Did I tell you, the luckiest guy in his audience was deaf and dumb?"

"No, I told you! That was my gag..."

Norman refused to pick up the gauntlet. "Neville (King) is doing okay.. he phoned yesterday.. I was at the hospital.. he told Lucy he's doing the summer in Turkey."

Lucy yelled from the kitchen. *"TORQUAY!"*

'Jesus' I thought..' is he still doing that old chestnut?' but I soldiered on.

"I heard Blackpool is closed," I declared "Dead. The only guy working there is "Chubby"... Fuck this fuck that...but that's up to him...No class... but there's no money in class anymore. Friend of mine went to see the Grumbleweeds... they're still doing Jimmy Saville..."

Norman screamed "Jimmy Saville... you're kidding...even Jimmy Saville doesn't do Jimmy Saville any more. What happened to Comedy?"

The old funster was getting morose. I asked. "So, why were in you the hospital?"

Norman slipped back into routine. "I've got Tetanus...Do you get that tetanus?"

"What, like lockjaw?" I replied. Am I kidding? This guy? LOCKJAW?

"How the hell can you get lockjaw in the ears," queried Norman.

"Tinnitus!" I yelled in mock irritation. "It's called Tinnitus...I've had it for years... only in one ear. I blame it on the War.... I was on a Destroyer.... on Russian Convoys."

Norman asked, "What's it like?"

"You've seen one War you've seen them all."

"Not the War... the Tetanus.....and Jimmy James did that gag a 50 years ago... when you were on Russian Convoys." Norman laughed "So, what's it like this Tettinus?".

"Tinnitus for Chrissake." I yelled; "They call it tinnitus...it's like a humming noise."

"All the time.... do you get it all the time?" asked Norman.

"Even when I'm asleep, sometime it keeps Jeannie awake all night." I confessed.

"Mine alternates," said Norman, "sometimes it's a ringing noise and other times it's a loud whistling noise. I spend half the day answering the phone and the other half throwing dogs out of the kitchen."

There was no stopping him now.

"The hospital sent me a note to go see the doctor. My doctor hates me... he's a German. He won't let me sit in the waiting room because I make the other patients laugh.... and being a German he doesn't like people laughing..... As soon as I arrive he has his receptionist send me straight in. A couple of weeks ago he told me I should stop masturbating. I said 'Why, is it contagious?' He said 'No, but it's upsetting the other patients in the waiting room'! So this time he said I had to just sit there and not speak...no jokes... no fooling around.... First he tests my chest with his stethoscope then he asks me which ear is the phone and forget the one with the dogs. I point to the telephone ear. Now he opens the desk drawer and he takes out this tuning fork... a huge tuning fork... it was like a blacksmiths anvil. Then he hits me on the knee with it ...It makes a loud boinnnnngggg.. then he sticks the pointed bit behind my ear.....

well, you know me... I have a great ear for music... soon as I heard 'b-flat' I grabbed the end of his stethoscope, put it to my lips and went into Sinatra's '*And now, the end is near*....' Miserable bastard threw me out.... told me to find another doctor."

Nobody can follow Collier...not when he's on a roll, and especially when he's doubling with Lucy. Nobody could follow that, not 'The Little Singing Angel'....not even Miss Mary Bagley and her guide dog... 'old Shep! And more important when someone else is paying for the call!

FINALE

Norman: *"Is that it then, Johnny... are we really dead?"*
Me: *"Yeah, well, you can't call this living, Norman...."*
Norman: *"Okay.. last one out dims the lights and closes the Curtains."*

....yesterday they told you you would not go far,
that night you open and 'there you are',
next day on your dressing
room they hang a star
let's go on with the show....
LET'S GO...

Johnny Hammond passed away on the
22nd of July 2007

CURTAIN CALL